Princeton and the Republic, 1768–1822

Princeton and the Republic, 1768–1822

THE SEARCH

FOR A CHRISTIAN ENLIGHTENMENT

IN THE ERA OF

SAMUEL STANHOPE SMITH

Mark A. Noll

☆

PRINCETON UNIVERSITY PRESS

PRINCETON, NEW JERSEY

1989

Library of Congress Cataloging-in-Publication Data

Noll, Mark A., 1946–
Princeton and the republic, 1768–1822: the search for a
Christian Enlightenment in the era of Samuel Stanhope
Smith / Mark A. Noll.
p. cm.
Bibliography: p.
Includes index.
ISBN 0-691-04764-2 (alk. paper)
1. Princeton University—History—18th century. 2.
Princeton University—History—19th century. 3. Higher
education and state—New Jersey—History. 4. Church and
education—New Jersey—History. 5. Smith, Samuel
Stanhope, 1750–1819. I. Title.
LD4609.N65 1989
378.749'67—dc19   88-39309

Publication of this book has been aided by grants from
the Lilly Endowment and Wheaton College

This book has been composed in Linotron Baskerville

Clothbound editions of Princeton University Press books are printed
on acid-free paper, and binding materials are chosen for strength and
durability. Paperbacks, although satisfactory for personal collections,
are not usually suitable for library rebinding

Printed in the United States of America
by Princeton University Press, Princeton, New Jersey

To Maggie

The circumstances attending the establishment of this College; the zeal for the promotion of literature, which was indicated by its erection, and which it served afterwards greatly to increase; and the many distinguished characters which it has contributed to form, render it, beyond all doubt, one of the most conspicuous institutions in our country, and one of those whose history and influence are most worthy of being traced.

—SAMUEL MILLER

A Brief Retrospect of the Eighteenth Century (1803)

Contents

Acknowledgments   xi

List of Abbreviations and Short Titles   xv

1 Introduction   3

2 Prologue, 1779: War, Heroism, Ruins   12

3 John Witherspoon Comes to Princeton: Promoting
   the Interests of the Redeemors Kingdom   16

4 The Legacy of Witherspoon: One of the Great Men
   of the Age   28

5 Samuel Stanhope Smith, 1751–1781: Labouring up
   the Hill of Science and Virtue   59

6 Princeton and the Nation, 1781–1794: A New Era in
   the Annals of Time   77

7 The College and Stanhope Smith, 1781–1794:
   Human Nature Susceptible of System   99

8 Transition and Continuity, 1795–1801: Glowing with
   Patriotism, as well as Pure Religion   125

9 Fire and Rebuilding, 1802–1806: An Asylum in This
   Day of Lamentable Depravity   157

10 The Republican Christian Enlightenment of Samuel
   Stanhope Smith: A Just Philosophy Grounded on
   Fact and Experience   185

11 Student Rebellion and New Trustees, 1807: Pillars of
   the Social Fabric Crumbling into Dust   214

12 The Domination of Ministers, 1808–1812: Not the
   Understanding, but the Heart   244

13   Ashbel Green and the New Regime: What Its Pious
      Founders Intended It to Be   272

14   Conclusion: Retrogression, the New Nation, and a
      Republican Christian Enlightenment   292

Appendix A   Number of Graduates, 1748–1830   301

Appendix B   Trustee Genealogies   302

*Appendix C   Number, Attendance, Participation: Board
      Meetings, 1779–1812*   303

Bibliography, with a Prosopography of the Princeton Circle   305
   MANUSCRIPTS   305
   THE PRINCETON CIRCLE   305
   ESSAY ON SECONDARY AUTHORITIES   322

Index   333

Acknowledgments

I began work on this book in the fall of 1978 at Northwestern University under a Fellowship for College Teachers in Residence from the National Endowment for the Humanities. The book was completed in 1987 while I was enjoying time freed from teaching by the Institute for Advanced Christian Studies, the Pew Charitable Trusts, and the National Endowment for the Humanities. For their support, I am grateful to the NEH, IFACS, and the Pew Trusts as well as to a number of other individuals and institutions who assisted in different ways over the nearly ten years it took an easily diverted scholar to finish the task.

At Northwestern T. H. Breen and the members of the NEH seminar provided exactly the right material and intellectual culture for getting under way. In the intervening years several colleagues and friends—Martha Blauvelt, Robert Calhoon, Joel Carpenter, Allan Fisher, Darryl Hart, Michael McGiffert, George Rawlyk, Harry Stout, Grant Wacker, and Robert Wuthnow—provided helpful critical comment on various writings related to this project. I have also benefited more than I can say from conversation, critical readings, and general encouragement offered by the true experts on the early history of Princeton. These include James McLachlan, the late Wesley Frank Craven, Ruth Woodward (who shared the files of the Princeton biography project), and especially John Murrin. Editors and referees of journals in which prelimary reports appeared—the *Princeton University Library Chronicle*, the *Westminster Theological Journal*, and the *Journal of the Early Republic*—often contributed more than they realized to my thinking.

George Marsden and Craig Noll enjoy the dubious distinction of having slogged through the considerably longer draft from which this book was hewn. I now enjoy the great pleasure of thanking them, on behalf of all who might read these pages, for the wisdom of their gentle criticisms. Nathan Hatch not only read much of this book in one shape or another but also contributed the perspective of his own study on the democratization of religion in the early republic as a refreshing counterpoint. Gifts of books, information, and hospitality made my work easier, and for them I am pleased to thank Randy Balmer, Lois Badgero, Earle E. Coleman, Darrell Guder, Craig and Margot Hammon, David M. Ludlum, and Harry Stout.

During the course of this project I have been the recipient of unfailing institutional courtesies. I owe a special debt to the librarians at Wheaton College, particularly to Dan Bowell for many works of supererogation, and to Ferne Weimer for allowing me to keep *The Works of John Witherspoon* checked out for what must be a record length of time. At Princeton, I appreciated the kindnesses of University Archivist Earle E. Coleman, Archives Assistant Cynthia McClelland, and the staff of the manuscript reading room at the Firestone Library. For similar help at the Pennsylvania Historical Society, the Presbyterian Historical Society, the Speer Library of Princeton Theological Seminary, and the Manuscript Room of the Library of Congress, I am likewise grateful. Wheaton College administrators, especially Ward Kriegbaum, Patricia Ward, and the chair of the history department, Tom Kay, went out of their way to provide much-appreciated aid. Student assistants Bob Lackie, Matt Floding, and John Stackhouse diligently researched matters relating to Princeton. Mrs. Bea Horne typed and managed the paper flow in Wheaton's history department with her accustomed diffidence and efficiency. During a year as the J. Omar Good Visiting Professor of Evangelical Christianity at Juniata College, Mrs. Anne Edgin eagerly typed several papers in which Princeton figured prominently.

With other historians, I am consistently amazed at the good graces of families who tolerate a preoccupation with far distant times. In my case, indulgent parents, Francis Noll and the late Evelyn Noll, regularly inquired about "the Princeton book." Parents-in-law, Ruth Packer and the late Robert Packer, generously allowed their New Jersey homes, first in Westfield and then in Whiting, to become staging areas for research trips to Princeton and Philadelphia. In the other generational direction, Mary Constance Noll could not yet read when the project began, but she has lived to do helpful proofreading on the final product. David Luther Noll is glad this book is finished so that I can write a mystery and (he thinks) make some money. Robert Francis Noll is still too young to worry much about the past, but he possesses the sort of exuberant disposition that even Ashbel Green would have enjoyed. In a special category is Maggie Packer Noll, who, for introducing

Acknowledgments

me to both New Jersey and conservative Presbyterians, must share some responsibility for this book. Much more, as wife, mother, co-worker, and heir together of the grace of life, she is substantially responsible for the meaning of my existence. Of her many gifts to me, the greatest, by far, is herself.

ADVENT 1987

Abbreviations and Short Titles

In citing works in the footnotes and in the Bibliography, I use the abbreviations and short titles listed below. I have abridged some of the lengthy titles from the period, silently if the abridgement occurs at the end of the title, with ellipses if more of the title is given after the abridgement.

Beasley, "Life" = [Frederick Beasley], "An Account of the Life and Writings of the Rev. Samuel Stanhope Smith," *Analectic Magazine*, n.s., 1 (June 1820): 443–74; 2 (July 1820): 3–18. Virtually the same document is attached as "A Brief Memoir of His Life and Writings" to *Sermons of Samuel Stanhope Smith*, 2 vols. (Philadelphia, 1821), 1:3–60.

Collins, *Witherspoon* = Varnum Lansing Collins, *President Witherspoon: A Biography*, 2 vols. (Princeton, 1925; reprinted in 1 vol., New York, 1969).

DAB = *Dictionary of American Biography*, 20 vols. (New York, 1928–1936).

FM = "Resolves and Minutes of the Faculty," PUA. Cited by date.

General Catalogue = *General Catalogue of Princeton University, 1746–1906* (Princeton, 1908).

HSP = Historical Society of Pennsylvania.

Life of Green = *The Life of Ashbel Green, V.D.M., Begun to be written by himself in his eighty-second year and continued to his eighty-fourth. Prepared for the press at the author's request by Joseph H. Jones* (New York, 1849).

Maclean, *CNJ* = John Maclean, *History of the College of New Jersey, from Its Origin in 1746 to the Commencement of 1854*, 2 vols. (Philadelphia, 1877).

Princetonians 1748–1768 = *Princetonians 1748–1768: A Biographical Dictionary*, ed. James McLachlan (Princeton, 1976).

Princetonians 1769–1775 = *Princetonians 1769–1775: A Biographical Dictionary*, ed. Richard A. Harrison (Princeton, 1980).

Princetonians 1776–1783 = *Princetonians 1776–1783: A Biographical Dictionary*, ed. Richard A. Harrison (Princeton, 1981).

PUA = Princeton University Archives, Seeley G. Mudd Manuscript Library, Princeton University.

PUL = Manuscript Division, Firestone Library, Princeton University.

PULC = *Princeton University Library Chronicle.*

Sprague, *Annals* = William B. Sprague, *Annals of the American Pulpit*, 9 vols. (New York, 1857–1869).

Thorp, *Lives* = Willard Thorp, ed., *The Lives of Eighteen from Princeton* (Princeton, 1946).

TM = Trustee Minutes of Princeton University, vol. 1, 1748–1796; vol. 2, 1797–1823, PUA. Cited by date.

Wertenbaker, *Princeton* = Thomas Jefferson Wertenbaker, *Princeton 1746–1896* (Princeton, 1946).

Witherspoon, *Works* = *The Works of the Rev. John Witherspoon*, ed. Ashbel Green, 4 vols. (Philadelphia, 1802).

WMQ = *William and Mary Quarterly*, 3d series unless other noted.

Princeton and the Republic, 1768–1822

Top, John Witherspoon by Charles Wilson Peale;
left, Samuel Stanhope Smith by Edward Ludlow Mooney;
right, Ashbel Green by Wooley. *From
Donald Drew Egbert*, Princeton Portraits
(*Princeton University Press, 1947*).

1

Introduction

★

WHEN SAMUEL STANHOPE SMITH arrived in Princeton on December 12, 1779, as the new professor of moral philosophy at his alma mater, the College of New Jersey lay in physical ruins. Yet the vigor of its intellectual vision made Princeton the most influential center of American learning south of the Hudson. When Smith resigned as the college's president on August 14, 1812, he left a fully restored and financially secure institution. Yet it was also a college with badly shaken intellectual foundations and seriously reduced influence in church and nation. This book attempts an explanation for the college's fortunes during Smith's years at Princeton, years that coincide almost exactly with the tenure of three college presidents. Smith was in his last year as an undergraduate when John Witherspoon, his predecessor, arrived from Scotland in 1768. He died at Princeton in 1819, only three years before the resignation of his successor, Ashbel Green.

The history of Princeton in these years is the story of a "circle" made up of the college's leaders and students. The inspiration for this circle, as both thinker and activist, was John Witherspoon, but at its center for many more years stood Stanhope Smith. Smith, whom no less a personage than George Washington commended as "both learned and good," provided the institution's day-to-day stability during much of Witherspoon's tenure and served as president himself from 1795 to 1812.[1] The Princeton circle took its character less directly, but no less importantly, from an extraordinary body of trustees, whose influence in church and state spread far beyond their homes in New York City, Philadelphia, and New Jersey. Students, who usually came to Princeton from well-positioned families in the mid-Atlantic and southern states and who

[1] *The Writings of George Washington*, ed. John C. Fitzpatrick, 38 vols. (Washington, D.C., 1931–1944), 35:283.

[3]

often left for distinguished careers as legislators, ministers, judges, merchants, and gentlemen, completed the circle.

The Princeton of Revolutionary America and the early national period offers grist for many mills. The college's own chroniclers have told its fascinating institutional history very well.[2] In addition, Princeton plays an important role in other stories, especially the interwoven history of republicanism, Calvinism, and the American Enlightenment and the closely related history of the Presbyterian church. This book is also organized as an institutional narrative, but it seeks to keep those more general matters always in view.

Historians have recently described the uncertainties of the Revolutionary and post-Revolutionary generations in vivid terms. Between 1760 and 1790, according to David Hackett Fischer, the American "social system . . . was torn to pieces." In succeeding decades, religious institutions labored to come to terms with what Nathan O. Hatch calls a "cultural ferment over the meaning of freedom." John Murrin writes of "one massive uncertainty" underlying political, social, and economic turmoil—whether "thirteen extremely heterogeneous societies with no tradition of continental unity [could] battle their way from colonialism to independence as something resembling a coherent nation." To Gordon Wood, "a common democratic revolution" had created "chaos" and was the occasion for "a social and cultural upheaval scarcely matched" in American history.[3] The history of the College of New Jersey in this period illustrates each of these uncertainties—social, religious, political, and cultural—as they affected the well-to-do, religiously and politically articulate Princeton constituency in the middle and southern states. Even more, it is a history that reveals a particularly decisive attempt to master the chaos through intellectual effort.

---

[2] See especially, Maclean, *CNJ*; Wertenbaker, *Princeton*; *Princetonians 1748–1768*; *Princetonians 1769–1775*; and *Princetonians 1776–1783*. A number of more specialized studies are cited at appropriate points in the course of the book and in the Bibliography. For the period covered here, the official name of Princeton College was the College of New Jersey. "Princeton Seminary" was the Theological Seminary of the Presbyterian Church in the United States of America at Princeton, New Jersey.

[3] David Hackett Fischer, *Growing Old in America*, expanded ed. (New York, 1973), 112; Nathan O. Hatch, "The Christian Movement and the Demand for a Theology of the People," *Journal of American History* 67 (1980): 545; John M. Murrin, "The Great Inversion; or, Court versus Country: A Comparison of the Revolution Settlements in England (1688–1721) and America (1776–1816)," in *Three British Revolutions: 1641, 1688, 1776*, ed. J.G.A. Pocock (Princeton, 1980), 376; and Gordon S. Wood, "Evangelical America and Early Mormonism," *New York History* 61 (1980): 361.

One of the chief tasks engendered by the uncertainties of the new age was the need to form a positive relationship between the Christian religion and the principles of the Revolution. For most Americans, Christianity amounted to a hereditary value system of great cultural significance. Even more generally, Revolutionary republicanism was an ideology with tremendous explanatory power. Everywhere in the new republic literate citizens were busy harmonizing the two faiths—Jefferson, with his enlightened religion and articulate social theory; Noah Webster, whose fears for the nation's religious destiny inspired his wide-ranging literary activities; jurists like Chancellor James Kent of New York, who invoked the Christian character of the new nation as a legal principle; ministers like Jedidiah Morse, who linked the spread of infidelity in Europe to the overthrow of republicanism in the United States; religious leaders from every region, who treated the Bible as a guidebook for the national destiny; and revivalists who preached New Birth and the well ordering of the nation as parts of one message.[4]

The confluence of the two value systems led to different results for different groups in the population. For Presbyterian efforts to evangelize and civilize the states from New York to the upper South, the interplay between Christian and republican convictions defined both failure and success.[5] The same could be said for Congregationalists in New England and for many others. In the effort to make sense of their lives, almost all educated Americans felt it necessary to take into account the legacy of both the Christian centuries and the meaning of 1776.[6]

[4] See Jefferson's letters on religious matters collected in *Jefferson's Extracts from the Gospels*, ed. Dickinson W. Adams, *The Papers of Thomas Jefferson, Second Series*, ed. Charles T. Cullen (Princeton, 1983), 317–416; Richard M. Rollins, *The Long Journey of Noah Webster* (Philadelphia, 1980); on Chancellor Kent, see Perry Miller, *The Life of the Mind in America from the Revolution to the Civil War* (New York, 1965), 66; Jedidiah Morse, *A Sermon, Exhibiting the Present Dangers, and Consequent Duties of the Citizens of the United States of America* (Charlestown, Mass., 1799); Mark A. Noll, "The Bible in Revolutionary America," in *The Bible in American Law, Politics, and Political Rhetoric*, ed. James Turner Johnson (Philadelphia, 1985); Donald G. Mathews, "The Second Great Awakening as an Organizing Process, 1780–1830," *American Quarterly* 21 (1969): 23–43.

[5] See especially Fred J. Hood, *Reformed America: The Middle and Southern States, 1783–1837* (University, Ala., 1980).

[6] In addition to works cited in n. 4 above, the following are representative of many works that explore this relationship: Marie Caskey, *Chariot of Fire: Religion and the Beecher Family* (New Haven, 1978); Stephen E. Berk, *Calvinism versus Democracy: Timothy Dwight and the Origins of American Evangelical Orthodoxy* (Hamden, Conn., 1974); Anne C. Loveland, *Southern Evangelicals and the Social Order, 1800–1860* (Baton Rouge, La., 1980); Sidney E. Mead, *The Old Religion in the Brave New*

At Princeton a third ingredient was integral to that effort. Through the leadership of John Witherspoon, the College of New Jersey became the first American center of the Scottish philosophy of common sense, a moderate form of the Enlightenment codified by a remarkable group of savants in Edinburgh, Glasgow, and the outlying parsonages of that northern kingdom.[7] Princeton leaders eagerly embraced the principles of the Scottish Enlightenment and employed them fulsomely to reconcile republicanism and Christianity. So armed, the Princetonians were supremely confident in their ability to chart connections between private principles and the well-being of society.

Until the first years of the nineteenth century, it seemed as if the Princeton authorities were succeeding in efforts to harmonize, under the canopy of republican patriotism, a traditional Presbyterian faith and the moderate Scottish Enlightenment. Graduates, they felt, were making the necessary contributions as statesmen and spiritual leaders to preserve the nation and its sacred heritage of liberty. They were holding tides of infidelity and anarchy at bay. Beginning with a great fire that gutted Nassau Hall in 1802, however, the Princeton circle suffered a series of devastating reverses. The bad thinking, bad religion, and bad politics sweeping the public at large now rolled over Princeton as well. Well-meaning clergymen, including influential college trustees, began to grow nervous about Stanhope Smith's enlightened faith. Most of all, the earlier synthesis of patriotism, faith, and science did not hold. Student unrest, which troubled Princeton as it did other American colleges in the early years of the century, climaxed in a great rebellion in 1807. As an assault on social order, this revolt was bad enough. As a symptom of the failure of the intellectual order that had guided the college over the previous generation, it was far worse. After the rebellion board members, who to that point had

World: Reflections on the Relation between Christendom and the Republic (Berkeley, Calif., 1977); Nathan O. Hatch, "_Sola Scriptura_ and _Novus Ordo Seclorum_," in _The Bible in America: Essays in Cultural History_, ed. Hatch and Mark A. Noll (New York, 1982); J. F. Maclear, "The Republic and the Millennium," in _The Religion of the Republic_, ed. E. A. Smith (Philadelphia, 1971); and Ernest Lee Tuveson, _Redeemer Nation: The Idea of America's Millennial Role_ (Chicago, 1968).

[7] Richard B. Sher, _Church and University in the Scottish Enlightenment: The Moderate Literati of Edinburgh_ (Princeton, 1985); Nicholas Phillipson, "The Scottish Enlightenment," in _The Enlightenment in National Context_, ed. Roy Porter and Mikuláš Teich (New York, 1981). The Enlightenment at Princeton was the "didactic" kind, described expertly in Henry F. May, _The Enlightenment in America_ (New York, 1976), 307–57.

been united in support of the school as a major vehicle for strengthening the nation, divided against themselves and turned their attention increasingly away from the college. It was a sign of Princeton's shifting fortunes that its board secured Smith's resignation in the summer of 1812 at the very moment when many of its most important members were founding a separate theological seminary to remedy weaknesses at the College of New Jersey.

The following pages tell the story of Princeton in this period largely from the perspective of Stanhope Smith and the college trustees. I have chosen to write the book primarily as an intellectual and religious history, set against the background of educational and political history, rather than the reverse. Others have studied political, organizational, educational, and denominational aspects of this period at Princeton.[8] But no full-scale work has yet investigated its patterns of thought.

The intellectual and cultural history of Princeton in this period is unusual for several reasons. Like many other colleges, Princeton experienced dramatic events over the course of its history. Unlike devotees of other institutions, however, members of the Princeton circle went to extraordinary lengths to define and debate the significance of such events.[9] In addition, the Princeton circle included

[8] David W. Robson, *Educating Republicans: The College in the Era of the American Revolution, 1750–1800* (Westport, Conn., 1985), 60–66, 113–14, 120–23, 161–68, 173–76; Jurgen Herbst, *From Crisis to Crisis: American College Government, 1636–1819* (Cambridge, Mass., 1982), 82–88; Steven J. Novak, *The Rights of Youth: American Colleges and Student Revolt, 1798–1815* (Cambridge, Mass., 1977), 20–24, 31–37, 79–83, 86–87, 115–23, 157–63; James McLachlan, "The *Choice of Hercules*: American Student Societies in the Early Nineteenth Century," in *The University in Society*, ed. Lawrence Stone, 2 vols. (Princeton, 1974), 2:449–94; the volumes in the *Princetonians* series; and Howard Miller, *The Revolutionary College: American Presbyterian Higher Education, 1707–1837* (New York, 1976), 66–69, 87–102, 164–89, and 259–65.

[9] On the intellectual situation at other colleges, see Daniel Walker Howe, *The Unitarian Conscience: Harvard Moral Philosophy, 1805–1861* (Cambridge, Mass., 1970); John R. Fitzmier, "The Godly Federalism of Timothy Dwight, 1752–1817" (Ph.D. diss., Princeton University, 1986), 160–211; and David C. Humphrey, *From King's College to Columbia, 1746–1800* (New York, 1976), 208–32. The contrast is instructive between the student rebellions that took place nearly simultaneously at Harvard and Princeton in early April 1807. While the Princeton revolt elicted an unusual amount of serious written justification from both sides, the Harvard incident featured little more than wanton vandalism; mature Harvard undergraduates did not take it seriously, and student publications arising from the incident were exercises in foolishness. Compare chapter 11 below with James R. McGovern, "The Student Rebellion in Harvard College, 1807–1808," *Harvard Library Bulletin* 19 (1971):

several individuals—most notably John Witherspoon and Stanhope Smith, but also a number of trustees—who were unusually articulate advocates of their political, religious, or scientific convictions.

Although Princeton's character as an elite institution meant that it did not necessarily represent the country as a whole, its location at the geographic and intellectual crossroads of the early republic ensured that its concerns were important to the nation. At the College of New Jersey in the years of Witherspoon, Smith, and Green, patriots defended the virtues of liberty, trustees and faculty labored to shore up the good order of society, Presbyterians gathered recruits for the ministry, and intellectually capable leaders worked from several angles to integrate the concerns of science, reason, and biblical revelation. Philosophical debates occurred in the context of political and social decisions. Teachers tried to communicate republican values to students, both appreciative and unruly, even as they took the measure of events in the wider world. Loyal Presbyterians looked to the college to advance the cause of Christ and of civilization.

That many also looked to Princeton as a bulwark of republicanism is a further recommendation of its significance. Most of the splendid recent discussion of Whig thought—J.G.A. Pocock and Caroline Robbins on its rich background in Britain and the Continent; Bernard Bailyn, Gordon Wood, and others on its outworking in the Revolutionary period; and the stimulating debate highlighted by the work of Lance Banning and Joyce Appleby on its evolution in the age of Jefferson—has not faced directly the question of how religion fit into the republican scheme.[10] At Princeton in the era of Stanhope Smith, however, religious considerations

341–55, and [Joseph Tufts], *Don Quixots at College; or, A History of the Gallant Adventures lately achieved by the combined students of Harvard University* (Boston, 1807).

[10] J.G.A. Pocock, *The Machiavellian Moment* (Princeton, 1975); Caroline Robbins, *The Eighteenth-Century Commonwealthman* (Cambridge, Mass., 1959); Bernald Bailyn, *The Ideological Origins of the American Revolution* (Cambridge, Mass., 1967); Gordon S. Wood, *The Creation of the American Republic, 1776–1787* (Chapel Hill, N.C., 1969); Lance Banning, *The Jeffersonian Persuasion* (Ithaca, N.Y., 1978); Banning, "Jeffersonian Ideology Revisited: Liberal and Classical Ideas in the New American Republic," *WMQ* 43 (1986): 3–19; Joyce Appleby, *Capitalism and a New Social Order: The Republican Vision of the 1790s* (New York, 1984); Appleby, "Republicanism in Old and New Contexts," *WMQ* 43 (1986), 20–34. For summaries, see Robert E. Shalhope, "Republicanism and Early American Historiography," *WMQ* 39 (1982): 334–56; and Isaac Kramnick, "Republican Revisionism Revisited," *American Historical Review* 87 (1982): 629–64.

were always central to the outworking of republican theory. Although my primary concern is how the republican convictions of the Princeton circle influenced its conception of theology and its analysis of social forces, a focus on the role of religion also enriches the more comprehensive story of American republicanism.

To study Princeton in this period is to study an institution that contributed a steady stream of leaders to the new nation. It is also to study a neglected figure whose influence reached much further than later historians have recognized. Samuel Stanhope Smith was among the first Americans to develop principles of the Scottish philosophy of common sense into an entire educational vision and to employ them for resolving knotty problems at the intersection of science and religion. He was also a key figure in transmitting principles of moderate Calvinism, scientific method, and Scottish philosophy to the West and South.[11] More generally, an intellectual history of Princeton in the early republic highlights a neglected strand of antebellum culture, the evangelical Calvinism that through Presbyterian institutions contributed to Manifest Destiny, the reforming impulse, missionary achievements, the Christian appropriation of science, and the moral tone of American politics.[12] In sum, I hope that this book bears out the conviction of a recent historian of education in the Revolutionary period "that colleges, then as now, were excellent windows through which to view aspects of the larger culture."[13]

[11] The most insightful work on Smith has been provided by Wesley Frank Craven, "Samuel Stanhope Smith," in *Princetonians 1769–1775*, 42–51; and by Douglas Sloan's chapter "Education, Progress, and Polygamy: Samuel Stanhope Smith," in *The Scottish Enlightenment and the American College Ideal* (New York, 1971), 146–84. On the Princeton influence in the South and West, see Hood, *Reformed America*; and Donald R. Come, "The Influence of Princeton on Higher Education in the South before 1825," *WMQ* 2 (1945): 359–96.

[12] For a sampling, see Sydney E. Ahlstrom, *A Religious History of the American People* (New Haven, 1972), 469–71; May, *Enlightenment in America*, 358–62; Hood, *Reformed America*; George M. Marsden, *The Evangelical Mind and the New School Presbyterian Experience* (New Haven, 1970); Theodore Dwight Bozeman, *Protestants in an Age of Science: The Baconian Ideal and Antebellum American Religious Thought* (Chapel Hill, N.C., 1977); E. Brooks Holifield, *The Gentlemen Theologians: American Theology in Southern Culture, 1795–1860* (Durham, N.C., 1978); William G. McLoughlin, *Cherokees and Missionaries, 1789–1839* (New Haven, 1984); Bruce Kuklick, *Churchmen and Philosophers from Jonathan Edwards to John Dewey* (New Haven, 1985), 66–79, 206–15; Gary Scott Smith, *The Seeds of Secularization: Calvinism, Culture, and Pluralism in America, 1870–1915* (Grand Rapids, Mich., 1985); and John Mulder, *Woodrow Wilson: The Years of Preparation* (Princeton, 1978), 229–77.

[13] Robson, *Educating Republicans*, xv.

Events at Princeton from the Revolution through the second decade of the nineteenth century point to several conclusions. First, the amalgam of republican, Enlightenment, and Christian values that John Witherspoon created in his early years at Princeton and that he passed on as an inspiring vision to Stanhope Smith, Ashbel Green, and the college trustees was an unstable entity. While it preserved in fruitful conjunction the main intellectual forces of early American history, it also contained a full range of ironic tensions. Not unlike the experience of the Puritans with the Half-Way Covenant more than a century before, when Princeton embraced a marginal secularization of religion in order to preserve religion as a force in public life, the results were ambiguous for both religion and the public.

Second, Stanhope Smith carried out the vision of Witherspoon as faithfully, under the circumstances, as could be expected. Yet despite Smith's abilities, his republican Christian Enlightenment failed. That failure was shown by the inability of Princeton teachers to communicate the full-orbed character of the synthesis to the students, who, in 1807 and on several other occasions, used the language of republicanism to overthrow their teachers' conceptions of virtue and order. The failure was also seen in Smith's inability to convince influential members of the Princeton board that his principles did not undercut the doctrines and practices of inherited Christian faith.

Third, both Smith and the more narrowly religious leaders who succeeded him exhibited a curious intellectual myopia concerning the Revolutionary vision. They continued to express confidence in John Witherspoon's synthesis of republican, Christian, and Enlightenment values, often by recalling the activities of Witherspoon himself, even after they confessed that the synthesis had not produced the virtue, piety, and social stability it promised, and even when they had begun to order their lives by other principles both more sectarian and more individualistic.

Finally, the scientific conventions of the moderate Enlightenment made it difficult for members of the Princeton circle to analyze their own situation accurately. With the advanced thinkers of their age, they believed that connections between private belief and public behavior were transparent, entirely accessible to empirical scrutiny and fully capable of lawlike description. This confidence in scientific method, however, led to a series of misjudgments concerning events at the college and the wider world. In particular, these misjudgments overestimated the motive force of religious and political convictions at the expense of other, less obviously ideological causes, with the result that a further misperception prevailed. What seemed to the Princeton leaders problems of religion or politics were often actually problems of their own appropriation of the Enlightenment.

Finally, this study raises at least one important theoretical question. If the republican Christian Enlightenment of John Witherspoon—and, in later variations, of Stanhope Smith and Ashbel Green—did not achieve what its proponents hoped it would, what may be concluded about the synthesis itself? That is, could an intellectual vision so heavily dependent on the self-revealing powers of nature, as defined by the Scottish philosophy, ever truly be integrated with an intellectual system incorporating Christian conceptions of revelation and the supernatural? I do not attempt a systematic answer to that question. Yet it remains an important one in light of how significant the Princeton of Witherspoon, Smith, and Green was in linking Christian and Enlightenment convictions, and in light of how significant these convictions, with the republicanism to which they were bound, have remained in the history of American religion, and indeed in the history of America.

2

Prologue, 1779

War, Heroism, Ruins

★

COMMENCEMENT AT the College of New Jersey on September 29, 1779, was only a shadow of previous celebrations. To be sure, the student speeches were well received, including one by the son of a trustee, Richard Stockton, Jr., who was well qualified to speak on his theme, "principles of true heroism." When the British had rolled through New Jersey in late November 1776, Richard, then twelve years old, was left behind to care for his family's Princeton estate. Some who heard his speech knew how ably the young Stockton had comported himself on that occasion, but others probably thought more of his father's heroism. Richard Stockton, Sr., had signed the Declaration of Independence as one of five New Jersey representatives to the Second Continental Congress. Five months later, in December 1776, he was captured by the British, who treated him with great brutality. Washington protested the harsh treatment, but Stockton won his freedom only by taking an oath of neutrality. This compromise, in turn, led to censure from some patriots. At the 1779 commencement Stockton also bore the marks of a harrowing operation for lip cancer, an affliction that would take his life seventeen months later.[1]

Whatever Richard Stockton's own thoughts during his son's oration, he probably reflected sometime during that day on the fate that made Princeton's thirty-second graduating class no larger than its first, his own, in 1748. Only ten students had attended the summer session in 1779, and a mere six were graduating that day. The commencement audience therefore had to be content with a

[1] "Richard Stockton [Jr.]," in *Princetonians 1776–1783*, 277–78; "Richard Stockton [Sr.]," in *Princetonians 1748–1768*, 10; Alfred Hoyt Bill, *A House Called Morven: Its Role in American History, 1701–1954* (Princeton, 1954), 35–50.

much shorter program of student speeches and debates than usual. A newspaper reported that a "numerous and respectable" crowd gathered for the ceremony, but it was nothing like the assemblies that had once thronged Princeton for the annual fall festivity. Only six years before, one of Princeton's largest graduating classes, with twenty-nine scholars, had done the day right.[2]

Still, college trustees had reason to take heart as they convened for a brief meeting that day. At least now it was possible to hold a commencement, as had not been the case in 1776 and 1777. Now they could muster a quorum, which had been impossible the previous September. And now something could be done to provide more regular instruction for the students who succeeded in reaching the campus.

Since the start of the war, President John Witherspoon had served nearly continuously in the Continental Congress. As a consequence, most of the instruction was left in the hands of William Churchill Houston, professor of mathematics and natural philosophy, himself a member of New Jersey's state assembly in 1777 and 1778. As of May 25, however, Houston too was part of New Jersey's delegation to Congress. In addition, the college had not been able to retain any junior faculty, or tutors, since 1777. At the September board meeting in 1779, the president himself took steps to remedy the situation: "Dr. Witherspoon proposed to the trustees to chuse a professor of Moral Philosophy—& recommended the Revd. Sam. S. Smith, at present, at the head of an Academy in Virginia," to fill the position.[3]

The choice, from almost any perspective, was a logical one. Smith's father, Robert, of tiny Pequea, Pennsylvania, was a respected figure in the Presbyterian church; a distinguished minister, educator, and patriot; and since 1772 a Princeton trustee. In his own right Stanhope Smith had been the leading member of Witherspoon's first graduating class in 1769, and in 1775 he married Ann Witherspoon, the president's oldest child. Smith was only twenty-eight when he was recalled to teach alongside his father-in-law, but he had already served faithfully as missionary and pastor in Virginia and had proven his mettle as an educator by successfully establishing Hampden-Sidney Academy in Prince Edward County.

The trustees who summoned Smith to Princeton were an ex-

---

[2] Wertenbaker, *Princeton*, 63.

[3] *Princetonians 1776–1783*, xix–xx; "William Churchill Houston," in *Princetonians 1748–1768*, 643–46; *Letters of Members of the Continental Congress*, ed. Edmund C. Burnett, 8 vols. (Washington, D.C., 1921–1936), 4:lvi; TM, Sept. 29, 1779.

traordinary group of talented, powerful, and visionary men. In 1779 most were working to secure national independence and create a new society. Witherspoon and the Monmouth County physician Nathaniel Scudder came to the 1779 board meeting from Philadelphia as members of the Continental Congress and returned to that body shortly after their business was finished in Princeton. Two of the board members absent from the September meeting, John Bayard and Jonathan Bayard Smith, held high office in Pennsylvania's new state government. Another absent trustee, Elias Boudinot, had just finished a term as Washington's commissary of prisoners, with responsibility for exchange and care of captured troops. Because most of the trustees lived in the New York–Philadelphia corridor, they had suffered unusual privations during the concentrated fighting that swept over New Jersey from November 1776 to June 1778. Board members also served under arms and as chaplains, and many had been called to public office. They were undergoing the experience that became, in the eye of memory, the meridian point of their lives.

Those who continued to serve on the Princeton board after the war regarded their trust as an opportunity to promote the ideals for which they had fought. They had learned the price of liberty. Two of their number paid for it with their lives. Nathaniel Scudder became the only member of the Continental Congress to die in battle when he fell during a skirmish with Loyalists in October 1781. One month later, another trustee, the Reverend James Caldwell, was killed in a military accident.[4] Instructed by principles of Revolutionary ideology and Calvinistic theology, the trustees were convinced they knew what liberty meant, what obligations it bore, and what privileges it bestowed. Some, it is true, took their responsibilities to the college more seriously than others. But all wanted to make Princeton an agent fulfilling their highest aspirations for the country. As dedicated Presbyterians, they also held lofty goals for the college as a center of Christian faith and learning.

Their choice of a professor at the 1779 board meeting had long-lasting significance. From the time he arrived in December 1779 until he retired thirty-three years later, Samuel Stanhope Smith was the administrative mainstay of the institution. Very soon after his return to Princeton in 1779, Smith became the college's intellectual heart as well. In him the trustees found a scholar, a patriot,

---

[4] Caldwell was famous for purportedly rallying patriots in a skirmish against the British at Springfield, New Jersey, by supplying hymnbooks for wadding paper and urging the troops, "Put Watts into them, boys!" ("James Caldwell," in *Princetonians 1748–1768*, 261).

and a Christian to carry on the work of Witherspoon. Over the years the trustees gave much to Stanhope Smith—prominence in the Presbyterian church, access to America's loftiest cultural circles, and a strategic influence over the elite youth of the middle and southern states. But they also asked for much in return—vigilant protection of moral and social order, careful guarding of the faith, and dedicated promotion of learning.

Even as they broadened and reaffirmed their initial confidence in Smith—through successive appointments as professor of moral philosophy, professor of theology, vice president, and president—the trustees also retained their own minds on the direction that the college should take. The board members who called Smith to Princeton, with only two exceptions, had passed from the scene by the time he retired in 1812. Yet throughout his tenure the trustees of 1779 and their successors never relinquished the conviction that they bore ultimate responsibility. Their hopes, their beliefs, their fears, and their maneuverings shaped Smith's oversight of the college and the college's wider role in the new nation. Still it was Smith—sometimes the servant of the whole board, sometimes the ally of one of its factions, sometimes without its support—who gave life to the college for the next third of a century.

In 1779, however, the needs of the present were more demanding than hopes for the future. Nassau Hall, the college building, was in ruins. The institution's accounts were muddled, its endowment devoured by inflation. The task of restoring facilities was a daunting one.

Straitened as circumstances seemed in Smith's early days as a professor, Princeton's fortunes were in fact on the rise. Nearly twice as many students appeared in 1780 as the ten who had attended in 1779.[5] Smith's presence bequeathed stability and continuity. The shift of active warfare to the south, and its cessation after 1781, eased the minds and encouraged the hearts of the Princeton circle. But most important, the college survived the war with its greatest asset intact. Samuel Stanhope Smith would direct Princeton's rapid recovery in the 1780s, but the inspiration for that rise remained the educational vision, the patriotic vigor, the virile Christianity, and the philosophical assurance of its president, John Witherspoon.

[5] Wertenbaker, *Princeton*, 64; and more generally, *Princetonians 1776–1783*, xx–xxiii.

3

John Witherspoon Comes to Princeton

Promoting the Interests of the Redeemors Kingdom

★

WHEN JOHN WITHERSPOON finally agreed in late 1767 to take up the presidency of the College of New Jersey, it brought an end to a period of uncertainty in both his life and the life of the college. Witherspoon himself served Princeton for twenty-six years, longer than his five predecessors together. The most significant aspect of his service was not its duration, however, but the stamp that his character impressed upon the institution. Under Witherspoon Princeton evolved in ways that deeply satisfied, even if they also occasionally perplexed, the doughty survivors among the serious men who had brought the college into existence and carried it through the trying experiences of its first two decades.

The arrival of Witherspoon gave Princeton trustees hope that a new day might be dawning for their institution.[1] The college, founded in 1746 and secured with a firm charter in 1748, had already become an important institution in the colonies. Except for Harvard and Yale it was granting more bachelor of arts degrees (an average of eighteen per year for the period 1760–1768) than any other American college. By 1766 its graduates were edging toward eminence in church and state. Even more than Yale and

[1] This chapter draws freely from Wertenbaker, *Princeton*, 3–79; *Princetonians 1748–1768*, xi–xxiv; Maclean, *CNJ*, 1:1–299; Leonard J. Trinterud, *The Forming of an American Tradition: A Re-examination of Colonial Presbyterianism* (Philadelphia, 1949), 169–241; L. H. Butterfield, *John Witherspoon Comes to America* (Princeton, 1953); Darrell L. Guder, "The History of Belles Lettres at Princeton" (Ph.D. diss., University of Hamburg, 1964), 107–37; Alison B. Olson, "The Founding of Princeton University: Religion and Politics in Eighteenth-Century New Jersey," *New Jersey History* 87 (1965): 133–50; and David C. Humphrey, "The Struggle for Sectarian Control of Princeton, 1745–1760," ibid. 91 (1973): 77–90.

Harvard it was a national institution, with students attending from New England and the South as well as from New York, Pennsylvania, and New Jersey.[2] Yet the institution's promising beginnings could not mask the uncertainties troubling the college as trustees began the search for a successor to President Samuel Finley, who had died in July 1766.

The most immediate worry was the question of leadership. In its first twenty years the college had displayed a voracious appetite for the pride of colonial Presbyterianism. Four of the church's most energetic leaders—Jonathan Dickinson (dead at age 59), Aaron Burr (dead at 41), Samuel Davies (dead at 37), and Samuel Finley (dead at 51)—as well as the theological luminary of the Congregationalists, Jonathan Edwards (dead at 54), had succumbed in the prime of life after coming to serve as the Princeton president.[3] While this succession of noteworthy leaders did spread the renown of the school from Edwards's Massachusetts to Davies's Virginia, the rapid turnover also destabilized the college. The raising of funds, the recruitment of students, the maintenance of discipline, the supervision of tutors—all felt the effects of swiftly changing leadership. Even more troubling, however, was the loss to the denomination of a full generation of its most effective leaders.

By its charter the College of New Jersey was an independent institution granting "free and Equal Liberty and Advantage of Education" to "those of every religious Denomination." The charter also set broad purposes for the school as a place "wherein Youth may be instructed in the learned Languages, and in the Liberal Arts."[4] But anyone with an eye to see knew that Princeton was a special preserve of the middle-colony, New Side Presbyterians, who favored heart religion over ecclesiastical precision and who

[2] Of the 301 students from 1748 to 1768 whose place of origin is known, 28 percent came from New England; 59 percent from New York, Pennsylvania, and New Jersey; and 13 percent from Delaware, Maryland, Virginia, North Carolina, and South Carolina. By contrast, almost all students in the period at William and Mary were from Virginia, 90 percent at Harvard from Massachusetts, and 75 percent at Yale from Connecticut (*Princetonians 1748–1768*, xix–xx).

[3] The importance of these leaders is suggested by the fact that the four Presbyterians accounted for 20 percent of the titles and 22 percent of the editions published by members of their denomination from 1706 through 1789. Only Gilbert Tennent among the Presbyterians published more than Dickinson, Davies, or Finley. For these figures I am indebted to a diligent student assistant, Matthew Floding, who derived them from Leonard Trinterud, *Bibliography of American Presbyterianism during the Colonial Period* (Philadelphia, 1968).

[4] "Charters of the College of New Jersey," in Wertenbaker, *Princeton*, 396–97.

incorporated revival into their theological traditions. Princeton's founders began their efforts to secure a charter hard on the heels of the death of William Tennent, whose "Log College" had been the model for other ventures by Presbyterians to instruct prospective ministers in the evangelical Calvinism of the New Side. Nine of the eleven laymen on its original board were Presbyterians, and eleven of the twelve ministers were members of the New Side Synod of New York. By 1756 only the governor of New Jersey (who chaired the board ex officio) was not a Presbyterian.[5] In addition, the college's first five presidents came exclusively from the factions that backed the colonial Great Awakening most wholeheartedly, migrants from New England and the Scotch-Irish generation trained in the Log Colleges. Princeton's early spokesmen were not dissembling when they promoted the institution as a broadly based school of the arts and sciences, but its overriding concern was clearly religious. Jonathan Dickinson, the first president, had said as much in 1747: "Our Aim in the Undertaking is to promote the Interests of the Redeemors Kingdom; and to raise up qualified Persons for the sacred Service to supply . . . qualified Candidates for the Ministry."[6] In this effort, the college had been successful. Princeton's first twenty-one classes (1748–1768) produced 158 ministers (or 47 percent of the graduates), 97 of whom served Presbyterian churches and, reflecting the New England connection, 41 Congregational. The great preponderance of these graduates carried away New Side or New Light convictions from Princeton.[7]

At the time of President Finley's death, the ecclesiastical situation was not as clear as it once had been. The bloom of the Presbyterian New Side lay withered in Princeton cemetery. Moreover, relations among Presbyterians were entering a new phase. In 1741 New Sides and Old Sides had parted ways, but after time banked the fires of revival and moderated the traditionalism of the conser-

[5] Humphrey, "Struggle for Sectarian Control of Princeton," 86, 88. For a general picture, see Howard Miller, "Evangelical Religion and Colonial Princeton," in *Schooling and Society*, ed. Lawrence Stone (Baltimore, 1976).

[6] Dickinson is quoted in Humphrey, "Struggle for Sectarian Control of Princeton," 83. The more general purposes are described in Aaron Burr, "Laws and Customs of the College" (ms., 1748), as discussed in Francis I. Broderick, "Pulpit, Physics, and Politics: The Curriculum of the College of New Jersey, 1746–1794," *WMQ* 6 (1949): 49; Princeton Trustees, *A General Account of the Rise and State of the College* (New York, 1752); and [Samuel Blair], *An Account of the College of New Jersey* (Woodbridge, N.J., 1764).

[7] *Princetonians 1748–1768*, xxii; *Princetonians 1769–1775*, xxvi–xxvii.

vatives, the two parties negotiated a reunion in 1758. Old antagonisms remained, but the hope was also growing for a unified Presbyterian advance.

Not surprisingly, the College of New Jersey was caught up in efforts to reunify the church. After Finley's death, Philadelphia Old Sides proposed to the Princeton trustees that the college name a president and one faculty member from their number. In return, the Old Sides offered to raise money for the school so that it could balance the faculty with two New Side appointees. The Princeton board brushed aside the attempted takeover. It had never so much as considered an Old Side as president; it had only rarely hired anyone with Old Side sympathies even as a tutor. The trustees, however, were not insensitive to the advantage that would accrue to the school if it could draw in Old Side support without jeopardizing its New Side commitments. Board members looked upon the church as a fount of good thinking, social order, and colonial health; they were therefore eager to do what they could for the college, even if this required some form of cooperation with the suspect Old Sides.[8]

The Presbyterian position in the colonies as a whole was also in flux during the 1760s. A new surge of Scottish and Scotch-Irish immigration had unloosed a flood of nominal Presbyterians to the west and south of the New York–Philadelphia center of previous Presbyterian settlement. The new settlers required ministers. At the same time that new immigrants were drawing Presbyterian attention away from New England, developments there were casting shadows upon the long-standing cooperation between Presbyterian New Sides and Congregational New Lights. The "New Divinity" of Jonathan Edwards's successors, Joseph Bellamy and Samuel Hopkins, still was attractive to some learned Presbyterians, but others thought it was drifting toward metaphysical obscurity. After Finley's death the Princeton Board did consider Samuel Hopkins as president. Yet they drew back, out of a growing sense that, however useful Hopkins's speculative divinity might be in his New England, he was not the man of the hour for the practical needs of the Presbyterians.[9]

[8] Butterfield, *Witherspoon Comes to America*, 1–36, reprints many of the letters that spell out this factional maneuvering.

[9] Trinterud, *Colonial Presbyterianism*, 129, 137, 226; William Warren Sweet, *Religion on the American Frontier, 1783–1840*, vol. 2, *The Presbyterians* (Chicago, 1936), 2. For the development of the New Divinity, see William Breitenbach, "The Consis-

Behind the various problems of personnel, regional diversity, ecclesiastical maneuvering, and theological emphasis lay basic questions concerning the college's institutional direction. From its inception trustees and presidents had promoted the College of New Jersey as an institution serving (1) religion, (2) the body politic, (3) social order, (4) good character, (5) learning, and (6) "the union of piety and science."[10] The pursuit of these overlapping interests defined the college's reason for existence and held up such a worthy ideal that the trustees in 1766 were not embarrassed to seek yet another dignified churchman to pursue them.

Princeton was to serve religion by supplying ministers to the church, by transmitting orthodox Christian faith, and by nourishing the piety of its charges. To accomplish these ends, college authorities spoke privately with students about their spiritual condition, conducted services of prayer twice a day, encouraged informal student devotions, lectured in divinity, and prayed for awakenings. They took almost as much care in designing means to serve political health and to support social order. The curriculum from its outset included systematic consideration of ethics and political theory. College regulations were designed to show students the importance of the rule of law. And especially at times of national emergency, trustees encouraged extraordinary rituals of patriotism. The college existed to defend liberty, train leaders of the state, and inculcate the personal virtue that they assumed was the foundation of social order and public morality.

From the start as well, college authorities took seriously their task in preparing gentlemen for the world. The school, with a few exceptions for talented plebians dedicated to the ministry, was largely a preserve of the elite. College laws, self-sustaining student societies, a special attention to public speaking, and an ever-present concern for honor provided the means to develop character and prepare students for stations of dignity in the world.

The college's curriculum, after preliminary work in classical languages and mathematics, featured serious-minded inquiry into the physical world (natural philosophy) and systematic study of humanity (moral philosophy). Observers from afar sometimes wondered if the clerics who presided at Princeton possessed the necessary expertise in the arts and sciences. The three presidents

---

tent Calvinism of the New Divinity," *WMQ* 41 (1984): 241–64; and Joseph A. Conforti, *Samuel Hopkins and the New Divinity Movement* (Grand Rapids, Mich., 1981).

[10] This was the title of John Witherspoon's inaugural address, which only rehearsed a long-standing theme at Princeton.

before Witherspoon who had served long enough to show their mettle—Burr, Davies, and Finley—silenced this speculation by their dedicated and skillful efforts in what would now be called "secular" subjects. They championed free inquiry, on the model of Bacon's induction, and did what they could to promote study in mathematics and natural philosophy (science). Yet they did so while maintaining orthodox assumptions about the unity of truth under God. Instruction in natural philosophy piously demonstrated the wonders of God in the physical world. Teaching in moral philosophy scientifically demonstrated the reasonableness of faith. Princeton was not as advanced in the pursuit of science as Harvard, which established a professorship in mathematics and natural philosophy in 1727, but it nonetheless had made a significant beginning, without, moreover, compromising its religious purposes in the process.[11]

In 1766 the trustees were again looking for someone to implement the several parts of the college's vision. Earlier presidents had stressed now one, now another of the general goals, without ever abandoning any of them. Samuel Davies's words to departing seniors in 1760 spoke for them all: "Serve your Generation. Live not for yourselves, but the Publick. Be the Servants of the Church; the Servants of your Country; the Servants of all."[12] Trustees may have sensed that they entertained a complex set of institutional purposes, yet they had gone beyond the place of desiring merely a Log College. They were pleased that Finley's last classes, of 1765 and 1766, included a full thirty-one graduates each, including several students who were already giving promise of distinction in public affairs (e.g., Luther Martin, Oliver Ellsworth) and the world of letters (e.g., David Ramsey), as well as in divinity (e.g., Jonathan Edwards, Jr., Samuel Kirkland).[13] On the other hand, they were not slackening their original religious purposes. The trustees of 1766 were still spiritual descendents of the colonial Great Awakening, in many cases the actual converts of Whitefield or Gilbert Tennent. They looked upon Harvard as an institution that had imperiled its religious direction by stressing too much the autonomy of learning and good character. Although many of them were

[11] Guder, "Belles Lettres at Princeton," 109–34; and George H. Bost, "Samuel Davies as President of Princeton," *Journal of Presbyterian History* 26 (1948): 165–81.

[12] *Princetonians 1748–1768*, xxiii.

[13] Edwards, Kirkland, and Ramsey were in the class of 1765; Ellsworth and Martin, the class of 1766 (*Princetonians 1748–1768*, 492–96, 502–7, 517–21, 555–59, 578–85).

Yale graduates, they feared that their alma mater was also sacrificing its religious birthright for a mess of dignified pottage. They may not have sensed how unstable the mixture of Princeton's goals actually was, but they knew that their next president would have to be a man of wisdom and skill to preserve the college's various purposes without doing damage to any of them. They hoped John Witherspoon would be their man. And, so it seemed, they were not disappointed.

JOHN WITHERSPOON was born in early February 1723, four years before the death of Sir Isaac Newton and nine years before the birth of George Washington.[14] His mother and his father, a minister of the Church of Scotland, provided an intellectually challenging home. At a very early age the young Witherspoon learned by heart large sections of the New Testament and many of Isaac Watts's hymns, perhaps developing as he did so the great facility for memorization that he retained throughout his life. Witherspoon was still quite young when he received the Master of Arts in 1739 from the University of Edinburgh. After more years of theological study he was licensed to preach and in January 1745 commenced ministerial service at the kirk in Beith, Ayrshire. A year later, after raising militia to repel the invasion of Charles Stuart, the Young Pretender to the British throne, Witherspoon was an observer at the Battle of Falkirk, where he was captured by rebel forces. He suffered a brief but severe imprisonment that brought on nervous disorders that plagued him for the rest of his life. Witherspoon's conscientious attention to pastoral labor, his solid preaching, and a taste for serious study solidified his reputation, and in June 1757 he moved to the larger, more prosperous Laigh Kirk in Paisley.

Before that time, however, Witherspoon had entered the wider world of theological controversy and set himself upon the course that would bring him to the attention of the Princeton trustees.

[14] For the life of Witherspoon before arriving in Princeton, I have relied especially on Collins, *Witherspoon*, 1:3–101. Also useful for that earlier period are A. L. Drummond, "Witherspoon of Gifford and American Presbyterianism," *Records of the Scottish Historical Society* 12 (1958): 185–201; George Eugene Rich, "John Witherspoon: His Scottish Intellectual Background" (Ph.D. diss., Syracuse University, 1964); Ashbel Green, *The Life of the Revd John Witherspoon*, ed. Henry Lyttleton Savage (Princeton, 1973); and Thomas Jefferson Wertenbaker, "John Witherspoon (1723–1794): Father of American Presbyterianism, Maker of Statesmen," in Thorp, *Lives.*

The general arena of this activity was the dispute between Moderate and Popular parties within the Church of Scotland. The specific occasion drawing Witherspoon into the fray was the publication in 1753 of his *Ecclesiastical Characteristics*, a satirical attack on those who "appropriate to themselves wholly the character of moderate men."[15]

The eighteenth-century dispute over Moderatism in the Kirk of Scotland represented an early chapter in the struggle between orthodox, confessional Protestantism and the moralistic, literary faith of the Enlightenment.[16] Moderates sought not an end to Christianity but its humanization. Inspired especially by the path-breaking moral philosophy of Francis Hutcheson (1694–1746), who taught at Glasgow for seventeen years, Moderates turned from divine revelation to a systematic examination of the human mind as the key to ultimate knowledge of the world. They championed "the moral sense," rather than outworn confessions, as the arbiter of truth and virtue. Moderates did not abandon preaching but looked upon the sermon as a form of dignified literature. Cultured, dignified, and enlightened, Moderates were at home in the company of Scotland's best families. Many of the elite, for their part, were ready to exercise traditional patronage rights to secure pastorates for Moderate ministers, who, with this support, exercised secure control of the Kirk's General Assembly.

Against the Moderates an Evangelical, or Popular, party arose to affirm the old creeds, to insist upon fervent preaching, and to champion the Bible. Evangelicals also complained bitterly about the abuses of privilege that kept Moderates in control of the General Assembly, even as they defended the traditional prerogative of the local congregation to veto the choice of its ministers. Witherspoon's *Ecclesiastical Characteristics* vaulted him into the leadership of this party. It was the most important of his several polemical pieces, which included also an attack on the stage, a fast-day sermon linking religious uprightness and national prosperity, and an exhortation assaulting cold sermon eloquence and clerical meddling in public affairs.[17] The thirteen "maxims" of the *Ecclesiastical*

---

[15] Witherspoon, *Works*, 3:209.

[16] Good general accounts of this struggle are found in Richard B. Sher, *Church and University in the Scottish Enlightenment: The Moderate Literati of Edinburgh* (Princeton, 1985); and Andrew L. Drummond and James Bulloch, *The Scottish Church, 1688–1843: The Age of the Moderates* (Edinburgh, 1973), 45–81.

[17] Collins, *Witherspoon*, 1:45, 52, 54–55; Witherspoon, "A Serious Inquiry into the Nature and Effects of the Stage," "Prayer for National Prosperity and for the Re-

Characteristics offered advice to ministerial candidates on how to get along in a Moderate world. The first counseled that "all ecclesiastical persons . . . suspected of heresy, are to be esteemed men of great genius, vast learning, and uncommon worth." Its fourth, on preaching, reminded the candidate that, in the pulpit, a Moderate's "authorities must be drawn from heathen writers . . . as few as possible, from Scripture." It also proposed that a Moderate "must be very unacceptable to the common people." In the course of this work, Witherspoon took direct aim at Moderate intellectual guides, including Leibnitz and Lord Shaftesbury, whose thought "has been so well licked into form and method by the late immortal Mr. H——n."[18] Witherspoon's satire, which in spite of heavy-handed moments still makes for enjoyable reading, was a particular triumph because it turned the Moderates' chosen weapons—humor, an eye for incongruity, and a patronizing savoir faire—to their own embarrassment. It went through five printings in two years and earned Witherspoon much admiration from Evangelicals as well as such lasting opprobrium from the Moderates that they succeeded in delaying his call to Paisley through protests in the presbytery.

Witherspoon's leadership of the Evangelicals rested on more than his wit. While he was engaged in poking fun at the Moderates, he was also preparing constructive theological works for the press. Major treatises on the relationship between justification and holy living (1756) and on regeneration (1764), together with occasional sermons, marked him as an effective theological spokesman. Some of the latter, like "The Absolute Necessity of Salvation through Christ," also carried on the attack against the Moderates, especially for their promotion of "the unnatural mixture . . . of modern philosophy with ancient Christianity."[19] Most such efforts, however, like the sermons "All Mankind by Nature under Sin" or "Christ's Death a Proper Atonement for Sin," were nonpolemical expressions of evangelical orthodoxy.[20] Witherspoon's theology was zealous, yet restrained; he appealed amply to Scripture but did not rely on sterile proof-texting. And he was especially eager to show how traditional Protestant concepts like justification and the

---

vival of Religion inseparably connected," and "The Charge of Sedition and Faction against good Men," in *Works*, 3:121–90; 2:453–77, 415–51.

[18] Witherspoon, *Works*, 3:211, 219, 229.

[19] Ibid., 2:340. The sermon was preached on Jan. 2, 1758.

[20] Ibid., 1:267–83, 331–48.

New Birth were always and everywhere of great practical significance.

Witherspoon also attempted to stay abreast of more formal academic work. In 1753, shortly before writing the *Ecclesiastical Characteristics*, he contributed to *The Scots Magazine* an essay that attacked Lord Kames, patron of Moderates and a Moderate author himself, for his opinions on the will. In this piece, which sketched positions he developed more fully as the Princeton president, Witherspoon painstakingly affirmed the faithfulness of our senses, moral and physical: "The ideas we receive by our senses, and the persuasions we derive immediately from them, are exactly according to truth, to real truth, which certainly ought to be the same with philosophic truth." The essay was not precise philosophically, nor did it receive wide attention, but it did reveal the young Witherspoon's capacity for academic discussion. It also provided at least some basis for Witherspoon's later claim that he had anticipated the fuller attacks on Berkeley and Hume mounted by Thomas Reid and other Scottish proponents of a common-sense realism. In addition, this essay became Witherspoon's introduction to America when it was sent by a colleague, John Erskine of Edinburgh, to Jonathan Edwards's friend and collaborator, Joseph Bellamy, for whose work Witherspoon had earlier expressed appreciation.[21]

SOON OTHER Americans came to learn about Witherspoon, including the Presbyterians Samuel Davies and Gilbert Tennent, who encountered his name in 1754 when they visited Scotland to raise money for the College of New Jersey. Shortly thereafter Witherspoon began to correspond with Samuel Finley, and perhaps other American Presbyterians.[22] When the Princeton trustees met in 1766 to select Finley's successor, they realized that no logical choice remained among the American New Side men. When they looked abroad, they were drawn immediately to Witherspoon. He was, of course, a champion of orthodoxy and a proponent of evangelical piety. But he was also at home in the world of learning. He was a magnanimous Presbyterian who had remained loyal to his General Assembly, when other Evangelicals had bolted in 1733

[21] Witherspoon, "Remarks on an essay on human liberty," *The Scots Magazine* 15 (1753): 165; Collins, *Witherspoon*, 1:41.

[22] George William Pilcher, ed., *The Reverend Samuel Davies Abroad: The Diary of a Journey to England and Scotland, 1753–55* (Urbana, Ill., 1967), 99; Butterfield, *Witherspoon Comes to America*, 12–13.

and 1761.[23] Witherspoon's very innocence of American factions gave him yet another advantage. Confident of his standing on the side of evangelical orthodoxy, the trustees could still make his appointment a gesture of conciliation to the Old Side by drawing attention to their willingness not to name yet another veteran of American factional strife. That Witherspoon had confounded the Moderates with their own weapons and that he had demonstrated the practicality of traditional piety were all the more reasons that his name inspired confidence in the Princeton trustees. It seemed, in short, as if they had found their man.

But first it was necessary to secure Witherspoon's acceptance. Although the board voted unanimously in November 1766 to name Witherspoon, for many months thereafter it was not certain that he would accept. Witherspoon seems to have been impressed enough by the prospect of serving religion and education in the New World, but Mrs. Elizabeth Witherspoon was reluctant to leave her settled round and, perhaps, the graves of the five children she had laid to rest in Beith and Paisley.[24] The urgings of trustee Richard Stockton, who was in Britain on business, and of Benjamin Rush, who was finishing his medical training at Edinburgh, were at first of no avail.

As a result, the disappointed Princeton trustees turned in 1767 to a twenty-six-year-old scion of the New Sides, Samuel Blair, Jr., whom they proposed as the head of a faculty to include two other New Sides and a solitary Old Side. Old Side leaders took offense, some trustees wondered in private if the school could survive, and Samuel Blair, who had only recently become an associate at Boston's Old South Church, accepted the position with grave reservations himself. Princeton's constituency felt the uncertainty; funds remained in short supply, and the number of students declined.[25] Finally, however, Rush won over Mrs. Witherspoon, Blair graciously stepped aside, the board reaffirmed its earlier choice, Old Side leaders were mollified, and trustees set plans afoot to welcome the Witherspoons in time for commencement in September 1768.

When the couple finally arrived in mid-August with their five

---

[23] Drummond and Bulloch, *Scottish Church, 1688–1843*, 41–42, 61–62.

[24] Collins, *Witherspoon*, 1:25 n. 19.

[25] Since most students entered college as sophomores or juniors, changes in administration could be reflected almost immediately in the size of the graduating class. The number of graduates sank to eleven each for 1767 and 1768, as compared to thirty-one each for the preceding two years. See Appendix A, which charts the number of graduates year by year.

surviving children, they were feted in Philadelphia, where a local printer issued a special edition of *Ecclesiastical Characteristics* to mark the occasion. The journey to Princeton became something of a triumphal procession when the gentry of Trenton and the trustees of the region turned out to escort the family from the Delaware River to Princeton. A mile from town the party was met by faculty, students, and local notables. The same night, August 12, students illuminated Nassau Hall with candles, and the Witherspoons settled into Morven, Richard Stockton's spacious home, until refurbishing of the president's house on campus could be completed. At the commencement on September 28, an unusually large crowd gathered to hear the new president declaim his inaugural in Latin on "the Connection & mutual influences of Learning & Piety."[26] For months thereafter Witherspoon remained an object of interest to the curious and of hopeful expectation to the friends of Princeton, the Presbyterian church, the liberal arts, and—increasingly—the liberties of the colonies.

The new president was not a disappointment. Rather, interest and expectation turned to respect and deference as Witherspoon unleashed a fearsome energy on his tasks. By 1775, when the outbreak of hostilities with Britain disrupted normal activities in the colonies, Witherspoon's reputation as a successful educator, an ecclesiastical statesman, and a defender of liberty was secure.

[26] No copy, unfortunately, exists of this address (Collins, *Witherspoon*, 1:133).

4

The Legacy of Witherspoon

One of the Great Men of the Age

★

THE SECRET of John Witherspoon's greatness did not lie on the surface. This "intolerably homely old Scotchman," as one visitor described him in 1787, was not a particularly striking figure. His portrait by Charles Wilson Peale reveals a friendly but unpresupposing countenance atop a nondescript frame of gentlemanly corpulence.[1] Neither was he an intellectual giant or a particularly consistent thinker. He won repute as a preacher, yet from the pulpit his Scottish burr rendered him nearly unintelligible in his adopted land. John Adams could understand his preaching only because debate in the Continental Congress had accustomed him to the accent.[2] Witherspoon was known as a philosopher, although in his work careful demonstration readily gave way to rough and ready assertions. He was regarded as the Revolutionary era's most important theologian-politician, even though, arriving in Princeton with lifelong ties to America's Calvinist theologians and little firsthand knowledge of the American political situation, he accepted his new country's dominant political fashions and rejected its best Reformed theology both without a moment's hesitation.

It was rather as a forceful personality and as a forthright spokesman for good sense that Witherspoon made his mark in America. Ashbel Green, student of Witherspoon and eventually himself president of the college, had regular contact with his mentor for

[1] Collins, *Witherspoon*, 2:161. The Peale portrait is reproduced after ibid., 182, and in Thomas Jefferson Wertenbaker, "John Witherspoon (1723–1794): Father of American Presbyterianism, Maker of Statesmen," in Thorp, *Lives*, 68.

[2] *Diary and Autobiography of John Adams*, ed. L. H. Butterfield, 4 vols. (Cambridge, Mass., 1961), 2:259.

more than a decade. Many years later, after Green had enjoyed considerable opportunity to meet the great men of America, he wrote that, "in promiscuous company, [Witherspoon] had more of the quality called *presence*—a quality powerfully felt, but not to be described—than any other individual with whom the writer has ever had intercourse, Washington alone excepted." Similar encomiums came from a wide range of contemporaries and have been echoed since, by none more effectively than Moses Coit Tyler: "This eloquent, wise, and efficient Scotsman—at once teacher, preacher, politician, law-maker, and philosopher, [was] upon the whole not undeserving of the praise which has been bestowed upon him as 'one of the great men of the age and of the world.' "³ The praise was indeed deserved, for Witherspoon did inspire confidence at a time of widespread dislocation, and he was a trustworthy man of affairs in an age of action. Healthy and active in America for barely twenty years, he yet became a mainstay in the defense of liberty and a major force in the organization of American Presbyterianism. He also rescued the College of New Jersey from uncertainty and made it a great national institution. Only after his passing did Princetonians, deprived of his charismatic person, find the complex allegiances of his life—as Calvinist preacher, Scottish philosopher, Whig patriot, eager scientist, and eloquent gentleman—almost more than they could bear.

IMMEDIATELY UPON assuming his new post in 1768, Witherspoon set about putting the college in order. He at once reorganized the local grammar school to make it an effective feeder for the college. He proposed a more formal arrangement to guide resident postgraduates in their professional studies. He traveled north, south, and west to secure funds and friends for the college. In his first year the college endowment doubled to over £5,000. His first trips sent him into New York, Pennsylvania, and New England, where he established immediate rapport with the New Side Presbyterians and the Congregational New Lights, but where he also won grudging commendation from other parties as well. Boston's Charles Chauncy, long a foe of revival, called him "a gentleman of good learning, strong powers, and a catholic, charitable Spirit." Closer to home, Witherspoon even received surpris-

³ Ashbel Green, *The Life of the Revd John Witherspoon*, ed. Henry Lyttleton Savage (Princeton, 1973), 58–59; Moses Coit Tyler, *The Literary History of the American Revolution, 1763–1783*, 2 vols. (New York, 1897), 2:320–21.

ingly warm praise from Francis Alison, a leader of the Philadelphia Old Sides, who only shortly before had attempted to take over the college for his own party: "The President is an active man, & a good Preacher; & has done much to procure funds. . . . I hear no great things of his superior knowledge in any Branch of Philosophy, but I think he will do better than any that they had of late years, or could have chosen in the bounds of our Synod." In late 1769 and again in February 1770, Witherspoon traveled to Virginia, where he received an even warmer welcome from the friends of religion and where he made a favorable impression on the Lees, the Washingtons, and other distinguished families.[4]

Witherspoon's presence also drew increasing numbers of students to the college. The size of Princeton's graduating classes soon approached that of Yale's, and Princeton herself enjoyed a higher yearly average of graduates in the last five years before the war (25 per year, 1772–1776) than at any time before the 1790s. All this was accomplished in spite of the fact that Witherspoon had tightened admission requirements. The board did not accept for long his original proposal that none be admitted except as freshmen for the entire four-year program. But it did back him by instituting more stringent entrance examinations, so that, while it was still possible to enter Princeton as a sophomore or even a junior, those thus admitted were better equipped to handle the advanced curriculum.[5]

Witherspoon's accomplishments at Princeton are made more remarkable by his simultaneous activity in church and society, for while he was righting the college, he was also laboring to regularize the Presbyterian church and to defend the prerogatives of the colonies. Witherspoon waited until April 1769 to present his ministerial credentials to the Presbytery of New Brunswick, but this delay did not keep that body from appointing Witherspoon a delegate to the May meeting of the Synod of New York and Philadelphia, nor the synod from asking him to head the Presbyterian

[4] Beverly McAnear, "The Raising of Funds by the Colonial Colleges," *Mississippi Valley Historical Review* 38 (1951–1952): 610; Wertenbaker, *Princeton*, 53–55; Collins, *Witherspoon*, 1:125–26; quotation from Chauncy, ibid., 114; quotation from Alison, L. H. Butterfield, *John Witherspoon Comes to America* (Princeton, 1953), 83.

[5] See Appendix A for a record of the number of graduates from Princeton in this period, and *Princetonians 1769–1775*, x, for the comparison with Yale (in the period 1769–1775, Yale had 188 graduates, Princeton 150). On academic standards, see Wertenbaker, *Princeton*, 90; and Ralph Ketcham, "James Madison at Princeton," *PULC* 28 (1966): 27.

delegation to the annual convention with the Connecticut Congregationalists.[6] Witherspoon's magnanimity, his evident good sense, and his experience in the General Assembly of Scotland made him an invaluable asset in the courts of American Presbyterianism, where he toiled faithfully until, with other like-minded colleagues, he brought his denomination to accept the more efficient centralization of its own General Assembly in the 1780s. Witherspoon's value to the Presbyterians also grew from his effective reconciliation of the colonial factions.

New Side Presbyterians were satisfied with Witherspoon because he was so obviously a man of evangelical piety. While his preaching was not moving like Samuel Davies's or finely honed like Edwards's, neither was it cold and formal like that of the Old Sides. In addition, Witherspoon actively opposed the speculative philosophy of Bishop Berkeley and David Hume, which many New Sides associated with infidelity. For their part, Old Sides were pleased that Witherspoon was not a rabble-rouser or a stiff-necked hyper-Calvinist. They appreciated his efforts to moderate the waves of religious enthusiasm that swept over the college in 1770 and 1772.[7] New Side and Old Side alike appreciated his forthrightness, his thoughtfulness, his ability to command a situation, and his sacrificial energy. Both were pleased as well that under Witherspoon Princeton seemed once again to be a thriving center for pastoral training. New Sides, who had noticed a tailing off of ministerial candidates under Davies and Finley, and Old Sides, who were troubled about the Presbyterian students who became Anglicans while at the College of Philadelphia, where Francis Alison taught, looked with satisfaction on this aspect of Witherspoon's work.[8] As a point of mediation between Old Sides and New, Witherspoon was more than meeting the hopes of those who had called him to America.

---

[6] Collins, *Witherspoon*, 1:123; *Records of the Presbyterian Church in the United States . . . 1706–1788* (Philadelphia, 1904), 389–400.

[7] Ashbel Green, himself a promoter of revivals at Princeton after 1812, played down Witherspoon's coolness toward the pre-Revolutionary revivals ("Dr. Witherspoon's Administration at Princeton College," *Presbyterian Magazine* 4 [1854]: 472). Maclean, *CNJ*, 1:389–90, pictures Witherspoon as cautious and reserved in the face of such enthusiasm.

[8] *Princetonians 1769–1775*, xxviii–xxix. Of 150 B.A.'s from 1769 to 1775, 72 (48 percent) became ministers, and of these a higher percentage than ever were entering the Presbyterian ministry. On Witherspoon's abilities to secure increased financial support from Presbyterians of all sorts, see Collins, *Witherspoon*, 1:123–24; and *Records of the Presbyterian Church, 1706–1788*, 396–97.

AS WITHERSPOON was rising to prominence in the church, he was also becoming an important figure in colonial politics. The Reverend John Rodgers, college trustee and minister of the Presbyterian church in New York City, had written to Witherspoon in December 1766, urging him to accept the Princeton post for the part he could play in that position "to advance the Cause of Christian Liberty by forming the Minds of Youth to proper Sentiments on this most interesting Subject." Witherspoon, foe of arbitrary ecclesiastical power in Scotland, wasted no time in fulfilling Rodgers's expectations. James Madison, Sr., directed his son and namesake to Princeton in the summer of 1769 largely because of Witherspoon's reputation as a friend of religious freedom. At his first Princeton commencement in September 1769, the younger Madison witnessed a further indication of Witherspoon's political involvement. The college had given honorary degrees since its founding, but only infrequently and most often to ministers. Witherspoon's arrival brought an immediate change. At the 1769 commencement Princeton bestowed six honorary degrees, including the college's first two Doctor of Laws. These went to two notable Pennsylvania statesmen: John Dickinson, author of the *Farmer's Letters*, a denunciation of all forms of taxation in America by the British Parliament and the most widely read political pamphlet of the decade, and Joseph Galloway, speaker of the Pennsylvania assembly. At the same commencement the college also bestowed an honorary master's degree on the Boston merchant John Hancock, who had become a colonial hero when, in June 1768, British customs officials seized his ship, *Liberty*, in Boston harbor for violating acts of trade.[9]

Succeeding commencements further indicated the stance of the president, who enjoyed a veto power over all student presentations. The 1770 gathering featured orations justifying American resistance to Great Britain, and that of 1771 an epic poem entitled "The Rising Glory of America," by Hugh Henry Brackenridge and Philip Freneau. Witherspoon encouraged, or at least countenanced, the heady patriotic activities of the Princeton undergraduates in the years before the war, including the ceremonial wearing of American cloth, the burning, in effigy, of Loyalists, the conducting of a tea party in imitation of Boston, and above all an

[9] Rodgers quotation, see Butterfield, *Witherspoon Comes to America*, 22; Irving Brant, *James Madison*, vol. 1, *The Virginia Revolutionist* (Indianapolis, 1941), 70; Douglass Adair, "James Madison," in *Fame and the Founding Fathers, Essays by Douglass Adair*, ed. Trevor Colbourn (New York, 1974), 126; *General Catalogue*, 398.

unending round of student speeches and debates on patriotic themes.[10]

When New Jersey patriots began to organize, Witherspoon was also in the forefront of their activity. In early 1774 a New Jersey committee of correspondence was formed to communicate with the other colonies and to inform its own citizens of British actions. Princeton's Somerset County, forming its own organization in July of that year, selected Witherspoon as one of its committeemen, thus setting the president on the path that led to his selection in June 1776 as a New Jersey delegate to the Continental Congress, his signing of the Declaration of Independence, and his lengthy service in the Congress from 1776 to 1783.[11]

Witherspoon's teaching at the college also broached political themes more directly than had hitherto been the case. From the first he included a full discussion of politics in his lectures on moral philosophy to juniors and seniors, lectures that promoted many of the prominent themes of the patriotic ideology. As political tension increased, Witherspoon in 1774 published his views to the public at large. A newspaper essay entitled "Thoughts on American Liberty" professed fidelity to the king but also stated in strongest terms the objection to Parliament's assertion that it had "full power and authority . . . to bind the colonies and people of *America* . . . in all cases whatsoever." Witherspoon responded that this claim was "illegal and unconstitutional." "We are firmly determined," he wrote, "never to submit to it, and do deliberately prefer war with all its horrors, and even extermination itself to slavery, rivetted on us and our posterity."[12] When war came, he used the congressional Day of Fasting, May 17, 1776, to preach a justly famous sermon, "The Dominion of Providence over the Passions of Men," which defended resistance to leaders who forgo justice, liberty, and common humanity, and which proclaimed God's ability to bring good out of the unrestrained excesses of Britain's tyranny.[13]

Witherspoon's involvement in the push toward independence did not please all of Princeton's supporters. Elias Boudinot, influential trustee and himself a sturdy advocate of American rights,

[10] Sheldon S. Cohen and Larry R. Gerlach, "Princeton in the Coming of the American Revolution," *New Jersey History* 92 (1974): 75–81.

[11] Collins, *Witherspoon*, 169, 177, 209, 212–19.

[12] Witherspoon, *Works*, 4:298–99.

[13] Collins, *Witherspoon*, 1:197–98; for a fine discussion of this sermon, see James H. Smylie, "Presbyterian Clergy and Problems of 'Dominion' in the Revolutionary Generation," *Journal of Presbyterian History* 48 (1970): 161–75.

yet doubted whether the clergy should be so active in politics. Boudinot, however, was practically alone with his scruples. The times demanded the services of every capable patriot; niceties of theory on the relationship between church and state could not be allowed to stand in the way. More representative of attitudes toward Witherspoon's involvement was John Adams's praise for the Princeton president, whom he called, after a visit in 1774, "as high a son of liberty as any man in America."[14] The citizens and political committees of New Jersey testified even more eloquently to his repute as statesman by returning him to office—Continental Congress, state senate, state assembly, New Jersey constitutional convention—as often as he would agree to serve.

THE CROWNING accomplishment of John Witherspoon's meteoric descent upon America was his new-modeling of instruction at the college. Friends of learning rejoiced to see Princeton regain financial stability under his leadership, friends of religion heralded his work among the Presbyterians, and friends of liberty cheered his contributions to their cause. These external activities, however, were no more than the visible reflection of the deep convictions that he put to work in restructuring education at Princeton. To be sure, Witherspoon set about his work within the framework of the college's traditional purposes. Yet by introducing a new means of integrating learning and faith, by committing the college so thoroughly to the ideology of the American Revolution and dedicating it so completely to the health of the new United States, and even by his own personal success in binding together the interests of learning, patriotism, and Christianity, Witherspoon altered the course of the college and defined its direction for at least the next century. It was a momentous development not just for the college but also for Presbyterians and, to a lesser extent, the new country as a whole.

Witherspoon bequeathed his intellectual, religious, and social vision to the Princeton circle during numinous times. His active career as president stretched from the mid-1760s and the Stamp Act crisis to the late 1780s, when both the nation (in the Constitution) and his church (in the formation of its General Assembly) made provision, with great expectation, for the future. The end of Witherspoon's life, in 1794, coincided with the beginning of the period when college, church, and nation faced the challenge of assimilat-

---

[14] Boudinot, see Collins, *Witherspoon*, 1:159, 206; Adams, see ibid., 166.

ing, and even defining, what had transpired in the Revolutionary era. That challenge, which for the Princeton circle amounted to working out the strengths and dealing with the hidden tensions of Witherspoon's achievement, defined both the triumphs and confusions of the college for a full generation after his passing.

On the surface, Witherspoon's adjustments in formal studies and in extracurricular education seemed more to further existing trends than to chart new paths. He did innovate by relying much more on lectures than had earlier presidents. But the subjects on which Witherspoon lectured—moral philosophy, divinity, history, and eloquence—were all well established at the college. Witherspoon was also only continuing the concerns of his immediate predecessors, Davies and Finley, when he gave added attention to student declamation, and when he hastened a transition from syllogistic, Latin, and ornamental oratory to forensic, English, and practical speeches.[15]

The same may be said for Witherspoon's promotion of natural philosophy, where Witherspoon's widely hailed efforts to advance science was the culmination of a long-standing institutional concern. Shortly before Witherspoon's arrival the trustees had authorized a professorship of mathematics and natural philosophy, pending the availability of funds. In 1771 Witherspoon's success at raising money made it possible to elevate a tutor, William Churchill Houston, into the science professorship. It also allowed Witherspoon to spend £250 for "Philosophical Apparatus" and, for £416.13.4, to purchase David Rittenhouse's orrery, an intricate working model of the universe that was the marvel of the age. In light of the scale of college finances—yearly tuition of £5 per student and a total annual budget of under £2,000 in Witherspoon's first years—the institution's commitment to science, urged on by its president, was impressive.[16] Witherspoon was also able to expand the library, which had not grown appreciably since Governor Belcher donated his personal collection in the 1750s. Previous

[15] The best discussion of Witherspoon's impact on the curriculum is Darrell L. Guder, "The History of Belles Lettres at Princeton" (Ph.D. diss., University of Hamburg, 1964), 141–211. See also Green, "Witherspoon's Administration at Princeton"; and Francis I. Broderick, "Pulpit, Physics, and Politics: The Curriculum of the College of New Jersey, 1746–1794," *WMQ* 6 (1949): 59–68. On Witherspoon and public speaking, see Elaine Pagel Paden, "The Theory and Practice of Disputation at Princeton, Columbia, and the University of Pennsylvania from 1750 to 1800" (Ph.D. diss., University of Iowa, 1943), 175–77.

[16] Guder, "Belles Lettres at Princeton," 156–57a; Broderick, "Pulpit, Physics, and Politics," 52, 60; Wertenbaker, *Princeton*, 108; Collins, *Witherspoon*, 1:109–11

presidents had added what they were able, but Witherspoon far exceeded their efforts by bringing along three hundred books from Britain and by consistently ordering more. Witherspoon seems to have placed a higher premium than before on work in English, and he increased the spirit of competition by offering extemporaneous exercises in translation to the lower classes and elaborate forensic competitions to juniors and seniors. He also began instruction in French as an elective.[17] In all, Witherspoon's alterations in the formal curriculum were substantial, but entirely in keeping with the college's earlier history. The more important changes lay beneath the surface and concerned content rather than form.

THE DEEPER significance of Witherspoon's tenure lay in his reorientation of intellectual activity around the principles of the Scottish Enlightenment, a shift that necessitated the displacement of intellectual patterns associated with Jonathan Edwards and New Side Presbyterian revivalism. The occasion for this substitution was Witherspoon's attack on the philosophical idealism of Bishop George Berkeley, but its effects went far beyond a technical philosophical dispute to alter the general character of the institution. In addition, Witherspoon's own practical activity led to a further alteration with great significance, namely, the replacement of the Christian ministry with patriotic public service as Princeton's primary contribution to morality, liberty, and social cohesion.

At first glance, Witherspoon's choice of a philosophical system seems a minor detail. When he arrived on campus, he found a faculty that was sustaining the college's traditional propensity for New England's evangelical Calvinism. At least one tutor had moved beyond Jonathan Edwards, whose Calvinism entailed a theological idealism, to Bishop George Berkeley, whose idealism was the cornerstone for an entire philosophical system. Witherspoon soon scotched all forms of idealism at Princeton through vigorous advocacy of the intuitive, realistic philosophy that he had learned at Edinburgh and studied while a pastor. During Witherspoon's last years in his native country, this general position was becoming known as a Scottish philosophy of common sense and was disseminated through the publication of learned treatises like Thomas Reid's *Inquiry into the Human Mind on the Principles of Common Sense*

[17] Wertenbaker, *Princeton*, 106–7; Green, "Witherspoon's Administration at Princeton," 468; Ketcham, "James Madison at Princeton," 29.

(1764) and popularizations like James Oswald's *Appeal to Common Sense in Behalf of Religion* (Part 1, 1766).[18]

Many years later Ashbel Green left a record of Witherspoon's early philosophical activity: "The Berklean system of Metaphysics was in repute in the college when he entered on his office. The tutors were zealous believers in it, and waited on the President, with some expectation of either confounding him, or making him a proselyte. They had mistaken their man. He first reasoned against the System, and then ridiculed it, till he drove it out of the college."[19]

Princeton's philosophical shift was not as personally traumatic as Green described it. Soon after arriving in Princeton, Witherspoon praised highly the work of his junior faculty, Joseph Periam, Jonathan Edwards, Jr., Ebenezer Pemberton, and James Thomson. He did not have as much good to say about the professor of theology and moral philosophy, John Blair, but still Witherspoon found him an agreeable person.[20] For our purposes, it is important to note that Witherspoon inherited a faculty with New England, or New Side, connections. Blair was a Scotch-Irish immigrant who had trained at William Tennent's Log College; Periam's father had migrated to America with revivalist George Whitefield; Jonathan Edwards, Jr., had stayed in New Jersey for education after his father's untimely death; Pemberton was a Rhode Islander who had prepared for college with his uncle, minister of a New Light church in Boston; and Thomson was from Massachusetts.[21] As such, it was not surprising that all of them favored the theology of Jonathan Edwards with its idealistic overtones. Periam even seems to have gone beyond the others to promote Berkeley's views. Since the faculty's Edwardsean idealism put them out of step with Witherspoon, it is not surprising that all of them left Princeton within a year of his arrival. Yet Witherspoon remained on cordial terms with all five as they moved on to other teaching or pastoral duties.[22]

[18] For a recent summary, see S. A. Grave, *The Scottish Philosophy of Common Sense* (Oxford, 1960).

[19] Green, *Life of Witherspoon*, 132.

[20] Witherspoon to Benjamin Rush, Oct. 8, 1768, in Butterfield, *Witherspoon Comes to America*, 80.

[21] *Princetonians 1748–1768*, 8, 399, 494, 513, 361.

[22] Ibid., 401, 361, 514, 494; *Princetonians 1769–1775*, xix; James Madison to his father, Sept. 30, 1769; in *The Papers of James Madison*, vol. 1, *16 March 1751–16 December 1779*, ed. William T. Hutchinson and William M. C. Rachal (Chicago, 1962), 45–47.

If Ashbel Green exaggerated the clash of personalities between Witherspoon and his original faculty, however, he did not exaggerate Witherspoon's distate for philosophical idealism. The implications of Witherspoon's stance are important enough to justify a brief excursion into the history of British philosophy in the eighteenth century.

Bishop George Berkeley had proposed that what humans commonly regard as the real world is in fact ideas in the minds of God and humans. He advanced this theory as an effort to fend off what he considered the latent materialism of John Locke's sensationalistic epistemology and to preserve the centrality of God in the knowing process. If, according to Locke, our knowledge is equivalent to ideas of sense and reflection, then, according to Berkeley, we do not need to believe in a self-standing material universe. In fact, to do so is to reduce the mind to a function of inert matter and make God irrelevant for the process of understanding the world. Berkeley's solution was to take Locke seriously in his conviction that we gain true knowledge through our ideas but then to argue that ideas must constitute all of reality. Berkeley also made the further point that our ideas of reality are consistent, regular, and predictable only because they are grounded in the all-encompassing mind of God.[23] Philosophical details were different, but a similar concern for the place of God in the human understanding of the world also loomed large for Jonathan Edwards.[24]

Scottish thinkers took great offense at Berkeley's proposals, and Witherspoon banished such notions entirely when he arrived at Princeton. His lectures on moral philosophy, prepared during his first years at the college, contained a vigorous counterattack: "Immaterialism takes away the distinction between truth and falshood [*sic*]. . . . The truth is, the immaterial system, is a wild and ridiculous attempt to unsettle the principles of common sense by metaphysical reasoning, which can hardly produce any thing but contempt in the generality of persons who hear it."[25] To be tainted with "immaterialism" of whatever sort was thus to go beyond the

[23] For recent, lucid summaries, see J. O. Urmson, *Berkeley* (Oxford, 1982); and John Dunn, *Locke* (Oxford, 1984).

[24] See Wallace E. Anderson, "The Development of Edwards' Philosophical Thought," in *The Works of Jonathan Edwards: Scientific and Philosophical Writings* (New Haven, 1980), 52–136; and Norman Fiering, *Jonathan Edwards's Moral Thought and Its British Context* (Chapel Hill, N.C., 1981).

[25] Witherspoon, *Works*, 3:377. On the composition of these lectures, see Green, "Witherspoon's Administration at Princeton," 467.

pale, regardless of what considerations, theological or otherwise, led to that conclusion.

Witherspoon also associated the unsound speculation that led to Berkeley's errors with the epistemological skepticism of David Hume. Hume, carrying Berkeley one step further, fastened on Locke's concepts of ideas as a barrier, rather than a bridge, to knowledge. If, Hume reasoned, all we know is our own ideas of the external world, then certainly such treasured assumptions as the connection between cause and effect, or such reassuring convictions as the belief that observing cause and effect in nature demonstrates the existence of God as First Cause, are not really descriptions of the world so much as statements about what happens in our minds. For Witherspoon this sort of skepticism was even more pernicious than Berkeley's immaterialism. It made nonsense out of efforts to understand the external world and to direct it toward moral, educational, or religious ends. Witherspoon's lectures in moral philosophy, which stated his objection to Hume's conclusions on cause and effect, also pointed to the antidote for immaterialism and skepticism—the principles of "common sense" propounded by the philosophers of Scotland.

> Everything that exists must have a cause. This . . . must itself be taken for an original sentiment of nature, or an impression necessarily made upon us from all that we see and are conversant with. About this and some other ideas great stir has been made by some infidel writers, particularly David Hume, who seems to have industriously endeavored to shake the certainty of our belief upon cause and effect, upon personal identity and the idea of power. . . . In opposition to this, some late writers have advanced with great apparent reason, that there are certain first principles or dictates of common sense, which are either simple perceptions, or seen with intuitive evidence. These are the foundation of all reasoning. . . . They can no more be proved than you can prove an axiom in mathematical science. These authors of Scotland have lately produced and supported this opinion, to resolve at once all the refinements and metaphysical objections of some infidel writers.[26]

Through such bold assertions Witherspoon rescued the College of New Jersey from Berkeley's idealism and Hume's skepticism.

[26] Witherspoon, *Works*, 3:395. Ashbel Green quoted Witherspoon on Hume as follows: he "was a man of extensive learning and an excellent historian, but of damna(ble) principles" (*Life of Witherspoon*, 274). For the rudiments of Hume's opinions, see D.G.C. MacNabb, "David Hume," in *The Encyclopedia of Philosophy*, 8 vols. (New York, 1967), 4:74–90.

New faculty members who joined him after 1769 either had no idealistic leanings, most having been students of Witherspoon himself, or kept them quiet if they did. They joined Witherspoon in a vigorous prosecution of Scottish philosophy, the intellectual foundation for his educational activity.[27]

As Witherspoon expounded it, the philosophy of common sense became the foundation for useful knowledge of every sort. Common sense defended the reality of the physical world and therefore allowed a wholehearted commitment to natural philosophy. It defined human relationships after the model of the physical sciences and therefore demonstrated the rationality of politics. It drew an analogy between external and internal sensations and therefore facilitated a science of morals. It regarded theology as dependent upon reason and therefore paved the way for an apologetic of scientific respectability.

Witherspoon's lectures in moral philosophy contain the distillation of his epistemology, ethics, and politics; his lectures on divinity do the same for that subject. The latter address particularly the relationship between theology and other fields of learning. Together these lectures show Witherspoon's debt to his Scottish upbringing. They also reveal a possible miscalculation by the Princeton trustees.

The board saw correctly that the Evangelical party, which Witherspoon championed in Scotland, shared a commitment to orthodoxy and piety with American New Side Presbyterians. But it also seems to have assumed that the division between Witherspoon's Evangelical party and its Moderate opponents was pretty much the same as that between the colonial New Sides and Old Sides. In fact, American New Sides were separated from Old Sides in both philosophy and theology, whereas Scottish Evangelicals shared much more the philosophical assumptions of their theological opponents. The results of this miscalculation are evident when the ideas of Old Side Francis Alison are compared with those of Witherspoon. Alison, an immigrant from Northern Ireland who graduated from the University of Edinburgh in 1732, seven years before Witherspoon, was an Old Side stalwart. At the College of Philadelphia he based his instruction in moral philosophy on the teaching of Francis Hutcheson, particularly on Hutcheson's efforts to study

[27] All twenty-one tutors appointed during Witherspoon's tenure were Princeton graduates, eighteen of them his own students. The professors under Witherspoon were W. C. Houston (Princeton 1768), Stanhope Smith (1769), Ashbel Green (1783), and Walter Minto, who was educated in Scotland (*General Catalogue*, 49–50, 28).

the moral sense scientifically. As early as 1759 Alison was dictating passages from Hutcheson's *Short Introduction to Moral Philosophy*, or *Compend*, to his students.[28] The anomaly is that Witherspoon, a biting theological opponent of Hutcheson in Scotland, and called to America as a theological alternative to Alison, taught the same moral philosophy, and from the same philosophical texts, as Alison and the Moderates.

Witherspoon, like Alison, put Hutcheson fully to use. The most recent and best student of the subject, Jack Scott, has detailed Witherspoon's extensive reliance on Hutcheson's two-volume *System of Moral Philosophy* (1755) for his lectures.[29] Witherspoon followed Hutcheson especially in his conception of ethics as a *natural* human *science*. With Hutcheson, Witherspoon placed great reliance on the ability of intuition to uncover the truth about human nature and the powers of virtue: "The principles of duty and obligation," he said early in his lectures on moral philosophy, "must be drawn from the nature of man." An examination of human nature discloses that people have an internal sense for virtue and beauty very much analogous to the external senses that communicate the reality of the physical world. According to Witherspoon, this "internal sensation is what Mr. Hutchinson [*sic*] calls the finer powers of perception." It includes "a sense of moral good and evil," or "conscience." When we study and cultivate this internal, moral sense, which all human beings possess, we are able to discern the nature of duty. And when we are able to do "what is dictated by the moral sense," we experience "a sense of moral excellence." Furthermore, Witherspoon shared Hutcheson's great faith, and the great faith of the Scottish Enlightenment generally, in an empirical approach to morality. If moral philosophers could only study their own natures carefully, Witherspoon felt that "a time may come when men, treating moral philosophy as Newton and his successors have done natural, may arrive at greater precision. It is always safer in our reasonings to trace facts upwards than to reason downwards upon metaphysical principles."[30]

---

[28] See especially Douglas Sloan, "Old Side Educator: Francis Alison," in *The Scottish Enlightenment and the American College Ideal* (New York, 1971), 88–94; and Caroline Robbins, " 'When It Is That Colonies May Turn Independent': An Analysis of the Environment and Politics of Francis Hutcheson (1694–1746)," *WMQ* 11 (1954): 215–16.

[29] Jack Scott, ed., *An Annotated Edition of Lectures on Moral Philosophy by John Witherspoon* (Newark, Del., 1982).

[30] Witherspoon, *Works*, 3:369, 378, 379, 381, 470. On the development of the idea of common sense, see the helpful discussion in Norman Fiering, *Moral Philos-*

Several things are noteworthy about Witherspoon's moral philosophy. First, its great confidence in intuition had wide ramifications for other areas of life. The Witherspoon who lectured on moral philosophy to Princeton students eventually was called to speak in higher assemblies, but even on the floor of the Continental Congress, his belief in the sense of the heart did not waver. Once, near the conclusion of an address on the wisdom of honoring an informal agreement with General Burgoyne, he suggested that "the law of nature and nations is nothing else but the law of general reason, or those obligations of duty from reason and conscience, on one individual to another antecedent to any particular law derived from the social compact, or even actual consent." Therefore, "a person of integrity will pass as sound a judgment on subjects of this kind, by consulting his own heart, as by turning over books and systems."[31] How do humans find their way in the world? By consulting the moral sense of their own hearts.

Second, it is important to realize that Witherspoon's moral philosophy reflects one aspect of Scotland's Enlightenment more than the other. While his lectures include a brief defense of perception and a brief rebuttal to Hume, they do not contain the full-orbed common-sense epistemology of the mature Thomas Reid, nor do they reflect a sophisticated common-sense approach to social theory or theology such as his successor, Stanhope Smith, developed after digesting the works of Reid and other scholars who published their most important work in the second half of the century. Witherspoon's concerns are rather those of Hutcheson's for a philosophy of the moral sense and for the ethical and political implications of that philosophy.[32] As a result, and because he was an eclectic rather than a systematic thinker, Witherspoon did not experience the clash of allegiances that the next generation faced as it assimilated the Scottish thought with greater thoroughness. For that generation, the great confidence in principles derived from human nature and from "the science of politics" would begin to strain against the hereditary Presbyterian commitments to divine

---

ophy at Seventeenth-Century Harvard: A Discipline in Transition (Chapel Hill, N.C., 1981), 285, 298–99.

[31] Witherspoon, Works, 4:328.

[32] Gladys Bryson, Man and Society: The Scottish Inquiry of the Eighteenth Century (Princeton, 1945), remains a fine introduction to these themes. For differences between ethical and epistemological applications of common-sense principles, see Mark A. Noll, "Common Sense Traditions and American Evangelical Thought," American Quarterly 37 (1985): 220–25.

revelation, a sense of the fall, and the authority of traditional confessions.

Third, and most significantly, Witherspoon's intellectual commitments place him at a fairly advanced stage in the development of what Norman Fiering has called "the new moral philosophy." With Hutcheson, Alison, and most other eighteenth-century moral philosophers, Witherspoon set aside the Augustinian distrust of human nature; in practice he denied that original sin harmed the ability to understand and cultivate natural virtue; he regarded the achievements of science as triumphs of empirical inquiry more than as insights into the effulgence of God's glory; and he pictured God more as the originator of material and moral order than as the constantly active creator of the world.[33]

Witherspoon's philosophical allegiance, regarded in this light, was no minor matter. It not only united him with Scottish Moderates and Old Side Presbyterians. It also divided him from the philosophical orientation of the New Side/New Light American Calvinists and complicated the implementation of Princeton's long-standing goals. In other words, when Witherspoon set in place a pattern of instruction grounded in Scottish moral philosophy, he materially altered Princeton's traditional approaches to ethics, epistemology, and the interconnections of knowledge. In particular, his commitment to Scottish common sense meant that there was no longer any room at Princeton for the influence of Jonathan Edwards. Nothing in the college's early history so significantly shaped its destiny.

IT DID NOT take long for Witherspoon to display his attitudes toward Edwardsean themes. During his first American autumn he traveled for funds into New England, where no less an observer than Old Light Charles Chauncy commented with surprised delight on Witherspoon's stance: "He is no friend to the grand and distinguishing Tenets of Mr. Edwards wch. have been almost universally imbibed in that part of the Country."[34] When revivals touched the college in 1770 and 1772, Witherspoon seems to have stepped aside in favor of transplanted New Englanders, like the Reverend Jedidiah Chapman of Orange, who fanned the flames. One zealous student, Ebenezer Bradford, who during the 1772 stir-

[33] Fiering, *Moral Philosophy at Seventeenth-Century Harvard*, with special reference to Witherspoon, 43.

[34] Collins, *Witherspoon*, 1:114. For other favorable comments by Chauncy, see *Princetonians 1748–1768*, 514.

rings called Witherspoon "a dull preacher," reported at length on the institution's attitude toward Joseph Bellamy, an acknowledged theological heir of Edwards. Witherspoon and the Reverend Elihu Spencer of Trenton, according to Bradford, were

> great enemies to what they call Eastward, or New Divinity, which was so much exploded by all in college, that when I came here, which was last fall, I was advised by a particular friend, not to let my sentiments be known by any means, alleging that it would be of great disservice to me. . . . The Dr. has lately been conversed with upon these things since they have made such progress in the College, and declares that he is neither for nor against them; however, he both preaches and converses in contradistinction to them.[35]

Witherspoon was sincerely committed to a Calvinistic creed, so it is hard to imagine that he opposed Edwards, Bellamy, and the New England style on strictly theological grounds. Rather, Witherspoon's coolness to "Eastward Divinity" almost certainly arose from the taint of idealism associated with Edwards, from the New Divinity's reputation as a speculative rather than a practical theology, and perhaps from a suspicion that Edwards's fiercely revelational ethics was not quite respectable in an age of reason and science. Whatever obscurity attends the reasons for Witherspoon's dismissal of New England theology, it is clear that he did cut the college loose from the pattern of thought promoted by Edwards.

Princeton, to be sure, had never been a thoroughly Edwardsean school, in spite of its manifold connections with New England Calvinism. Its early presidents, with the exception of Edwards, were ministerial activists rather than philosophical theologians, and so were satisfied to encourage piety and to nurture learning in general terms. They tended to be educational eclectics who followed Yale and the English dissenting academies, without inquiring closely into internal relationships among science, divinity, and moral philosophy. Aaron Burr, for example, used Henry Grove's *Moral Philosophy* as a college text, although Grove deprecated the idea that God providentially recreated the world each and every moment, a tenant standing near the heart of Edwards's idealistic

---

[35] Bradford to Bellamy, Apr. 18, 1772, in *Proceedings of the New Jersey Historical Society* 6 (1851–1853): 174, 176. Bradford was a somewhat unstable person who, despite his comments in 1772, remained at Princeton after his graduation to read theology with Witherspoon in preparation for the ministry (*Princetonians 1769–1775*, 272–76).

conception of God and the world.[36] Yet in their general orientation, the early Princeton presidents aligned themselves with Edwards's combination of Calvinistic revivalism and theistic-centered
learning. In particular, they would have held implicitly, as Edwards held explicitly, that the world is not primarily matter in motion, that knowledge does not begin from a human tabula rasa,
that ethics is not a value-free science, that Christian virtue is altogether different from the natural expressions of the moral sense,
and that divine providence and Christian revelation provide the
indispensable framework for educational endeavors.[37]

With Witherspoon this orientation is changed. Convictions he
shared with the Scottish realists like Thomas Reid, which were useful in rebutting Berkeley and Hume, committed him to Cartesian
assumptions about authority and Lockean views of knowledge. In
practice, Witherspoon began theoretical inquiry with Descartes's
denial of inherited authority and with Locke's assumption that
matter in motion grounded knowledge of the external world. Under Hutcheson's influence, and in spite of his manifest religious
sincerity, Witherspoon sharply divided the testimony of the moral
sense from the testimony of revelation. Moral philosophy itself,
Witherspoon contended in the first paragraph of his lectures, is
worthy of the name "*Philosophy*, because it is an enquiry into the
nature and grounds of moral obligation by reason, as distinct from
revelation." To be sure, he asserted at length that "the discoveries
of reason cannot be contrary to" the Bible and that "there is nothing certain or valuable in moral philosophy, but what is perfectly
coincident with the scripture." He also was at pains to show that
truly virtuous actions reflect the will of God. But Witherspoon's
orthodoxy did not prevent him from also asserting, as he began
his discussion of ethics, that "the principles of duty and obligation
must be drawn from the nature of man." Nor did it stop him from
emphasizing "how we derive either the nature or obligation of
duty" from an examination of "human nature."[38]

[36] Broderick, "Pulpit, Physics, and Politics," 45–46, 50; Wertenbaker, *Princeton*,
80–86; on Grove, see Fiering, *Moral Philosophy at Seventeenth-Century Harvard*, 218–
19; on Edwards's intellectual position, see Anderson, "Development of Edwards'
Philosophical Thought," 52–136.

[37] For general interpretations of this religious position, see Leonard J. Trinterud,
The Forming of an American Tradition: A Re-examination of Colonial Presbyterianism
(Philadelphia, 1949), 169–95; and Howard Miller, "Evangelical Religion and Colo-
nial Princeton," in *Schooling and Society*, ed. Lawrence Stone (Baltimore, 1976).

[38] Witherspoon, *Works*, 3:367, 471, 369, 380.

As if conscious of the direction in which he was taking instruction at Princeton, Witherspoon paused at the outset of his lectures to note that "an author of New-England, says, moral philosophy is just reducing infidelity to a system." That author was Cotton Mather, who had criticized the drift of eighteenth-century moral philosophy for its equation of natural and regenerate virtue. For his part, Jonathan Edwards, whose body was resting less than a mile from Nassau Hall in the Princeton cemetery, had honored the natural exploration of the moral sense but had denied that its study yielded true virtue, which came only from the touch of grace. Witherspoon passed over such objections with a shrug— "But however specious the objections [to Moral Philosophy], they will be found at bottom not solid."[39]

Witherspoon exalted a value-free science of ethics to the place in morality that Edwards had reserved for grace. In addition, his desire to demonstrate the rationality of Christianity testified to the exalted status he reserved for independent scientific inquiry. Witherspoon devoted part of one chapter in his lectures on moral philosophy to showing the scientific respectability of Christian faith, and it was the predominant theme of his lectures on divinity.[40] Those lectures assured the students that reason contains no inherent criticism of revelation, that the positive teachings of Scripture reflect both sound reason and "the state of human nature," and that revelation is necessary to provide the truth concerning those matters for which reason is not sufficient. Witherspoon's remarks on divinity do include brief reflections on the standard topics in Calvinistic dogmatics, but his overriding concern is to demonstrate the reasonableness of the faith.[41] On the other hand, he is only marginally interested in analyzing individual dogmas or in attempting to join the individual parts of the faith into a cohesive whole. Thus, unlike Edwards, who labored so diligently in his books *Free Will* and *Original Sin* to derive an integrated theology comprehending both God's undeviating will and the moral respon-

[39] Ibid., 367; Scott, *Lectures on Moral Philosophy by Witherspoon*, 64, 68; Jonathan Edwards, *The Nature of True Virtue*, intro. William K. Frankena (1765; reprint, Ann Arbor, Mich., 1960); Fiering, *Jonathan Edwards's Moral Thought*.

[40] Witherspoon, "Lectures on Moral Philosophy," in *Works*, 3:394–96; Sloan, *Scottish Enlightenment*, 119–22, provides a fine summary of Witherspoon's purposes in his "Lectures on Divinity."

[41] In the 1802 Philadelphia edition of his "Lectures on Divinity," Witherspoon's preliminary remarks take up fourteen pages, his various arguments for the truth of Christianity forty-three pages, and his exposition of the heads of doctrine forty-eight pages.

sibility of humans, Witherspoon passed over the problem of the will almost cavalierly: "I could never see any thing satisfactory in the attempts of divines or Metaphysicians to reconcile these two things, but it does not appear difficult to me to believe precisely in the form of our confession of faith—to believe both the certainty of God's purpose and the free agency of the creature. Nor does my being unable to explain these doctrines form an objection against one or the other."[42] His interests, rather, lay in demonstrating that reasonable inquiry could verify the faith.

By providing Princeton with a philosophical basis derived from Scottish moral philosophy and by removing a New England tradition strongly under the influence of Edwards, Witherspoon brought Princeton into the mainstream of eighteenth-century higher education. Theological commitments notwithstanding, he advanced the "new moral philosophy" at the expense of an older practical theology that stretched back from Edwards through the Puritan William Ames and John Calvin to Augustine. From the newer perspective, Witherspoon could treat virtue as a subject of natural scientific inquiry rather than as a product of divine grace. It allowed him to demonstrate through reason and science the truthfulness of revelation instead of presupposing revelation as the foundation for science and reason. If his new moral philosophy lacked the cohesion of Edwards's theistic conception of the world—if for Witherspoon nature and grace, science and revelation, were beginning to go their own ways—he still was able to champion both faith and learning, divinity and science, as compatible forms of truth. The fact that Witherspoon was so manifestly a man of sincere piety and of stalwart theological conviction and that he subscribed *ex animo* to the Westminster Confession of Faith made for genuine continuity with Princeton's past. Underneath a common commitment to broadly Calvinistic theology, however, a change was taking place at Princeton from idealism, metaphysics, and conversion to realism, ethics, and morality, a change that profoundly affected the college and its place in the wider world.

JOHN WITHERSPOON'S POLITICAL convictions did not contribute new attitudes to the Princeton circle so much as they height-

---

[42] Witherspoon, *Works*, 4:91; contrast the position of Edwards as summarized in Fiering, *Moral Philosophy at Seventeenth-Century Harvard*, 145. On Edwards's efforts to pose an integrated theory of sovereign divine will and human moral responsibility, see the chapter "Morality and Determinism" in Fiering, *Jonathan Edwards's Moral Thought*, 261–321.

ened the application of traditional concerns. From its beginnings
the College of New Jersey had been a center of dissent, and so it
continued, with varying degrees of intensity, to Witherspoon's accession. Samuel Davies, especially, had been an ardent advocate of
British liberties during the French and Indian War, and he had
infused his brief administration with a manifest political spirit.
Samuel Finley had kept his political sentiments more to himself,
but graduation exercises during his administration, as under Davies, featured oratory praising patriotic virtues and discussing public affairs in place of the theological and philosophical declamations that had predominated under President Burr.[43]

Witherspoon's fund-raising tours throughout the colonies seem
to have quickened his latent political convictions. From the first his
lectures in moral philosophy dealt directly with practical political
topics, and from the first he encouraged students to declaim on
current affairs. In 1772 the trustees even felt it necessary to cau-
tion him about the unrestrained political fervor that surfaced at
commencement.[44] But as a body the board shared the Whig convictions of Witherspoon and his students, and so were not unduly
alarmed at their new president's forceful political advocacy.

Witherspoon's lectures on moral philosophy presented a coherent political theory for the first time at Princeton. As with his ethics, Witherspoon's convictions were very much in keeping with
those of Francis Hutcheson and his American disciples like Francis
Alison. Witherspoon certainly knew the explicit discussion "When
It Is That Colonies May Turn Independent" from Hutcheson's
System of Moral Philosophy and also the exposition of natural rights,
social compact, and governmental corruption with which it was associated.[45] Witherspoon followed Hutcheson in regarding society
as "a voluntary compact" arising from a condition where "men are
originally and by nature equal, and consequently free." He argued
as well that "reason" and "common utility" showed the purpose of
society to be "the protection of liberty, as far as it is a blessing."
From this Hutchesonian perspective, Witherspoon addressed the
pressing issues of his day: "We must obey and submit to [rulers]

[43] Alison B. Olson, "The Founding of Princeton University: Religion and Politics
in Eighteenth-Century New Jersey," *New Jersey History* 87 (1965): 133–50; Broderick, "Pulpit, Physics, and Politics," 57; on Davies in the French and Indian War, see
Nathan O. Hatch, *The Sacred Cause of Liberty: Republican Thought and the Millennium
in Revolutionary New England* (New Haven, 1977), 41.

[44] Cohen and Gerlach, "Princeton in the Revolution," 79.

[45] Robbins, "Environment and Politics of Francis Hutcheson," 214, 218–19.

always, till the corruption becomes intolerable. . . . Dominion . . . can be acquired justly only one way, viz. by consent. . . . The causes of commencing war are . . . the violation of any perfect right—as taking away the property of the other state, or the lives of its subjects, or restraining them in their industry, or hindering them in the use of things common, &c."[46] Since Witherspoon came to these Whig conclusions scientifically, from an external analysis of social conditions and an internal reflection on the moral sense, they carried great weight in an age of reason and ethical sensitivity.

Witherspoon's political views brought him into fullest harmony with other defenders of American rights. Again, his position closely resembled that of Francis Alison, who had been a determined foe of an American Anglican bishop before moving on to a general distrust of Great Britain. The Scottish mentors of Alison and John Witherspoon had contributed substantially to the radical dissenting views that shaped the American perception of British tyranny.[47] Witherspoon had only to make his opinions known to be linked with other friends of liberty, whether those like Alison, who shared his Scottish education, or those like the well-known Founders, who had acquired republican convictions in America.

It was no surprise, then, that when political tensions came to a climax, Witherspoon gave himself wholeheartedly to the American cause. In May 1775 he drafted a letter to the churches of the Synod of New York and Philadelphia, calling on Presbyterians to remember that the House of Hanover itself now held the throne because Englishmen overthrew the corrupt James II in 1688. A year later his fast-day sermon of May 17 and an address to Scots in America with which it was published argued that, since Britain demanded unconditional colonial submission, the defense of colonial freedom could not be separated from a defense of colonial independence.[48] Nor was it surprising that, with Witherspoon's

---

[46] Witherspoon, *Works*, 3:419, 420, 437, 470.

[47] See James F. McAllister, Jr., "Francis Alison and John Witherspoon: Political Philosophers and Revolutionaries," *Journal of Presbyterian History* 54 (1976): 33–60. On the Scottish contribution to republican civic humanism, see Caroline Robbins, *The Eighteenth-Century Commonwealthman* (Cambridge, Mass., 1959), 177–220; J.G.A. Pocock, *The Machiavellian Moment: Florentine Political Thought and the Atlantic Republican Tradition* (Princeton, 1975), 497–505; and Pocock, *Virtue, Commerce, and History* (Cambridge, 1985), 123–41, 248–53.

[48] Witherspoon, "A Pastoral Letter from the Synod of New-York and Philadelphia, To the Congregations under their Care . . ." and "The Dominion of Providence Over the Passions of Men . . . To which is added, an Address to the natives of Scotland residing in America," in *Works*, 3:9–15, 17–60.

predilections and Princeton's dissenting heritage, the college became known as a "seminary of sedition" to those who doubted the
wisdom of independence. For their part, the young men who studied with Witherspoon, and who in many cases were drawn to
Princeton for its reputation as a champion of dissent, rendered
extraordinary service to the cause of independence. From the 335
students in Witherspoon's first fifteen classes (1769–1783), only 5
were open Loyalists, while the list of those who provided military,
diplomatic, religious, or legislative aid to the cause was nearly as
long as the roll of graduates.[49]

It is somewhat harder to assess the impact of Witherspoon's political theory on the Princeton circle than it is to describe the considerable results of his practical political involvements. Yet the intellectual changes he brought to the college still can be glimpsed in
his theoretical approach to public affairs. For one, Witherspoon's
wholehearted commitment to republican values and to American
independence reinforced the college's attachment to middle-colony Presbyterians and its break with New England New Lights.
Aaron Burr, Jonathan Edwards, and at least some of Edwards's
followers had held such high views of the church and such con-
suming views of the need for conversion that they made more of
the division between church and world than did Old Side Presbyterians or the New Sides who were not from New England.

Ashbel Green's father, Jacob, a transplanted New Englander
and an ardent follower of Edwards, who pastored a Presbyterian
church near Morristown, New Jersey, provides an instructive contrast to Witherspoon. Green regularly criticized failings among patriots during the war, even while devoting great energy to the new
country. Witherspoon, on the other hand, spoke of the conflict in
black-and-white terms. The cause of America filled his entire ho-
rizon, leaving very little room, at least until the 1780s, for self-crit-
icism.[50]

[49] Cohen and Gerlach, "Princeton in the Revolution," 87; David W. Robson, *Educating Republicans: The College in the Era of the American Revolution, 1750–1800* (Westport, Conn., 1985), 67–70; Howard H. Peckham, "*Collegia Ante Bellum*: Attitudes of College Professors and Students toward the American Revolution," *Pennsylvania Magazine of History and Biography* 95 (1971): 67; *Princetonians 1769–1775*, 550; *Princetonians 1776–1783*, 467.

[50] Mark A. Noll, "Observations on the Reconciliation of Politics and Religion in Revolutionary New Jersey: The Case of Jacob Green," *Journal of Presbyterian History* 44 (1976): 293–307. The most extreme example of Witherspoon's attitude was his humiliating treatment of printers who published Loyalist works, as described tellingly in Timothy M. Barnes and Robert M. Calhoon, "Moral Allegiance: John

More obviously, Witherspoon's political theory reflected another change of emphasis with lasting consequences. It was a long-standing commonplace at Princeton, and most other centers of learning in the eighteenth century, that social welfare rested on the virtues of a population. Early Princetonians and the New England Edwardseans differed from the commonplace only in their insistence that social well-being was best served by a supernaturally infused virtue, by the regenerating grace of God. Whatever natural benevolence could accomplish, a supernatural virtue was necessary for true social welfare.[51] While still in Scotland Witherspoon himself took special pains to attack the idea that a merely natural morality could be the basis of social health.

> It is not, indeed, to be wondered at, that not only this nation, but the protestant states of Europe in general should be brought under the rod, as they have so shamefully departed from that purity of faith and strictness of morals which was the glory of the reformation. How many have of late been ashamed of the cross of Christ, and the doctrine of the grace of God? And what hath been substituted in their room? A pliant and fashionable scheme of religion, a fine theory of virtue and morality. A beautiful but unsubstantial idol, raised by human pride, adorned and dressed by human art, and supported by the wisdom of words. And hath it not, in this, as in every preceeding age, in this, as in every other christian country, whenever it gained any credit, been the fore-runner and brought fast at its heels a deluge of profaneness and immorality in practice?[52]

When Witherspoon addressed this same connection between personal virtue and social well-being in his lectures at Princeton, however, he sounded less like his predecessors and his own Scottish sermon and more like the moralists of human nature whom he had earlier denounced. The fourteenth of his moral philosophy lectures, on jurisprudence, sounded a traditional Edwardsean note: "If, as we have seen above, virtue and piety are inseparably connected, then to promote true religion is the best and most effectual way of making a virtuous and regular people. Love to God, and love to man, is the substance of religion; when these prevail, civil laws will have little to do." But in his fourth lecture, Wither-

---

Witherspoon and Loyalist Recantation," *American Presbyterians: Journal of Presbyterian History* 63 (1985): 273–83.

[51] Bernard Bailyn, *The Ideological Origins of the American Revolution* (Cambridge, Mass., 1967), 32–33, 67; Edwards, *Nature of True Virtue*.

[52] Witherspoon, "Prayer for National Prosperity and for the Revival of Religion Inseparably Connected" (1758), in *Works*, 2:472.

spoon described "piety" as a product more of human nature than of divine grace.

> From reason, contemplation, sentiment and tradition, the Being and infinite perfection and excellence of God may be deduced; and therefore what he is, and commands is virtue and duty. Whatever he has implanted in uncorrupted nature as a principle, is to be received as his will. . . . We ought to take the rule of duty from conscience enlightened by reason, experience, and every way by which we can be supposed to learn the will of our Maker, and his intentions in creating us such as we are.[53]

The result was not impiety, for Witherspoon still held that "the nature and will of God is so perfect as to be the true standard of all excellence, natural and moral."[54] It was rather that Witherspoon's politics followed the form of his ethics by grounding the virtue that made for social health in the *natural powers* of humanity.

It is difficult to tell whether Witherspoon's political theory or the mere excitement of the times did more to alter the vocational choices of Princeton students. For whatever reason, the college certainly became, in Thomas Jefferson Wertenbaker's words, "the school of statesmen" during the Revolutionary generation. Witherspoon's cultivation of practical subjects like history, science, and composition, his efforts to increase the library's holdings in contemporary affairs, his concern to transform rhetoric from an academic into a public exercise—all were intended to make Princeton graduates, whether ministers or statesmen, more effective in their public careers. His efforts, however, bore much more fruit in producing the latter than the former.[55]

It should not be thought that Witherspoon's commitment to ministerial education was insincere. Shortly after arriving in Princeton, he instituted regular instruction in divinity for undergraduates, and especially for postgraduate students considering the ministry. These lectures began with a moving personal confession that asked his auditors to contrast Witherspoon's previous circumstances ("long accustomed to preach to a crouded audience of from twelve to fifteen hundred souls . . . and all subject to my pri-

---

[53] Ibid., 3:447–48, 388. Earlier in the lecture Witherspoon cited Hutcheson specifically to define "conscience" as simply "a sense of moral good and evil" (pp. 378–79).

[54] Ibid., 387.

[55] Wertenbaker, *Princeton*, 80; Green, "Witherspoon's Administration at Princeton," 468–69.

vate oversight and discipline") with his current lot ("now to have such a thin and negligent assembly, and mostly composed of those who think themselves under no obligation to attend, but when they please"). Yet for such a sacrifice there would be "an ample recompense," if only Witherspoon were "made instrumental in sending out faithful labourers into the harvest."[56] Witherspoon's "recompense" soon included a large number of Princeton graduates who went on to dignified service as Presbyterian ministers. According to Ashbel Green, Witherspoon once told him at a meeting of the General Assembly, "You can scarcely imagine the pleasure it has given me in taking a survey of this Assembly to observe that a decided majority of all the ministerial members have not only been sons of our college, but my own pupils."[57]

Notwithstanding the sincerity of Witherspoon's commitment to clerical training, the beginning of the war witnessed a sharp reduction in the number of graduates presenting themselves for the ministry. Only seventeen of eighty-two Princetonians from the classes of 1776–1783, or 21 percent, became ministers, and in Witherspoon's last ten years, 1784–1794, only 13 percent of 222 students.[58] The implications of this decline would loom large in the tenure of Samuel Stanhope Smith. At this stage it is important to realize that, while Witherspoon labored diligently with ministerial candidates, he also redirected instruction in such a way as to make political service the natural product of educational practice. Special revelation and the supernatural workings of grace remained a part of his personal concern, and very much part of his concern

[56] Witherspoon, *Works*, 4:10.

[57] Quotation from "John Witherspoon," in Thorp, *Lives*, 85. In 1789 the new General Assembly of the Presbyterian Church reported 188 ministers; 97 were graduates of Princeton, and 52 had been students of Witherspoon (Elwyn A. Smith, *The Presbyterian Minister in American Culture: A Study in Changing Concepts, 1700–1900* [Philadelphia, 1962], 92).

[58] *Princetonians 1776–1783*, xxxi; *Catalogue of All Who Have Held Office in or Have Received Degrees from the College of New Jersey at Princeton* (Princeton, 1896). (Unlike the more comprehensive *General Catalogue* of 1908, the 1896 catalogue continues an older practice of italicizing the names of students who entered the ministry.) Of Witherspoon's 114 students who became ministers, 75 graduated before the war (Smith, *Presbyterian Minister*, 93). The other educational center of colonial Calvinism, Yale College, was also seeing fewer of its students enter the ministry during this same period. But the proportion at Yale did not drop as fast: 25 percent of the graduates became ministers for 1778–1792, and the number did not dip below 20 percent until the second decade of the nineteenth century (Steven J. Novak, *The Rights of Youth: American Colleges and Student Revolt, 1798–1815* [Cambridge, Mass., 1977], 136).

for ministers, but they no longer meant as much for the curriculum. Whether this change, the exciting example of the president's own political service, or the general temper of the age was responsible, the training of ministers at Princeton became a secondary concern during the Witherspoon years.[59]

WITHERSPOON WAS a larger-than-life figure to his contemporaries. Any one of his great achievements—on behalf of the Presbyterians, his country, or the College of New Jersey—would have been enough for the lifetime of a single individual. Yet he won renown in each of these areas after coming to America well into middle age. His accomplishments, and the winsome force of his strenuous personality, made him a revered figure in his own lifetime and a venerated memory long thereafter. Of all his deeds, the restructuring of intellectual and cultural values at Princeton was the most prodigious. For Witherspoon did nothing less than to draw the Princeton circle into the main currents of developments for American society and Western learning. Through his efforts the college became a highly regarded nursery for the republican principles of the new nation. And it became a leader in promoting modern scientific learning. It did so, moreover, without seeming to abandon the configuration of purposes that had governed the school since its inception.

Witherspoon, that is, seemed to exemplify each of the Princeton circle's fundamental concerns. He was an evangelical Christian who told his divinity students, "Religion is the grand concern to us all, as we are men;—whatever be our calling and profession, the salvation of our souls is the one thing needful." No one could question his service to the body politic. Nor could anyone who knew about college expenditures for scientific equipment and faculty doubt his devotion to learning. With his predecessors Witherspoon also refused to segment his religion and his scholarship: "I would therefore begin," he implored his students, "by earnestly beseeching you to keep clear views of the importance of both piety and literature, and never suffer them to be divided. Piety, without literature, is but little profitable; and learning, without piety, is pernicious to others, and ruinous to the possessor." And his extant lectures, whether in moral philosophy, eloquence, or divinity,

---

[59] Even Ashbel Green was forced to admit that some observers felt Witherspoon's religious zeal had flagged because of the political excitement of the war (*Life of Witherspoon*, 273).

leave ample evidence of a concern to build character and through sound character to preserve social order.[60]

Witherspoon also succeeded in uniting the Princeton circle in his efforts. "Our great advantage," he wrote in a promotional pamphlet from 1772, "is the harmony of the board of trustees, and the perfect union in sentiment among all the teachers, both with the trustees and with one another." Witherspoon, if anything, was underestimating the support of the board, for he enjoyed its full confidence in almost every area of his activity. Minor matters aside, like concern for rabble-rousing at commencement, the trustees were pleased with his work and with the direction in which he was leading the college.[61] He had successfully revived its finances, its enrollment, and its prestige. From Princeton's heritage and his own contributions, he had forged an education combining Christianity, patriotism, and science. And he had demonstrated the value of such an education to church, state, society, and the world of thought. As the war began and brought with it violent changes at Princeton, the trustees could look back with great satisfaction on Witherspoon's performance. Although he had been in America less than a decade, he had given the school a vitality and an intellectual stature it had never known before.

A number of considerations, however, obscured the true dimension of Witherspoon's work at Princeton. Witherspoon's larger-than-life reputation hid the fact that his service as an active educator was actually quite short. He arrived in 1768; his lectures were completed by 1772 and never substantially changed thereafter.[62] He soon turned to the public conflict over colonial rights, which absorbed his energy and the energy of many in the Princeton circle for nearly two decades. From 1776 to 1783 Witherspoon was regularly absent from Princeton in service to the Continental Congress and the New Jersey legislature; from 1779 he lived a mile outside of town on his farm, Tusculum, while Stanhope Smith occupied the president's house on campus. Efforts to organize the Presbyterian General Assembly occupied much of his time from

---

[60] Witherspoon, *Works*, 4:11 (both quotations). On these emphases in Witherspoon's thought, see the fine discussion in Fred J. Hood, *Reformed America: The Middle and Southern States, 1783–1837* (University, Ala., 1980), 10–18.

[61] Witherspoon, "Address to the Inhabitants of Jamaica," in *Works*, 4:200. Expressions of favor from the board are spread liberally throughout the TM.

[62] Green, "Witherspoon's Administration at Princeton," 467; Scott, *Lectures on Moral Philosophy by Witherspoon*, 2; Varnum Lansing Collins, ed., *Lectures on Moral Philosophy by John Witherspoon* (Princeton, 1912), xxi–xxiii, where Collins notes that a 1772 student transcript is substantially the same as printed versions from the early nineteenth century.

1784 to 1789. Ill health and failing eyesight reduced the vigor of his presence for more than a decade before his death in 1794. In addition, the events of the war so badly disrupted the college that Princeton's physical environment was not restored for nearly twenty years.

It was, therefore, only during the early 1790s that the Princeton circle resumed the course that Witherspoon had pioneered in the years before the war. The interim, while of extraordinary significance for impressing the virtues of liberty upon the college, had not been a normal period of educational activity. Witherspoon's declining health and his death removed him from active leadership at precisely the time when Princeton resumed pursuit of the goals he had defined two decades before. It was thus not Witherspoon but his colleagues on the board and his successor, Samuel Stanhope Smith, who carried the responsibility for putting his educational purposes to work in a nonrevolutionary situation. When they addressed this task, they found that Witherspoon's legacy included unresolved tensions and unassimilated contradictions concerning the college and its place in the world.

The rest of this book is the story of how Samuel Stanhope Smith, the trustees of his generation, and then Ashbel Green attempted to deal with those tensions and contradictions in the context of ongoing developments in church, nation, and the world of thought. When difficulties arose in the years after Witherspoon's death, neither Smith nor the trustees blamed him for their troubles or even gave any indication that they felt he was somehow responsible. Yet they could have. For what Witherspoon left—besides the brilliant record of his public service, the revered memory of his character, the powerful example of his devotion to piety and learning, and the sterling reputation he had won for the college—was a number of extraordinarily weighty, yet unresolved questions.

To sketch these issues here is to set the framework for the college's history through the administrations of Witherspoon's students Stanhope Smith and Ashbel Green and, to a lesser extent, through the presidencies of James McCosh, F. Landey Patton, and Woodrow Wilson.[63] And it is to suggest the places where Princeton's internal history intersected the larger stories of republican politics, Presbyterian theology, the American Enlightenment, and the search for order in the early republic.

[63] J. David Hoeveler, Jr., *James McCosh and the Scottish Intellectual Tradition: From Glasgow to Princeton* (Princeton, 1981), 219–20; and John M. Mulder, *Woodrow Wilson: The Years of Preparation* (Princeton, 1978), 145, 163.

The fundamental issue was the integrated education upon which Princeton had prided itself since its founding. Could the college remain a nursery of both piety and science, a place at once to train ministers and statesmen, a promoter of character, social order, Presbyterian orthodoxy, and political well-being? Or had Witherspoon left a legacy with irreconcilable elements? The specific issues touched particularly the college's commitments in science, philosophy, and republican politics.

Witherspoon had given a new prominence, indeed a virtual hegemony, to scientific inquiry—in natural philosophy as the way to discover the physical world, in ethics as the way to put the moral sense to work, and in divinity as the way to verify both the existence of God and the doctrines of Protestant orthodoxy. For a Presbyterian minister at the American center of evangelical Calvinism, he had reduced theology and Christian revelation to surprisingly marginal positions. Such subjects remained vocationally useful to ministers and were the wellspring of personal piety, but they offered very little to either natural or moral philosophy. Was it possible to sustain this dependence of theology upon philosophy and still maintain the institution's traditional service to piety generally and its specific role as a training ground for Presbyterian ministers? How would trustees react when they began to sense the tension? By embracing a more secular position openly and abandoning Princeton's earlier commitments in religion? By reimposing the single-minded piety of the Burr era and playing down the pursuit of modern learning? Or by attempting to juggle, as Witherspoon had, the supernaturalism of traditional Calvinism and the implicit naturalism of Enlightenment thought?

Witherspoon's energy made republican principles and Whig conceptions of social order the norm at Princeton. Would this republicanism reduce the college's efforts in religion, science, and character formation to merely instrumental aids in the service of liberty? Was republicanism, in fact, fully compatible with traditional orthodoxy? Did it provide a secure base for forming character and stabilizing society? If, as indeed happened, a "contagion of liberty,"[64] rooted in Revolutionary principles, spread to the Princeton campus itself, how would college authorities, who considered themselves friends of order as well as stalwarts of the Revolution, respond?

To ask these questions is to suggest the difficulty in making a final assessment of Witherspoon's intellectual activity. For all his

---

[64] Bailyn, *Ideological Origins of the American Revolution*, 230.

directness, and despite the ease with which historians have fit him into the historiography of the American Revolution, Witherspoon remains an enigmatic figure.[65] The Scottish minister who read Joseph Bellamy's works with delight, urged ministers not to meddle in politics, denounced Francis Hutcheson, opposed ecclesiastical patronage as tyrannical, and mobilized troops against the Rebellion of '45 was also the American college president who banned Bellamy's works from his campus, joined legislative assemblies, modeled his collegiate instruction on Hutcheson, supported a moderate establishment of religion, and championed the Rebellion of '76.[66] A partial explanation of this ambiguity must include the observation that, while in Scotland, Witherspoon's antiestablishment "populism" was associated with theological conservatism. In America, by contrast, his republicanism was shared by representatives of every position on the theological spectrum. Nonetheless, "sea change" still seems the only appropriate phrase to describe the two stages of Witherspoon's career.

By the time the college board entrusted Samuel Stanhope Smith with the responsibility for carrying out its mission for Princeton, Witherspoon was a fading presence. Yet his great accomplishment—uniting at one place in a cohesive educational system the values of high Whiggery, naturalistic moral philosophy, Calvinistic orthodoxy, honorable citizenship, and social order—set the character of a Princeton education and decisively shaped the values of the Princeton circle. It was up to those who remained, to the board and to Smith, to sustain that character and the achievement of Witherspoon when he was no more.[67]

[65] For example, H. James Henderson, "The Structure of Politics in the Continental Congress," in *Essays on the American Revolution*, ed. Stephen G. Kurtz and James H. Hutson (Chapel Hill, N.C., 1973), 160; and Marshall Smelser, *The Winning of Independence* (New York, 1973), 132.

[66] A similar list of contrasts was assembled in Brant, *James Madison*, 1:74. The best attempt to show the consistency of Witherspoon's career is an essay stressing ongoing continuities in wider worlds of revivalism and enlightened learning; see Ned Landsman, "John Witherspoon and the Problem of Provincial Idenitity in Eighteenth-Century America," in *Scotland and America in the Age of Enlightenment*, ed. Richard B. Sher and Jeffrey Smitten (Edinburgh, forthcoming).

[67] It is only fair to say that my opinion of Witherspoon's intellectual achievement and long-term influence is not wholly favorable. Douglas Sloan was certainly correct, when he wrote of Witherspoon's efforts to unite naturalistic science and traditional theology, that "the ultimate result . . . appears to have been beneficial neither to science nor to theology, and to have robbed both of a needed inner dynamic and self-direction" (*Scottish Enlightenment*, 240).

5

Samuel Stanhope Smith, 1751–1781

Labouring up the Hill of Science and Virtue

S AMUEL STANHOPE SMITH was born on March 15, 1751, in Pequea, Pennsylvania, about forty miles west of Philadelphia in Lancaster County, where his father had only that year assumed responsibility for the Presbyterian church.[1] A child (as his first biographer reported) of "prompt parts and virtuous dispositions," Smith was well suited for the academic course that his parents set for him.[2] They, in turn, were both well-respected Presbyterians, whose interests provided a channel for the considerable talents of their son.

Robert Smith (1723–1793) was born in Ireland of Scottish parents and migrated in 1730 to the colonies, where his education took place under the supervision of Samuel Blair in Faggs Manor, Chester County, Pennsylvania. Blair, a founding trustee of Princeton College, an affecting preacher of heart religion, and a leader of the colonial Great Awakening, conducted one of the more successful of the several Presbyterian academies that at midcentury offered rigorous classical and theological training to the aspiring sons of Scottish immigrants. At about age fifteen, Robert Smith was converted under George Whitefield, whose ministry left an extraordinary impression on the young man. More than forty years later Smith visited scenes of revival in Virginia and evaluated their effectiveness by how thoroughly they measured up to standards set by Whitefield.[3] At Faggs Manor Smith acquired not only learning

---

[1] Wesley Frank Craven corrects the frequent error, found even on Smith's gravestone, that he was born in 1750 (*Princetonians 1769–1775*, 42).

[2] Beasley, "Life," 413.

[3] William Henry Foote, *Sketches of Virginia, Historical and Biographical (First Series)* (1850; reprint, Richmond, 1966), 409; Samuel Holt Monk, "Samuel Stanhope

for the ministry but also a wife, Elizabeth, the daughter of his teacher. He took with him as well the friendship of the large Blair clan, which included a number of prominent divines.

Robert Smith quickly became established as a faithful servant of Presbyterian interests, a capable teacher, a forceful preacher of revival, and a loyal patriot. He seems to have had a great capacity for faithful institutional service, missing only four annual meetings of his denomination's highest assembly from 1753 until his death, attending regularly the sessions of the Princeton board after his election in 1772, and conducting a not inconsiderable grammar school at Pequea. As many as thirty pupils at a time studied the rudiments of Latin, Greek, science, mathematics, and theology under his direction; over fifty ministers, including Stanhope and two other sons, received their first formal learning from his hands during the forty years he conducted the school. For his labors on behalf of the church, he was named moderator of the Synod of New York and Philadelphia in 1774, he received the honorary D.D. from Princeton in 1786, and in 1790 he was asked to serve as the second moderator of the Presbyterian General Assembly. Unlike his son Samuel Stanhope, Robert Smith enjoyed good health throughout his life, missing only one Sunday in the pulpit throughout his entire preaching career.[4]

Robert Smith also differed from his son, who would come to champion a more dignified faith, by energetically promoting revival. While the older Smith did help to heal the Presbyterian schism occasioned by the Great Awakening, his sympathies were clearly with the revivalistic, or New Side, party.[5] His published sermons reveal him as an effective orator and an uncompromising champion of the divine initiative in salvation. "Grace is a principle of spiritual life infused into the soul by the Holy Ghost," he asserted in 1767, a position from which he never wavered.[6] Robert

Smith (1751–1819): Friend of Rational Liberty," in Thorp, *Lives*, 88; Jacob Newton Beam, "Dr. Robert Smith's Academy at Pequea, Pennsylvania," *Journal of the Presbyterian Historical Society* 8 (1915): 154; Wesley Frank Craven, "John Blair Smith," in *Princetonians 1769–1775*, 344.

[4] Beam, "Robert Smith's Academy," 150; *Records of the Presbyterian Church in the United States 1706–1788* (Philadelphia, 1904), 450; *General Catalogue*, 401; *Minutes of the General Assembly of the Presbyterian Church in the United States of America from . . . 1789 to . . . 1820* (Philadelphia, 1847), 22; Sprague, *Annals*, 3:173.

[5] Witness his plea to hard-line Scottish separates that, "instead of *jangling and Debates*, we might *join Hands to Hand, seeking the Way to Zion, with our Faces thitherward, weeping as we go!*" (*The Detection Detected* [Lancaster, Pa., 1757], 136).

[6] Robert Smith, "The Principle of Sin and Holiness," in *Sermons and Essays by the*

Smith, in sum, embraced the Savior as Whitefield, Jonathan Edwards, and the colonial New Lights had made him known.

Smith was also a patriot who believed that God took a special interest in the political fortunes of his English and American children. During the French and Indian War he professed to see God's special working in the raising of William III "to deliver the Protestants . . . in *Britain*, from the slavish yoke of *popish* Tyranny," in the more recent triumphs at Louisbourg and on the Continent, and in the beneficent rule of George II. "How evident may we see the Hand of God in all these successes."[7] Less than twenty years later, he took a different stance toward George II's successor, and on two occasions he helped transport provisions from the Pequea area to Washington's forces. Yet though loyalties had changed, Smith still could observe God's hand sustaining his chosen people. The thanksgiving proclaimed by Congress for December 13, 1781, gave him the opportunity to exult that "the glorious Sovereign of the earth and heavens hath lifted up a banner for you, O ye highly favoured Americans! and hath saved you by his right hand." Smith concluded this address by observing that, since "the cause of America is the cause of Christ," his hearers had special reason to praise God and heed his commandments.[8]

The heritage that Robert Smith communicated to his son defined the lifelong interests of Samuel Stanhope Smith. The son would give less place to religious ardor and exhibit greater skill in learning, but he too would be committed to a providential understanding of America, to the values of an academic life, and to the verities of traditional Christian faith. Times would change, and the reputation of the son would eclipse that of the father. Yet Stanhope Smith never entirely left the world that his father's teaching first opened up for him.

STANHOPE SMITH was a precocious child, even in a century marked by the intellectual exploits of the very young. At age six in 1757 he began serious study with his father, rapidly mastered Latin and Greek, and soon began the mathematical and scientific

---

Tennents and Their Contemporaries (Philadelphia, 1855), 312. The same note was still prominent late in life (e.g., *Three Sermons, on the Nature and Excellency of Saving Faith; Delivered at Pequea, in August and September, 1791* [Lancaster, Pa., 1791]).

[7] Robert Smith, *A Wheel in the Middle of a Wheel, or, Harmony and Connexion of Various Acts of Divine Providence* (Philadelphia, 1759), 35, 48.

[8] Beam, "Robert Smith's Academy," 159; Robert Smith, *The Obligations of the Confederate States of North America to Praise God* (Philadelphia, 1782), 4, 33.

studies that led him to eventual renown. He had been baptized by Samuel Finley, the New Side stalwart and colleague of his father, who was Witherspoon's predecessor as president of the New Jersey college. From an early age Stanhope showed more interest in the business of his elders than in the rough-and-tumble play of his fellows. Before he left for college at age sixteen, he publicly joined the church, an early age for such a step. He excelled in the academic competitions for which his father's grammar school was famous and early on began to be treated as a leader among men. It apparently was his custom while still very young to gather brothers, sisters, and neighborhood children to conduct his own version of divine service, and later to take turns with his mother in leading family worship while his father was away.[9] Smith's commanding presence, even as a child, was one of the sources for a rivalry that developed with his younger brother, John Blair (b. 1756), and that would color the relationship between these prominent divines until the younger's death in 1799.[10] In spite of this strain, the childhood of Stanhope Smith presaged a distinguished career.

Smith's years as a student did nothing to dim his prospects. He took his place in Princeton's junior class in the fall of 1767 and proceeded to a series of academic triumphs. James Madison, who arrived at the college shortly before commencement in 1769, reported home that Smith, as "the greatest *Scholar*" of his class, had been designated the chief orator for the occasion.[11] In both learning and demeanor Smith cut a distinguished figure. All agreed that Robert Smith was fortunate to secure his son as an assistant in the Pequea grammar school in 1769 while the young man began preparation for the ministry. In a similar way Smith dignified the position of Princeton tutor to which he was called in 1770, while he continued ministerial training with Witherspoon.

For Smith's later career, two developments in his early years at Princeton stand out with special importance. The first was intellectual, namely, his conversion under Witherspoon to the Scottish

[9] Beasley, "Life," 445–46; Charles Greer Sellers, Jr., "John Blair Smith," *Journal of the Presbyterian Historical Society* 34 (1956): 204.

[10] Sellers, "John Blair Smith," 204–5; Craven, "John Blair Smith," in *Princetonians 1769–1775*, 342–46. The rivalry between the brothers eventually may have affected the history of Princeton, since John Blair Smith was closely allied with Ashbel Green and Archibald Alexander, who later harbored suspicions of their own concerning Samuel Stanhope Smith.

[11] Madison to his father, Sept. 30, 1769, in *The Papers of James Madison*, vol. 1, *16 March 1751–16 December 1779*, ed. William T. Hutchinson and William M. C. Rachal (Chicago, 1962), 45.

philosophy of common sense. The second was personal—the growing recognition by his peers that Smith was an individual of uncommonly elegant bearing.

Smith's early theological training inculcated the values of revivalist Calvinism. Given Jonathan Edwards's commanding presence among colonial Calvinists, this training predisposed its adherents both to philosophical idealism and a certain suspicion of new conventions in eighteenth-century thought.[12] The exact content of Robert Smith's instruction in theology is not known, but it no doubt contained a healthy dose of Edwards and his followers, as well as standard Reformed divines from the Continent.[13] Smith's first instruction at Princeton fortified this earlier training, perhaps to the point of exaggeration. He arrived at Princeton during a year of transition, after the death of Samuel Finley and before the arrival of Witherspoon. Instruction at the college was under the general oversight of John Blair, Smith's cousin and a divine of New Side sentiments. Smith seems also to have been instructed by tutor Joseph Periam, the most self-conscious follower of Jonathan Edwards on a faculty dominated by Edwardsean sentiments. Periam's advocacy of Berkeley's philosophy may have been an eccentric intellectual hobbyhorse, or it may have been a means of combating the materialism and the egotism that Berkeley, and also Edwards, espied in the widespread appropriation of Newton and Locke. In any event, Smith appears to have absorbed idealist notions from Periam, although it is not clear how Smith related these to theological principles. So bold was Smith's advocacy of immaterialism that his father was worried.[14]

As he did for the college as a whole, John Witherspoon made quick work of his brightest pupil's dalliance with Bishop Berkeley. Frederick Beasley, class of 1797, an Episcopal educator and long-time friend of Stanhope Smith, probably received the story of Witherspoon's arrival and its impact from Smith himself. Beasley eventually became an ardent Lockean with no sympathy whatever for idealism, so he may have overdramatized Witherspoon's impact on Smith to serve his own philosophical purposes. Nonetheless, his account, the first and fullest description of Stanhope

---

[12] On those conventions, see Norman Fiering, *Jonathan Edwards's Moral Thought and Its British Context* (Chapel Hill, N.C., 1981).

[13] For a general picture of these educational resources, see Howard Miller, *The Revolutionary College: American Presbyterian Higher Education, 1707–1837* (New York, 1976), 79–96.

[14] *Princetonians 1748–1768*, 399–402; and Beasley, "Life," 448.

Smith's intellectual conversion, catches the excitement of the event.

> Accordingly, Mr. Smith, although captivated, at first, by the specious fallacies of the bishop of Cloyne [Berkeley], had too much sober sense and penetration to be long held in bondage by the silken chains of such a fantastic theory. Dr. Witherspoon arrived from Scotland, and bringing with him, we are told, the recently broached principles of [Thomas] Reid, [James] Oswald and [James] Beattie, furnished him with a clue by which he was conducted out of the dark labyrinth into which he had been betrayed by bishop Berkeley and his disciple, professor Periam. From the cloudy speculations of immaterialism, he was now brought back to the clear light of common sense. Nature was again reinstated in her rights, and the external world, which had been banished for a while, returned and resumed its place in creation.[15]

The consequences for Smith and the future of Princeton can hardly be overstated. Smith's later prominence at the institution meant that Witherspoon's vision for collegiate education would dominate Princeton long after he had left the scene. When Smith began to lecture on moral philosophy at Hampden-Sidney, when he completed his course of lectures as a Princeton professor, and when he published them at the end of his active service, he was only making good on the promise of his undergraduate experience. Smith's embrace of common-sense philosophy had a profound influence on the picture of the world that he would communicate to undergraduates for forty years. The dictates of common-sense intuition, especially of the universal moral sense, provided a key for integrating modern learning and Christian faith, even as they allowed Smith to modify certain features of inherited Calvinism. They also provided Smith with the means to harmonize studies in the various disciplines, to defend religion against its cultured despisers, and to grasp the meaning of contemporary political developments. Witherspoon's success at winning over his first valedictorian to common-sense principles was, in short, one of the great events in the early history of Princeton and, because of Princeton's importance in the middle and southern states, an event of no small significance for American high culture in the early republic.

The second memorable development of Smith's collegiate career was his emergence as a figure of unusual personal dignity. Whether from his intellectual and religious precocity, the nature

---

[15] Beasley, "Life," 449–50; on Beasley, see Elizabeth Flower and Murray G. Murphey, *A History of Philosophy in America*, 2 vols. (New York, 1977), 1:306.

of his upbringing, his great success at college, forebodings about his health, or for other reasons, Smith's character attracted unusual attention. Already as a sixteen-year-old undergraduate he was marked, as a modern biographer phrased it, by "fastidiousness of dress and decorum." Under Witherspoon, Princeton came to place greater stress on belles lettres and on dignified speechmaking, two subjects that Smith found immensely rewarding. Frederick Beasley reported that in those years "the works of Pope, Swift and Addision, which were now read with avidity, served to form his taste upon the best models and imbue his mind with the principles of polite literature." Long after his graduation Smith continued to affect the neoclassical pose.[16]

The resulting character became an object of diffident respect, and also of some resentment. William Paterson, the future Supreme Court justice and college trustee, studied at Princeton while Smith was a tutor and also competed with him for the affections of Richard Stockton's niece. To the undergraduate Paterson, Smith was a self-satisfied prig. "Smith, tutor Smith," he wrote in a satirical poem,

> so wond'rous civil,
> Compound odd of Saint and Devil . . .
> Proud of his learning and his parts
> The case exact of all upstarts—
> Proud of his beauty too; I swear
> He is all lovely and all fair;
> Proud of his manners, 'tis most true
> (We must e'en give the devil his due)
> In manners he excels; he came
> From Pequea, land of wond'rous fame,
> Where learning wit and genius shine
> Ecce Signum, I am divine![17]

Throughout his career Smith's dignity was a mixed blessing. It regularly earned him the respect of students and others but also served to set him apart from ordinary social intercourse. His polish became an ornament to the office of college president, even as it prevented him from exercising the intuitive sway that the rough-and-ready Witherspoon enjoyed.

Smith's course of formal study was pointed toward ordination as a settled pastor and perhaps also, for one of his attainments, to the conduct of a grammar school. During his last year as tutor, Smith

[16] Monk, "Samuel Stanhope Smith," 90; Beasley, "Life," 453–54.
[17] Monk, "Samuel Stanhope Smith," 91.

was licensed to preach by his father's New Castle Presbytery, and we may assume that he was beginning to look for a ministerial call. A break in his never robust health intervened, however, and set in motion the chain of circumstances that turned Smith more directly toward an educational career. In 1773 he contracted an intermittent fever and experienced other symptoms of tuberculosis, a malady from which he was never entirely free. To find a more suitable climate for his health, as well as to exercise his calling, he traveled to Virginia and offered himself for service as an itinerant in the western counties, where Presbyterians were only beginning to gain a foothold.

SMITH'S ARRIVAL in Virginia in 1773 coincided with discussions within the Hanover Presbytery concerning the pressing need for higher education. The presbytery, stretching across the central part of Virginia and straddling the Blue Ridge Mountains, owed its existence to the labors of New Side revivalist Samuel Davies (1723–1761). When Davies accepted the call to the College of New Jersey, he left behind high standards of faith and learning. Davies's Virginia colleagues, who faced the challenge of ministering to growing numbers of nominally Presbyterian immigrants from Scotland and the north of Ireland, set several plans in motion during the early 1770s to provide schools for ministers and public leaders. In 1774 the Hanover Presbytery authorized a "seminary" in Augusta County, west of the mountains. To this insitution they called William Graham, Princeton class of 1773 and a friend of Stanhope Smith. Shortly after authorizing Graham's academy, the presbytery also began a work east of the Blue Ridge in Prince Edward County. This venture it committed into the hands of Stanhope Smith. In early 1774 the Hanover Presbytery began to raise money for its new "Prince Edward Academy"; in February it named Smith the rector; by September he was advertising for students in the *Virginia Gazette*. The academy was to feature "the System of Education . . . which is adopted in the College of *New Jersey*; save that a more particular Attention shall be paid to the Cultivation of the *English* language." Smith's advertisement also emphasized "the most *catholic* Plan" of the school and its eagerness to ensure "Parents, of every Denomination," that their sons would enjoy the form of worship they desired.[18]

---

[18] *Virginia Gazette*, Oct. 7, 1775, as reproduced in E. T. Crowson, "Samuel Stanhope Smith: A Founder of Hampden-Sydney College," *Virginia Cavalcade*, Autumn

This assertion was not mere rhetoric, since it reflected both Smith's actual sentiments and a more mundane reality. For an educational institution to flourish in Virginia during the 1770s, support was necessary from members of the Church of England. The Hanover Presbytery recognized that fact of life and named several Anglicans to the school's board. It was this new board which, in deference to the spirit of the times, renamed the school "Hampden-Sidney Academy" to honor two statesmen, John Hampden and Algernon Sidney, who, over a century before, had helped the Puritans shake off the rule of an earlier English tyrant.

Meanwhile, Smith continued to preach as a supply pastor and itinerating evangelist and to set his personal house in order. In June of 1775 he returned to Princeton to marry Ann Witherspoon, who would become the mother of his nine children. In October Smith was ordained and installed as the minister of two churches near the academy, which he continued to serve until his departure from the area. Already before he embarked on his career as an educator, Smith enjoyed a reputation for what one contemporary called "his impressive and pathetic addresses."[19]

Classes at Hampden-Sidney Academy began in January 1776, and the school was an immediate success. Enrollment reached 110 that same summer, which led Smith to engage three other recent Princeton graduates as instructors, including his brother John Blair Smith and his brother-in-law David Witherspoon.[20] None of the Princetonians had ever seen so many students at their alma mater. Under Smith the new academy made its way in an increasingly tumultuous world. Students and their parents expressed pleasure at the quality of instruction. College buildings eventually appeared, though not without frustrating delays. More difficult than raising buildings was raising money. The Virginia burgesses refused an appeal for a subsidy, and a lottery fell flat. But the greatest difficulty was the war.

There was never a hint of suspicion about the institution's loy-

---

1974, 58. For this period of Smith's life, I have relied on Crowson's article; J. D. Eggleston, "Hampden-Sydney Opened as a College in 1776," *Record of the Hampden-Sydney Alumni Association* 18, no. 4 (July 1944): 14–16; Alfred J. Morrison, *The College of Hampden-Sidney: Calendar of Board Minutes, 1776–1876* (Richmond, Va., 1912); A. J. Morrison, *College of Hampden Sidney: Dictionary of Biography, 1776–1825* (Hampden Sidney, Va., 1921); and Foote, *Sketches of Virginia*. On Graham, see *Princetonians 1769–1775*, 289–94.

[19] Gilbert Morgan to Samuel Miller, no date [ca. 1819], Samuel Miller Papers, PUL.

[20] Collins, *Witherspoon*, 2:204–5.

alties. Smith himself spoke widely on behalf of independence. He even exploited the republican thirst for liberty by petitioning the Virginia assembly for the same liberties in religion at home that the colony was seeking in its struggle with Great Britain.[21] And in September 1777 Smith responded to an appeal by Governor Patrick Henry and formed the Hampden-Sidney student body into the Prince Edward County Militia. A British fleet carrying General Howe and his army was approaching Virginia, and the Hampden-Sidney students, under the command of John Blair Smith, joined other patriots to defend the coast. But General Howe turned aside for Philadelphia, and Governor Henry disbanded his militia. The troops from Prince Edward County returned, insofar as it was possible, to their studies.

The most serious difficulties created by the war were not ideological but practical. Because of its disruption the school's trustees could not meet for several years. The rapid depreciation of Continental currency made it impossible for the college to board students. And the full enrollments of 1776 dwindled drastically. The academy was struggling, but it had made a good beginning that redounded to the credit of the Hanover Presbytery, its "catholic" board, and its rector, Stanhope Smith.

DURING HIS stay in Virginia Smith's correspondence with the new state's rising political leaders gave him an opportunity to try out his thinking on social and more strictly intellectual concerns. When Thomas Jefferson introduced a "bill for the more general diffusion of knowledge" to the Virginia House of Delegates in December 1778, Smith took an immediate interest. Jefferson's proposal, with its eloquent theoretical defense of public education, called for a three-tiered program of publicly funded schooling: "All the free children, male and female," in each carefully defined locality were to receive three years of basic study; the best male students were to have further instruction paid for at county "grammar school-houses"; and the best of these students were to be supported for a three-year course of study in the higher sciences at the College of William and Mary.[22]

Soon after this proposal appeared, Smith wrote a deferential letter to Jefferson, whom he had not met, to point out difficulties in

[21] The petition is reproduced in Foote, *Sketches of Virginia*, 326–27.
[22] *The Papers of Thomas Jefferson*, vol. 2, *1777 to 18 June 1779*, ed. Julian P. Boyd (Princeton, 1950), 526–35.

the bill. A second letter followed Jefferson's prompt reply. Smith was worried that, unless the measure took account of "the variety of religious sentiments that exist in the state," it would fail. While he bemoaned "the jealousy of parties" and "the partialities of sects" as "the disgrace of science," Smith felt that Jefferson's scheme must take account of interconfessional strife, particularly between Episcopalians and Presbyterians. "The Baptists and Methodists," Smith conceded, "content themselves with other kinds of illumination than are afforded by human science." His own position was entirely that of an enlightened servant of learning who regretted that "few are possessed of that cool and philosophic temper, and that confinement of sentiment that is necessary to overcome this unhappy [i.e., sectarian] influence." His proposal was for Episcopalian and Presbyterian friends of science to join together in running William and Mary, thereby encouraging a liberality of religious sentiment throughout the entire system. Smith's "extreme love of peace, and of that benevolence which my religion recommends, and of enlarged and liberal inquiry in matters of science," encouraged him to think that it could be done if the Episcopalians would "descend a little from that pride and insolence" and the Presbyterians "relax somewhat of that rigour and austerity that have hitherto characterized them."[23]

Jefferson evidently responded with respect, but also with the observation that Smith's plan presupposed the continuation of a religious establishment, something that Jefferson's further plans for William and Mary hoped to avoid. (His letter is unfortunately lost.) Smith responded that "the reasons for a public religion have always appeared to me inconclusive" and that it might therefore be better for the assembly to establish two universities in different parts of the state to prevent an unofficial establishment from gaining control of education by manipulating the single capstone of the system.[24]

In the event, Jefferson's bill did not pass, and education in Virginia continued under the normal eighteenth-century hodgepodge of private and public authorities. Yet Smith's letters on the subject did reveal his liberality of mind, his indisposition against sectarian religious strife, and his willingness to work with Episcopalians that, for weal and woe, would also mark his later career at Princeton.

An exchange of letters with James Madison during this same pe-

[23] Smith to Jefferson, [Mar. 1779?], ibid., 247–48.
[24] Smith to Jefferson, Apr. 19, 1779, ibid., 253.

riod provided an occasion for Smith to try out ideas, this time not on educational policy but on moral philosophy. Madison, who was one day younger than the Hampden-Sidney rector, had become acquainted with Smith during his years as a Princeton student, and he resumed the friendship when Smith settled in Virginia. With Madison, Smith stood on easy terms. They had apparently conversed on philosophical subjects while at Princeton and continued to do so in Virginia. In late 1777 or early 1778, Smith asked for Madison's reactions to an informal treatise on the weighty issues of free will and determinism. "You have frequently attacked me on the knotty question of *liberty* & *necessity*," Smith wrote, adding the hope that "it may prove a relaxation to you in the midst of other business, to attend to a few metaphisical ones."²⁵ Madison at the time had already served one term in the new Virginia assembly and, in 1778, was placed by the assembly on the Governor's Advisory Council. Yet as an indication of his capacious intellect, he still took time to respond.

The oddest aspect of the exchange was that Smith, the Presbyterian minister and sprout from a Calvinist family tree, argued the libertarian position, while Madison, a layman of the Episcopal church, seems to have defended the necessitarian. The oddity dissolves when Smith's case is examined, however, for he turns out to be applying, with considerable astuteness, the philosophical principles he had so solidly embraced under Witherspoon.²⁶ The question of free will and determinism, as Smith saw it, must be decided by studying "the common [sen]sations of the human mind." Put most simply, "the idea of *power* seems to be so plain & well-defined, that none but a philosopher too enamoured of the product of his own brain, is capable of denying it. And when this idea is acknowledged, as by plain & unsophisticated reason & experience I think it must[,] the *liberty of moral action* necessarily follows. . . . Human liberty is as evident & undelusive as the principle of our nature." Furthermore, once this deliverance of the moral sense is perceived, it is everywhere confirmed by a scientific procedure: "Experiment in morals as well as in phisics is the only proper source

²⁵ Smith to Madison, sometime between Nov. 1777 and Aug. 1778, *Papers of James Madison*, 194.

²⁶ Madison also engaged in a postgraduate course of study directed by Witherspoon, but he seems to have picked up as much from the traditional elements in Witherspoon's theology as from the more modern elements of his philosophy, at least for the issue Smith raised (James H. Smylie, "Madison and Witherspoon: Theological Roots of American Political Thought," *PULC* 22 [1961]: 118–32).

of truth, & guide of reasoning. . . . Experiment appears to favour the conclusion . . . that, in the common course of life no particular motive hath a necessary & irresistable power over the Will."[27]

Smith was well acquainted with Jonathan Edwards's arguments on the subject, for Witherspoon had directed his reading to Edwards and other prominent divines.[28] But to Madison, Smith countered Edwards's argument that willing proceeds ineluctably from the strongest motive by suggesting that *"liberty consists* in such a *proportion* of external objects to the *principles of human nature,* as [a]lways to raise so[me] *emotion* or *desire* sufficient to be a *motive* or *volition,* but not to determine the *will* with *absolute necessity."* Before he ended the exercise, Smith took pains to disassociate his thoughts from principles "so vigorously maintained by the Arminians." And he reminded Madison, "I am here talking only as a philosopher." "As a Divine," he conceded, "I might say that the strength of vicious habit might require some heavenly assis[t]ance or afflatus to make [virtuous motives] always effectual."[29]

Madison's reply is lost, but from Smith's second letter on the subject, written September 15, 1778, it appears that the young public servant pressed the arguments of Edwards as a rejoinder to the position of the young minister.[30] Edwards had argued that Arminian convictions about human freedom involved several absurdities, including an arbitrary self-determination of the will and an infinite regression of motive. However Madison put his case for the Edwardsean views, Smith denied that his own position entailed either of these problems. Moral intuition was the clincher: "Altho we are not able to explain the idea of *moral liberty,* & that innate *energy* of mind that is involved in it, so as to be exempt from all questioning and doubt, yet we have as clear a sentiment of nature to appeal to, as is the case of colour." Before he closed this second letter on free will, Smith protested, as he did also to Jefferson, his abhorrence of sectarianism. "As the world goes, it has become necessary to assume some name, & to class yourself ever with those

[27] Smith to Madison, sometime between Nov. 1777 and Aug. 1778, 195, 196, 197, 199, 203. At the very end of the letter, Smith asked Madison if he knew of any arguments for the existence of God that were better than "a kind of indelible sentiment of the heart" (p. 211).

[28] Beasley, "Life," 453.

[29] Smith to Madison, sometime between Nov. 1777 and Aug. 1778, 209, 210, 211.

[30] Irving Brant, *James Madison,* vol. 1, *The Virginia Revolutionist* (Indianapolis, 1941), 121–22, with reference to Jonathan Edwards, *Freedom of the Will* (1754); the definitive edition of this work is that of Paul Ramsey (New Haven, 1957).

you despise." Yet he hoped for better things, especially for "a favourable opportunity to unite some of our religious parties, if their leaders were sufficiently catholic."[31]

The Smith who speaks in the letters to Jefferson and Madison is a person of obvious ability and manifest public spirit. He is furthermore an individual of considerable intellectual sophistication whose speculations on the will are already more searching than anything he had heard from his mentor Witherspoon. At the same time, it is also obvious that the development of Witherspoon's positions is moving Smith into unexplored territory. Even at this early stage there is an obvious division between Smith's public position as a New Side minister and his private speculations as a philosopher. A whiff of dilettantism also attends his recreational enjoyment of philosophical speculation. It is already possible, as Douglas Sloan once put it very well, that Smith was living up "to Witherspoon's own ideal of the evangelical gentleman and ministerial man of letters with more success than the plain old doctor ever could."[32]

The new directions in which Smith was carrying the legacy of Witherspoon did nothing, however, to undermine his effectiveness in Virginia. His elegance, diplomacy, and catholicity boosted the fortunes of Hampden-Sidney. As a stately, serious-minded, dignified, and handsome young man, he quickly won a wide personal following. Forty years after Smith left the state, the memory of those early days remained. At the time of Smith's death, a Virginian wrote, "They say there never has been a man in Virginia under similar circumstances so popular. Tho young, a presbyterian, and a preacher from the north he was universally known, loved and revered." Reports about Smith's later career—that he had become a partisan Federalist, that he was tempting orthodoxy—clouded the earlier memory, but his Virginia friends could remember when his reputation was simply above reproach: "For a young man his gravity and weight of character, his piety as a man of prayer, his affections and tenderness, his eloquence, learning and talents, the confidence and attachment of his friends[,] appear to have given Dr. Smith as Minister of the Gospel in Virginia, a popularity as great perhaps greater than anywhere else."[33]

The only serious difficulty in Smith's Virginia career was his

[31] Smith to Madison, Sept. 15, 1778, *Papers of James Madison*, 256–57.

[32] Douglas Sloan, *The Scottish Enlightenment and the American College Ideal* (New York, 1971), 168.

[33] Gilbert Morgan to Samuel Miller, no date [ca. 1819].

health. In 1777 he experienced a recurrence of tubercular symptoms, due, Frederick Beasley concluded, to his "arduous duties in the seminary" and "the frequency and vehemence of his mode of preaching."[34] A trip to the waters of Sweet-Springs in western Virginia seems to have improved matters, but he continued to be susceptible to further incapacity, especially when overworked.

For the rest, Smith's activity in Virginia gave Witherspoon and the Princeton trustees every indication that he would be a major asset to his alma mater. Witherspoon kept abreast of Smith's progress through correspondence with his children. Other trustees learned of Smith's excellences through more public means. Perhaps they had even been told about the way Smith could defend learning as a sacred duty. At least one future stalwart of the Presbyterian interest, Moses Hoge, never forgot the words that Smith delivered to his grammar school, that, "while sanctified learning is the greatest blessing, unsanctified learning is the greatest curse."[35] Such sentiments, combined with Smith's manifest ability, were surety enough for the Princeton board.

IN SPITE of Princeton's confidence in him, Smith may have entertained doubts about Princeton, once he confronted the seriousness of the college's situation.[36] When Smith returned on December 12, 1779, the brutal effects of war still lay heavy on the village of some sixty to seventy dwellings and its college. The British had occupied the town from December 7, 1776, to January 3, 1777. They had not been kind to either the community or the college, for both bore the stigma of sedition. Redcoats used the college building, Nassau Hall, as a barracks and stable. They stripped the chapel and the town church for firewood. And they plundered the libraries of the president and the college; some of the books eventually ended up in North Carolina with Cornwallis's army. During the Battle of Princeton, on January 3, 1777, the British broke Nassau Hall's windows to fire out, and American artillery savaged the building firing in. After the British abandoned the town, it looked, in Benjamin Rush's words, like "it had been desolated with the

[34] Beasley, "Life," 458.

[35] Quotation from Foote, *Sketches of Virginia*, 555.

[36] The following description of the college's state after the war draws on Wertenbaker, *Princeton*, 60–69; *Princetonians 1776–1783*, xxi–xxii; *Life of Green*, 136–37; TM, Apr. 16, 1778; Apr. 21–22, and Sept. 29, 1779; Sept. 27–28, 1780; and Varnum Lansing Collins, *Princeton* (New York, 1914), 78–82.

plague and an earthquake, . . . the college and church are heaps of ruins."[37]

What Princeton's enemies had not destroyed, its friends did. Continental troops barracked in the college for the next five months, and then for over a year the Americans used Nassau Hall as a hospital. Even Rittenhouse's famous orrery, which the British had spared, fell prey to "the fingering of the American troops," who ruined it almost beyond repair.[38] In 1779 the young Ashbel Green was living in Morris County, only a short distance from the college. He reported that "the dilapidation and pollution of the college edifice, when left by its military occupants, extended to every part of it, and rendered it utterly unfit . . . for the residence of students."[39]

The destruction of the college would not have been as debilitating if funds had remained for repairs, but the war ruined the endowment as well. In 1777 the trustees patriotically invested college reserves in United States Loan Office certificates, but these soon became nearly worthless. The Continental Congress on November 6, 1779, finally harkened to Witherspoon's insistent plea for compensation with a grant of 19,357 Continental dollars, worth no more than 5 percent of face value because of the weakness of congressional issues. The trustees at their April 1779 meeting had set other fund-raising efforts in motion, which (apart from £238 turned in by Robert Smith the next year) were not immediately productive. College expenses were still modest by later standards, but financial affairs were nonetheless in extremis.[40] A chaotic bookkeeping system complicated an already desperate situation.

By the time Smith arrived, the trustees had begun repairs under the supervision of Witherspoon, Richard Stockton, Sr., and the Reverend Elihu Spencer of Trenton. But things were moving slowly. In 1781 when Ashbel Green entered the college, only two of Nassau Hall's four floors had been restored. And the shortage of funds continued to be a crippling problem. Smith came to

---

[37] Monk, "Samuel Stanhope Smith," 93; L. H. Butterfield, *John Witherspoon Comes to America* (Princeton, 1953), ix–x; Alfred Hoyt Bill, *The Campaign of Princeton, 1776–1777* (Princeton, 1948), 112–13; *Life of Green*, 137; Rush quotation, see Wertenbaker, *Princeton*, 61.

[38] *Life of Green*, 136. A picture of Rittenhouse's orrery is found in Brooke Hindle, *The Pursuit of Science in Revolutionary America* (Chapel Hill, N.C., 1956), following p. 194.

[39] *Life of Green*, 137.

[40] TM, Apr. 22, 1779; Sept. 28, 1780.

Princeton under the provision that Witherspoon would cede half his salary and the presidential house on campus for the new professor. Smith moved into the house immediately, but it was many years before he enjoyed the salary. As an old man, he recalled that in his "ardent, & as it appears too unworldly zeal for the restoration of [Nassau Hall] . . . , I supported my family for nearly five years on the proceeds of land in Virginia left in the care of my brother, to be sold on my account, & gradually remitted to me, while the income from the students, which at that period passed thro my hands, was almost wholly expended on the buildings."[41]

These were difficult days, but also days of lofty ambitions and bracing national aspiration. Witherspoon, though largely preoccupied with affairs of state, still found time to issue a confident circular after the September 1779 board meeting, announcing the resumption of classes and the provision of a full staff. It heralded the availability in the curriculum of French, which Smith had taught in Virginia, a subject with obvious political attraction at that stage in the war with Britain. In addition the advertisement promised a program of studies with "great attention paid to every branch of English Education."[42]

In spite of financial strain, Smith made an excellent first impression. With Witherspoon absent much of the time and with William Churchill Houston continuing to serve in Congress and also beginning his own legal practice in New Jersey, college instruction rested largely with Smith. He was officially the "professor of divinity and moral philosophy," but his responsibilities ranged much more broadly. In his teaching and in the society of Princeton, Smith was an immediate success.

RICHARD STOCKTON, signer of the Declaration of Independence, graduate of Princeton's first class, and mainstay of the college, finally lost his battle with cancer on February 28, 1781. In the absence of John Witherspoon, who was attending his duties at the Congress, Mrs. Annis Boudinot Stockton turned to Smith for the funeral sermon. Mrs. Stockton suggested the text for the occasion (Psalm 119:96) but allowed Smith to develop it as he saw fit. The result was a fulsome eulogy to Stockton, but also an occasion for Smith to champion convictions and habits of character that he was cultivating at the college.

[41] Smith to Ashbel Green, ca. 1819, Gratz Collection, HSP.
[42] *New Jersey Gazette*, Oct. 13, 1779, quoted in Maclean, *CNJ*, 1:325.

According to Smith, Stockton had been a dedicated believer, for whom Christ was the most important thing, but he was also "one of the fathers of learning and eloquence." Stockton's faith, moreover, was solid and dignified. It almost went without saying that it had led him to extensive research "into the principles of morals and religion." Yet it was also a "liberal" faith, neither petty-minded nor sectarian. It had comported well with that "flowing and persuasive eloquence" for which he was admired. And it had motivated his lengthy service to Princeton College, where he worked "to confirm the footsteps of those who were here labouring up the hill of science and virtue." Stockton also displayed great fortitude in the face of his physical calamities. Most important, Stockton exemplified that harmony of reason and grace, wisdom and religion, dignity and morality that the signer's generation had defined and that they had called Witherspoon to promote at the college.[43]

When Smith delivered this sermon, he was two weeks short of his thirtieth birthday. He had not yet made a name for himself as a man of science. His service to the emerging nation had been limited because of youth and precarious health. And the skills of his oratory as well as the dignity of his manner had won only local fame. Witherspoon, the master in political, ecclesiastical, and educational arenas, still dominated the college. It was, however, already clear that in Stanhope Smith Princeton possessed an able assistant and, perhaps in years to come, a worthy successor to the venerable Scot. His personal qualities were of the highest order. His academic vision blended faith and reason in pleasing harmony. His heart was set on service to the public. He seemed already to justify the faith that Richard Stockton and his colleagues on the board had exercised in calling him back to Princeton.

In 1781 Witherspoon, Smith, and the trustees faced great difficulties in restoring their institution from the ravages of war. Yet repair of the institution's physical condition was proceeding apace. Before long Smith would step into a larger world as resolute champion of the harmony of science and religion, he would be recognized from Boston to the Carolinas as a worthy successor to Witherspoon, and soon the institution would aspire to intellectual heights unimagined before the war.

[43] Smith, *A Funeral Sermon, on the Death of the Hon. Richard Stockton, Esq.* (Princeton, 1781), 13, 38, 41, 38, 42, 24.

6

Princeton and the Nation, 1781–1794

A New Era in the Annals of Time

PRINCETON AUTHORITIES never entertained the least doubt that the College of New Jersey would participate fully in reconstructing American life after the Revolution. Indeed, they acted as if their institution would both embody that effort and inspire an expanding group of citizens for the task. As individuals, Princeton trustees and faculty were deeply engaged in forming the new nation. They took part in creating government for the towns, many of the new states, and the nation. They labored to stabilize the economy and preserve social order. They hoped to fulfill the promise of republicanism while working to prevent its corruption. They wanted to bring Christianity and civilization to the raw edges of the expanding country. More specifically in their activity on behalf of the college, they hoped to demonstrate the utility of knowledge. At Princeton, science would be harmonized with Christian faith and inspired by republican virtue to sustain the health of nation, church, and society.

THE PRESIDENT and faculty were Princeton's most visible representatives, but to an unusual degree the institution also reflected the character of its trustees.[1] From the time of its establishment under a firm charter in 1748, the College of New Jersey was governed by a board of twelve ministers and eleven laymen. One layman, the governor of New Jersey (who chaired the board), and one minister, the president of the college (the vice chairman),

---

[1] In this section I draw on biographical information for the Princeton trustees as contained in the sources cited in the Bibliography. A fuller portrait of the board's members is found in my essay "The Princeton Trustees of 1807: New Men and New Directions," *PULC* (Spring 1980): 208–30.

served ex officio, while the other twenty-one members constituted a self-perpetuating body. Board members were drawn from New Jersey, New York City, and the Philadelphia area. With the establishment of the new United States and the new General Assembly of the Presbyterian Church, several members assumed national prominence. The board was a mature deliberative body, distinguished in church and state. It was predominately, but not exclusively, Presbyterian. Its members had all favored independence. With a very few exceptions, trustees sided with the Federalists after the emergence of political parties. Board members were joined by ties of blood, occupation, and geography. Perhaps most important, the trustees with whom Stanhope Smith worked in his long career at the College of New Jersey were men who had made their mark in the Revolutionary War and whose participation in the founding of the new country remained the pivot of their lives.

Fifty-eight men served on the board in the years between Stanhope Smith's appointment in September 1779 and his resignation in August 1812. Thirty-two were ministers: one Episcopalian, one Associate Reformed, two who held pastorates in both Dutch Reformed and Presbyterian churches, and twenty-eight Presbyterians. Of the Presbyterians, nine had been elected moderator of the colonial Synod of New York and Philadelphia. Princeton trustees played crucial roles in forming the General Assembly in 1789 and served as moderators of the General Assembly for its first three years. The first two stated clerks of the General Assembly were also Princeton trustees, as was the first moderator of the General Synod of the Associate Reformed Church.

If the clerical members of the board were distinguished in the Presbyterian church, the laymen were distinguished in the nation. The twenty-six lay trustees of the Smith era included one member of the Stamp Act Congress, one signer of the Declaration of Independence in addition to John Witherspoon, one justice of the United States Supreme Court, two delegates to the United States Constitutional Convention, ten members of the Continental Congress, five representatives to the United States House of Representatives, four United States senators, sixteen members of provincial or state assemblies, and state and municipal officeholders too numerous to mention. All but one of the candidates who received serious consideration from the combined houses of the New Jersey legislature in its annual choice of governor from 1776 to 1813 were already members of the Princeton board before they stood for office. Until 1803 the board always had at least one of its members serving concurrently in the United States Congress.

Family connections, business and vocational associations, and the Presbyterian church linked the Princeton trustees to each other. (See the genealogies, Appendix B.) But an even stronger, if more nebulous, bond had been forged among them by their common effort in creating the American nation. Of the forty-eight Smith trustees old enough to have participated in the War for Independence, fourteen (including three future clergymen) had served under arms, twelve of the ministers had been chaplains, and at least another eleven had offered significant noncombatant assistance to the cause.

Participation in the American Revolution amounted to much more than a casual series of incidents to be endured and quickly forgotten. Trustees joined a number of the new institutions and participated joyfully in the celebrations that kept Revolutionary patriotism alive. Six of the veteran officers belonged to the Society of Cincinnati, and several enlisted in Washington Benevolent Societies when these arose in the early nineteenth century. Laymen like Elias Boudinot and William Paterson as well as ministers like John Rodgers, Ashbel Green, and J. F. Armstrong preached patriotic homilies on the Fourth of July and exploited fast days for rekindling the patriotic spirit. Their biographers were regularly impressed with how enduring and how weighty the memories of the Revolution remained.[2]

Trustees united not only in general approval of the Revolution but in the specific belief that God had accomplished it. In this view they expanded upon the republican Christianity that had been so prominent among Presbyterians and other Christian patriots during the war itself. The political strife and the international tumult that followed from the mid-1790s only heightened the trustees' sense of God's providential protection during the earlier period. Several of the board members who eulogized Washington spoke of the divine activity that enabled the Father of his Country to lead the people to safety. Newark's Alexander MacWhorter was most direct: Moses was able to deliver "the chosen tribes . . . from the fangs of a cruel tyrant, from bondage and slavery, and conduct them to a promised land. . . . He never murmured under all his burdens, toils and adverse trials, till he had accomplished all that

[2] For example, biographies of John Woodhull, Ashbel Green, and James Armstrong, in Sprague, *Annals*, 3:305, 392, 488–89.

God intended by him; so our American Moses."[3] Two weeks before Stanhope Smith resigned in the summer of 1812, Joseph Clark struck the same note in a fast sermon before his New Brunswick congregation: "In many parts of our history, a striking resemblance may be traced to that of the Israelites." Forefathers had come from oppression to a good land, "heathen" were subdued, the new settlements received "the peculiar smiles of a kind providence," they enjoyed protection when their "liberties were threatened, and the country invaded by a foreign power," a deliverer was raised up to lead the armies, liberties were restored and territories increased, and the land was blessed with peace and plenty.[4]

So completely did trustees view the Revolution as a providential event that they often merged the interests of the country and the fate of the Kingdom of God. This conviction encouraged trustees to praise Washington not only as a great national leader but also as "an uniform professor of the christian religion" and, in later paeans, as an opponent of "the contagion of infidel philosophy."[5] It even went as far as to encourage some trustees to glimpse the dawning of the millennium in the outworking of Revolutionary principles. So George Duffield in 1783 told how, in America, "our God erected a banner of civil and religious liberty . . . far removed from the noise and tumult of contending kingdoms and empires— far from the wars of Europe and Asia, and the barbarous African coast." And, he hoped, "Here, also, shall our Jesus go forth conquering and to conquer, and the heathen be given him for an inheritance, and these uttermost parts for a possession." Elias Boudinot was still voicing these same sanguine views of the eschatological future as late as 1793.[6] Later, after visions of godly order dissolved into partisanship and war, the eschatological metaphors were more pessimistic. Yet the belief that the United States was to play a leading role in the End of the Age never wavered.

The Princeton trustees of the Smith era, especially those who

[3] Alexander MacWhorter, *A Funeral Sermon . . . for the universally lamented, General Washington* (Newark, N.J., 1800), 9.

[4] Joseph Clark, *A Sermon Delivered in the City of New-Brunswick* (New Brunswick, 1812), 9.

[5] MacWhorter, *Funeral Sermon*, 3n; Clark, *A Sermon*, 14. Similar claims from a trustee about Washington's personal faith are found in John B. Romeyn, *A Funeral Oration* (Poughkeepsie, N.Y., 1800), 4.

[6] "George Duffield," in *Princetonians 1748–1768*, 52; Boudinot, "Oration before the Society of the Cincinnati in the State of New Jersey" [July 4, 1793], in *The Life, Public Services, Addresses, and Letters of Elias Boudinot*, ed. J. J. Boudinot, 2 vols. (1896; reprint, New York, 1971), 2:356–78.

mattered most in the direction of the school, were a tightly knit body. Members enjoyed respected positions in society, they were overwhelmingly evangelical and Presbyterian, most of them were Federalists, and they shared a great number of connections beyond their common concern for the College of New Jersey. But most of all they shared memories of the times that had tried men's souls.

EVENTS TOWARD the end of the War for Independence ensured that Princeton leaders would align their aspirations for the new nation and for their college, if in fact their extensive service for the patriot cause had not already achieved that end. At least 230 sons of Princeton offered some kind of military service to their new country before 1783, and the college produced only 13 known Loyalists.[7]

When Congress proclaimed a day of national thanksgiving for April 19, 1783, to celebrate the peace treaty ending the war, John Witherspoon improved the occasion at Princeton with a sermon on Psalm 3:8, "salvation belongeth unto the Lord." As Witherspoon recalled the events of the late war, he pointed to the steady intervention of providence that had turned American weakness into strength and British superiority into defeat. In spite of British brutality, manifest especially in disgraceful treatment of prisoners, God overruled to unite the fractious colonies, to provide a uniquely capable military leader, and to grant success on the field of battle. "Nothing appears to me more manifest than that the separation of this country from Britain, has been of God; for every step the British took to prevent, served to accelerate it, which has generally been the case when men have undertaken to go in opposition to the course of Providence, and to make war with the nature of things." It remained for Witherspoon only to remind his auditors to thank God and to recall the moral underpinnings of republican social theory. "Whatever state among us shall continue to make piety and virtue the standard of public honor, will enjoy the greatest inward peace, the greatest national happiness, and in every outward conflict will discover the greatest constitutional strength."[8]

Earlier that same month, news of the Treaty of Paris moved

[7] *Princetonians 1748–1768*, 676–77; *Princetonians 1769–1775*, 549–50; *Princetonians 1776–1783*, 467.

[8] Witherspoon, *Works*, 3:79, 85. On the festivities of this day, see Collins, *Witherspoon*, 2:125n.

Elias Boudinot, who was rapidly becoming the most influential layman among the Princeton trustees, to expand upon the significance of independence: "The Contemplation of this Epoche, almost overcomes me at times. It opens a new Scene to Mankind, and I believe is big with inconceivable Effects in the political & I hope in the moral World."[9] As Witherspoon and Boudinot expressed these sentiments in April 1783, they did not know that their college would soon become the stage upon which representatives of the independent American states would play out the last act in the inauguration of America's grand republican experiment.

Elias Boudinot was presiding over the Continental Congress in Philadelphia on June 20, 1783, when a mutinous group of soldiers from the Maryland Line, assigned to guard duty in Philadelphia and Lancaster County, surrounded their meeting place, the Pennsylvania State House. This hard-drinking band had heard that Congress planned to discharge them without settling back pay, and so they were taking matters into their own hands. After a standoff lasting three hours, the legislators passed peacefully through the mutineers and then called upon Pennsylvania to disperse the rioters. When nothing happened, Congress resolved to leave Philadelphia, a "sink of Toryism and Extortion," as one of the delegates put it.[10] Boudinot, and eventually Stanhope Smith, on behalf of the Princeton trustees and faculty, offered Nassau Hall as a temporary home, and the Congress speedily agreed.[11] From late June 1783 until the receipt of the final Treaty of Paris in early November, the Continental Congress shared that partially rehabilitated building with the faculty and the approximately fifty students then in residence at the college. And so it came to pass that the mythos of the new nation imbued even more thoroughly the ethos of the college.

Congress had no sooner arrived at Princeton than it joined the college for a gala celebration of the Fourth of July. For the first time that year the two student societies had chosen orators for the

---

[9] Boudinot to James Searle, Apr. 1, 1783, in George Adams Boyd, *Elias Boudinot: Patriot and Statesman, 1740–1821* (Princeton, 1952), 119–20.

[10] John C. Miller, *Triumph of Freedom, 1775–1783* (Boston, 1948), 675.

[11] Boyd, *Boudinot*, 124–26. On Congress's move and its stay in Princeton, see also Collins, *Witherspoon*, 2:130; Eugene R. Sheridan and John M. Murrin, ed., *Congress at Princeton: Being the Letters of Charles Thomson to Hannah Thomson, June–October 1783* (Princeton, 1985); Varnum Lansing Collins, *The Continental Congress at Princeton* (Princeton, 1908); and *Journals of the Continental Congress, 1774–1789*, 34 vols. (Washington, D.C., 1904–37), 24:410, 423, 425.

day. The nominee of the American Whigs, who spoke on "the superiority of a republican government over any other form," was Ashbel Green, later the most influential clerical trustee during Smith's presidency, and in 1812 his successor.[12] Congress attended these exercises and then joined the society orators at a banquet hosted by Boudinot and his sister, the widow Annis Stockton, at Morven. After a sumptuous repast President Boudinot toasted each of the thirteen states to the accompaniment of artillery fire. Later skyrockets and other fireworks lit up the campus.

The advent of Congress dramatically transformed Princeton. "From a little obscure village," Green wrote his father, "we have become the capital of America. Instead of almost silence in the town, nothing is to be seen or heard but the passing and rattling of wagons, coaches, and chairs, the crying about of pine apples, oranges, lemons, and every luxurious article both foreign and domestic."[13] Yet in the face of such excitement, life at the college did go on. Students recited lessons and, after Witherspoon returned in July from an inspection of newly purchased lands in Vermont, juniors and seniors went back to lectures in history and chronology, eloquence, and moral philosophy.

Late in the summer the college hall was the scene of Congress's festive reception of General Washington, who had been called from his encampment at Newburgh, New York, to consult on the nature of a peacetime military establishment. Elias Boudinot, as presiding officer of the Congress, remained seated, with his hat on his head, when the general entered to an otherwise tumultuous welcome. The Congress, after anguished discussion of protocol, had decided that such a gesture was necessary to demonstrate the superiority of civilian power over the corrupting influence of the military, even when administered by the hallowed Washington. Boudinot's remarks, as also Witherspoon's welcome on behalf of the town and college, repeated the glorious phrases that the Princeton president had uttered in his April sermon of thanksgiving.[14]

[12] Jacob N. Beam, *The American Whig Society of Princeton University* (Princeton, 1933), 140; *Life of Green*, 142. Additional information on that gala day is found in Boyd, *Boudinot*, 128; and Alfred Hoyt Bill, *A House Called Morven: Its Role in American History, 1701–1954* (Princeton, 1954), 56.

[13] Quoted in Collins, *Witherspoon*, 2:130, with information on Witherspoon's activity from the same citation.

[14] *Journals of the Continental Congress*, 24:492–94, 521–23. For the speeches, see Collins, *Witherspoon*, 2:126 n. 5, 131–32. On Washington's stay, see also Boyd, *Bou-*

The arrival of Washington, however, was only a prelude to the climax of Congress's stay in Princeton. The 1783 commencement, on September 24, and the board meetings that followed sealed these numinous events upon the consciousness of the Princeton circle. A British officer attended the exercises incognito and later reported to Lord North that the ceremony was a farce that enabled Witherspoon, "the political firebrand," to go on poisoning "the minds of his young Students and through them the Continent."[15] For nearly everyone else it was an unalloyed triumph.

Ashbel Green, the valedictorian, led the graduating seniors in the customary series of speeches and debates. The scene in Princeton's Presbyterian church, however, was anything but customary. A special stage provided room not just for the faculty and graduates but also for members of Congress, the ministers of France and Holland, and General Washington. Green's praise for the general was so fulsome that Washington colored with embarrassment. Yet the next day he shook Green's hand and complimented him on the address.[16] For their part, the trustees requested Washington to sit for a portrait by Charles Wilson Peale, an assignment agreeable to all parties. The result was a painting for the ornate frame that once had held a portrait of George II, the very portrait that had been decapitated by a cannon ball during the Battle of Princeton. It hangs in the central room of Nassau Hall to this day. Washington, in response, gave the college fifty guineas.[17]

At the same commencement trustees bestowed honorary doctorates of divinity on stalwarts for American liberty from Connecticut, England, and Scotland. They also accepted a gift of £100 from Gov. John Dickinson of Delaware to endow an essay competition for students on questions intended to sustain the meaning of those days, like "What are the most proper measures to be adopted by a government for promoting and establishing habits of piety and virtue among a people?"[18]

The intensity of that summer could not, of course, be main-

---

dinot, 131; Bill, *House Called Morven*, 57; James Thomas Flexner, *George Washington in the American Revolution (1775–1783)* (Boston, 1968), 518–20; and Douglas Southall Freeman, *George Washington: A Biography*, vol. 5, *Victor with the Help of France* (New York, 1952), 451–52.

[15] Collins, *Witherspoon*, 2:133–34.

[16] *Life of Green*, 164, with pp. 143–44 on Green's veneration for Washington; Boyd, *Boudinot*, 134. The full text of Green's speech is found in Collins, *Continental Congress at Princeton*, 273–77.

[17] TM, Sept. 24–25, 1783.

[18] Ibid., Sept. 26, 1783.

tained. Elias Boudinot was worried, even as the board finished its September sitting, that "neither our Legislatures nor People at Large are acting with prudence." He feared that recent successes would be spoiled unless "wisdom and firmness and temperate councils" could somehow prevail.[19] As soon as official word arrived that the treaty had gone into effect, Washington left for Mount Vernon, and Congress simply went home, leaving much unfinished business. Princeton, with several other towns and cities, asked to be chosen as the permanent site for the United States government, but all were disappointed when Congress decided to reconvene in Philadelphia. Graduating seniors dispersed from the college, and after the fall recess a new group of students arrived. Life went on.

But before the Congress adjourned, Boudinot issued a proclamation on October 18 setting aside the second Thursday of December as another day of public thanksgiving to glorify God for the successful completion of the peace. Difficulties in realizing the promise of independence were foreboding. Yet despite grave problems, the exalting vision did not decay. The leaders of Princeton as well as of the nation were filled with hope.

On December 11, in response to Boudinot's proclamation, John Rodgers, leader of New York City's Presbyterians and one of the most influential members of the Princeton board, preached a sermon on Psalm 126:3, "The Lord hath done great things for us; whereof we are glad." Rodgers had been forced to flee from the city during the conflict and had returned to his regular charge only that autumn. Despite the disruption of his family, the ruin of his church, and the dispersion of his congregation, Rodgers had not wavered during the war. In the summer of 1779 he had proclaimed that, in the present struggle, "our *All is at stake. . . .* The liberties of thousands yet unborn are in our hands." Rodgers's moral support for the cause and his active service as a chaplain earned him the enmity of Loyalists, one of whom claimed that Rodgers "had given more encouragement to rebellion, by his treasonable harangues from the pulpit, than any other republican preacher, perhaps, on the continent."[20] Now in December 1783 he

[19] Boudinot to Robert Livingstone, Sept. 27, 1783, in Edmund C. Burnett, ed., *Letters of Members of the Continental Congress*, vol. 7, *January 1, 1783, to December 31, 1784* (Washington, D.C., 1934), 314.
[20] John Rodgers, *Holiness the Nature and Design of the Gospel of Christ. A Sermon, Preached at Stockbridge, June 24, 1779* (Hartford, 1780), vi. The Loyalist was Thomas Jones, *History of New York during the Revolutionary War*, ed. E. F. DeLancey, 2 vols.

rose to speak on "The divine Goodness displayed, in the American Revolution."

Rodgers's thanksgiving discourse rehearsed at great length the acts of providence that had established the new nation. Like Witherspoon earlier in the year, Rodgers reminded his listeners of the need to persevere in virtue. God had not "broken our connexion with that people [Great Britain], long practiced in the arts of venality, and grown old in scenes of corruption," merely to allow Americans to sink under profligacy, luxury, and disunity. He had rather gaven a task to the citizens of the new country to make good on a providential beginning: God "has, by the revolution we this day celebrate, put all the blessings of liberty, civil and religious, within our reach. Perhaps there never was a nation, that had the fair opportunity of becoming the happiest people on earth, that we now have."[21]

The war was over. The hand of God had gained the victory for a people inspired by the vision of a moral republic. Now it was time to strengthen the institutions—governmental, ecclesiastical, and educational—that would fulfill the extraordinary promise of the Revolution. It was time to see if those who stood before the open door of liberty could enter in.

MEMBERS OF the Princeton circle did not minimize the magnitude of the challenges they faced. They realized that great efforts would be necessary to repair the wounds of war, create the frameworks of government, and educate citizens in their responsibilities as republicans.

The problems began at home with the fiscal ruin and physical debility of the college itself. A young Dutchman, G. K. van Hogendorp, passed through Princeton in 1784 and, while generally impressed with the teaching, was also struck by the disadvantages under which the college labored: "When paper money depreciated[,] the College, like many rich men, lost a great deal of property by a legal fraud. . . . Only part of the Building is repaired since the peace." The next year a friend wrote Ashbel Green, who was vacillating between a pastoral call in Philadelphia and the offer of a

---

(New York, 1879), 2:3, as quoted in L. H. Butterfield, *John Witherspoon Comes to America* (Princeton, 1953), 90 n. 51.

[21] John Rodgers, *The Divine Goodness Displayed, in the American Revolution* (New York, 1784), 10, 37.

professorship at Princeton, that he should chose the ministry. One of the reasons—the college "is poor, very poor."[22]

Although the trustees by this time were working hard to augment their funds, they were largely unsuccessful. The most ill-fated effort took place in 1783 and 1784, when the board sent Witherspoon and trustee Joseph Reed, president of Pennsylvania's Supreme Executive Council, to raise money in Britain. Even though Reed bore his own expenses, the results were, in Witherspoon's words, "very unsuccessful." Britons were in no mood to assist a college that had supported the late rebellion, and Witherspoon reported to the board on October 1, 1784, that the journey had garnered a paltry £5 14s.[23] To add woe upon woe, a shipboard accident cost Witherspoon one of his eyes, a loss that soon affected the sight of the remaining eye and thus reduced even further his day-to-day involvement with the college.

Nothing daunted, the trustees persisted in their pursuit of funds. Special appeals went out to the Presbyterian Synod of New York and Philadelphia that could, it was hoped, recognize the college's importance for "our civil & religious interests." The board encouraged its own members to solicit money aggressively. It asked Congress for western lands and for payment on debts from the war. So short was money that the board even made a rule in September 1792 requiring trustees who nominated individuals for honorary degrees to bear the cost themselves for inscribing the diploma and sending it through the post. As late as 1796 the college justified an appeal for support to the New Jersey legislature on the grounds that it "is now reduced to extreme necessity" because of losses from the war.[24]

The college's financial difficulties in the decade after the peace were but a microcosm of difficulties afflicting the Presbyterian interest more generally. Both redcoats and patriots had found the churches of New York, Philadelphia, and New Jersey convenient sites for hospitals, barracks, and redoubts. Into the 1790s many of

[22] Gijsbert Karel van Hogendorp, *The College at Princetown, May 1784*, ed. Howard C. Rice (Princeton, 1949), 2; unknown correspondent to Green, Nov. 22, 1785, Gratz Collection, HSP.

[23] TM, Oct. 22, 1783; Sept. 30–Oct. 1, 1784; A. L. Drummond, "Witherspoon of Gifford and American Presbyterianism," *Records of the Scottish Historical Society* 12 (1958): 197–98.

[24] TM, Oct. 1, 1784; Aug. 2, 1785; Apr. 19, 1786; Sept. 28, 1791; Sept. 27, 1792; Apr. 10, 1793; *The Memorial and Petition of the Trustees of the College of New-Jersey* (n.p., 1796), right col.

these buildings still were not satisfactorily repaired. Increased Scotch-Irish immigration into New Jersey, Pennsylvania, and further south increased the demands on a clerical contingent already strained to meet the pastoral needs of their charges. Minutes of the Synod of New York and Philadelphia were filled during the 1780s with worries about the unwieldiness of synodical organization, the shortage of funds, the difficulty in finding adequately trained recruits for the ministry, failed opportunities to establish churches, and the unmet needs of a growing constituency.[25]

Four of the eight meetings of the synod from 1781 to 1788 were chaired by men who were serving concurrently as college trustees, and members of the Princeton circle were active in numerous services to the synod. Stanhope Smith, for example, was the clerk in 1781 and 1782, and he served on several of the committees that brought about its reorganization at the end of the decade.[26] Struggles of the church and those of the college, in short, were simply parts of one effort to spread the bountiful effects of responsible Christian civilization.

College authorities did not give in to discouragement during this difficult period. To be sure, after the establishment of a new government under the Constitution, some made a point of contrasting its virtues with the earlier weaknesses of the Confederation. Stanhope Smith, for instance, felt that framers of the Confederation had been deceived "by that elevated and sublime virtue which was displayed at that time [the Revolution] by the whole mass of the people" and so created a government unduly influenced by principles of pure democracy. Under the Confederation the country "resembled a giant paralized, and laid upon his back." During the Confederation period itself, Smith expressed some uneasiness with "the spirit of high, and perhaps licentious liberty, in the country" that reduced the effectiveness of the churches, and with "our extreme idea of liberty" that encouraged ostentation among the people, weakness in the Congress, and the official neglect of religion.[27]

[25] Martha Tomhave Blauvelt, "Society, Religion, and Revivalism: The Second Great Awakening in New Jersey, 1780–1830" (revision of Ph.D. diss., Princeton University, 1974), 69; William Warren Sweet, *Religion on the American Frontier, 1783–1840*, vol. 2, *The Presbyterians* (Chicago, 1936), 2; *Records of the Presbyterian Church in the United States of America . . . from . . . 1717 to . . . 1788* (Philadelphia, 1841), 499–548.

[26] *Records of the Presbyterian Church, 1717–1788*, 489, 493, 517–18, 547.

[27] Smith, *The Divine Goodness to the United States of America. A Discourse on the Subjects of National Gratitude* (Philadelphia, 1795), 12, 11; Smith to Charles Nisbet, Nov.

With the rest of his Princeton colleagues, however, Smith was not so much pessimistic about the course of American affairs as he was eager to see how things would turn out.

The transition from winning the war to erecting a virtuous republic was not a smooth one, yet during the decade that passed after the victory at Yorktown in 1781, the hopes of the Princeton leaders continued to rise. Practical difficulties remained, but great breakthroughs also occurred at the end of the decade in both church and nation. They seemed to suggest that the uncertainties of the mid-1780s constituted only a momentary delay in the realization of the Revolution's highest ideals. The establishment of a more secure national government under the Constitution, the return of Washington as leader of his people, and the nearly simultaneous organization of the Presbyterians into a General Assembly were auguries for good. The Revolution had intimated the goal. Through Washington's first term as president it seemed to the Princeton circle as if fulfillment lay within reach.

Princeton officials saw the fate of their college writ large in the events of church and state, if for no other reason than that graduates and trustees of the college played key roles in writing the Constitution and creating the Presbyterian General Assembly. Trustees were not exaggerating when they reminded the New Jersey legislature in 1796 that their graduates had led the fight for independence and continued to be leaders in American society "from Vermont to Georgia."[28] The successful establishment of the national government and of a smoothly functioning church, in turn, heightened expectations for realizing their fondest hopes for the republic.

The reorganization of the Presbyterian church was intended to accomplish several things—to make local congregations more self-conscious participants in general Presbyterian tasks, to provide for greater harmony and cooperation at the regional level, and above all to enable the denomination more readily to meet the challenge of western expansion. The principal means of accomplishing these tasks was to replace the old synod with a General Assembly and to create four new regional synods to oversee more closely the ongoing work of the denomination. Each of the four synods—New York and New Jersey, Philadelphia, Virginia, and the Carolinas—

26, 1784, and Feb. 4, 1785, in Michael Kraus, "Charles Nisbet and Samuel Stanhope Smith—Two Eighteenth Century Educators," *PULC* 6 (1944): 25, 33.

[28] *Memorial and Petition of the Trustees*, left col.

contained three to five presbyteries. Some of the presbyteries, especially in the West, reported more congregations clamoring for pastors than it had churches with regular ministers. The streamlined organization of a General Assembly would make it possible to meet the needs of the West, even as it enhanced denominational cooperation in the settled East.[29]

In the Presbyterian reorganization, Princeton leaders took the main parts. The two individuals most influential in the formation of the General Assembly were Witherspoon, who wrote several of the key documents erecting the new body, and New York's John Rodgers, who served on every one of the committees responsible for the new plan of government.[30] The last moderator of the Synod of New York and Philadelphia in 1788, who appointed himself, Witherspoon, and Stanhope Smith to several committees putting final touches on the reorganization, was trustee John Woodhull of Freehold. Witherspoon was asked to preach the opening sermon of the first General Assembly in May 1789 and to direct that body until a moderator could be elected. That moderator for the first General Assembly was John Rodgers. His successor in this influential chair for 1790 was Robert Smith, and in 1791 John Woodhull. In 1790 the assembly appointed Ashbel Green its stated clerk, or administrative secretary, a position he held for twelve years. Two years later Green became a chaplain to the United States Congress as a quasi-official representative of the Presbyterian interest. The bond between church and college is suggested by the fact that, during the last decade and a half of Witherspoon's tenure at Princeton (1780–1794), the four most active clerical trustees were John Woodhull, John Rodgers, Ashbel Green, and Robert Smith. Furthermore, John Bayard and Isaac Snowden, the most active laymen on the board during that same period, were both delegates to the Presbyterians' first General Assembly. The point to be made is that the high hopes these men held for the new General Assembly were closely related to their great expectations for the college.

Princeton's involvement in the establishment of the Constitution, though still substantial, was not as direct. Two trustees, Gov. William Livingstone and William Paterson, were members of the New Jersey delegation to the Constitutional Convention in 1787,

---

[29] For figures on the supply of ministers in 1788, see Leonard J. Trinterud, *The Forming of an American Tradition: A Re-examination of Colonial Presbyterianism* (Philadelphia, 1949), 306.

[30] Ibid., 292–93; Collins, *Witherspoon*, 2:223–24; *Life of Green*, 260.

where Paterson acted as chief defender of state integrity. Nine of the fifty-five delegates to the convention, including its guiding spirit, James Madison, were graduates of Nassau Hall. The convention's committee that hammered out the compromise between the Virginia plan of representation by population and Paterson's New Jersey plan of representation by state unit included five of these Princeton graduates. Thirty-one Princeton graduates were members of the state conventions that ratified the Constitution. And Princeton alumni from New England to Georgia were active at every level of state and national government to implement the new structure ordained by the Constitution.[31] With such a stake in the new government, it is little wonder that the spirits of Princeton officials rose and fell with the perceived health of the nation.

During the 1780s and even more in the first years under the Constitution, these spirits were very high. An extraordinary sanguinity within the Princeton circle overcame hereditary religious antagonisms and, indeed, sectarianism and partisanship altogether. Most striking at the time was an unusual willingness to overlook ancient standoffs between Christian bodies. So we find Stanhope Smith praising the good citizenship of America's Roman Catholics in 1785 and Elias Boudinot advising a ward that it would be no great disaster if he converted to Rome.[32] In the winter of 1793–1794, Smith assured a prospect for the Episcopalian ministry, John Henry Hobart, that Princeton was an excellent place for him to read theology, since the teachers, primarily himself, were not in the least interested in proselytizing for the Presbyterian interest.[33] These passing remarks were straws in the wind. They suggest how confident the Princeton leaders were that the new national mood could overcome centuries of Catholic-Protestant strife and also smooth over the rank conflict that had divided the Episcopal church from America's other denominations during the Revolutionary period.[34]

[31] Compromise committee, *Princetonians 1748–1768*, 581; state conventions, ibid., 674–75; *Princetonians 1769–1775*, 548–59; *Princetonians 1776–1783*, 465. In addition to public servants cited in these volumes, extensive lists of Princeton graduates active in political life are found in Maclean, *CNJ*, 1:358–61.

[32] Smith to Nisbet, Feb. 4, 1785, 32; Boudinot to John Caldwell, May 2, 1790, Elias Boudinot Collection, PUL, partially quoted in Boyd, *Boudinot*, 145–46.

[33] Smith to Hobart, Nov. 18, 1793, and undated letter, winter 1793–1794, in Arthur Lowndes, ed., *The Correspondence of John Henry Hobart, 1757–1797* (New York, 1911), cix, cxii.

[34] On that conflict, see Carl Bridenbaugh, *Mitre and Sceptre: Transatlantic Faiths, Ideas, Personalities, and Politics, 1689–1775* (New York, 1962).

The glow from antagonisms ameliorated shone also over politics. Here the contrast is not so much with what had been as with what would come. By 1800 most of the Princeton leaders were determined Federalists and even more determined anti-Jeffersonians. But at least until 1792 or 1793, scarcely a hint of the future could be seen. James Madison's contribution to the Constitutional Convention was the occasion for his alma mater to bestow the LL.D. in September 1787.[35] Such recognition for a son of the college might only be expected, even in light of later disengagement between Princeton and the Democratic-Republicans. Much more remarkable was the cordiality displayed between Thomas Jefferson and John Rodgers's rising young colleague in the New York Presbyterian church, Samuel Miller, who later became an influential trustee. In 1793 Miller sent Jefferson an address in which he recommended several of the Virginian's causes. Jefferson's polite reply opened a correspondence that continued sporadically for over a decade, in spite of the fact that, already in the early 1790s, Miller was beginning to move in the orbit of Ashbel Green and others who became arch-Federalists.[36]

Trustee actions in bestowing the honorary higher degress reinforced the expansive spirit of the times. Besides the honor to Madison in 1787, the college gave its LL.D. to Charles Pinckney of South Carolina, a supporter with Madison of the Constitution and a future Jeffersonian, and the honorary D.D. to a Connecticut Congregationalist, a Maryland Episcopalian, two Lutherans, an Anglican, and a minister of the German Reformed Church. During the next three years the college indicated something of its commitment to natural and applied science, to patriotism, to cosmopolitanism, and to religion by honoring David Rittenhouse, famed creator of the orrery; a naturalist and a jurist from Scotland; two Frenchmen, Lafayette and the director of the treasury in the Revolutionary government; and supporters of the Constitution in New Jersey and South Carolina. The commencement of 1791 proved, however, to be the high point of nonpartisanship, when the college bestowed the LL.D. upon Secretary of the Treasury Alexander

[35] See the letters of congratulation from Boudinot (Aug. 27, 1788, Elias Boudinot Collection, PUL) and Witherspoon (quoted in Irving Brant, *James Madison: Father of the Constitution, 1787–1800* [Indianapolis, 1950], 230–31).

[36] Jefferson to Miller, Sept. 3, 1793, Samuel Miller Papers, PUL. Much later, Miller repudiated "everything that I ever said or wrote in [Jefferson's] favor" (Samuel Miller, Jr., *The Life of Samuel Miller*, 2 vols. [Philadelphia, 1869], 1:129–33, quotation 132).

Hamilton and Secretary of State Thomas Jefferson and the D.D. upon an antirevivalist Connecticut Congregationalist, the evangelical Anglican John Newton (author of "Amazing Grace"), and a member of Scotland's seceder antiburgher church.[37]

The catholicity manifest in the board's dispersal of honors did not long survive the early 1790s. While it lasted, it was a remarkable testimony to the Princeton expectation that leaders of church and state could overcome deep-seated differences to create a republic not just of virtue, religion, and civil order but also one supported by learning, piety, and patriotism from beyond the American shore.

WE ARE not left to infer the character of Princeton expectations from scraps of out-of-the-way information. Several times from 1789 to 1793, influential leaders of the Princeton circle expressed unambiguously their understanding of the United States' providential past and their anticipation of a uniquely glorious future. From these statements—a prayer on July 4, 1789, by Ashbel Green; John Woodhull's sermon that same year, giving thanks for the ratification of the Constitution; and Fourth of July addresses in 1793 by Elias Boudinot, Alexander MacWhorter, and Samuel Miller—it is possible to construct a composite picture of what Princeton officials in this halcyon period felt about the history of their country and its prospects for the future.

At the outset these leaders took for granted the cosmic significance of the American experiment. July 4, 1776, as MacWhorter put it most dramatically, was not only "the nativity of our nation" but a day that "forms a new era in the annals of time." Mac-Whorter, who had learned how to address a crowd from George Whitefield, waxed evangelistic about "this wonderful, this auspicious day . . . the birth-day of freedom—the greatest blessing, one accepted [*sic*], ever ushered into our world."[38] Other Princeton figures were slightly more restrained, but all agreed that God had exercised an extraordinary providence in bringing the United States through the war and establishing the new nation.[39] In 1789

[37] *General Catalogue*, 401–3.

[38] Alexander MacWhorter, *A Festival Discourse, Occasioned by the Celebration of the Seventeenth Anniversary of American Independence* (Newark, N.J., 1793), 7, 10.

[39] For example, John Woodhull, *A Sermon, for the Day of Publick Thanksgiving . . . November 26, 1789* (Trenton, 1790), 6–7; Boudinot, "Oration before the Cincinnati," in *Life and Letters*, 2:358, 361; and Green, *An Oration, Delivered July 4, 1789*

Ashbel Green tallied the record of that providence in a characteristic summary: safe settlement in a fruitful new world, "deliverance
from tyranny and oppression," success in populating a previously
"heathen land," unexpected military triumphs against Great Britain, and the raising up of Washington. To this list could now be
added the Constitution, "a righteous and energetic system of government," with "pure, unadulterated principles."[40]

The inevitable result for Christians so deeply impressed with the
divine activity on their behalf was to glimpse the dawning of the
millennium. In 1789 Woodhull averred that God's past goodness
to the nation should lead American citizens "to look out for the
glory of the latter day; or rather, to look around, and see if it do
not already dawn." Boudinot in 1793 was more cautious, but no
less expectant in looking for America's "great principles" to usher
in "that happy state of the world, when, from every human breast,
joined by the grand chorus of the skies, shall arise with the pro-
foundest reverence, that divinely celestial anthem of universal
praise—Glory to God in the highest—Peace on earth—Good will
towards men."[41]

In those days of great hope Princeton authorities, though soon
to entertain drastically different opinions, thought they could observe the spread of liberty around the globe, especially in France,
the "great and powerful ally" that had played such a vital role in
the war.[42] John Woodhull had received news of the liberation of
the Bastille and probably of the "Declaration of Rights" before his
paean to the Constitution in November 1789. To Woodhull,
France's assistance in the War for Independence had been the result of God's special intervention. Now it seemed "that a bounteous
providence is about to *reward* them with blessings, in some respects
similar to those which they have assisted in procuring for us."[43]
Even as late as July 1793, several months after word of Louis XVI's
execution had reached America, Samuel Miller urged wholehearted support for France. Europe's "convulsive struggles" were
hastening the spread of Christianity and human happiness. "Es-

---

... *To which is added, A Prayer delivered on the same occasion, by the Rev. Ashbel Green*
(Philadelphia, 1789), 26–27.

[40] Green, *A Prayer*, 26–28. For an even more rapturous view of the Constitution,
see MacWhorter, *Festival Discourse*, 11–12.

[41] Woodhull, *Sermon for Publick Thanksgiving*, 28; Boudinot, "Oration before the
Cincinnati," 378. An illuminating summary of the rise of millennial expectation ca.
1790 is found in Ruth Bloch, *Visionary Republic: Millennial Themes in American
Thought, 1756–1800* (New York, 1985), 150–86.

[42] Green, *A Prayer*, 28.

[43] Woodhull, *Sermon for Publick Thanksgiving*, 13.

pecially," asked Miller, "can we view the interesting situation of our AFFECTIONATE ALLIES, without indulging the delightful hope, that the sparks, which are there seen rising toward heaven, though in tumultuous confusion, shall soon be the means of kindling a general flame, which shall illuminate the darkest and remotest corners of the earth, and pour upon them the effulgence of ten-fold glory?" Miller added a lengthy note to the published version of his sermon defending this enthusiasm for the French Revolution, which suggests that uneasiness was in the air.[44] But that the younger colleague of John Rodgers and a rising light among the Presbyterians could speak with such favor about the French cause at this date was a revealing indication of a more general mood.

Princeton leaders knew no bounds in their praise for liberty and in their devotion to the nation that embodied the blessings of independence. Woodhull regarded the establishment of the United States as the occasion for the transportation to America of Europe's hereditary greatness, what he called empire: "O Empire! millions hail thee welcome! And while the British yoke lies broken beneath thy feet, may liberty be seated at thy right hand, and justice, mercy and truth, be enthroned in thy heart; and thus mayest thou dwell with us, till time shall be no more!" MacWhorter, who would pause to ask his listeners to celebrate Independence Day as Christians, with "chaste and pure temperance," nonetheless could not temper his own enthusiasm for the meaning of the day: "Happy the time—happy the place—happy the land that gave her birth, and thrice happy the hour, more than Jubilee year, in which INDEPENDENCE, Heaven-born INDEPENDENCE was assumed!"[45]

These hymns to liberty were not merely expostulations in the excitement of a moment. Rather, the Princeton love of liberty was embedded deeply in the moral cosmology of classical republicanism. Communal goodness ensured the blessings of freedom; public virtue guaranteed the triumphs of the American Revolution. Even at their most ecstatic moments in this felicitous period, the Princeton leaders paused to rehearse the ineluctable bond between moral and social order. Woodhull concluded his praise for the Constitution with the observation that "God usually, and I believe always, treats nations, considered as public bodies, according to their gen-

[44] Samuel Miller, *Christianity the Grand Source, and the Surest Basis, of Political Liberty: A Sermon Preached in New-York, July 4th, 1793* (New York, 1793), 30–31, 32–34n.

[45] Woodhull, *Sermon for Publick Thanksgiving*, 15; MacWhorter, *Festival Discourse*, 11, 10. Similar ecstasy is found in Green, *A Prayer*, 30; and Boudinot, "Oration before the Cincinnati," 361.

eral moral character." Boudinot was even more direct in reminding his listeners, "On your virtue, patriotism, integrity, and submission to the laws of your own making, and the government of your own choice, do the hopes of men rest with prayers and supplications for a happy issue."[46]

Samuel Miller, the most politically liberal clergyman in the Princeton circle during this period, yet made the most conservative statement of these republican verities. As the title of his 1793 sermon suggests, "Christianity the Grand Source, and the Surest Basis, of Political Liberty," Miller also drew an explicit link between religious and republican health. As Miller expounded his theme, "the general prevalence of real Christianity, in any government, has a direct and immediate tendency to promote, and to confirm therein, political liberty." All knew that corruption and vice led to oppression, since "human depravity is the life and soul of slavery." Conversely, the fruits of the Holy Spirit "stand equally opposed to the chains of tyranny, and to the licentiousness of anarchy."[47] Miller's continued enthusiasm for France set his 1793 sermon apart from the other Princeton utterances, yet it nonetheless announced most clearly the governing assumptions of the Princeton worldview. Not just virtue, but Christian virtue, was the key to social well-being.

Princeton enthusiasm for the course of the nation did not long survive the Fourth of July, 1793. Perceptions of events at home and abroad changed drastically well before the turn of the century. Yet Princeton leaders never wavered in upholding two crucial convictions of this earlier, more optimistic period. First, God himself had given the United States an opportunity for public morality, order, and prosperity without precedent in the history of humankind. But, second, a moral law dictated that healthy republics required a foundation of private virtue and Christian faith. To this second unquestioned assumption, the Princeton authorities added a specifically intellectual dimension. They believed that the exercise of observation and reason, employed with scientific rigor, could perceive the cause-and-effect relationships that determined the well-being of a society as surely as Sir Isaac Newton had assigned effects to causes in the physical world.[48]

The result in later years was that Princeton leaders came natu-

[46] Woodhull, *Sermon for Publick Thanksgiving*, 23; Boudinot, "Oration before the Cincinnati," 365.

[47] Miller, *Christianity the Grand Source*, 12, 13, 19.

[48] The nature of these scientific assumptions is explored at some length below in chapters 7 and 10.

rally to regard turmoil in society, difficulties in the church, and even stress at Princeton College as conditions revealing a decline in virtue, an abandonment of religion, and a loss of former glory. They knew what millennial prospects the Revolution had once opened up, they understood well the relationship between moral deep structures and social surface structures, and they possessed the techniques of moral science to trace tremors in the American edifice to cracks in the foundation. The optimism of 1789–1793 soon faded. The millennial dawn verged toward an apocalyptic nightmare. But until long after the tenure of Samuel Stanhope Smith, no major figure in the Princeton circle questioned the moral and religious blueprints inspired by the Revolution and ratified in the making of the Constitution.

IN ALL of their expectations for national life under the Constitution, the primary place of learning was unmistakable. Princeton leaders with great unanimity looked upon the American Revolution as an educational event. Stanhope Smith wrote in 1784 that revolutions were certainly disruptive, yet "when we consider that human society can advance only to a certain period before it becomes corrupted, and begins to decline, and that letters always decline with virtue, revolutions are perhaps the necessary scaffolding by which science and human nature must gradually arrive at their summit." Boudinot proclaimed that "the child of the poorest laborer, by enjoying the means of education," could look forward to participating in government at even the highest levels. "Science here flourishes in these walks of freedom," according to Mac-Whorter, who perceived a natural cohesion between the interests of learning and the glories of the republic.[49]

Samuel Miller agreed that, with American independence, "the interests of science emerged from the clouds, which until that hour had sat thick and deep upon them," but also went on to specify the function of education in the development of America. The science that arises with freedom teaches "all these republican principles," like equality of rights and obligations, civil and religious liberty, and the reign of law, "which are calculated to call forth the best energies of man . . . and to build up the fabric of national happiness." Schools existed, as Ashbel Green put it in 1789, to be "nurseries of sound literature, of true patriotism, and of undissembled piety." Although Green's optimism soon began to sour, he pro-

[49] Smith to Nisbet, Nov. 26, 1784, 20; Boudinot, "Oration before the Cincinnati," 374; MacWhorter, *Festival Discourse*, 14.

claimed the same educational ideals in 1795, when he affirmed that governments could never do better for its citizens than by providing schools where "all classes of them have their minds enlightened by information, and formed to habits of honesty, industry, and a reverence for virtue." Once again it was Miller who explained the specific role for religion in making education work for the social good: "Teach them [children] to acknowledge the God of heaven as their King, and they will despise submission to earthly despots. Teach them to be Christians, and they will ever be free."[50]

Stanhope Smith, the man entrusted by the Princeton trustees with the realization of these ideals at the college, shared them fully himself. Three times during the decade 1786–1796 in letters to Benjamin Rush, he expressed his great faith in the glorious end to which proper education could lead. Most revealing was his statement in February 1792, when commenting on the virtues taught by warfare. Battle, Smith concluded, was one of God's means for contributing to "the improvement of arts . . . improvement of manners . . . the improvement both of talents & of virtue." He ended, "There is therefore no need of any other millennium than the general progress of science & civilization."[51] Training for war was not part of the curriculum at Princeton, but in all other respects the college existed for the very purposes that the Princeton circle ascribed to science and learning—to teach republican values, encourage piety, and support the establishment of a virtuous society.

In the earliest days of the new country, Princeton officials entertained high hopes for education at all levels. They were especially gratified that the College of New Jersey, more and more under the active leadership of Stanhope Smith as Witherspoon faded from the picture, was making definite progress in its efforts to serve the interests of science, religion, and the republic.

[50] Samuel Miller, *A Sermon . . . July Fourth, 1795* (New York, 1795), 15; Green, *A Prayer*, 30; Green, *A Sermon Delivered . . . the 19th of February, 1795, Being the Day of General Thanksgiving* (Philadelphia, 1795), 34; Miller, *Christianity the Grand Source*, 37.

[51] Smith to Rush, Feb. 19, 1792, Library Company of Philadelphia, HSP. See also Smith to Rush, May 10, 1786, as quoted in Douglas Sloan, *The Scottish Enlightenment and the American College Ideal* (New York, 1971), 174; and Smith to Rush, May 13, 1796, Library Company of Philadelphia, HSP. From the latter letter: "The reciprocal influences of civilization & of piety will probably tend to bring on that final & happy order of ages which religion hath predicted."

7

The College and Stanhope Smith, 1781–1794

Human Nature Susceptible of System

PRINCETON TRUSTEES could take considerable satisfaction in the years immediately after the Revolutionary War that their college was being restored. Progress was slow, but still the faculty was inculcating republican virtues, preserving the institution's religious character, and providing models for the socially productive use of science. John Witherspoon, Stanhope Smith, and their junior colleagues were putting the discipline and curriculum of the college in order, and Smith was emerging as a consequential intellectual leader in his own right. The nature of that leadership became clearer over the last fifteen years of Witherspoon's life as Smith overcame illness, began to make a mark on the undergraduates, and published his first religious and philosophical works. This period of apprenticeship also revealed hints of the tension within Smith between the worlds of Presbyterian propriety and Enlightenment gentility that would eventually have a telling effect on Princeton's stance in the young republic.

MUNDANE REALITIES usually dictated the actions of trustees and faculty as they guided the school during Witherspoon's last years. Student pranks—from an explosion of gunpowder outside the door of a tutor's room in January 1786 to a calf in chapel in July 1790—relieved the tedium and allowed the faculty to test its theories of discipline. On this score Witherspoon was almost always effective.[1] Under his direction the college instituted a graded series

---

[1] On the gunpowder, see journal of John Rhea Smith, Jan. 3, 1786, Peter Force Collection, Manuscript Division, Library of Congress; for the calf incident, see FM, July 2, 1790. On Witherspoon's effectiveness as a disciplinarian, see Collins, *Witherspoon*, 2:154, 218–20.

of punishments to restrain the Princeton scholars, from private admonishment through public censure to suspension or expulsion. The regulations were spelled out in a new edition of the college laws published in 1794, which also specified the curriculum, requirements for regular public speaking, and standards for religious observance. The young men were not to bring alcoholic beverages into their rooms without the "express permission" of a professor, nor were they to frequent "a tavern, beer-house, or any place of such kind" without similarly specific leave. Students were expected to yield "immediate and implicit obedience" to lawful commands from college authorities, and they were to open their doors to college officers or pay for repairs if doors had to be forced. More generally, "lying, profaneness, drunkenness, theft, uncleanness, playing at unlawful games or other gross immoralities" were to receive punishments suited "to the nature and heinousness" of the offense.[2]

Princeton standards proved acceptable to an expanding constituency. Through the 1780s the number of students rose steadily (17 or 18 present in 1780; 40 in 1782, 68 in 1784, 90 in 1786), tailed off slightly at the end of the decade (72 in the summer of 1790), and then increased again. In September 1792 a total of 37 students received the B.A., more than at any previous commencement in the school's history. By 1793 the three restored stories of Nassau Hall, with 42 student "chambers," were filled nearly to capacity.[3]

Mere numbers, however, meant less to the Princeton officials than their ability to provide a first-rate education. Modifications in the classical curriculum appeared slowly, but efforts were made to bring studies up-to-date and to employ them more directly for promoting the institution's goals. When van Hogendorp visited the college in 1784, the freshman year was still entirely given over to the classics. But sophomores were spending more of their time on history, logic, geography, arithmetic, English grammar, and rhetoric than on Homer and Horace. Juniors concentrated on natural philosophy and mathematics, theoretical (Euclid, algebra, trigo-

---

[2] *Laws of the College of New-Jersey: Reviewed, Amended, and Finally Adopted, by the Board of Trustees, in April 1794* (Trenton, 1794), quotations from 29, 30, 35.

[3] Precise numbers on attending students are difficult to come by. The figures here are from Wertenbaker, *Princeton,* 64; FM, summer session, 1790 (72 students, divided 16 seniors, 31 juniors, 20 sophomores, and 5 freshmen); Henry Lyttleton Savage, ed., *Nassau Hall, 1756–1956* (Princeton, 1956), 19; and the graduates listed in *General Catalogue.*

nometry) and applied (mensuration, navigation, surveying). Seniors concluded their study with lectures in moral philosophy ("Comprehending Ethics Politics and Jurisprudence"), readings in Locke and Montesquieu, and special attention to eloquence and criticism. All four classes also had regular assignments in religion and public speaking.[4]

The most striking feature of this curriculum was its imitation of Scottish models, which in the eighteenth century featured a balance between study of the classics and more modern concern for science and contemporary high culture. In 1794 Smith explained to Benjamin Rush, an outspoken critic of the classical curriculum, that, while he himself valued a thorough study of the ancient languages, he wished as Rush did "that the french language were become an indispensable part of education." Problems of finances and staffing notwithstanding, Smith affirmed to Rush that already "in figures & mathematical science, perhaps this college does not yield to any on the continent."[5]

Princeton's effort to adjust its curriculum to the times, to keep in the intellectual forefront, depended heavily on its promotion of science broadly conceived. Smith himself became a leader during the 1780s in the effort to defend the harmonies of physical science (or natural philosophy), mental science (or moral philosophy), theological science (systematic reflection on Christianity), and political science (the lineaments of republicanism). Scientific reasoning—which meant empiricism, induction, and rigorous logic applied to a much broader range of subjects than would come to be the case after the mid-nineteenth century—enjoyed privileged status in the minds of the Princeton leaders, especially Stanhope Smith. They believed in its power to ferret out the secrets of the world—human nature, politics, history, religious and ethical experience, as well as chemistry, astronomy, and applied mathematics. They also believed in the power of scientifically derived knowledge, not only to enlighten the mind, but also to strengthen the will and inspire the heart. Smith's comments to Benjamin Rush on training in the classical languages included the suggestion that languages are best

[4] Gijsbert Karel van Hogendorp, *The College at Princetown, May 1784*, ed. Howard C. Rice (Princeton, 1949), 3–5; this curriculum is virtually the same as described in the 1794 *Laws*, 36–37. For a general summary, see Darrell L. Guder, "The History of Belles Lettres at Princeton" (Ph.D. diss., University of Hamburg, 1964), 207–12.

[5] Smith to Rush, Nov. 10, 1794, Library Company of Philadelphia, HSP. For general Scottish influences on Smith, see Douglas Sloan, *The Scottish Enlightenment and the American College Ideal* (New York, 1971), 149–50, 172.

studied at an early age, for this provides "a kind of experimental way of acquiring the first principles of moral philosophy, which consist in tracing the active and intellectual powers of man."[6]

This comment, with all its assumptions about the beneficial moral and social results arising from formal learning, reflected widespread, if less articulate, beliefs of the entire Princeton circle. Its confidence in the powers of scientific knowledge flowed naturally from Witherspoon's convictions. His was a moderate, didactic Enlightenment, certainly restrained by traditional Calvinism, but an Enlightenment nonetheless. For Stanhope Smith the light of modern learning shone even more brightly.

Increased enrollment and heightened expectations of financial stability, though never quite achieved, enabled the college to maintain a third professor throughout this period, in mathematics and natural philosophy. William Churchill Houston, however, never resumed full-time teaching after the war, and so the trustees in 1785 named the young Ashbel Green to fill this chair. Green possessed an agile intellect and a basic grasp of his subjects. Moreover, he had proven himself an outstanding tutor during the two years after his graduation in 1783. Yet Green was still an amateur, interested more in the ministry than in natural philosophy. When an opportunity arose in May 1787 to take a junior position at Philadelphia's strategic Second Presbyterian Church, Green accepted it readily.[7] This resignation, however, enabled the board to make its first serious appointment in natural science, for the opening coincided with the arrival in the middle states of an experienced Scottish astronomer who was looking for work.

Walter Minto (1753–1796) was Princeton's first professional scientist.[8] A native Scot trained at Edinburgh and Pisa, Minto had taught mathematics at the University of Edinburgh, pursued his interests in local history, received an LL.D. from Aberdeen, and published several small papers in astronomy. The attractions of America's newly defended freedoms drew him across the ocean. Minto did not find preliminary discussions with Princeton satisfactory, so he began teaching at a secondary school on Long Island.

---

[6] Smith to Rush, Nov. 10, 1794. Smith's wording suggests that by this time he was familiar with Thomas Reid's *Essays on the Intellectual Powers of Man* (1785) and *Essays on the Active Powers of Man* (1785), works that expanded and refined the Scottish philosophy of common sense.

[7] Maclean, *CNJ*, 2:213.

[8] See Luther P. Eisenhart, "Walter Minto and the Earl of Buchan," *Proceedings of the American Philosophical Society* 94 (1950): 282–94; Collins, *Witherspoon*, 164n.

Soon, however, he was won over to the Princeton offer by "Old Witherspoon," who, Minto reported to a Scottish colleague, "begged me to do them the honor & the favor to come & they promise themselves a large increase of students from my being there." For their part, the trustees found the presence of Minto a chance to realize their ambitions. The board, "considering the importance to the interest & reputation of the institution of perfecting the course of mathematical and philosophical science," named Minto to a professorship of mathematics and natural philosophy in September 1787.[9]

Minto seemed the perfect man for the job. Not only was he learned, cultured, and European, but he could also articulate to students and others the interconnections among science, religion, and republicanism that were the great concerns of the Princeton authorities. He had been a friend of American liberty in the old country and now took an immediate delight in prospects for the nation's political future. His inaugural address at the commencement in 1788 warmed the hearts of his employers by noting that only a "civilized society" improves "the Arts and Sciences" and by complimenting them as "for-ever dear to the wellwishers to the cause of learning and of the liberties of mankind."[10]

Even more, this inaugural address exhibited a method of uniting natural philosophy and natural theology that, if it did not use language customary to all the trustees, still won their approval. Minto's address, entitled "The Progress and Importance of the Mathematical Sciences," offered an occasion to rehearse the slow advance of the human mind until the recent unfolding of "the active genius of man" with Copernicus, Descartes, and others who paved the way for Isaac Newton, "a man without an equal in the history of human genius." Newton's reputation, moreover, rested not just on his mathematical brilliance but also on the fact that his research "conducted him" to "the Supreme Cause of All." Newton's life, as well as that of many other prominent mathematicians,

9 Minto to the Earl of Buchan, Oct. 28, 1787, in Eisenhart, "Walter Minto," 288; TM, Sept. 26, 1787. For early expressions approving Minto, see Witherspoon to the Earl of Buchan, May 24, 1788, in Eisenhart, "Walter Minto," 289; and Ashbel Green, "Dr. Witherspoon's Administration at Princeton College," *Presbyterian Magazine* 4 (1854): 472.

10 Minto, *An Inaugural Oration; or, The Progress and Importance of the Mathematical Sciences* (Trenton, 1788), 8, 49. Minto's letter to the Earl of Buchan on Oct. 28, 1787, expressed great delight in the prospect of swift passage for the the new Constitution (Eisenhart, "Walter Minto," 288).

demonstrated how clearly science was useful to faith. "Natural philosophy in particular, by leading us in a satisfactory manner, to the knowledge of one almighty, all-wise, and all-good Being, who created, preserves and governs the universe, is the very hand-maid of religion." These were welcome words at Princeton as were also Minto's instructions concerning proper forms of reasoning: "None but self-evident truths are admitted as first principles." Such principles opened a broad and safe way to use the best modern learning for religion and morality. If anyone had missed the outline of these benefits in the speech itself, Minto repeated them with unmistakable clarity in his closing prayer, where he petitioned "the Supreme Being" to "prosper the interests of science and literature in the United States of America: to make those interests ever subservient to the promotion of liberty, happiness and virtue."[11]

Practical problems kept Princeton from fully entering into the way that Minto marked out and that Stanhope Smith was outlining in his own work at the same time. Scientific equipment proved hard to obtain. The board took note in September 1790 that "a proper apparatus is absolutely necessary for the successful cultivation of, & instruction in, several parts of natural philosophy" and put in motion a fund-raising plan to purchase the needed equipment. Smith acted on his own toward the same end as soon as he assumed full responsibility for the college.[12] Such practical matters, however, seemed to be the only difficulties that kept Princeton from realizing its lofty scientific goals.

LIFE AT the college involved more, of course, than the discipline of students and formal study. Princeton authorities also wanted to promote respect for religion and for the nation's republican ideals. As would become more obvious to some Princeton supporters after the turn of the century, religious ardor at the college had cooled in the wake of the Revolution. Ashbel Green, the best source on this subject, was not an altogether unbiased witness, for when he became president in 1812 with a mandate to revive religion, it was advantageous for his purposes to exaggerate the spiritual decline of preceding years. Yet Green's statement that there was no "religious revival" at Princeton from 1773 to 1814 accords well with other evidence. Even Green, who was ever reluctant to

---

[11] Minto, *Inaugural Oration*, 15, 22, 26, 36–37, 30, 50.

[12] TM, Sept. 28, 1790; Smith to Ashbel Green, Dec. 12, 1794, Gratz Collection, HSP.

cast aspersions on Witherspoon, did report "that the feverency of his piety suffered some abatement during our revolutionary war."[13]

To be sure, at Princeton there was never any institutional carelessness about religious practice. The College of New Jersey was a distinctly Protestant enterprise firmly committed to traditional Presbyterianism, and it would remain so long after Stanhope Smith departed the scene. Trustees spent an inordinate amount of time at their meetings superintending the institution's "charitable funds," the endowments reserved for young men preparing to be ministers. They also displayed an ever-present concern for religious faith and practice in their oversight of the college. The *Laws* of 1794 stipulated that students were to behave "with gravity and reverence" during the daily services of morning and evening prayer.[14] According to the preference of their parents (which meant, for practical purposes, Presbyterian or Episcopalian), students on Sunday were to attend worship and recite a catechism or other religious lesson in the afternoon.

Students left various records of their collegiate religious experiences. A number who later became prominent clergymen reveled in this aspect of life at Princeton. Others seem to have become discriminating sermon-tasters, like the student in 1786 who early in the year complained that Stanhope Smith in the pulpit was "not very animated" and preached with "a disagreeable monotony," who some weeks later found it worth recording that Witherspoon gave a sermon "of an hour," and still later in the same year was pleased when tutor Ashbel Green took responsibility for the Sunday sermon—"a fine figure in the pulpit & a fine voice and a good sermon & everything very good, but a little affectation."[15] More generally, Christian observance seems to have been simply an unquestioned feature of the college environment.

Religion, because it was so ingrained in the lives of those making up the Princeton circle, did not seem to require assiduous cultivation. It was a normal part of college life. Only later, when other matters went awry, would Princeton officials bring religion into fo-

[13] Green to William Sprague, Apr. 10, 1832, in Sprague, *Lectures on Revivals of Religion* (1832; reprint, London, 1959), 130–32 of Appendix; for the same sentiments, see Green, *The Life of the Revd John Witherspoon*, ed. Henry Lyttleton Savage (Princeton, 1973), 273.

[14] *Laws* (1794), 28.

[15] John Rhea Smith, Jan. 8, Feb. 19, and Mar. 5, 1786, Peter Force Collection, Library of Congress.

cus as a cause of specific concern or cultivate its practice as an agent for reform. Well before that time, however, Princeton authorities had made the promotion of another set of quasi-religious values the object of explicit and detailed attention.

Because Princeton was so thoroughly allied with the cause of American independence, it is little wonder that national celebrations loomed large at the college. Even before the Declaration of Independence, students and faculty demonstrated solidarity for the cause by wearing American-made clothing on ceremonial occasions, by participating in local demonstrations against the British, and by an endless round of republican declamations. On July 9, 1776, national independence was celebrated in fine style: "Nassau Hall was grandly illuminated," according to a contemporary account, "and independency proclaimed under a triple volley of musketry, and universal acclamation for the prosperity of the United States . . . , with the greatest decorum."[16] Patriotic celebrations only grew in importance as the years progressed. In the spring of 1778, the whole town of Princeton was illuminated to celebrate the alliance with France. In 1781 more elaborate rejoicing greeted the news of Cornwallis's surrender at Yorktown.[17] Celebration of July Fourth remained the highlight of the year, as it was in 1783 with Congress at the college. Three years later, students were somewhat annoyed that the faculty insisted on their dining in the college commons, instead of providing their own feasts as they had in the past. Yet "the Punch, ham & green peas which (mirabile dictu) we had on this membl day" dispelled the irritation. The full round of activities—two long orations in the morning, more punch in the afternoon, six more speeches at 5 o'clock, "the discharge of 3 rounds from a cannon in the campus"—sufficed to "assure more general satisfaction than had been felt before."[18]

Observation of the Fourth continued to be a highlight of the student year through Smith's tenure as president. Shortly after his

[16] From the *Philadelphia Evening Post*, in Alfred Hoyt Bill, *A House Called Morven: Its Role in American History, 1701–1954* (Princeton, 1954), 38. On the same day, see Collins, *Witherspoon*, 1:222; and Sheldon S. Cohen and Larry R. Gerlach, "Princeton in the Coming of the American Revolution," *New Jersey History* 92 (1974): 83, where the date is incorrectly stated as July 19.

[17] Bill, *House Called Morven*, 46, 53.

[18] John Rhea Smith, July 4, 1786, Peter Force Collection, Library of Congress. On the superiority of July Fourth to all other holidays, including religious observances, see Wertenbaker, *Princeton*, 210.

entrance into the sophomore class, fifteen-year-old James Iredell of Edenton, North Carolina, wrote home concerning July 4, 1804. It "was celebrated with great magnificence. The college windows were decorated with laurel and cannon were fired at intervals during the whole day." At one o'clock the students sat down to "an elegant dinner when compared to our common fare," at which they enjoyed "punch & wine, of which we drank very freely not a small quantity. After dinner," he went on, "'Hail Columbia' & a song on Contest were sung or rather roared out by the students, enlivened as they were by copious draughts of punch." At two o'clock, four orators from each society declaimed on the meaning of the day. In the evening the college was "illuminated," and "an elegant display of fireworks" took place. Next came the ball, celebrated with "much formality & ceremony," although Iredell was not pleased that "there were very few handsome girls there." After dancing the ladies retired, but the students "about two o'clock . . . sat down to supper & continued at table till day break. When we returned to college very few of us were in a condition to tell what we had been doing the night before."[19]

These days of national celebration, especially the Fourth, were vital parts of a Princeton education. On such occasions and in sharp contrast to the rest of the school year, students functioned as adults. They were encouraged to eat and drink with few restraints, to stage entertainments, and to rehearse in public speeches the glories of liberty. The rituals of patriotism—music, fireworks, cannons, rifles, and special illuminations—as well as its fervent republican rhetoric let students share momentarily in the excitement experienced by their elders when they had created the nation. If students were too young to defend liberty in person, Princeton authorities nonetheless found a way to enlist them as participants in its ritual celebration and as fellow workers in proclaiming republican truths to a new generation.

Instruction in republican patriotism, though less formal, was no less significant to Princeton experience than the stated curriculum and organized Christian worship. Together these elements created the means by which faculty and trustees hoped to inculcate their most cherished values to leaders of the rising generation. Increasingly, however, it was Stanhope Smith rather than John Witherspoon who took the lead in organizing the college's internal life

[19] James Iredell to Henry A. Donaldson, July 7, 1804, transcript in James Iredell Papers, PUA.

and articulating the commitment to republicanism, religion, and learning that defined the Princeton circle as a whole.

THE TRUSTEES testified to their growing confidence in Smith by leaving him in charge during 1783–1784 when Witherspoon undertook his quixotic search for funds in Great Britain. Also in 1783 they officially broadened his professorial responsibilities to include theology as well as moral philosophy. Three years later the board formalized a de facto state of affairs by naming Smith vice president of the college.[20]

Well beyond the college circle Smith was also being recognized for his extraordinary demeanor, the great personal dignity that enhanced his learned elegance. During the late 1780s the visiting Frenchman Moreau de Saint Mery went out of his way to comment on Smith's exceptionally grand appearance, a trait that also captured Archibald Alexander's attention during his first visit to a Presbyterian General Assembly in 1791. When Alexander first spied Smith, he "saw a person whom I must still consider the most elegant I ever saw. . . . The thought never occurred to me that he was a clergyman, and I supposed him to be some gentleman of Philadelphia, who had dropped in to hear the debate."[21] Smith's studied calm, which served as an emblem of the rational harmonies to which he was devoting his life, was one of the traits that enhanced his reputation at Princeton and beyond.

Another was his ability to provide reassuring personal direction for at least some students. Smith's friend and biographer Frederick Beasley admitted that Smith's "coolness, reserve, and even stateliness in demeanor" erected a barrier to warm friendship.[22] Yet with at least a few students, and even more with the young tutors, Smith unbent far enough to render significant personal support. Again the testimony of Ashbel Green is important, for in spite of many later differences, Green as an old man could still recall fondly Smith's paternal encouragement of his own career. In 1783 or 1784, while serving as tutor, Green told Smith that he was experiencing difficulty in making the choice between law and the church. Smith warned the young man frankly that "theology . . . is not the road either to fame or wealth" but that it was the best

[20] TM, Sept. 29, 1786. The *General Catalogue* (1908) provides an incorrect date, 1789, for Smith's appointment as vice president.

[21] Moreau, from Bill, *House Called Morven*, 61; James W. Alexander, *The Life of Archibald Alexander* (Philadelphia, 1855), 99.

[22] Beasley, "Life," 16.

means "to do good." This timely advice, backed by other prompt-ings in due season, was critical for the course of Green's later life. Smith seems to have offered similar support to others as well.[23]

While Smith's years as Witherspoon's understudy witnessed his growing stature as a respected educator, they were not untouched with difficulty. Smith's health continued to be frail, with periods of severe illness in the summer and fall of 1782, in 1784, in 1792, and perhaps at other times. He came close to death in 1782 from a recurrence of consumption, an episode that he later described to Benjamin Rush in riveting detail. Over a period of several days Smith hemorrhaged heavily each afternoon from his lungs, effu-sions that stopped only when he was bled from the arms or legs. Smith could sense the onset of the hemorrhages and requested his physicians to bleed him before the flow began. When they refused out of consideration for the quantity of blood already lost, Smith lanced himself when he felt the blood rise in his lungs. The crisis left Smith enervated for several months but also succeeded in end-ing the hemorrhages. Smith's assessment of the episode to Rush was characteristic: "I am sure I write to a gentleman who knows that religion with philosophy are able, by long habit & reflexion, to overcome the weak & unworthy parts of nature. And as I have just returned from an encounter with death, I may take the liberty to say that, to a mind who studies to make the God of life & death her friend, he is the less terrible the nearer you approach him."[24]

Illness continued, however, and Smith seems to have anticipated the recurrence of tuberculosis, since he always kept a lancet for bleeding on his person. When Witherspoon was absent in Britain in 1784, one of the tutors usually took charge of morning and eve-ning prayers because of Smith's inability to perform this func-tion.[25] Not until the late 1780s did Smith recover more completely from this episode, and even then he was never strong.

Matters of health were not Smith's only uncertainties in these days. On more than one occasion he entertained possibilities of

[23] *Life of Green*, 146.

[24] Smith to Rush, Jan. 14, 1782, Library Company of Philadelphia, HSP; Smith, "An Account of the good Effects of copious Blood-letting in the Cure of an Hem-orrhage from the Lungs: in a Letter from the Rev. Dr. Samuel S. Smith, President of the College of New Jersey, to Dr. Benjamin Rush," *Medical Museum* 2 (1806): 1–6. On Smith's general health in this period, see Beasley, "Life," 464; and Samuel Holt Monk, "Samuel Stanhope Smith (1751–1819): Friend of Rational Liberty," in Thorp, *Lives*, 94.

[25] On the lancet, see Smith to Rush, Nov. 7, unspecified year, Library Company of Philadelphia, HSP; *Life of Green*, 132; Maclean, *CNJ*, 2:208.

occupation elsewhere, as both a minister and educator. In the year of Witherspoon's death he told Green that he found "some circumstances here disagreeable to me" and asked about the possibility of filling a vacancy in the Market-Street Presbyterian Church in Philadelphia. Smith also told Green that he would have accepted a call to a New York pastorate two years before if his health had not stood in the way. The exact nature of Smith's uneasiness in Princeton is not clear, but it evidently was not resolved immediately by his elevation as Witherspoon's successor, for in 1796 he expressed considerable interest in the presidency of the new University of North Carolina.[26] The uncertainty surrounding Smith's place of employment was certainly not unexpected for someone of his talents and ambition. Yet along with difficulties in his health, it dispels the picture of Smith as Witherspoon's patient heir apparent. These things also introduce a note of dissonance to his own activity at Princeton. He was a creature of the college, but not entirely.

DURING THE ten years before Witherspoon's death, a basic division in Smith's character came increasingly into focus. On the one hand, he was a rising light in the church, active in the deliberations of his denomination's regional and national courts, busy as a professor of theology directing the apprenticeship of aspiring ministers, and visible at Princeton as a spokesman for the Presbyterian interest. On the other hand, Smith's private correspondence reveals him as an acolyte of the Enlightenment, offended by dogmatic intolerance, distressed by the effect of democratic excess on learning, and committed to a nearly unbounded faith in reason. Smith himself seemed to hold the two sides of his character together with little strain, and his early writings displayed an ability to combine orthodoxy and Enlightenment. Implications of Smith's two loyalties for the Princeton circle were, therefore, not at all clear in the 1780s and 1790s. But since they later became the source of controversy and confusion, it is more than germane to explore their development at an earlier date.

Smith's standing as an orthodox Calvinist owed more to his name, position, education, and associations than to his explicit activities. Lacking evidence to the contrary, it was easy to assume that this son of Robert Smith—an intellectual heir of John Wither-

---

[26] Smith to Ashbel Green, Mar. 17, 1794, Samuel Stanhope Smith Collection, PUL; R.D.W. Connor, Louis R. Wilson, and Hugh T. Lefler, *A Documentary History of the University of North Carolina, 1776–1799*, 2 vols. (Chapel Hill, N.C., 1953), 2:52, 58–60, 445–46.

spoon, a scion of the New Side, and a theology professor at the College of New Jersey—stood with the firmer Calvinists. In addition, Smith's relationships during his early years at Princeton with the more orthodox members of his denomination were friendly and supportive. His public opinions on religion were undeniably sound.

Smith traveled to New England during the fall vacation of 1790 to celebrate a recent return to health.[27] While in Boston he preached three sermons that were eventually published. They encouraged Christians to beware of slander and other "small faults" as dangers threatening spiritual well-being and impeding the work of the Holy Spirit. The first of these, "On the Guilt and Folly of Being Ashamed of Religion," asked hearers to consider how such shame kept some from becoming Christians and how it led others to turn away from morality to vice. It concluded with the dread reminder that at the last judgment Christ would be ashamed of those who in this life had been ashamed of him.[28] The sermons do not offer the single-minded piety characteristic of Jonathan Edwards, George Whitefield, or even Robert Smith and John Witherspoon, but they were, in their discursive fashion, no less heralds of standard eighteenth-century evangelicalism. For all the public knew, the sentiments in these sermons represented the beginning and end of Stanhope Smith's religion.

Private correspondents, however, knew more. In letters to Benjamin Rush and his cousins Samuel and Susan Shippen Blair, as earlier in his letters to Jefferson and Madison, a different persona emerges. Here we meet "the epitome of eighteenth-century gentility and rationality," in Douglas Sloan's apt characterization.[29] A continuing exchange with Rush reveals a Smith eager to give rational science and natural and moral philosophy the fullest possible sway.

The letters with the Blairs, written between 1786 and 1791, are quite different. With occasional contributions from Smith's wife and Samuel Blair, Smith and Susan Shippen Blair exchanged lofty, neoclassical sentiments in epistles apparently intended for simple personal pleasure. Blair, Smith's maternal cousin, was the clergyman who as a young man had been chosen to head Princeton itself

[27] Smith, "Effects of copious Blood-letting," 4.
[28] Smith, *Three Discourses* ["On the Guilt and Folly of Being Ashamed of Religion," "A Sermon on Slander," and "On the Nature and Danger of Small Faults"] (Boston, 1791).
[29] Sloan, *Scottish Enlightenment*, 184.

when negotiations with Witherspoon temporarily collapsed. At that time Blair was an associate minister of Boston's Old South Church, where he had been called after graduating from Princeton and serving as a college tutor. Since the early 1770s, Blair and his wife, the daughter of Philadelphia physician William Shippen, Sr., had lived a life of semiretirement in Germantown, interrupted by service as a chaplain during the war and by occasional preaching responsibilities. Blair's physical and mental health, injured by shipwreck and by deprivations during the Revolution, was not good. During the time of the Smith-Blair correspondence, his standing with the Presbyterians also received a blow when he announced his belief in the doctrine of universal salvation.[30] For both the Smiths, busy at Princeton with a growing family and a full range of duties at the college, and the Blairs, laboring under several sorts of difficulties themselves, the exchange offered a much needed divertissement. Smith became Cleander, his wife Emelia, and Susan Blair Fidelia. The letters, filled with what now appears to be cloying imitation of Pope, flew back and forth between Princeton and Germantown.[31] It was to these intimate friends, the Blairs and Rush, that Stanhope Smith expressed opinions that would eventually affect the future of the college as well as cloud his good standing among the Presbyterians.

Smith's letters displayed, for instance, a considerable degree of dissatisfaction with the strictures of Presbyterian orthodoxy. He for one was not disposed to let his mind be fettered by blind adherence to authority. In 1792 he cautioned Rush not to reveal to "some serious champions of orthodoxy" Smith's musings on the benefits of warfare, and he made light of Rush's standing with regard to "the creed of bigotry." Two years later Smith worried that, since Princeton was not "as independent in its friends as it ought to be," plans for educational reform would have to go slowly.[32]

These passing hints of uneasiness became more definite in Smith's reaction to the Presbyterian censure of Samuel Blair. Early

---

[30] *Princetonians 1748–1768,* 302–6.

[31] David F. Bowers, "The Smith-Blair Correspondence, 1786–1791," *PULC* 4 (1943): 123–34. The children of Samuel Stanhope and Ann Witherspoon Smith were as follows: Elizabeth (1776–1847), John Witherspoon (1778–1829), Frances Ann (1780–1807), Ann Maria (1782–?), Harriet (1784–1794[?]), Susan Frances (1785–1849), Mary Clay (1787–?), Robert Blair (1789–1789), and Caroline Laurens (1792–?); Samuel Stanhope Smith File, PUA.

[32] Smith to Rush, Feb. 19, 1792; Nov. 10, 1794; both Library Company of Philadelphia, HSP.

in 1788 Smith told Blair that he could not agree with him. Yet he spent more time denouncing the spirit of those who attacked Blair than he did in addressing the issue itself. Smith did "not intend to wrap myself in a shroud of orthodoxy with lifeless acquiescence in established systems," nor did he propose "to fight for God as if the Devil were in me." Rather, "reason and charity" were his means to promote "the cause of truth and piety."[33] Later that same year Smith scorned the Philadelphia Presbytery, which had censured Blair, for displaying "the narrowness and weakness of the human mind, in a country and an age in which one would think there were sufficient lights to deliver it from such illiberal darkness."[34] At least two members of the Philadelphia Presbytery, John Bayard and Ashbel Green, might have been surprised to hear such a reaction from one whom they had selected to assist the theological education of undergraduates and the clerical training of graduates at the college they served as trustees.

Smith's letters with the Blairs came to an end in 1791, in part because rumors were spreading about the relationship between himself and Susan Blair. Smith protested to Blair in January 1788 that the hyperorthodox "have made you a *heretic*, and me a *rake*." His 1791 sermon in Boston on the evil of slander probably was his formal response to the gossipers.[35] Yet the end of this literary conceit by no means warned Smith off from his commitment to a more enlightened approach to science, faith, and moral responsibility.

Apart from his published writings, Smith gave fullest expression to such sentiments in letters to Benjamin Rush, who stood on intimate terms with many members of the Princeton circle. Rush, a graduate of the college in 1760, was a classmate of Samuel Blair and of longtime Princeton trustee Jonathan Bayard Smith. During his medical studies in Scotland he assisted in the negotiations that brought Witherspoon to Princeton. And he retained a lively interest in college matters throughout his life. He was married to the sister of Richard Stockton, Jr., and thus closely connected with the kin network that played such a large role in the college during the Smith years. Rush, like Stanhope Smith, was a scion of New Side Presbyterianism, having studied with, and been deeply influenced by, almost all its major leaders, including Samuel Finley, Samuel

---

[33] Smith to Blair, Jan. 27, 1788, in Sloan, *Scottish Enlightenment*, 169.

[34] Smith to Blair, July, no day, 1788, quoted in William H. Hudnut, III, "Samuel Stanhope Smith: Enlightened Conservative," *Journal of the History of Ideas* 17 (1956): 543.

[35] Smith to Blair, Jan. 27, 1788, 169; Monk, "Samuel Stanhope Smith," 98.

Davies, and Gilbert Tennent. Yet also like Smith, Rush was a man of worldly wisdom who placed the promotion of liberty, morality, and science above sectarian religious concern. Rush's list of services to his nation was a long one, from suggesting the title "Common Sense" to Tom Paine for his famous tract in 1776, through signing the Declaration of Independence and laboring mightily for a host of philanthropic causes, to patching up the rupture between John Adams and Thomas Jefferson. Rush was always a serious-minded Christian, but increasingly unconcerned about creeds or traditional denominational loyalties. After the war he moved from Presbyterianism to Episcopalianism to Unitarianism and finally to an amorphous nondenominational Trinitarian belief.[36] This is the man to whom Smith opened his mind most fully on intellectual questions over the last twenty years of the eighteenth century and who remained a treasured friend until his death in 1813.

It was to Rush that Smith expressed the confidence that the spread of learning would both defend American liberty and hasten the millennium. With Rush, Smith discoursed grandly over a great array of subjects, unfettered by either sectarian dogmatism or illiberal petty-mindedness. War and peace, the social effects of philosophical reasoning, female education, the death penalty, style in English prose, free will and necessity, death, the relationship of humidity to complexion, modern and ancient languages—all were matters that Smith contemplated with Rush as auditor, confidant, and disputant.[37] Rush's own writing in medical and social topics was a prime reason for Smith to be confident "that the sons of America will arise to vie with the philosophers of the old world." Likewise, Rush's philanthropy raised hopes for the growth of the new nation out of barbarism. The persona that Smith opened to Rush was by no means antireligious. It was rather one that blurred traditional distinctions between the realm of the spirit and the life of the mind. "Divinity and philosophy," he told Rush shortly after becoming president of Princeton, "when enlightened by the same spirit, naturally fall into the same train of thought." Smith looked forward to the day when all would recognize "that the chair of the philosophical society [Rush was a leading member of Philadel-

---

[36] *Princetonians 1748–1768*, 318–25. Donald D'Elia, *Benjamin Rush: Philosopher of the American Revolution* (Philadelphia, 1974), contains the most perceptive account of Rush's religious life.

[37] Smith to Rush, Feb. 19, 1792; Jan. 14, 1783; Aug. 27, 1787; Apr. 10, 1787; Aug. 3, 1790; Feb. 25, 1798; Dec. 5, 1796; Feb. 19, 1792; May 13, 1796; Nov. 10, 1794; all Library Company of Philadelphia, HSP.

phia's American Philosophical Society] is as orthodox as the pulpit of Princeton [where he himself preached]."[38]

As events after 1802 would make clear, not everyone in the Princeton circle melded confessional religion and enlightened learning so readily. An internal struggle over the school's destiny arose between those who agreed with Smith and those with less sanguine views on the harmony of traditional faith and Enlightenment science. In the years immediately after the Revolution, however, such conflicts were unknown. John Witherspoon, who combined piety and the Enlightenment with consummate ease, still lived. Smith and Smith's future antagonists like Ashbel Green were both clearly protégés of the Old Doctor. The needs of the new nation, especially the prospect of grounding republican virtue in a bedrock of faith and science, demanded the unreserved cooperation of all. Moreover, Smith himself was demonstrating to the world that there was no cause for alarm over Princeton's intellectual course. In fact, quite the reverse was true. Especially in a tour de force published in 1787, he showed with convincing finality that the best modern learning pointed, not to the conflict, but to the harmony of science, faith, and republican order.

SHORTLY BEFORE his death Smith reminisced about the circumstances that led to the writing of his *Essay on the Causes of the Variety of Complexion and Figure in the Human Species.*[39] Smith had long been interested in the reasons why different human groups varied in skin color, posture, and facial characteristics. This interest may have been stimulated by his acquaintance with the Indian missions sponsored by the New Side Presbyterians in New Jersey and Pennsylvania, his associations with early opponents of slavery like Samuel Miller, or his contact with blacks in Virginia and to a lesser extent in New Jersey. In 1818, however, Smith said only that he was drawn to the subject "perhaps, originally, from a sceptical doubt," presumably concerning the biblical account of a common descent of all people from Adam and Eve. In the eighteenth century this long-standing assumption about the origin of humanity was being questioned by savants like Voltaire, who held that the

[38] Smith to Rush, Apr. 10, 1787; Aug. 8, 1787; May 13, 1796; all Library Company of Philadelphia, HSP.

[39] Smith, *An Essay on the Causes of the Variety of Complexion and Figure in the Human Species. To which are added Strictures on Lord Kaims's Discourse, on the Original Diversity of Mankind* (Philadelphia, 1787).

different races testified to the multiple origins of humanity.[40] Smith's desire to approach the subject scientifically was long-standing.[41] The occasion for organizing his thoughts on the subject was offered by David Ramsey, who sometime in 1785 or 1786 shared a coach to Philadelphia with Smith and Witherspoon. During the ride Smith entertained his companions with speculations on the causes of racial diversity. Ramsay, Princeton class of 1765, medical student of Benjamin Rush, renowned historian of the Revolution, and like Stanhope Smith a son-in-law of Witherspoon, happened also to be a member of Philadelphia's American Philosophical Society.[42] Through his influence Smith was elected an honorary member and then invited to deliver the society's oration on February 28, 1787.

The book that resulted was a learned, yet relatively brief disquisition that interacted fruitfully with several other eighteenth-century discussions of the subject. Smith began by assuming that "variety in human nature, is effected by slow and almost imperceptible gradations." All but three or four of his pages developed the argument that climate and social conditions are fully adequate to explain both current differences between human races as well as the historical process by which the different races descended from one human pair. The essay was significant as a pioneering American effort in physical anthropology and for its consideration of the place of blacks in a white society, aspects of the work that have been learnedly considered by several modern scholars, especially John C. Greene and Winthrop Jordan.[43] For our purposes, however, the *Essay* is most important not so much for its contribution to anthropology or racial theory as for its stated intent and its illustration of larger concerns within the Princeton circle.

[40] Smith to Ashbel Green, undated (annotated in Green's hand, "about the 18th month before his death," hence ca. Feb. 1818), Gratz Collection, HSP. Splendid treatment of the general subject, along with a full description of Smith's contribution, is found in two works by John C. Greene: "The American Debate on the Negro's Place in Nature, 1780–1815," *Journal of the History of Ideas* 15 (1954): 384–96; and the chapter "The Sciences of Man: Physical Anthropology," in Greene's *American Science in the Age of Jefferson* (Ames, Iowa, 1984), 320–42.

[41] See Smith to Nisbet, Nov. 26, 1784, in Michael Kraus, "Charles Nisbet and Samuel Stanhope Smith—Two Eighteenth Century Educators," *PULC* 6 (1944): 22–23.

[42] *Princetonians 1748–1768*, 517–21.

[43] Smith, *Essay on the Causes of Variety* (1787), 3. For Greene's works, see n. 40. Winthrop Jordan provided an illuminating introduction to the second edition of Smith's *Essay* (New Brunswick and New York, 1810), published by the Harvard University Press in 1965.

Smith made his purposes entirely clear. He wanted to show that good science supported divine revelation, but even more that the unity of humanity was essential for a moral philosophy of *common* sense. Modern commentary on Smith's *Essay* has focused mostly on the second edition, which Smith brought out in 1810, a work nearly three times as long as the original. In the later edition Smith was no less definite about what constituted good science, but he did shift the burden of his substantive argument. In the first edition the preservation of the procedures of moral philosophy was the main theme, while the defense of revelation played a complementary role. The second edition reversed the emphasis. The longer second edition, with its heightened concern to defend religious tradition, has naturally drawn the attention of modern scholars, but in so doing they have missed something of what Smith's first edition meant for its author and the intellectual environment of the late 1780s.[44]

Smith's 1787 *Essay* began with a brief definition of proper science as a procedure eschewing "arbitrary hypothesis." Rather, genuine science took place when careful students observed "the operations of nature with minute and careful attention." Moreover, it was simply "unphilosophical" to recur to hypothesis, when a "proper investigation" could account for a phenomenon "by the ordinary laws of nature."[45] Firmly grounded in method, Smith proceeded to make his case. Climate, as observed in the various habitats of North America, changed complexion, and these

[44] For descriptions of Smith's work as primarily a vindication of Christian revelation, see Jordan, "Introduction" to Smith's *Essay on the Causes of Variety* (Cambridge, Mass., 1965), xv; Greene, "American Debate on the Negro's Place," 384; Hudnut, "Samuel Stanhope Smith," 544; and M. L. Bradbury, "Samuel Stanhope Smith: Princeton's Accommodation to Reason," *Journal of Presbyterian History* 48 (1970): 195. More sensitive to Smith's actual purposes is Monk, "Samuel Stanhope Smith," 93–95.

[45] Smith, *Essay on the Causes of Variety*, 1–2. This short introduction to Smith's 1787 edition contained only brief and indirect reference to the religious implications of his subject: "Many philosophers have resolved the difficulty [variety of complexion and figure] . . . by having recourse to the arbitrary hypothesis that men are originally sprung from different stocks, and are therefore divided by nature into different species. But as we are not at liberty to make this supposition, so I hold it to be unphilosophical to recur to hypothesis." By contrast, in 1810 Smith expanded his introduction to a full four pages in order to show how the work united religion and philosophy "by bringing in science to confirm the verity of the Mosaic history" (*Essay on the Causes of Variety* [1810; reprint, 1965], 3, with full introduction 3–60. All citations to the 1810 edition are from the Winthrop Jordan edition of 1965.

changes were transmitted to future generations. While habitation in a cooler climate eventually produced lighter skin, life in the tropics produced the opposite. Civilized society, again as Smith had observed on several occasions with Africans and Indians living in white society or with individuals descended from red or black ancestors, brought bodily form and color close to that of the northern Europeans, who constituted the norm of comeliness. No good reason existed for postulating a supposed separate origin for the various races when observable fact demonstrated the changes that environment worked on the human form.

Smith's brief conclusion spelled out what he expected his argument to accomplish. It protected the Bible's account of a common human ancestry, but it also provided a foundation for moral philosophy. Smith thus guarded the two most important intellectual values he had inherited from Witherspoon—Christian faith and a philosophy of common sense. He did so, in addition, while showing the utility of that inheritance. The preservation of moral philosophy was especially critical, since it made possible a whole range of ethical, political, social, and religious explorations. Smith's conclusion deserves to be quoted at length, for only by such quotation can we observe his harmonious blending of religious and philosophical concerns and, especially in this edition of the *Essay*, Smith's overriding attention to the philosophical. He had canvassed "the causes of the principle varieties of person that appear in the different nations of the earth." And he was eager to spell out the implications.

> I am happy to observe, on this subject, that the most accurate investigations into the power of nature ever serve to confirm the facts vouched by the authority of revelation. A just philosophy will always be found to be coincident with true theology. The writers who, through ignorance of nature, or through prejudice against religion, attempt to deny the unity of the human species do not advert to the confusion which such principles tend to introduce. The science of morals would be absurd; the law of nature and nations would be annihilated; no general principles of human conduct, of religion, or of policy could be framed; for, human nature, originally, infinitely various, and, by the changes of the world, infinitely mixed, could not be comprehended in any system. The rules which would result from the study of our own nature, would not apply to the natives of other countries who would be of different species; perhaps, not to two families in our own country, who might be sprung from a dissimilar composition of species. Such principles tend to confound all science, as

well as piety; and leave us in the world uncertain whom to trust, or what opinions to frame of others. The doctrine of one race, removes this uncertainty, renders human nature susceptible of system, illustrates the powers of physical causes, and opens a rich and extensive field for moral science. The unity of the human race I have confirmed by explaining the causes of its variety.[46]

That the burden of Smith's concern in 1787 was philosophical receives further testimony from the "Strictures" he directed against Lord Kames in an appendix that was one-third as long as the *Essay* itself. Henry Home, Lord Kames (1696–1782), was a Scottish jurist and essayist closely associated with leaders of the Scottish Enlightenment. He was a Moderate Presbyterian and thus suspected by Witherspoon's Popular, or Evangelical, party. Yet Kames also promoted ideas not strictly in keeping with the ameliorating temper of the Moderates.[47] His *Essays on the Principles of Morality and Natural Religion*, first published in 1751, attempted to rebut Hume's skepticism about proofs for the existence of God; later editions of that work contained ideas on human volition bearing some similarities to Jonathan Edwards on the will.[48]

The work to which Smith responded was Kames's "Preliminary Discourse concerning the Origin of Men and of Language," a preface to his *Sketches of the History of Man* (1774). In this book Kames argued that a straightforward observation of the races led to the conclusion that "there are different species of men as well as of dogs." Such a conclusion did not seem impious to Kames, for he suggested that God had specially "fitted" or "qualified" the different human species to their different environments. The one bar that Kames saw to this theory was the account in Genesis, where all people are described as descending from Adam. Kames found the solution to this problem in the Bible's story of Babel, where God dispersed humanity into different groups and different languages. Babel and God's subsequent outfitting of the dispersed people to their various new habitats, therefore, provided sufficient

[46] Smith, *Essay on the Causes of Variety* (1787), 109–10.

[47] On Kames, see *Dictionary of National Biography*, 9:1126–28; Arnand Chitnis, *The Scottish Enlightenment* (London and Totowa, N.J., 1976), 55–56; Gladys Bryson, *Man and Society: The Scottish Inquiry of the Eighteenth Century* (Princeton, 1945), 64–66; and Elmer Sprague, "Home, Henry," in *The Encyclopedia of Philosophy*, 8 vols. (New York, 1967), 4:61–62.

[48] Paul Ramsey, ed., *The Works of Jonathan Edwards: Freedom of the Will* (New Haven, 1957), 14–15 n. 1, 443–52.

reason for explaining the division of humanity into different species.[49]

Curiously, Stanhope Smith read Kames's argument as the work of an infidel. He felt that Kames had written disingenuously, that his deference to revelation was insincere, that he really wanted readers to conclude (in spite of Kames's own biblical exposition) that a philosophy antagonistic to revelation proved the multiple origin of humanity. Smith's counterattack ridiculed Kames for employing weak authorities, for misreading nature, and for substituting philosophy for "the light of truth and reason."[50] Smith's own careful observations and the painstakingly verified accounts of individuals adjusting successfully to new environments proved that all humanity was of one species.

This conclusion, supported by even more forceful assertions about the scientific proof for revelation in the 1810 edition, made Smith a champion of Christianity in the eyes of many of his contemporaries. A student in the class of 1806, gazing back from the mid-nineteenth century to his first meeting with Smith, wrote rapturously of the reputation this tract had won for the Princeton president. "The press every where teemed with high wrought eulogisms & the church received it with unbounded admiration because it had vanquished & overwhelmed an host of infidel writers who had ridiculed the idea that the diversified tribes of men had sprung from one pair."[51] The actual achievement, however, was not this clear-cut, as a closer examination of Smith's "Strictures" indicates.

The real burden of Smith's concern was not to establish the reliability of Mosaic history or any other narrowly religious assertion but to verify "the doctrine of one race."[52] The real difference with Kames was a difference in natural theology. God's goodness appeared for Kames in the providential creation of diverse human "kinds" adjusted to different environments. For Smith, on the other hand, "the goodness of the Creator appears in forming the

[49] Kames, "Preliminary Discourse," in *Sketches of the Natural History of Man*, vol. 1 (Edinburgh, 1778), 20, 22, 75–83.

[50] Smith, *Essay on the Causes of Variety* (1787), separately numbered "Strictures," 17.

[51] Undated reminiscence by member of the class of 1806, 8, John Maclean Papers, PUA. Samuel Miller also praised the work in *A Brief Retrospect of the Eighteenth Century*, 2 vols. (New York, 1803), 1:117.

[52] Smith, *Essay on the Causes of Variety* (1787), "Strictures," 30, with reference to this "doctrine" also on pp. 23, 28.

whole world for man, and not confining *him*, like the inferior animals, to a bounded range. . . . The divine wisdom is seen in mingling in the human frame such principles as always tend to counteract the hazards of a new situation."⁵³ Kames denied the possibility that science and revelation diverged by postulating two providential interpositions, Babel and the separate shaping of human species. He also made a concerted effort to harmonize the explicit biblical record and his scientific conclusions. Smith denied the same possibility by dispensing with special providence altogether and by resting his case entirely on science. And he casually dismissed the need to harmonize his discoveries in natural philosophy with the biblical history of Babel.⁵⁴

To make such a move while presenting his argument as a defense of revelation and orthodoxy required considerable rhetorical finesse. At one point Smith was forced to read Kames's description of the "miracle" at Babel as "the effect of chance." At another point, Smith himself dispensed with the biblical record. In his effort to prove that diversity in language could arise from the savage state "naturally," Smith turned from Scripture ("I am not now going to explain the history of Babel") to an ad hominem attack on Kames, who "no doubt, most devoutly and fervently disbelieves all miraculous interpositions of the Deity." Against both Kames and the Bible, Smith suggested that it was "in *the nature of things*" (Smith's emphasis) that "man would become savage, and language would become divided." Since, Smith suggested, "independent tribes naturally give rise to diversity of tongues, thus, perhaps, the speech of men was at first one—it became gradually divided into a multitude of tongues." While Smith does not show how his cosmology accords with the story of Babel, he scores his opponent for despising revelation.⁵⁵

The only thing that can explain Smith's argument against Kames is his determination to preserve "the doctrine of one race."⁵⁶ This teaching is in fact the burden of the *Essay* in 1787. Whether Smith's distortion of Kames's arguments was deliberate or not, the result

⁵³ Ibid., 6.

⁵⁴ Sloan, *Scottish Enlightenment*, 151 n. 12, also recognizes that Kames had a greater place for divine revelation than did Smith.

⁵⁵ Smith, *Essay on the Causes of Variety* (1787), "Strictures," quotations 17, 18, 24, 30. Smith later abridged this argument for his *Lectures . . . on the Subjects of Moral and Political Philosophy*, 2 vols. (Trenton, 1812), 1:104–5.

⁵⁶ Smith, *Essay on the Causes of Variety* (1787), "Strictures," 28 and 30, where the same phrase apears.

was the same.[57] As compared with Kames, who wrestled seriously with the biblical record, Smith rested his case on the exclusive use of natural philosophy and was much less indebted to revelation. Smith's overriding concern was to defend the possibility of universally valid moral philosophy.

Although the effort of 1787 won praise for its general intelligence and its orthodoxy, Smith intended it primarily as a scientific and philosophical work. Near the end of his life he recorded his pleasure that Dugald Stewart, successor to Thomas Reid as leader of the Scottish common-sense philosophers, and Georges Cuvier, France's great naturalist, had approved the 1787 edition.[58] At that late date Smith did not even mention the essay's apologetic significance. The fact is, however, that at Princeton in 1787 no clear distinction existed between a work of moral philosophy exemplifying the most rigorous exercise of Enlightenment thought (as defined by the Scottish tradition) and one defending the interests of religion. Witherspoon had drawn the two together. Smith was now attempting to see how they could advance in tandem.

Witherspoon had promoted the idea that the principles of his Scottish philosophy could lead to a just understanding of "nature"—physical, human, and social—quite apart from the record of revelation. To pursue such a course assiduously was now to arrive at verified knowledge and also wisdom for action. "The rules which . . . result from the study of our own nature," as Smith phrased it at the end of his *Essay*, make possible a "science of morals" that in turn provides "general principles of human conduct, of religion, or of policy."[59] Such principles were the very things that in 1787 a new nation, independent, yet threatened by disorder within and predators without, desperately required. Public order and the health of the republic demanded "a science of morals."[60] Because Smith could demonstrate that humanity was a unit,

[57] A possible cause for Smith's antagonism toward Kames is the latter's earlier differences with Witherspoon. Witherspoon attended the 1756 General Assembly of the Scottish Kirk when Kames was censured along with David Hume for heretical opinions (Collins, *Witherspoon*, 1:41; and Richard B. Sher, *Church and University in the Scottish Enlightenment: The Moderate Literati of Edinburgh* [Princeton, 1985], 65–74), and Witherspoon's 1753 essay in *The Scots Magazine* on human liberty was directed against Kames.

[58] Smith to Green, ca. Feb. 1818.

[59] Smith, *Essay on the Causes of Variety* (1787), 109.

[60] Smith's *Essay* appeared in the same year as the writing of the Constitution, and so at least a few of his readers might have seen a connection between his "science of morals" and "the science of politics" described by both Alexander Hamilton (*Fed-*

such a science was possible. As a bonus, moreover, the same vigorous reasoning also verified the truth of Christian revelation.

Smith's 1787 *Essay* was a signal effort. It exemplified the finest scientific procedures. It vindicated a philosophy of common sense. It defended Christianity. And it made possible the construction of rational liberty. The work was the most striking intellectual performance by a member of the Princeton circle to that time. It was the first full application of the philosophical principles enunciated by Witherspoon. By demonstrating the legitimacy of common-sense reasoning, it preserved an approach to society and politics that would be immensely significant for more than a generation in the middle and southern states. And it anticipated the way in which Smith later expanded upon the harmonies of Christianity, the Enlightenment, and republicanism to several generations of students and through a series of important textbooks.

The *Essay* also highlights issues that came to define the later history of the Princeton circle. First, it championed the fundamental harmony of traditional Christianity and moral philosophy as Witherspoon construed it. No one at Princeton during the lifetime of Stanhope Smith would ever deny that harmony, but the boldness with which he affirmed it led to a growing uneasiness among his fellow trustees and, much later, to questions by historians about the feasibility of such a harmonization. Second, the *Essay* assumed that, once the unity of humanity had been confirmed, moral philosophy could prepare the world for public virtue. The note of urgency was not entirely, or even primarily, intellectual. Smith and his colleagues needed the unity of human nature because they needed a philosophy for public moral order.[61] Yet once possessing such a philosophy, they seemed to assume that it would be relatively easy to secure a virtuous public. The progress of moral philosophy was expected to lead to progress in public morality, first in the college and then in the nation. And so it seemed that it would for a few brief years between the ratification of the Constitution and the outbreak of political conflict in Washington's second

---

eralist No. 9) and James Madison (*Federalist* No. 47) in their arguments for the Constitution.

[61] On the importance of the concept of a unified human nature for James Madison and other architects of the Constitution, see Douglass Adair, " 'That Politics May Be Reduced to a Science': David Hume, James Madison, and the Tenth Federalist," in *Fame and the Founding Fathers: Essays by Douglass Adair*, ed. Trevor Colbourn (New York, 1974), 95–96; and Morton White, *Philosophy, the Federalist, and the Constitution* (New York, 1987), 86–89, 206.

administration. In 1787, Smith's *Essay* seemed to clinch the harmony of Presbyterian Calvinism and the moderate Scottish Enlightenment and to ensure the public effectiveness of a commonsense moral philosophy. In reality, however, Smith had only defined an agenda of perplexity for the Princeton circle.

In 1787 the difficulties in the Witherspoon-Smith agenda lay in the future. At that time the *Essay* showed that Witherspoon's colleague was proving himself admirably. And he continued to do so, with public acclaim and success at the college for the rest of Witherspoon's life. Little wonder then that, when the old president died at his country home, Tusculum, on November 15, 1794, while awaiting receipt of the day's last newspaper, the college continued on its course without interruption. Soon the trustees formalized the succession that Stanhope Smith's accomplishments had made a foregone conclusion.

In 1794 the Princeton board knew its own mind on religion, education, and the nation. Stanhope Smith had become an efficient exponent of their convictions. And considerable capital remained to be spent from the legacy of Witherspoon. For a few years the great goals seemed almost tangibly within reach.

8

Transition and Continuity, 1795–1801

Glowing with Patriotism, as well as Pure Religion

THE DEATH of John Witherspoon had little apparent effect on the college. Day-to-day instruction, from which the president had withdrawn some time before, proceeded apace under the competent direction of Smith, Minto, and the tutors. The number of students did decline in the years immediately after the Old Doctor's death but soon recovered. By the early nineteenth century enrollments reached record levels. The loss of a leader like Witherspoon had an inevitably depressing effect on the institution, but Stanhope Smith's growing reputation compensated in some measure for the loss. Moreover, all recognized that the course Smith took in guiding the college was the one that Witherspoon himself had set.

Matters of greatest moment at Princeton in Smith's early years as president had less to do with educational details than with developments beyond the quiet hills of central New Jersey. Warfare in Europe and political strife at home, attended by accumulating portents of moral dissolution, loomed large. The heady self-congratulation that followed the establishment of national government under the Constitution gave way to fear and self-doubt. Excesses of optimism were replaced by excesses of alarm. Not long after Smith took the helm of the college, these altered circumstances in the larger world made their presence felt at Princeton. But in spite of mounting turmoil, Smith and his colleagues largely succeeded in keeping the college on its course. Amid war and the threat of war from Europe, social and moral decay in America, concentrated assaults on public order, and even the success of Democratic-Republicans in the election of 1800, the college remained a haven of Christian decorum, Enlightenment good sense, and republican order. Stanhope Smith enjoyed a lengthy honeymoon with the board and the Princeton constituency. Not until after the turn of the century did events at the college fully reflect the chaos of the world at large and thereby call into question the new president's conduct of the school.

WHEN THE trustees met in May 1795 for the first time after Witherspoon's death, they heard a memorial sermon from John Rodgers and arranged for its publication. The board took the prudential step of drawing up a more specific "system of rules" to define the duties of college officers and then proceeded unanimously to elect Stanhope Smith as president. After "prayer made suitable to the occasion," Smith took the prescribed oath. The next item of business was Ashbel Green's report on a subscription begun in Philadelphia, at the request of the new president, to purchase a "chemical apparatus." Then the board asked Green to consult with David Rittenhouse about the repair of his orrery, and the meeting "concluded with prayer."[1] The tone of the new administration—science balanced by piety—was set.

If the trustees needed reassuring that Smith was the man for his new responsibilities, their confidence was no doubt boosted by three impressive public addresses that Smith delivered in the year of his inauguration. Each testified eloquently to the new president's personal capabilities and the vigor of his intellect. Each also reflected the blend of commitments that had marked the work of Witherspoon and that the board had confirmed as their purpose for the institution.

The first was a sermon preached at Princeton in early January on a fast day appointed by the Synod of New York and New Jersey. Smith acknowledged the chastisement of natural disasters, foreign wars, and Indian attack on the frontier, but was most concerned about "a certain *fever* and *delirium* of liberty . . . at war with all decency and subordination." Especially perverse were those, who, under cover of words like "*patriotism, and the love of the people,*" promoted "the purposes of ambition or of party." From such evils, which all understood to refer to the Democratic Societies and their guides such as Thomas Jefferson, it was indeed time to repent. Still, the nation's leadership was in good's hands. Washington was protecting the country from damaging involvement in European affairs and had masterfully suppressed the recent "insurrection,"

[1] TM, May 5–7, 1795.

which again all recognized as the Pennsylvania Whiskey Rebellion. In sum, the reasons for fasting were manifest, but firm government in reliable hands as well as the reasonableness of the "universal system of moral discipline" kept Witherspoon's heir apparent from undue alarm.[2]

Only six weeks after the fast, Smith was called to preach at Philadelphia's Third Presbyterian Church for a day of thanksgiving proclaimed by President Washington to note the restoration of domestic tranquillity after the disturbances in Pennsylvania. Smith expatiated upon his theme, *The Divine Goodness to the United States*, in terms that other Princeton trustees were also using that very day.[3] God was to be praised for raising up and preserving the United States of America and petitioned to preserve the new nation from faction, demagoguery, an unrestrained press, and entanglements abroad. As many of his colleagues were prone to do on such occasions, so Smith also took pains to describe the great utility of religion for a republic. While "the gospel of Christ is the most precious gift which God hath bestowed upon mankind," it is also "the surest basis of virtue and good morals, without which free states soon cease to exist." Smith's thanksgiving discourse was distinguished from contemporary efforts by its reflection on the utility of scholarship. It was "the business of the philosopher to trace the relations of causes and effects" and so to note that "every event in society, as well as nature, may be referred to some adequate cause incorporated into the system of the universe" by "God, the first mover of all." Elias Boudinot described the address to a Massachusetts correspondent as "the most elegant political Sermon ever delivered in this City." The audience rushed to subscribe for the printed edition, since "never was a Sermon delivered here with more applause."[4]

Smith's third major address of 1795 was his inaugural on September 30, 1795, delivered in Latin at his first commencement as president. A generation before, in 1768, Witherspoon had opened

[2] Smith, *A Discourse on the Nature and Reasonableness of Fasting, and on the existing Causes that call us to that Duty* (Philadelphia, 1795), 24, 27, 17.

[3] Smith, *The Divine Goodness to the United States of America. A Discourse on the Subjects of National Gratitude ... a Day of General Thanksgiving and Prayer* (Philadelphia, 1795). See also, Ashbel Green, *A Sermon Delivered ... the 19th of February, 1795, Being the Day of General Thanksgiving* (Philadelphia, 1795).

[4] Smith, *Divine Goodness to the United States*, 29, 31, 8; Boudinot quoted in Clifford K. Shipton, "Samuel Stanhope Smith," in *Biographical Sketches of Those Who Attended Harvard College in the Classes 1768–1771* (Boston, 1975), 235.

his first commencement with a "Learned & elegant Latin Oration on the Connection & mutual influences of Learning & Piety." Now Smith returned to the same theme by asking "whether . . . it be profitable to connect piety with all the other arts which belong to a liberal education?"[5] While Smith's answer was predictable, the eloquence of his address, not to speak of the power of his argument, made this a memorable event, at least for those students who had applied themselves to their classical studies and those assembled dignitaries who had not outgrown their Latin. Smith assured his guests that God was the source of all goodness and all wisdom, while also conceding that wicked men were able to pervert "the most excellent endowments of mind" to evil ends. He catalogued a long list of noble historical examples where "piety and a veneration for God have been almost uniformly connected with the most excellent endowments of mind, and these cultivated and adorned by learning." Especially noteworthy were "those illustrious restorers of the mathematicks," at whose head stood Isaac Newton, "the most perspicuous of all; who despising and setting aside all the theories of men, drew the science of nature from nature herself." Quite obviously Witherspoon's dream of "turning the Newtonian trick" for the whole curriculum still lived.[6]

The heart of Smith's concern, no less than his agenda for the College of New Jersey, appeared in a single paragraph. On the one side, religion, learning, and morality were joined together by the tightest bonds; on the other, they sustained the health of the nation. "Learning and a polished manner of life and also power, riches, and glory [come] from probity of morals." In the past, however, "riches begat luxury, and luxury licentiousness, and a corruption of morals invaded all the people . . . and all arts being neglected, they degenerate into ignorance, and at the same time into imbecility and want." Smith's peroration defined both his purposes and the standards with which he would be measured if, for whatever reason, the institution failed to exhibit the disciplined order

---

[5] Smith, *Oratio Inauguralis . . . Habita in aedibus Collegii Neo-Caesariensis* (Trenton, 1817), published with Smith's oration on the death of Washington. I have used a manuscript translation of this address made in 1817 by David McKinney of Belle Fonte, Pennsylvania, housed at the Presbyterian Historical Society, Philadelphia; quotation from p. 2. For the correct date of this address, see Maclean, *CNJ*, 2:6. On Witherspoon's address, see Collins, *Witherspoon*, 1:113.

[6] *Oratio Inauguralis* (McKinney translation), 4, 11, 13. For "the Newtonian trick," see Charles A. Beard, "Written History as an Act of Faith," *American Historical Review* 39 (1934): 223.

that was the fruit of learning connected to piety. "From my very soul I exhort you all of whatever age, that you preserve holy and untouched, this bond of union between piety and learning, lest dire experience may at length teach us, that these things, which when united are a mutual support, being disjoined and separated would bring ruin upon one another—From which may God long preserve us in Nassau-Hall."[7]

IN SMITH'S first years as president, Nassau Hall was safe. The new president carried on where the old had left off. To be sure, Smith's accession did coincide with heightened Princeton fears about events in the wider world, but the college, at least until after the turn of the century, was reaping the good fruit of educational fidelity rather than sowing a whirlwind of decay.

The most notable early achievements were scientific. Very early in his tenure Smith organized an appeal to the New Jersey legislature that, when the college promised to liberalize its board to include some non-Presbyterians, yielded a grant of $4,800.[8] Although this grant could barely begin to fund Smith's plans for Princeton, it was no mean gift at a time when the annual tuition, room rent, and fees for an individual student were still less than $50.[9] Smith, however, was thinking big. He wanted to spend $6,000 alone on "philosophical apparatus," but the New Jersey grant was supposed to cover building repairs and library acquisitions as well as scientific equipment. Still, Smith resolved to go on by raising money from private subscriptions. As he put it to a correspondent in late February 1796, "If I live, I am resolved, if possible, to have in future one of the best apparatuses on the continent."[10] Later that same year Smith spelled out his goals more

---

[7] *Oratio Inauguralis* (McKinney translation), 5, 10.

[8] TM, Jan. 13 and Apr. 13, 1796; *The Memorial and Petition of the Trustees of the College of New-Jersey* (broadside, [1796]), with copy in Maclean, *CNJ*, 2:13–17. On the stipulation of the legislature for more non-Presbyterians on the board, the trustees were as good as their word, but no better. The next two vacancies were filled by Episcopalians, Joshua Maddox Wallace and the Reverend Charles Henry Wharton, but these two residents of Burlington, New Jersey, were close friends of Elias Boudinot and regarded the world much as he did. Thereafter for many years all new trustees were Presbyterians once again.

[9] Other expenses (board, firewood, laundry, and candles) came to $120–$130 per year. See *Laws of the College of New-Jersey* (Trenton, 1794), 37; and the broadside circular distributed to parents from ca. 1796 to 1806, listing expenses of $171.21 for a year (no title, Evans no. 30863 for 1796, under "Princeton University").

[10] Smith to friend of his daughter Frances, Feb. 27, 1796, in Maclean, *CNJ*, 2:24.

completely to Benjamin Rush. "The time is ... now come, or nearly so," he felt, to propose "that the study of languages, except modern ones, shall cease after the Freshman class—unless as mere exercises of taste or imitation—& that three entire years be employed in the different branches of art & science." Although the college was hamstrung, as Smith admitted in the same letter, by "the poverty of our circumstances, & the small number of our teachers," it did indeed seem that progress was being made toward the goal of a refined, enlightened education.[11]

The trustees, for their part, were cooperating. They added a professor of chemistry in 1795, who, with Smith and Minto, gave the college three genuine professionals for the first time in its history. The dip in enrollment late in the decade meant that the board could not immediately replace Walter Minto as professor of mathematics when he died in 1796. But it did take other measures to compensate. The first one thousand dollars from the New Jersey grant was designated for the use of the chemistry professor. Soon the board was trying to find more room on campus for scientific equipment. Individual board members also joined Smith in soliciting funds and equipment for scientific purposes from associates in America and overseas.[12]

In 1799 the board also agreed to a plan that admitted a group of students for just the scientific and English-language subjects. The year before Smith could inform Rush that he had succeeded in arranging matters so that "almost the whole of the three last years" was given over to English-language instruction "in the most *useful* branches of literature & science."[13] From developments much later, it is clear that some trustees had their doubts about reducing the classical content of the curriculum. At the time, however, there were no objections. The board specified more explicitly in 1800 the content of the new scientific course and in 1801 authorized the first five certificates for the special program.[14] The president's desire to modernize the curriculum was succeeding.

To aid in reaching his goals, Smith enjoyed an energetic and capable faculty. Princeton's professor of chemistry, the first person

[11] Smith to Rush, Dec. 5, 1796, Library Company of Philadelphia, HSP.

[12] TM, Apr. 1, 1799; Smith to Samuel Bayard in London, Dec. 26, 1796, in Douglas Sloan, *The Scottish Enlightenment and the American College Ideal* (New York, 1971), 161.

[13] TM, Sept. 25, 1799; Smith to Rush, Feb. 25, 1798, Library Company of Philadelphia, HSP.

[14] TM, Sept. 23, 1800; Sept. 29, 1801.

to hold such a position in the United States, was an able young Scot, John Maclean, who had studied at Glasgow, Edinburgh, London, and Paris, before the love of American liberty drew him, as Walter Minto before, to America. Maclean not only was a good teacher, whom the visiting Benjamin Silliman described as "a man of brilliant mind, with all the acumen of his native Scotland." He was also a public champion of sound natural philosophy who, if less directly than Stanhope Smith, also wanted to demonstrate the harmony of science and faith.[15]

Soon after he began his duties at the college, Maclean published *Two Lectures on Combustion*, in opposition to the theories of Joseph Priestley. This substantial pamphlet argued in favor of Lavoisier's conclusion that changes in the function of oxygen explained combustion and against Priestley's theory that combustion could be accounted for by a liberation of the substance phlogiston. Maclean rehearsed arguments on both sides of the controversy before concluding in favor of Lavoisier. Maclean's comments on Priestley's methods went further, however, to suggest problems with the latter's materialistic philosophy and his Unitarian religion as well as his phlogistic science. "Indeed," said Maclean, "you may adopt it [Lavoisier's antiphlogistic theory] with safety; for from being a plain relation of facts, it is founded on no ideal principle, on no creature of the imagination; it is propt by no vague supposition, by no random conjecture; it is dependent upon nothing whose existence cannot actually be demonstrated; whose properties cannot be submitted to the most rigorous examination; and whose quantity cannot be determined by the tests of weight and measure."[16] In similar manner, Smith had earlier taken the measure of Lord Kames's scientific method and found it wanting. Maclean in his role as a chemist did not pause to draw the fruitful conclusion. Yet the implications were clear: proper reasoning was based on the facts of experience and careful induction. The weaknesses of Priestley's science exemplified the weaknesses of his thought more generally. Sound natural philosophy showed the mistakes in Priestley's view of God as well as in the radical political principles that made him the darling of the Jeffersonians.[17]

[15] Quotation from Silliman in John C. Greene, *American Science in the Age of Jefferson* (Ames, Iowa, 1984), 165; on John Maclean, see *Dictionary of Scientific Biography* (New York, 1973), 8:612–13.

[16] John Maclean, *Two Lectures on Combustion* (Philadelphia, 1797), 116.

[17] Some Princeton animus against Priestley may have arisen from the knowledge that Priestley had written against Thomas Reid and the whole Scottish effort to

If the college's achievements in intellectual activity were not enough, Smith also emerged more clearly as a spiritual leader during his early years as president. In 1799 he was named moderator of the Presbyterian General Assembly, the same year in which that body selected him, along with ten other current or future Princeton trustees, as charter members of its corporation.[18] When Smith offered a collection of his sermons to the public in 1799, the list of 256 subscribers testified amply to the eminence he had achieved. Most of the college trustees and many of Smith's former students naturally put down for a copy, but the subscribers included ten United States senators, sixteen congressmen, two Episcopal bishops, two justices of the New Jersey Supreme Court, the director of the mint, one justice of the United States Supreme Court, one United States district attorney, and the "Ambassador from the Batavian Republic."[19] Some of these dignitaries were members of the Princeton circle, but many were not.

The sermons themselves represented an effort to add the refinements of style to the treasured religious truths of the Princeton tradition. In a substantial introduction Smith spelled out his thoughts on the genre. It was now difficult to make sermons interesting, since the world had become so conscious of cultivated style. Smith's solution was to add "elegance" to "simplicity." To this end he used the model of French preachers, whose sermons often contained a "fervor" lacking among the English. Smith apologized to readers who looked for a fuller use of the Bible in his arguments or for a more specific consideration of profound theological truths. His purpose was to reach "a much larger class" than was interested in such matters, and so he proposed to mingle "remarks drawn from the philosophy of human nature . . . with the illustrations of divine truth." Philosophy would accompany him into the pulpit.[20]

Smith's texts came from the Old Testament wisdom literature,

construct a philosophy from common-sense principles; see Richard B. Sher, *Church and University in the Scottish Enlightenment: The Moderate Literati of Edinburgh* (Princeton, 1985), 311–12. A good summary of Priestley's views is found in the article by John Passmore, in *The Encyclopedia of Philosophy*, 8 vols. (New York, 1967), 6:451–55.

[18] *Minutes of the General Assembly of the Presbyterian Church in the United States of America from . . . 1789 to . . . 1820* (Philadelphia, 1847), 161, 173–74.

[19] Smith, *Sermons* (Newark, N.J., 1799), 493–96.

[20] Ibid., iii–vi. On Smith's indebtedness to French models, see A. Owen Aldridge, "Massillon and S. S. Smith: French-Inspired Sermons in Early American Literature," *French-American Review* 6 (1982): 147–59.

Gospel passages illustrating the virtues of Jesus, and practical sections in the Pauline epistles. They contain much that would have warmed the heart of Robert Smith or his mentor George Whitefield. At the same time, themes from the Enlightenment were leavening the old gospel of revivalistic Calvinism. A number of the discourses were not so much biblical expositions as moral essays in the style of Addison and Steele or Samuel Johnson—for example, "On Industry," "The United Influence of Reflection and Sacred Reading in Cultivating and Purifying the Morals," and "On the Pleasures of Religion." Classical allusions abounded. And a strong religious utilitarianism ran through the volume: Smith recommended Bible reading "for the direction and government of our conduct." The three "pleasures of religion" he noted were "satisfaction to the mind," "pleasures to the heart," and "security and peace."[21]

Confrontation with an offended God, which was the burden of his father's preaching, or mystical union with the Incarnate Christ, a theme prominent with earlier Princeton presidents Samuel Davies and Jonathan Edwards, was not Smith's central concern. No longer, as with these earlier Princeton voices, was self-assertive pride the "cause of infidelity." For Smith it was rather vice, ignorance, and vanity.[22] His enemies were not theologians who misinterpreted the doctrines of grace but ethical theorists and popular politicians whose opinions deranged the moral and social order. Smith thus singled out for special criticism David Hume, "the most philosophic of modern infidels"; Tom Paine, whose "historical and critical" inaccuracy in *The Age of Reason* exceeded even the errors of Voltaire; the Scottish thinkers Lord Kames and Lord Monboddo, for erroneous views on the origins of humanity and language; and Rousseau, whose "writings still continue to diffuse a baneful poison through society."[23] The sermons were an accomplished performance, simple yet elegant, sincere yet gracious. No one could miss in them the message of Calvinistic piety, even if Princeton's new leader pronounced this message with a heightened attention to literary refinement and an emphasis on the temporal advantages of religion that had not been heard so clearly at the college before.

In Smith's early years, leaders in the Princeton circle, as well as

[21] Smith, *Sermons*, 210, 278, 281, 288.
[22] Ibid., 5, 30, 40.
[23] Ibid., 31, 32n, 36n, 44.

those beyond, were pleased with the new president. Not that gain-sayers were absent entirely. Isaac Weld, Jr., an Englishman touring North America, stopped by for a visit in July 1796 and was decidedly unconvinced that the college amounted to anything. He found seventy students whose level of maturity and academic attainments "better deserve the title of a grammar school than a college." To Weld the library was "most wretched, consisting for the most part, of old theological books, not even arranged with any regularity." As far as Princeton's vaunted scientific pretensions, Weld cast aspersions on Rittenhouse's dilapidated orrery and the fragmentary parts of "a philosophical apparatus." Stanhope Smith's heart would have bled if he had known how Weld described the cabinet for natural history: "Two small cupboards . . . contain a couple of stuffed alligators, and a few singular fishes, in a miserable state of preservation the skins of them being tattered in innumerable places, from their being repeatedly tossed about."[24] Other would-be critics had difficulties with Smith himself. About this time the story began to circulate that John Blair Smith, out of exasperation with his sibling's airs, told him, "Brother Sam, you don't preach Jesus Christ and Him crucified, but Sam Smith and him dignified."[25]

The overwhelming consensus, however, moved in the other direction. Smith had inherited a thriving institution and had made it stronger. He was a leading philosopher, a dignified preacher, and an expert at demonstrating the harmony between learning and faith. Under his leadership the college boded fair to ascend from the heights to which John Witherspoon had brought it.

Philip Lindsley, who came to Princeton in 1802, enjoyed a singular vantage point on Smith and his work, since he later served as a tutor under Smith and as a professor under Smith's two successors, before becoming the president of Cumberland College in Nashville, Tennessee. When Lindsley arrived at the college, Smith was reputed to be "the most eloquent and learned divine among his contemporaries." "From our childhood," Lindsley went on, "we (the students) had never heard the Doctor's name pronounced but with praise. We came to the College, therefore, prepared to look

[24] Isaac Weld, Jr., *Travels Through the States of North America* (London, 1799), as quoted in *PULC* 4 (1943): 122.

[25] Among the several sources repeating this story is Samuel Holt Monk, "Samuel Stanhope Smith," in Thorp, *Lives*, 100. Maclean, *CNJ*, 2:133, argues that it came not from Smith's brother but from "a rude and ignorant man of the coarser sort, a better judge of strong drink than of sound doctrine."

up to him as the great man of the age. . . . He daily grew in our esteem. . . . We never questioned his sincerity and uprightness. We revered him as a faithful Christian minister,—far above reproach or suspicion."[26] Even granting the mellowing effect of the more than forty years that intervened between Lindsley's first association with Princeton and the writing of this testimony, it still speaks clearly of Smith's esteem at the time.[27]

By 1800 and the fifth anniversary of Smith's succession, almost all acknowledged that the institution had made a successful transition. Enrollments were up, and the quality of both instruction and instructors was high. Students, while exhibiting some of the irresponsibility that was upsetting the wider world, seemed to benefit from their time at Princeton. The better sort of parents continued to send their sons to the college, where most of them applied themselves seriously to their studies before embarking on lives of exemplary service in the world. The later eminence of graduates is no sure guide to the quality of instruction received when young, but it was reassuring to the Princeton circle that, after the passing of Witherspoon, its graduates continued to reach almost the same heights as his famous scholars had achieved: for example, from the classes 1795 through 1801, two attorneys general of the United States, one secretary of state, the first federal commissioner of Indian affairs, one director of the Bank of the United States, several members of the Senate and Congress, a few ambassadors, numerous judges and district attorneys, many officials of high rank in the states, a number of college professors and presidents, and a healthy sprinkling of distinguished clergymen. Well indeed could Smith urge graduating seniors in 1797 to practice the industry that "will be essential to your success if you would rise to eminence in any liberal profession, or serve your country with distinction in any respectable department of church and state," for, as he observed, "one or another of these objects I presume is your aim."[28]

THE SUCCESS of the college during Smith's early years was all the more remarkable in light of developments in the country as a

[26] Sprague, *Annals*, 3:342.

[27] For other encomiums, see the comments of George Washington to his ward and namesake, George Washington Custis, a Princeton student in 1796 and 1797, *The Writings of George Washington*, vol. 35, *March 30, 1796–July 31, 1797*, ed. John C. Fitzpatrick (Washington, D.C., 1940), 283, 451, 510, and the praise from Smith's biographer Beasley ("Life," 470, 14, 16).

[28] On the graduates, see Maclean, *CNJ*, 2:112–17; Smith, *Sermons*, 160.

whole. Over a short span of years at the end of the eighteenth century, Princeton perceptions of the world changed dramatically. The college, with its delicately balanced concern for Christian teaching, philosophical excellence, and republican virtue, had once been a torch anticipating the dawn. Now it became a beacon fire holding back the night.

Where before Princetonians had hailed the rising glory of America, they now bewailed its collapse. Where they had looked with eager expection to the results from "a Constitution of Order . . . which embraces all the dignities of man . . . in the highest and most perfect degree," they now turned away from direct political involvement.[29] Where they had glimpsed the millennium, they now perceived a cataclysm. Their expectation was turned to doubt, their hope to despair.

The occasions for this change were both domestic and foreign, both political and religious.[30] As early as the first year of Washington's second term, 1793, events in France presaged a greater evil to come. The execution of the king, radical reforms promoted by left-wing Jacobins, the outbreak of war on a large scale in Europe, and eventually the Reign of Terror disillusioned the supporters of Princeton who had glimpsed the spread of liberty in the French Revolution. Rumblings from afar were magnified by the conduct of Citizen Genet in the United States during 1793 and 1794. Public affairs stabilized briefly in succeeding years when President Washington took firm action to quash the Whiskey Rebellion in western Pennsylvania and when Chief Justice John Jay negotiated what seemed to Federalists a successful treaty with Great Britain. Yet the political legacy of these events—especially Washington's sharp denunciation of Democratic Societies at the time of the Whiskey Rebellion and the acrimonious contentions over the Jay Treaty—did nothing to reassure Princeton leaders about the nation's fate. When Washington in his Farewell Address called for a course of national prudence, avoiding foreign entanglements and eschewing partisan factions at home, his words were received warmly at the

[29] Alexander MacWhorter, *A Festival Discourse, Occasioned by the Celebration of the Seventeenth Anniversary of American Independence* (Newark, 1793), 11.

[30] For a general picture of this period, I have benefited from John C. Miller, *The New American Nation Series: The Federalist Era, 1789–1801* (New York, 1960); Marshall Smelser, "The Jacobin Phrenzy: Federalism and the Menace of Liberty, Equality, and Fraternity," *Review of Politics* 13 (1951): 457–82; and Smelser, "The Jacobin Phrenzy: The Menace of Monarchy, Plutocracy, and Anglophilia, 1789–1798," ibid., 21 (1959): 239–58.

College of New Jersey. Yet events after Washington left the scene were not reassuring. Partisan strife continued, and degeneration seemed to be spreading out from France to contaminate the United States. Moral decay, as illustrated by French efforts to bribe American negotiators in 1798 (the XYZ affair), and military peril, exemplified by the quasi-war on the high seas at the end of the decade, both loomed large. Most of the members of the Princeton circle understood fully why John Adams and the Federalists promoted the Alien and Sedition Acts and could only regard the Kentucky and Virginia Resolutions, which protested these acts, as impudent.

If these political upsets were not bad enough, Americans—especially in the corridor between New York and Philadelphia—seemed to be receiving special signs of divine chastisement. Disease was an obvious manifestation. Five times in the decade after 1792, and every year from 1797 through 1799, yellow fever ravaged Philadelphia, to the great distress of the Princetonians living in that city. In 1798 a mysterious illness carried off over 2,000 members of New York City's churches in little more than three months, including 186 adherents of the united Presbyterian church of John Rodgers and Samuel Miller.[31]

Religious pollution also abounded. Here the great cause of alarm was Tom Paine, who in 1794 and 1795 published the two parts of his notorious *Age of Reason*, a work attacking the supernatural elements of Christian faith generally, and the Calvinistic interpretation of religion specifically. For the leading publicist of the American Revolution to turn against the faith was a great blow that preoccupied the Princeton circle for many years.[32]

Acting in character, the Princeton leaders did not hesitate to bemoan the souring conditions of their world. Ashbel Green's sermon on May 9, 1798, a fast day appointed by President Adams, was a typical public statement. Green, the most active clerical trustee on the Princeton board during this period, energetically drove home his text from 2 Chronicles 15:2 ("the Lord is with you while ye be with him"). Green did not equivocate: "The nation that

---

[31] *Life of Green*, 272; for numbers of New York dead, see Samuel Miller, *A Sermon, Delivered February 5, 1799 . . . as a Day of Thanksgiving, Humiliation, and Prayer on account of the removal of a Malignant and Mortal Disease* (New York, 1799), 36.

[32] For the general offense at this book, see Gary B. Nash, "The American Clergy and the French Revolution," *WMQ* 22 (1965): 402–3; and James H. Smylie, "Clerical Perspectives on Deism: Paine's *The Age of Reason* in Virginia," *Eighteenth-Century Studies* 6 (1972–1973): 203–20.

adheres to the laws of God shall be protected and prospered by him, but the nation that forsakes and disregards those laws he will destroy." God will protect a "*characteristically pious* nation, but not one that is *characteristically* impious." Christianity lies behind "those civil institutions and those excellent social dispositions and habits which have rendered our country the envy of the world." But now impiety threatens the ruin of this great nation, "so intimately is religion and morality connected by a *natural bond*, or rather by the *divine constitution*, with the safety and prosperity of nations." Without mentioning him by name, Green praised President Adams, commending "in a Christian nation . . . the rulers" who "recommend Christianity by their practice and example" and who pass laws to suppress vice. Tom Paine, on the other hand, had introduced disaster. Again without mentioning names, Green showed how ridicule of the Trinity inspired the general "infidelity" and "profaneness" of the day. God was apparently using France, "the most powerful, the most active, and the most insidious nation on earth," to chasten "this guilty age—this age of *infidel reason*."[33]

A note survives from a parishioner, John Eby, who wrote Green to express his deep gratitude. "At a time like this, discourses so well adapted—glowing with patriotism, as well as pure religion, cannot fail of doing much good, and must be peculiarly grateful to all those who have the spirits of men—who love their country, or who venerate the Supreme Being."[34] Eby spoke for himself, but he could well have been a mouthpiece for the Princeton board, since its members shared fully Green's beliefs in the connection between personal virtue and public weal. Also in 1798, for example, the Presbyterian General Assembly, with at least nine Princeton trustees concurring, sent a report to its churches concerning the "scenes of devastation and bloodshed, unexampled in the history of modern nations" and of "that bursting storm, which threatens to sweep before it the religious principles, institutions, and morals of our people."[35]

[33] Green, *Obedience to the Laws of God, the sure and indispensable Defence of Nations* (Philadelphia, 1798), 7, 17, 33, 44, 17, 48.

[34] Eby to Green, May 10, 1798, Gratz Collection, HSP.

[35] *Minutes of the General Assembly*, 152–53. For similar fearful assessments of the times in the late 1790s, see Alexander MacWhorter, *The Blessedness of the Liberal: A Sermon Preached . . . before the New-York Missionary Society* (New York, 1796), 22; Samuel Miller, *A Discourse, Delivered April 12, 1797 . . . before the New-York Society for Promoting the Manumission of Slaves* (New York, 1797), 7; and Miller, *Sermon on Removal of a Disease*, 16–26. Samuel Miller and Ashbel Green even selected the same text (2 Timothy 3:1, "in the last days perilous times shall come") for exposition in this

While Ashbel Green and other ministers were busy venting their distress in sermons, Elias Boudinot, Princeton's foremost lay trustee, who served as director of the mint until 1805, was taking steps of his own to counter the danger. As early as 1795 Boudinot completed a massive refutation of Paine's *Age of Reason*, entitled *The Age of Revelation; or, The Age of Reason shewn to be an Age of Infidelity*. It was a behemoth of a book, setting forth a long series of arguments to defend the Virgin Birth, "The Divine Mission of Jesus Christ," the resurrection, and the authenticity of the Bible. Its urgency depended upon Boudinot's assessments of the times, which suffered under "the melancholy prevalence of a spirit of infidelity," and also on his analysis of the future, where many prophetic signs pointed to the rapidly nearing "second coming of Christ."[36] Boudinot's alarm grew as he observed events at home and abroad in the last years of the century. The activity of the Democratic-Republicans, the opposition to the Jay Treaty, and the rise of Napoleon, who seemed ready to check the power of the pope (to Boudinot, the Antichrist), were all "signs of the Times."[37] When Jefferson, Burr, and the Democratic-Republicans triumphed over Adams and the Federalists in 1800, Boudinot was resigned and philosophical. "Nothing short of fatal experience, will open the Eyes of the deluded Multitudes" to the evils of the "Jacobins." Boudinot resolved to "submit entirely to [God's] will." At the same time, he determined to do his duty, which, in that bleak hour, meant supporting Jefferson (whose "principles are bad") over the Princeton alumnus Aaron Burr (whose principles are "ten times worse") in the deadlocked electoral college.[38] Aided by a trust in Providence and his ability to grasp the prophetic meaning of current events, Boudinot kept his head. But that the world in which he had taken so many important responsibilities,

period: Miller, *A Sermon, Delivered May 9, 1798, Recommended . . . as a day of general Humiliation, Fasting, and Prayer* (New York, 1798); Green, *A Pastoral Letter from a Minister in the Country* (Philadelphia, 1799), 8.

[36] Elias Boudinot, *The Age of Revelation; or, The Age of Reason shewn to be an Age of Infidelity* (Philadelphia, 1801), xvii, for date of composition; quotations, iv, 34.

[37] See Boudinot to Samuel Bayard, Oct. 17, 1795, Wallace Papers, HSP; Boudinot to Bayard, Apr. 22, 1797, Stimson Boudinot Collection, PUL; Boudinot to Elisha Boudinot, Jan. 6, 1798, Stimson Boudinot Collection, PUL. For other apocalyptic speculations at the time, see Samuel Miller, *A Sermon, Delivered before the New-York Missionary Society . . . April 6th, 1802* (New York, 1802), especially 46–47; John B. Romeyn, *Two Sermons* (Albany, 1808), 12–28; and Charles Henry Wharton to Elias Boudinot, Aug. 1, 1809, Stimson Boudinot Collection, PUL.

[38] Boudinot to Elisha Boudinot, Jan. 7, 1801, Thorne Boudinot Collection, PUL.

including oversight of the College of New Jersey, was decaying rapidly, there could be no doubt.

SEVERAL EXPLANATIONS are possible to interpret the rapid swing in Princeton perceptions of the world. The simplest is that they were rationalizing the loss of political power. Since the Princeton circle lay almost entirely within the Federalist orbit, it is not surprising that its members reacted with alarm.[39] They were social conservatives, classical republicans, whose political leaders were tasting defeat. As disappointed Federalists, the Princetonians were not interested in fine distinctions among Jeffersonianism, unrestrained democracy, the ravages of the French Revolution, and brazen impiety. Richard Stockton, Jr., for one, regularly called all of his opponents "jacobins." In the election of 1798, William Paterson was the leader of the New Jersey Federalists who saw their opponents, in the words of a Federalist newspaper, as the vanguard of "French impiety, and all the horrors of French despotism, rapacity and violence."[40] By 1798 "French impiety" had become a byword for the irreligion and disorder that an unregulated pursuit of freedom and an unrestrained employment of reason brought about. The earlier hope that France's Revolution might follow the beneficent course of America's was no more.

The even more fervent hope that American politics, rooted in the luminous experiences of the Revolution, might avoid the internecine strife of Europe also dissolved when unseemly partisanship followed in the wake of Washington's retirement. Scorn for the party spirit that seemed to be engulfing the new nation animated especially laymen on the board, like William Paterson, who became known as the "avenger of Federalism" for his active prosecution of Democrats under the Alien and Sedition Laws. He regularly looked upon opponents of the Adams administration, like Congressman Matthew Lyon, whom he sentenced to four months in prison and a one-thousand-dollar fine, as little more than traitors. Once he proclaimed that "the love of country is full of benignity, benevolence, and peace, whereas the [love?] of party is intolerant

[39] Moreover, most Princetonians were the "Old Federalists," described in David Hackett Fischer, *The Revolution of American Conservatism: The Federalist Party in the Era of Jeffersonian Democracy* (New York, 1965).

[40] Alfred Hoyt Bill, *A House Called Morven: Its Role in American History, 1701–1954* (Princeton, 1954), 77; J. R. Pole, "Jeffersonian Democracy and the Federalist Dilemma in New Jersey, 1798–1812," *Proceedings of the New Jersey Historical Society* 74 (1956): 282.

and delights in blood. In France we have seen it rage like an infuriate monster."[41] Some of the trustees slowly accommodated themselves to the necessity for political parties, but as late as 1812, a minister, Joseph Clark, was calling his community to repentance for "the unhallowed, destructive passions" of political infighting and "the rage of party spirit."[42] What else could such Old Federalists do, when the world was passing them by, but bewail their fate?

The sudden swing in attitudes toward the world also raises questions about the tone of Princeton discourse. The rhapsodies of the late 1780s and early 1790s were turned overnight into perfervid jeremiads. Prophetic speculation veered from exaltation to gloom. Extreme gave way to extreme. Princetonians, with other Americans of their religious views and social station, were susceptible to heights of millennial expectation and depths of apocalyptic gloom. Their view both of history and of society predisposed them to extreme opinions on current events. The times, with a full share of violence in the name of principle, exacerbated the tension. Perhaps the forces without and the insecurities within were simply too great.[43]

This psychological analysis, like the political explanation, has much to recommend it. Both, however, may be subsumed under a more general interpretation that calls attention to the complicated effect on the Princeton circle of what are now styled ideologies.[44]

[41] On Paterson, see *Princetonians 1748–1768*, 439; and Michael Kraus, "William Paterson," in *The Justices of the United States Supreme Court 1789–1969: Their Lives and Major Opinions*, ed. Leon Friedman and Fred L. Israel, 4 vols. (New York, 1969), 1:171. The quotation is from an undated Fourth of July address, ca. 1800, William Paterson Papers, Manuscript Division, Library of Congress.

[42] Joseph Clark, *A Sermon Delivered in the City of New-Brunswick* (New Brunswick, 1812), 16.

[43] The tensions are well traced in Gordon S. Wood, "Conspiracy and the Paranoid Style: Causality and Deceit in the Eighteenth Century," *WMQ* 39 (1982): 401–3; Ruth Bloch, *Visionary Republic: Millennial Themes in American Thought, 1756–1800* (New York, 1985), chap. 9, "Francophobic Reaction and Evangelical Activism"; Peter Charles Hoffer, *Revolution and Regeneration: Life Cycle and the Historical Vision of the Generation of 1776* (Athens, Ga., 1983), chap. 3, "History as Process vs. History as Order: Generativity, 1789–1815"; and John R. Howe, Jr., "Republican Thought and the Political Violence of the 1790s," *American Quarterly* 19 (1967): 147–65.

[44] It may cost more than it is worth to use the debated term "ideology" instead of an ordinary phrase such as "assumptions concerning the workings of the world." Yet some definitions of ideology are helpful, if taken not as universal reifications but as approximate general descriptions of the way beliefs function to shape perceptions and inspire actions. Such useful definitions include Clifford Geertz's no-

For members of the Princeton circle, four such ideologies—overlapping, reinforcing, occasionally contradicting—may be identified.

The first was *classical republicanism*, narrowly defined. This set of convictions and perceptions—described so ably by Bernard Bailyn, Gordon Wood, and other recent interpreters—centered on a fundamental distrust of unchecked power.[45] The grasp of an arbitrary monarch, the machinations of a venal parliament, the overweening aspirations of a state church, the wanton enthusiasms of a democratic mob—all threatened social stability and heralded the decline of civilization. Unchecked power, these "real Whigs" argued, nourished corruption, which in turn fed the maw of unrestrained power. Let authority get out of hand, and the hard-won trophies of English liberty, every vestige of natural right—not to speak of the rule of law itself—stood in mortal jeopardy. The Revolution had both proven the validity of this social analysis and impressed it deeply upon the consciousness of the new country's guiding elite, including the Princeton circle.

The second ideology was more narrowly intellectual. It involved the beliefs described by Henry May as *the Didactic Enlightenment*.[46] Following the lead of eighteenth-century Scottish moralists, leaders at Princeton came to regard scientific methods as privileged avenues to truth. With their Scottish mentors, Princetonians embraced the vision of rational, perceptible order that also inspired Newton and Locke, and they opposed vigorously the disillusioning or revolutionary ends to which European skeptics and radicals carried the Enlightenment. As advocates of the better sort of Enlightenment, the Princeton circle possessed the certainty that they could discover the ends and means of social relationships. From the same source they derived the confidence that a carefully

---

tion of ideology as "a cultural system" (*The Interpretation of Cultures* [New York, 1973], 193–233, especially 213 n. 30), or George M. Frederickson's definition of ideology as "the set of principles, programs, and goals that reflect the way a social group applies its values and attitudes to the problems it faces at a particular time" (quoted in Nathan O. Hatch, *The Sacred Cause of Liberty: Republican Thought and the Millennium in Revolutionary New England* [New Haven, 1977], 9n).

45 Bernard Bailyn, *The Ideological Origins of the American Revolution* (Cambridge, Mass., 1967); Gordon S. Wood, *The Creation of the American Republic, 1776–1787* (Chapel Hill, N.C., 1969).

46 Henry F. May, *The Enlightenment in America* (New York, 1976), 307–57 on the "Didactic Enlightenment," 3–101 on the "Moderate Enlightenment" of Newton and Locke.

crafted education could mold the rising generation to secure the common good.

The third ideology was less influential at Princeton, but nonetheless a factor, namely, the strand of *liberal republicanism* that played a complementary role to classical Whig thought through the time of the Revolution and that emerged as a more dominant, if also more partisan, influence at the end of the century.[47] This worldview is usually associated with Jefferson and other opponents of the Federalists, but some of its elements were also found at Princeton. The bond in Stanhope Smith's thought between confidence in science and optimism about the future shared at least something with a similar bond in Jefferson. The belief in the expanding economic potential of America that most of the Princeton leaders espoused also partook of this spirit. The turn after 1800 by some of the Princetonians to a more individualistic conception of religious conversion was also related to a liberal picture of social atomism. While liberal republicanism never had the direct influence among Princetonians that classical Whig thought and the Didactic Enlightenment exerted, it nonetheless was present to some degree.

The fourth and perhaps most powerful ideology for the Princeton circle was *the Christian faith*.[48] With New England Congregationalists and a few other Americans, the Princeton Presbyterians had come to understand their own story as a continuation of the biblical narrative. Almost all members of the Princeton circle were attached sincerely to the spiritual, transnational aspects of Christianity. Almost all believed as well that the history of the church in the New World carried a special providential significance. God had

[47] See especially Joyce Appleby, *Capitalism and a New Social Order: The Republican Vision of the 1790s* (New York, 1984); and Appleby, ed., "Republicanism in the History and Historiography of the United States," *American Quarterly* 37 (special issue, fall 1985): 461–598.

[48] Despite the great amount of literature on Christian groups and activities in the early history of the United States, I am not aware of significant works devoted to interpreting the inner dynamics of Christian thought for the period after Edwards and before the Second Great Awakening. The early sections of Perry Miller, "The Evangelical Basis," in *The Life of the Mind in America from the Revolution to the Civil War* (New York, 1965); Theodore Dwight Bozeman, *Protestants in an Age of Science: The Baconian Ideal and Antebellum American Religious Thought* (Chapel Hill, N.C., 1977); E. Brooks Holifield, *The Gentlemen Theologians: American Theology in Southern Culture, 1795–1860* (Durham, N.C., 1978); Fred J. Hood, *Reformed America: The Middle and Southern States, 1783–1837* (University, Ala., 1980); and Donald Mathews, *Religion in the Old South* (Chicago, 1977), come closest to providing such treatment.

not only caused the light of the gospel to shine in America. He had also manifested special mercies in nurturing pure religion, creating Christian institutions, and shaping culture in accord with gospel principles.

The Christianity of the Princeton circle paralleled classical republicanism in its depiction of a cosmic struggle between good (righteousness/liberty) and evil (sin/tyranny). It shared with the Didactic Enlightenment a confidence in the Author of Nature and the reliability of God-given reason. It also stood with liberal republicanism in defending the dignity of individuals and the potential for their development. Yet Princeton Christianity was always much more than a gloss on other ideologies. As Christians, Princetonians believed in the fundamental truthfulness of the Bible. They held without wavering to the conviction that the law of God established moral standards for both individuals and society. And they firmly believed that the Christian faith offered a word of hope—a message of salvation—for putting men, women, and their institutions right with God and with the world he had made. The religion of Princeton was no freer from cultural coloration than religion in other times and places. Yet throughout the era of Samuel Stanhope Smith, to a degree difficult to imagine in our more secular times, it was an all-encompassing window to the world and a driving engine of action very much on its own terms.

Each of these ideologies exerted considerable influence in the Princeton circle during this period. Extremes of rhetoric resulted when several value systems coincided to anticipate either impending utopia or accelerating doom. Political and social events were the occasions that triggered Princeton judgments, but the nature of those judgments depended upon the ideologies through which perceptions were filtered. These ideologies, in turn, are the key to understanding both continuities and discontinuities in how Princetonians viewed the world.

EVENTS LATE in the 1790s called forth a very different analysis of current events from members of the Princeton circle than had prevailed short years before. One conviction, however, grew stronger—the belief that the social well-being of a republic depended upon the virtue of its citizenry. If anything was changing in this regard, it was the heightened attention payed to religion as the key to sustaining virtue. The utilitarian calculus found in both Ashbel Green's fast sermon of 1798 and Stanhope Smith's discourses published in 1799 testified to this increased attention. This same concern drove Elias Boudinot to combat Tom Paine, for Boudinot held that, if the youth of America really took to heart the message of *The Age of Reason*, they would become "enemies to the religion of the Gospel" and so introduce "the dissolution of government and the bonds of civil society."[49] Christianity was the only effective remedy against the depravity that, as Samuel Miller put it, "is the source of all disorder and misery."[50]

The increasing stress on religion as the prime guarantor of public virtue had important implications for thoughts about education. Trustees of Princeton College never wavered in affirming the value of learning, but they did modify their judgments. Events were pushing the college's leaders toward the affirmation, not just that education itself could prepare a citizenry for its republican duties, but that education, to fulfill its lofty purposes, must function within the reassuring boundaries of religion. This refinement of earlier views, which had tended to see education per se as a boon to the republic, exerted a far-ranging impact on the story of Princeton in the new century.

William Paterson, a layman, and Samuel Miller, a minister, made the strongest assertions at the turn of the century about the evils that higher learning might encourage if it was not guided by sound religious principles. "Schools and seminaries of learning," said Paterson in a Fourth of July address, were very important "for supporting good government, promoting the interests of virtue and religion, and the causes of genuine and rational freedom." Nonetheless, ignorance was not the worst enemy to "genuine republicanism." Rather, it was knowledge put to evil uses, which had turned Europe inside out and was now threatening America. "For behold the demon of false philosophy, vain and proud, and covered with the spoils and blood of the fairest portion of Europe, hither bends his course."[51] Samuel Miller said much the same on several occasions during the same period. The fast proclaimed by President Adams in May 1798 became the occasion for a full state-

---

[49] Boudinot, *Age of Revelation*, xxiii. Boudinot held that the process would work in reverse if Christians spread the message of Christianity as contained in the Bible; see his *Address of the New-Jersey Bible Society to the Publick* (New Brunswick, 1810), 6: "If the knowledge of revealed truth tends to elevate the minds of men; to rescue them from depression and debasement . . . , then, what friend to his country, what lover of humankind, can hesitate, for a moment, to encourage the widest possible spread of the holy scriptures?"

[50] Miller, *Sermon before New-York Missionary Society*, 51.

[51] Paterson, undated address, ca. 1800.

ment of the theme. Miller valued eduation highly but not without qualification. Science is a great gift to "illuminate the mind," but "unless regulated and directed by holy principles," it would feed "the pride of presumptuous reason, and the deceitfulness of a vain philosophy," and in general promote "those *doctrines of devils*, which are calculated only to corrupt and destroy."[52]

The awareness that some higher learning was but the "doctrines of devils," that learning must be carefully checked by religion to ensure its social utility, represented a momentous realization in the Princeton circle. John Witherspoon had proclaimed an ideal of intellectual neutrality, learning open to all and leading, with the employment of proper method, to truth supporting religion and undergirding the commonwealth. Although Witherspoon had never squared this proposition neatly with his evangelical Calvinism and its insistence upon the supremacy of Christian wisdom, he nonetheless had made a forceful case for the autonomy of scientific procedures. Stanhope Smith was only following this lead when he attempted to demonstrate from nature alone that all humanity was descended from a common source. The Princeton trustees as a body testified to their belief in this same proposition by their arduous efforts at promoting instruction in natural philosophy and by their manifold testimonies to the values of education for a republic. Until nearly 1800 trustees seemed barely to entertain the thought that such efforts could subvert true religion and "genuine republicanism" as well as support them. By 1800, however, some of them had grown concerned about that very possibility.

This changing perception of the place of learning introduced a wedge that separated the Princeton leaders who remained content with Witherspoon's conception of an autonomous science from those leaders who began to promote specifically religious means for restraining learning and preserving the nation's virtue. Much else was involved in the turn of Presbyterians to revival and voluntary societies in the nineteenth century, but the growing belief among individuals like Miller and Paterson that education by itself did not necessarily lead to virtue was part of the story.[53] Even as

[52] Miller, *Sermon, May 9, 1798*, 18. Miller returned to this theme repeatedly, e.g., *Sermon on Removal of a Disease*, 13–14; *Sermon before New-York Missionary Society*, 51; *A Brief Retrospect of the Eighteenth Century*, 2 vols. (New York, 1803), 2:442.

[53] On increased Presbyterian interest in revivals, see especially Martha Tomhave Blauvelt, "Society, Religion, and Revivalism: The Second Great Awakening in New Jersey, 1780–1830" (revision of Ph.D. diss., Princeton University, 1974); and Lois

they maintained their solicitous care for the College of New Jersey, some members of the Princeton circle began in the 1790s to devote more attention to Christian voluntary agencies—to promote missionary work at home and abroad, to free the slaves, and to achieve other goals as well.[54] Promoters of these enterprises harbored no ill will toward the College of New Jersey. Yet a straw was in the wind. Suspicion of education that was unrestrained by religion would soon channel energies away from traditional institutions toward new Christian agencies as superior means to promote religion and preserve society. When that day arrived, the consequences for a college under the guidance of an enlightened student of John Witherspoon would be considerable.

Altered circumstances in the wider world led to more immediate problems as well. Simply put, the few Democratic-Republicans on the Princeton board who did not regard events in the late eighteenth century as calamities were bound to differ with those who did.[55] A subtler but more powerful tension was also bound to arise within the Federalist majority. In this group those, like Stanhope Smith, who continued to believe that reason, science, and natural philosophy deserved a privileged status, were destined to clash with those who saw a greater need to protect higher education from the error at loose in society.

The strain from this tension did not appear immediately. Yet an important issue was coming to the fore: how much did the military convulsions in Europe, the partisan debates over American foreign policy, the political infighting at home, altered social circumstances, and the perception of declining public virtue disturb the delicately balanced synthesis of Christian, Enlightenment, and republican convictions inherited from Witherspoon? Differing an-

---

W. Banner, "Presbyterians and Voluntarism in the Early Republic," *Journal of Presbyterian History* 50 (1972): 187–205.

[54] For example, MacWhorter, *Blessedness of the Liberal* (1796); Miller, *Discourse for the Manumission of Slaves* (1797); and Miller, *Sermon before New-York Missionary Society* (1802).

[55] The most prominent Democratic-Republican trustee, Gov. Joseph Bloomfield, gradually reduced his interest in Princeton after the political controversies of the late eighteenth century. Bloomfield attended 93 percent of the board meetings and was active in 87 percent for the period 1795–1801; for 1802–1806, attendance declined to 80 percent and activity to 60 percent; for 1807–1812, attendance declined further to 68 percent and activity to 11 percent. ("Activity" here means that a trustee performed at least one significant task on behalf of the board at any one sitting.)

swers to this question defined the history of Princeton in the early nineteenth century.

FOR HIS PART, Stanhope Smith shared the disgruntlement of his colleagues at the dismal state of the world in the 1790s. Even before Witherspoon's death, he expressed alarm at the prospect of "democratic frenzy" raised by the activities of Citizen Genet. Nor was he reluctant to chastise those who saw no need for a strong navy during the perilous days of 1794, when England and France both seemed intent on gobbling up American ships.[56] Yet as late as his fast and thanksgiving sermons of 1795, Smith could still offer a general benediction to the country and its progress.

Smith's attitude began to change toward the end of the decade, especially because of the rise of the Democratic-Republicans. When in 1799 Jedidiah Morse sent a copy of his thanksgiving sermon to Smith, the sermon in which Morse detailed the pernicious activities of the Bavarian Illuminati as the cause of America's woe, he found a receptive ear. Smith responded by asking Morse whether the Congregationalists and Presbyterians could not "discern the signs of the times, & . . . awaken to some zealous & combined effort to withstand the torrent of infidelity & immorality that is overspreading our country?" To other New England correspondents after the beginning of Jefferson's administration, Smith complained about "the present imbecile, and double dealing administration" that was throwing everything "into the vortex of popular passion and folly" and thereby destroying the nation through "false hood and *low cunning.*"[57] Jefferson's first year as president only confirmed Smith's worst fears. The Democratic-Republicans had introduced "the principle of national imbecillity & disorganization," which left the country defenseless against France and Britain. Smith apologized to New Jersey's Senator Jonathan Dayton, to whom he communicated these thoughts in December 1801, "for entering so far into political speculation." But he could not forbear wondering about the ability of "the *patricians* yet . . . to

[56] Smith to John Beatty, Dec. 23 and 24, 1793; Mar. 6, 1794, all Presbyterian Historical Society, Philadelphia.

[57] Smith to Morse, Feb. 24, 1799, Samuel Stanhope Smith Collection, PUL. Smith to Timothy Pickering, ca. 1801; and Smith to Pickering, after 1801, quoted from Pickering Manuscripts, Massachusetts Historical Society, in Shipton, *Biographical Sketches of Harvard Classes 1768–1771*, 235, 236. The best study of the Illuminati scare remains Vernon Stauffer, *New England and the Bavarian Illuminati* (New York, 1918).

save the republic, when the *tribunes* shall have urged it to the brink of ruin."[58]

Smith, in short, was as troubled by the march of current events as his colleagues on the Princeton board. Together they made sure that the college's stance would not be in doubt. No longer, for example, were honorary degrees distributed across the political spectrum. The college bestowed six LL.D.'s from 1795 through 1801, all to active Federalist leaders (like Hamilton's successor as secretary of the treasury, Oliver Wolcott) or distinguished anti-Jeffersonians (like Timothy Pickering of Massachusetts). In a rare entry into the political fray, Smith even went as far as to serve as a presidential elector for John Adams in 1801.[59] More characteristically he remained on the political sidelines but at the same time left no doubt about his serious disapproval of Jeffersonian triumphs.

Despite the crisis in public virtue, however, Smith's expectations for education did not change. Unlike William Paterson and Samuel Miller, he did not seem concerned about the effects of infidelity on philosophy. As he would throughout his life, Smith still represented learning as an unsullied means for promoting religion and public good.[60] The only qualification he offered, in his *Essay* of 1787 as well as in the textbooks published after the turn of the century, was the provision that learning be guided by proper methods and that it shun hypothetical speculation, while cleaving to the inductive ordering of experience. The thought that philosophy itself could be perverted to ignoble ends never appears in his letters or his books.

Smith's attitude toward the heretics of his day suggests the cast of his thinking. With most of the other Princeton leaders, Smith abominated philosophical impieties, like the materialism of Priestley or the many deranged ideas belched out of revolutionary France, almost as much as he scorned political radicalism, especially as embodied in the philosophy of Jefferson. So firm was Smith's belief in the mutually supporting affinities of sound learning, Christian piety, republican virtue, and elegant style, however, that he often assumed that an infelicitous *form* of argument refuted its *substance*. That is, bad men could not speak well, since a pleasing discourse belonged by its nature to the side of virtue and

[58] Smith to Dayton, Dec. 22, 1801, Samuel Stanhope Smith Collection, PUL.

[59] *General Catalogue*, 403–5; on Smith as elector, see Monk, "Samuel Stanhope Smith," 87; and Maclean, *CNJ*, 2:138.

[60] See Smith to Rush, May 13 and Dec. 5, 1796, both Library Company of Philadelphia, HSP.

piety. So Smith in 1796 calmed Ashbel Green's fears about Joseph Priestley's arrival in America with the assurance that the latter's errors would not have much impact, since Priestley "is neither a good orator, nor a very brilliant writer."[61] When Smith reviewed Jefferson's first annual message to Congress in 1801, he concluded that the new president would never succeed in gaining the influence of the virtuous Washington or Adams, in part because his political convictions were so degenerate, but also in part because his prose was so labored. "When he attempts nothing more than a plain & simple style as in his correspondence with the french & british ministers, he seems capable of writing with perspicuity & propriety: but when he aims at a superior strain of eloquence, he becomes both puerile & laboured."[62] In sum, Smith's confidence in the virtue of learning was all but unbounded, his respect for the morality of the intellect unalloyed.

Although this steady confidence in the deliverances of reason as such eventually alienated Smith from some Princeton trustees, it was nonetheless a position shared by others. Elias Boudinot, for example, agreed with Samuel Miller that the End of the Age was fast approaching and with William Paterson that the Democratic-Republicans were a grave menace, yet he also stood more or less with Stanhope Smith in believing that learning and piety enjoyed a natural harmony. Thus, to silence Paine, it was enough to adduce "sufficient evidence," "rational inquiry," and "the revelation of God in the natural world . . . arising from experience." In short, "the rules of *common sense*" would destroy Paine's contentions utterly.[63] Differences on these matters among the Princeton trustees were subtle. Was properly grounded learning always good and always an opponent of evil and error, as Smith and to a large extent Boudinot held? Or was it possible that learning itself could become a tool of infidelity and disorder if it were not restrained by religion, as Paterson and Miller had come to think? This difference of perspective was never spelled out, and yet it constituted one of the fundamental issues that came to divide the loyalties of the Princeton circle.

ALTHOUGH TRUSTEES and the faculty succeeded in preserving

---

[61] Smith to Green, Mar. 20, 1796, Samuel Stanhope Smith Collection, PUL. He said much the same thing about Condorcet the next year (Smith to Green, no day or month, 1797, ibid.).

[62] Smith to Dayton, Dec. 22, 1801.

[63] Boudinot, *Age of Revelation*, vi, ix, 30.

Princeton College as a haven in an increasingly disorderly world, aftershocks from disturbances in the nation occasionally made themselves felt on the campus before the end of the century. Trustees, for example, were greatly distressed when the faculty reported in April 1799 that dueling had made its appearance on campus. The board confirmed the expulsion of the chief culprit, expressed its shock at this "gross and monstrous violation of the Laws both of God and man," and recorded its being "deeply affected with the information . . . whereby it appears that these false and wicked principles in regard to personal honor which are the foundation of the practice of duelling are obtaining in the college." Trustees dispatched Elias Boudinot to reprimand three other students involved in the affair, but they then permitted the malefactors to continue at the college.[64]

Other disquieting events soon followed. In February 1800 three seniors were suspended for disrupting morning chapel, where, in the general student opinion, the room was too cold and the prayers too long. Many of the scholars felt the punishment was overly harsh and expressed their displeasure by creating a disturbance in Nassau Hall. The unrest lasted for several days and came to an end only when President Smith appealed personally for calm. But then two weeks later, one of the suspended students returned, as Smith told the trustees, "and violently assaulted one of the tutors." This incident in turn precipitated a new round of disorder.[65]

A similar standoff occurred in early 1802. On the first day of the new year, the faculty suspended five students for various acts of drunkenness, disorder, and mischief during "the Christmas holydays." The next day a committee of six students (including two future members of the American Philosophical Society) presented a petition urging the faculty to reconsider its actions concerning four of the suspended students. When the professors returned this memorial as "disrespectful & improper," the student committee returned with a new petition explicitly rejecting "Jacobinism" and "Jacobinical methods." But this statement too the faculty found unacceptable. Upon receiving that word, some students again rioted. More ominously, "a combination was entered into by them not to perform any of the exercises of the College until the persons suspended should be admitted." But the professors stood fast, and soon they received yet a third document renouncing the strike,

[64] TM, Apr. 11, 1799.
[65] Ibid., Apr. 9, 1800; Wertenbaker, *Princeton*, 137.

commending the faculty's "general prudence & mildness in administering the Laws," promising obedience to college regulations, and respectfully renewing the request to review the suspensions. Stanhope Smith and his colleagues were now satisfied, they did reconsider the suspensions, and life returned to something like normal.[66] Yet Princeton authorities could not have been reassured by these signs of contagion from the wider world.

Still, they could be pleased with the general temper and demeanor of their charges. When occasion demanded, students showed that they were internalizing the values of their elders. News of French duplicity in the XYZ affair reached the campus in 1798, and students immediately sent an address to President Adams offering themselves for combat against the enemy. They had rejoiced to see the French throw off the yoke of tyranny but now were saddened at that nation's reckless grasp for empire. Similar expressions of republican zeal appeared regularly in declamations before the student societies and in student compositions. Nicholas Biddle, class of 1801 and future president of the Bank of the United States, was a typical example. Paine and Jefferson, he wrote when a student, were "paving the way for scenes similar to those that have been acted in France." Like the older members of the Princeton circle, he too feared for his nation: "The fires of discord rage with dreadful fury, and unless extinguished by the wisdom of citizens may involve our country in one general conflagration."[67] Students, it seemed, were learning their lessons.

WITHIN A SIX-MONTH period at the turn of the century, members of the Princeton circle were provided extraordinary occasions for summing up their perceptions of the world. When George Washington died on December 14, 1799, the country as a whole responded with an outpouring of sermons, discourses, and memorials, hundreds of which were eventually published.[68] Six trustees of the Stanhope Smith era, including the president himself,

[66] FM, Dec. 31, 1801; Jan. 1, 2, and 9, 1802. In a letter of Jan. 25, 1802, Benjamin Rush congratulated his son, James, for steering clear of "the late insurrection" (L. H. Butterfield, ed., *Letters of Benjamin Rush*, 2 vols. [Princeton, 1951], 2:842).

[67] Wertenbaker, *Princeton*, 208–9; Thomas P. Govan, "Nicholas Biddle at Princeton, 1799–1801," *PULC* 9 (1948): 56, 57.

[68] On these memorials in general, see Robert P. Hay, "George Washington: American Moses," *American Quarterly* 21 (1969): 780–91; and James H. Smylie, "The President as Republican Prophet and King: Clerical Reflections on the Death of Washington," *Journal of Church and State* 18 (1976): 233–52.

spoke and then published orations to mark the great man's passing. These addresses presented a common picture of the nation and its destiny. To the members of the Princeton circle, Washington had been God's special agent to guide the nation through the perilous days of its birth. Washington was honorable, noble, and patriotic. He embodied morality, he respected the ways of God, and he was indeed "an uniform professor of the christian religion." Since Washington had honored God, God had honored him. Through the leading of Providence he became Moses guiding his people to a promised land, even as he was also "the Cincinnatus of his age" for scorning self-aggrandizement.[69] Washington ever avoided the sectarian factionalism that was now tearing the country asunder. He therefore deserved the glory that is the highest honor of republics to bestow upon their citizens.[70] How could Americans benefit from the passing of this national institution? They should recognize that "the calamities that we experience now" are God's judgment for sinfully forsaking the honorable course that Washington had pioneered.[71] Yet, although current affairs presented a bleak aspect, hope remained. Stanhope Smith described the path to such hope in the conclusion of his address to the assembled officers of the state of New Jersey at the capitol in Trenton: "Divine Providence which prepares these great souls who are the defenders and saviours of the nations, will continue the succession of them, while those nations continue to respect religion and virtue."[72]

Less than six months after Washington's death, Stanhope Smith, as the retiring moderator, was called upon to preach the opening sermon of the Presbyterian General Assembly. This address, given in Philadelphia on May 15, 1800, was another virtuoso performance. The text, Jude 3 ("earnestly contend for the faith which was once delivered unto the saints"), spoke to the need for battle in that historical moment. "A deluge of infidelity in the old world"

---

[69] Alexander MacWhorter, *A Funeral Sermon . . . for the universally lamented, General Washington* (Newark, N.J., 1800), 3n, 9–10, 13. Whatever Washington's actual religion (probably no more than a cool respect for the Author of Nature, as explained in Paul F. Boller, *George Washington and Religion* [Dallas, 1963]), Christian republicans had to make him an ardent believer because of the central role they assigned to religious faith in shaping the virtue without which republics floundered.

[70] Stanhope Smith, *An Oration upon the Death of George Washington* (Trenton, 1800), 40.

[71] Ira Condict, *A Funeral Discourse . . . for paying solemn honor to the memory of Gen. George Washington* (New Brunswick, 1800), 19.

[72] Smith, *Oration upon the Death of Washington*, 43–44.

now rolled "its fearful tide to the new," imperiling "religion and governments themselves." With this assessment the commissioners to the General Assembly, as well as the leaders of the Princeton circle, concurred. Not quite as apodictic was the solution that Smith offered, though most of the broader Presbyterian constituency probably still agreed. "God has connected the knowledge of truth," Smith affirmed, "with the practice of duty, and the duties with the happiness of human nature." This connection meant that, if people could be trained to be good, they would grow up to benefit church and society. But if training were neglected, they would foment disorder in every sphere of life. The need of the hour, then, was for "a virtuous and pious education, conducted with prudence, and persevered in with steady and constant wisdom." Especially the training of ministers in the arts and sciences would counteract the poisons of infidelity. Despite the doubts of a few of Smith's colleagues, for him sound learning still led unerringly to religious and social health. "True piety" was the most vital thing for a minister, but next, and "and not much less important," was "sound science, and general literature, that he may be able to . . . acquire that ascendency over the minds of men, which acknowledged virtue, a luminous eloquence, and extensive information alone can give."[73] To Smith the crisis in public affairs was an occasion to draw together more tightly true religion, civic virtue, and the beneficial science of the Enlightenment. In 1800 other Princeton leaders, though equally the heirs of Witherspoon and of Witherspoon's convictions, nonetheless were beginning to suspect the nature of that alliance. As yet, however, no alternative existed to Smith's vision, so thoroughly had the triumphs of Witherspoon defined the course of the Princeton circle.

AS THE COLLEGE of New Jersey entered the new century, its officers could be pleased at its position in the nation, the church, and the society. Their ranks were still joined; the march to enlightened Christian faith and virtuous republican citizenship was steady. Stanhope Smith did not possess Witherspoon's rough-and-ready charisma, but he had nonetheless emerged as an important leader. One of Smith's students provided a retrospective portrait of this man who led Princeton into the nineteenth century.

[73] Smith, "The Connexion of Principle with Practice; or, The Duty of Maintaining Sound and Evangelic Principles in the Church," appended to *A Comprehensive View of the Leading and Most Important Principles of Natural and Revealed Religion* (New Brunswick, 1815), 534, 519, 522, 523, 536.

When we first saw him he was perhaps six feet high & well proportioned & perfectly erect: his countenance was beautiful, his forehead lofty: his dark eye beaming with intellectual fire & his voice more powerful & melodious than any other pulpit orator we ever heard. . . . His lectures on philosophy which we studied in the senior class were characterized by great research, conclusive reasoning, & great originality of thought—advanced with all the graces of polished style. . . . As presiding officer of the College he was surpassed by none of his predecessors.[74]

Perhaps not all the trustees agreed with this student, but most would have concurred that, when on January 14, 1800, Smith arose to declaim his memorial sermon for Washington in the New Jersey state house before the governor, military and civilian leaders, the Order of the Cincinnati, and "an immense assembly with countenances sad," he "was then in the meridian of his intellectual power."[75] Infidelity may have become a "deluge," but Princeton, under the sure hand of its leader, kept steadily to its course.

Even at that pregnant moment, however, contrary forces were stirring. The very day before Smith memorialized Washington, another key member of the Princeton circle was putting ideas on paper that amounted to an implied criticism of Smith and his leadership at the college. Ashbel Green of Philadelphia's Second Presbyterian Church was no less devoted to the program of Witherspoon than was Smith and no less committed to the harmony of learning and faith. Yet he also was coming to share with Samuel Miller and William Paterson a growing conviction that education per se could be dangerous if it were not securely rooted in religion. Moreover, this figure of considerable talent and unlimited organizational energy was looking more and more to voluntary organization, instead of inherited colonial institutions, as the preferred means for promoting true religion and republican social order.

And so on January 13, 1800, Green wrote a long letter to the Reverend E. D. Griffin in Newark that contained the earliest hints of what would become a growing effort by ministers in the Princeton circle to strike out in new directions for the promotion of religion and social order. Specifically, Green raised the idea of a theological seminary independent of the College of New Jersey, a proposal with far-ranging implications for questions of learning, faith, and social well-being. Green had evidently spoken with Grif-

---

[74] Untitled and undated reminiscence by a member of the class of 1806, John Maclean Papers, PUA, 7, 9.
[75] Ibid., 12.

fin and Samuel Miller about the need for a new institution of higher learning that could be preserved from "the fate of those that have gone before it." Green asked Griffin to keep quiet about these plans for the moment, yet urged him to see what "a few individuals" might think about "a plan to educate men for the ministry in an institution by themselves."[76]

Green's still-amorphous ideas of January 1800 amounted to the first serious questioning within the Princeton circle of Smith and what he could accomplish through an intellectualist approach to the education of Christian republicans. In 1800 these thoughts were no more significant than a cloud the size of a man's hand. But when the thunder that disturbed the wider world finally resounded over Princeton during the first decade of the nineteenth century, the deluge from without would quickly be matched by storms within. Together they placed in jeopardy the vessel that John Witherspoon had guided, with universal approval, into the uncharted seas of the new republic.

[76] Green to Griffin, Jan. 13, 1800, Gratz Collection, HSP. The discovery of this letter makes it possible to correct my earlier misstatement that Green's first thoughts on a separate seminary were written down in Mar. 1805 (Mark A. Noll, "The Founding of Princeton Seminary," *Westminster Theological Journal* 42 [1979]: 76).

9

Fire and Rebuilding, 1802–1806

An Asylum in This Day of Lamentable Depravity

★

PRINCETON DID NOT have to wait long to experience the disorders of the age. Less than two years after Stanhope Smith explained to the General Assembly how sound education promoted religion and public virtue, the very future of the College of New Jersey was placed in jeopardy. A great fire that devastated the campus in 1802 signaled the eruption of irreligion and public disorder at the college. With heroic effort the college recovered from this disaster and in the process boldly reaffirmed its reasons for existence. Yet the experience left the community shaken. To rebuild Nassau Hall was a difficult task. To restore equilibrium to Princeton's sense of its mission proved even more difficult.

IN EARLY March 1802 the United States Congress, with its new Jeffersonian majority, completed its repeal of the Federalist Judiciary Act that had been passed the previous year. The action materially reduced the power that the original measure had bestowed upon John Adams's Federalist appointees to the bench and directly affected the daily responsibilities of a Princeton trustee, Associate Justice of the Supreme Court William Paterson. At about the same time, another son of the college, Aaron Burr, Jefferson's vice president, was approaching Federalists with proposals for his own political advantage. To Princetonians, such events illustrated the derangement of the times.[1]

The disorder so manifest in the political sphere arrived in

---

[1] A good overview of the period is found in Dumas Malone, *Jefferson the President: First Term, 1801–1805* (Boston, 1970), 121–24.

Princeton at one o'clock in the afternoon of March 6, 1802. As the
bell called students for dinner in the refectory, fire appeared at
several places on the roof of Nassau Hall. Despite valiant efforts to
extinguish the blaze, it could not be halted. The building was gutted, and its contents destroyed. All but one hundred of the college's three thousand books, the extensive libraries of the two student societies, and most of the students' personal possessions were
lost. President Smith's immediate reaction, as recorded by an undergraduate, was to bemoan the conflagration as "the progress of
vice and irreligion."[2]

Four days later, even before the trustees could gather for an
emergency session, Smith wrote Jedidiah Morse to inform Boston
of the disaster. "Direct proof" was lacking, but still it seemed certain that the fire was "communicated by design." Smith was just as
certain that the fire was "one effect of those irreligious & demor-
alizing principles which are tearing the bands of society asunder
& threatening in the end to overturn our country." Yet the forces
of disorder and infidelity had not triumphed beyond recall, for
"the college of Princeton," Smith told Morse, "will be immediately rebuilt, probably in a better state than it was, & its discipline
rendered still more strenuous & exact, to meet the spirit of the
times." Already subscriptions were being opened in Philadelphia
and New York, and Smith hoped Morse would spread the news to
his friends in Boston who might be prepared to contribute as the
opportunity afforded. "Friends of religion & of old principles"
were rallying to the aid of the college, "the last bulwark of old principles to the South of your state."[3] Beleaguered the college was, but
it would rise again.

The themes that Smith enunciated to Morse were the themes
that Princeton's other leaders sounded as well. When the board
met on March 16, it too concluded that "the edifice of the College
was *intentionally set on fire*." Relying, however, on "the smiles of
Heaven" and "the benevolence of its numerous friends and the
friends of virtue and learning," it resolved to rebuild as rapidly as
possible. The trustees instructed Smith to prevent seven suspected
troublemakers from returning to the college and asked a committee to prepare a stricter code of student regulations. The board
made extensive plans to solicit funds, and it prepared a special re-

[2] Wertenbaker, *Princeton*, 126.

[3] Smith to Morse, Mar. 10, 1802, Samuel Stanhope Smith Collection, PUL. Wertenbaker, *Princeton*, 127–28, concludes that the fire started because of improperly
cleaned chimneys.

quest for support from the Presbyterian General Assembly in order "to render the College of New Jersey an asylum for the soundest principles of religion in an age in which . . . the hosts of impiety are directing against them their whole force."[4] An address to the public dated March 18, 1802, appealed to "the Friends of Religion," "the Friends of Science," "the Friends of Civil Liberty," "the Alumni of the College," and "the Wealthy and Benevolent of Every Description" to repair the damage left by this fire that "was the effect of design." The College of New Jersey had been founded "to cherish the principles, and extend the influence of evangelical piety" and thereby also to serve "the interests of civil society." The sum required to rebuild was large, at least forty thousand dollars, but the aims of the institution were worthy of such an expense. The trustees were determined "to make this institution an asylum for pious youth, so that in this day of general and lamentable depravity, parents may send their children to it with every reasonable expectation to safety and advantage."[5]

The decision to begin the summer semester in early May, as scheduled, testified to the resolution of the trustees. Students would have to board in the town and meet for classes in public inns until Nassau Hall was restored, but the college would not give in to the evil forces that conspired for its undoing. When the students assembled on May 6, the board asked Ashbel Green to address them on its behalf. Green's firm words reflected the general mood of the trustees. The board was so determined to maintain order that it was "ready to dismiss the whole college rather than to suffer the least infringement or contempt of its authority." Green also presented a revised version of the laws that set out in great detail what the college expected of the students. At the end of his address, Green also introduced a new ceremony in which students were asked if they had read the laws and if they could "solemnly pledge your truth and honor to obey them." If students would honor their oaths, Princeton still could fulfill the goals of its founders, despite the corruption in the wider world. The college existed to promote "science in union with evangelical piety" and to demonstrate "the importance of this union to society." With such a goal, and with its record of success in the past, Green was confident that Princeton could still be a place where parents might send their

[4] TM, Mar. 16–19, 1802.

[5] *Address of the Trustees of the College of New-Jersey, to the Inhabitants of the United States* (Philadelphia, 1802), 3n, 1, 4.

sons "with a reasonable expectation that their religious principles will be guarded, their morals carefully inspected, the habits of order, industry and due submission to superiors formed and established, while science shall enlighten their minds and exertion invigorate their faculties."[6]

And so they set about rebuilding. The task involved great labors in raising funds. Even more important, it involved recommitment to the founding vision that all still took to be the vision of John Witherspoon. Further occasions of disorder could only indicate that the vision was not being implemented, that someone was letting down the side.

Immediately after the fire the friends of Princeton began to contribute to its restoration. At their special meeting in late March, the board commissioned several of its own members to seek funds through what the agents called "begging tours"—Alexander MacWhorter in New England, Joseph Clark in South Carolina, and Stanhope Smith toward Washington, D.C.[7] Even before the school reconvened in early May, the results were encouraging. The village of Princeton and its environs contributed nearly $8,000 in cash and materials within two weeks of the fire. Without even a formal solicitation, sixty-five people connected with Harvard College sent word that they had subscribed $4,274.72. Even though Smith called himself "the worst beggar in the world," he yet reaped a bountiful harvest in Baltimore and Washington. In Washington, Smith secured a pledge of $500 from the wayward alumnus Aaron Burr and of $100 from Thomas Jefferson, a sum that seemed to disappoint Smith, who yet opined that such a meager gift "perhaps . . . is excusable on the score of the great number of applications made to him."[8]

---

[6] TM, May 5, 1802; Green, *An Address to the Students and Faculty of the College of New-Jersey, Delivered May 6th 1802—the day on which the students commenced their Studies, after the burning of the College Edifice* (Trenton, 1802), 4, 15, 9, 5. Green's words echoed those of a college founder, William Tennent, who professed himself ready to burn down Nassau Hall rather than let it slip from its Presbyterian moorings (Wertenbaker, *Princeton*, 87).

[7] TM, Mar. 18, 1802.

[8] Smith to Benjamin Rush, Mar. 20, 1802, Samuel Stanhope Smith Collection, PUL; Smith to Boudinot, Apr. 15, 1802, Presbyterian Historical Society. Burr had still not paid up when Smith wrote a gentle reminder about his pledge on Jan. 2, 1804 (Samuel Stanhope Smith Collection, PUL). A recent graduate, Edward Thomas, informed wrongly that Jefferson had pledged only fifty dollars, vented the sort of opinion that his Princeton connections reinforced: "Was aid solicited by an institution where infidelity and disaffection ruled, he would, no doubt, have felt

Smith was back in Princeton for the opening of the summer semester on May 6, but the board in late September asked him to make an even longer tour through the South during the winter of 1802–1803. Other board members received similar commissions, but even by that date it was obvious that the fire had been a disguised blessing. The college enjoyed more sympathy with the public than the board realized, students were returning in healthy numbers, and the restoration of Nassau Hall was proceeding rapidly. At the same September meeting the board also asked Ashbel Green to step in as interim president for the winter semester during Smith's absence. Though a routine measure at the time, this move was fraught with implications for the future, since it gave Green an opportunity to observe the effects of Smith's instruction firsthand and also to implement reforms that Green felt would better serve the mission of the school.[9]

Fund-raising, however successful, was arduous business. In June 1802, the sixty-seven-year-old MacWhorter wrote a discouraged letter from Boston complaining that the New Englanders were more willing to donate books than cash. MacWhorter was "quite tired of my business" and had concluded, "Begging is a work of mortification." Joseph Clark reported from near Fort Royal, Virginia, in February 1803 that, while money was coming in, the strain was beginning to tell: "I am weary, really I am weary & ardently desire once more to be at rest with my family & people."[10] The dangers could rise beyond tedium and fatigue. Judge John Bryan of Virginia, who volunteered to help Joseph Clark raise money in that state, contracted "a violent bilious colic" in December 1802 that proved fatal. In that same month Smith lost six hundred dollars in a robbery.[11]

For all the sacrifice, the reward was very great. Elias Boudinot, as usual, questioned the practical competence of the clergy, fearing that the incoming funds would be mismanaged—but they were not. By November 1802 Alexander MacWhorter, now safely re-

---

pleasure in granting assistance" (Thomas to Nicholas Biddle, June 9, 1802, in Thomas P. Govan, "Nicholas Biddle at Princeton, 1799–1801," *PULC* 9 [1948]: 61). Unlike Burr, Jefferson paid his pledge.

[9] TM, Sept. 30, 1802; see FM, Nov. 23, 1802 through May 12, 1803, for Green's reforms.

[10] MacWhorter to Green, June 9, 1802, North Carolina Manuscripts, HSP; Clark to Green, Feb. 19, 1803, Moore Collection, PUL.

[11] W. Frank Craven, "Joseph Clark and the Rebuilding of Nassau Hall," *PULC* 41 (1979): 58, 63; and Wertenbaker, *Princeton*, 129–30.

turned to Newark, could effusively thank contributors in Boston and report that "Divine providence has smiled upon us amazingly in our calamity."[12] Something more than forty-two thousand dollars was eventually raised—a sum roughly four times the college's annual budget in the early part of the century.[13] With these gifts Nassau Hall was fully restored, and enough money was left over to build an observatory for John Maclean and two new buildings, to the north and south of Nassau Hall.[14]

The only serious hurdle impeding the drive for funds was the attitude of some Jeffersonians. Joseph Clark reported on more than one occasion that the college's reputation as a Federalist bastion made it difficult to secure contributions in Virginia.[15] From Maryland the Reverend William Mackay Tennent reported much success "among the federal Gentlemen," but slow going elsewhere. Still, even the political standoff was not complete. Tennent was pleased that "there are also some very good Democrats whose prejudices I have endeavored to remove & in some instances have been successful—From one of them I received $50."[16] The reputation of Stanhope Smith and his colleagues as "friends of order" went before, but public sympathy for Princeton still ran deep.

THE FUND-RAISING efforts were not merely successful on their own terms. They also sparked increased confidence by parents, with the result that enrollment boomed. While the number of students dropped slightly immediately after the fire, there was soon an impressive recovery, so much so that the college graduated thirty-nine students in 1804, the most ever in its history. The next year that number rose to forty-two, and in 1806 to a breathtaking

[12] Boudinot to Elisha Boudinot, July 13, 1802, Thorne Boudinot Collection, PUL; MacWhorter to Jedidiah Morse, Nov. 8, 1802, Gratz Collection, HSP.

[13] TM, Apr. 4, 1804, mention the $42,000 figure; Maclean, *CNJ*, 2:52, listed the total as $44,317.86. Maclean's state-by-state breakdown of gifts reflects something of Princeton's national reputation. The most money came in from New Jersey ($9,697), but Pennsylvania yielded over $6,000, Maryland over $4,000, and Massachusetts, New York, and Virginia over $3,000 each. By comparison, most of the outside funds secured for Yale College under President Timothy Dwight (1795–1817) came from Connecticut (Brooks Mather Kelley, *Yale: A History* [New Haven, 1974], 127).

[14] Wertenbaker, *Princeton*, 130–32. The building to the south of Nassau Hall still stood in 1987 as Stanhope Hall.

[15] Clark to Ashbel Green, Feb. 19, 1803; and Craven, "Clark and Rebuilding of Nassau Hall," 63.

[16] Tennent to Ashbel Green, May 23, 1803, Moore Collection, PUL.

fifty-four, representing all but one of the seventeen states in the Union. The number of young men on campus soared from around one hundred before the fire to nearly two hundred by 1806.[17]

In addition, income from student fees and gifts enabled the board to make an unprecedented expansion of the faculty. Already in September 1802 a professor of languages was added to assist tutors with freshmen and sophomores. In 1803 the board appointed a professor of theology, an action with far-ranging consequences that will require detailed attention. And in 1804 the board named one of its own members, the Reverend Andrew Hunter, a relative by marriage of Elias Boudinot and Richard Stockton, to serve as professor of mathematics and astronomy.[18]

The augmented faculty joined the trustees in reaffirming the traditional stance toward learning and its public utility. At the board's request, Stanhope Smith wrote a general circular to the public in 1804, announcing "the perfect restoration of the College Edifice lately destroyed by fire, with many improvements in its structure" as well as "several new buildings, which have greatly increased the advantages for study." The circular thanked God and the "public-spirited individuals" who had made it possible and then stressed the commitment of the college to instruct its students in "the Principles of the Christian Religion." He also emphasized the special provisions for would-be ministers—the new professor of theology, the availability of scholarships, reduced fees for room and board, and opportunties for personal instruction from the president. "The Friends of Religion and Learning" could rejoice in the restoration. They would certainly agree with the board that "just sentiments of the nature, as well as a full conviction of the truth of religion," were "the surest basis of public morals"; and they could rest assured that the benevolence of the public "will stimulate [the trustees'] exertions to render [the college] still more useful to their country, and to the church."[19]

[17] Other colleges were also growing rapidly at the start of the nineteenth century, due in part to the better economic conditions that prevailed until Jefferson's embargo of 1807. Yale, which had averaged about thirty-seven graduates a year under President Ezra Stiles (1777–1795), saw that figure rise to over fifty in the period 1795–1817 under President Dwight (Kelley, *Yale*, 128, 138). On graduates from the College of New Jersey, see *General Catalogue*; and for attendance early in the nineteenth century, Lowell H. Harrison, "A Young Kentuckian at Princeton, 1806–1810: Joseph Cabell Breckinridge," *Filson Club History Quarterly* 38 (1964): 291.

[18] TM, Sept. 30, 1802; Dec. 8, 1803; Apr. 5, 1804.

[19] Smith, *College of New Jersey* (n.p., [1804]), 1, 2, 3, 6.

For their part, the trustees seemed fully to support efforts by the faculty to improve the quality of instruction, especially in science. At its September 1805 gathering the trustees witnessed a dramatic confluence of the commitments undergirding the institution. On their own initiative President Smith and other faculty had purchased "a very valuable Cabinet of Natural History" in New York. This treasure, a collection of biological and animal specimens likened to Charles Willson Peale's famous museum in Philadelphia, had cost $3,000, a sum that Smith now asked to be reimbursed. Whereupon Elias Boudinot "rose in his place" and offered to donate one thousand acres of New York land to the corporation if the board would accept the president's terms.[20] It was the first and last time in eighteen years of recording the board minutes that Professor Maclean described the physical action of a trustee. Witherspoon's dream of "the Union of piety and science" seemed several steps closer to reality.

As if in response to heroic efforts by the Princeton circle, even the wider world seemed to be improving. Despite fears at the election of Jefferson and Burr in 1800 and despite continued grumbling about the sad course of events in the world, Princeton was adjusting to new realities. Elias Boudinot, now clearly the dominant laymen on the board, waxed hot and cold as he studied the signs of the times. Reports of religious revivals were encouraging in the summer of 1802, when he also felt that Napoleon's restoration of religious freedom in France might be the biblical "resurrection of the Witnesses" and thus a sign presaging the End. Eighteen months later he was nervous again about the possibility of France's invading Great Britain, and before too long he was also worried about Aaron Burr's rumored designs against the Union.[21] But Boudinot's vacillation on the meaning of public affairs was the equivalent of optimism from a more sanguine individual. Several of the board's ministers in fact looked upon the rising tide of revivals across the country as a very good sign. Ashbel Green was so encourged by reports of missionary activity sponsored by the Presbyterians and other bodies that he could tell the General Assembly in 1804 that, despite widespread "inattention to the ordinances of

[20] TM, Sept. 26, 1805. Boudinot's land was in Broome County, New York, an area not settled to any significant degree until 1848; newspaper account of the lands in *Endicott Daily Bulletin* (N.Y.), ca. Oct. or Nov. 1950, filed with Elias Boudinot Collection, PUL.

[21] Boudinot to Elisha Boudinot, July 13, 1802; Dec. 27, 1803; Jan. 9, 1807; all Thorne Boudinot Collection, PUL.

religion" in some regions, revival fires were blazing in many places—the Ohio Territory, the South, and the Presbyterian Synods of New York, New Jersey, and Albany.[22]

At the college it even seemed possible that the political antagonisms of the recent past might be overcome. To be sure, some southern Democrats still took offense at Smith's instructions in political science. As one such student from Virginia put it in September 1804, the president was "directly hostile to republican principles" and "stigmatizes" their supporters as "jacobins and anarchists . . . demagogues and disorganizers."[23] Yet other Jeffersonians reported that the college was a tolerant place where they could get along easily.[24] When Joseph Cabell Breckinridge, the son of Jefferson's attorney general, arrived as a student in December 1805, after visiting Jefferson in Washington, he reported no hostility to the political position of his family. His only difficulties were adjusting to new patterns of instruction and loose habits of student spending.[25] After the turn of the century the board even broadened its gift of honorary degrees. Most of the laymen so honored were staunch Federalists, like John Marshall (1802). But the board also unbent far enough in 1803 to bestow an LL.D. on its own alumnus, Aaron Burr, and in 1806 gave the same degree to John Quincy Adams, still nominally a Federalist but already moving toward an alliance with the Democratic-Republicans.[26]

In sum, political relaxation on the Princeton board was another sign of the institution's stability. The effects of the fire had been overcome, and then some. The college had never enjoyed more students or a larger faculty. The outpouring of gifts had at last brought relief from the financial struggles dating back to the Revolution. Princeton's commitment to the promulgation of religion and science in harmony, and to the appplication of that harmonious learning for the good of society, seemed to be as strong as ever. Well might Stanhope Smith exult to David Ramsay in September 1805 as he described with pride Princeton's new cabinet of natural

[22] Green, *Glad Tidings; or, An Account of the State of Religion, within the bounds of the General Assembly of the Presbyterian Church in the United States of America; and in other parts of the world* (Philadelphia, 1804), 3.

[23] William Garnett to Thomas Ruffin, Sept. 24, 1804, in *The Papers of Thomas Ruffin*, ed. J. G. de Roulhac, vol. 1 (Raleigh, N.C., 1918), 56.

[24] David Allen to John Breckinridge, Jan. 9, 1802, in Harrison, "Young Kentuckian at Princeton," 288–89.

[25] Ibid., 289–97.

[26] *General Catalogue*, 404–7.

history. The newly strengthened faculty was making "every exertion of which our finances will admit, for the advancement of every branch of science, & of Natural Science particularly."[27] The commitment to science, combined with the commitment to religious instruction, provided a stable intellectual base to match the spectacular physical reconstruction. But once again, as before in the history of the College of New Jersey, surface appearances did not necessarily reflect the underlying reality.

THE SIMPLE truth was that, though the college was enjoying a remarkable physical recovery, the effects of the fire had also exacerbated hidden tensions. One problem, strain on faculty resources, resulted simply from success at attracting so many students to the restored Nassau Hall. But other developments raised profounder doubts, at least in the minds of several influential trustees. These doubts concerned specifically the declining number of graduates entering the ministry and the way Stanhope Smith was synthesizing faith and reason. A combination of problems, all intensifying during the early years of the nineteenth century, set the stage for the manifest crisis that followed the rebellion of 1807.

Princeton's most obvious difficulty after the fire was an overworked faculty. Even with new professorships, the work expected from each teacher was becoming oppressive. In April 1804 Smith prepared an account of faculty activities in which he described the instruction of the 153 students in attendance the previous semester. Smith himself taught the senior and junior classes in eleven different subjects, ranging from belles lettres and composition to metaphysics and the laws of nature and nations. For his courses in moral philosophy and "Revealed Religion," Smith also provided written lectures. He spent from ten to fourteen hours each week hearing the upper classes recite. In addition, he superintended evening prayers and the student orations that followed, he chaired the numerous meetings of the faculty, he directed the Monday evening meetings of the theological society, he ate in the refectory in rotation with the other professors, he was chief disciplinary officer, and he received and answered a minimum of six hundred

[27] Smith to Ramsay, Sept. 29, 1805, Samuel Stanhope Smith Collection, PUL. Augustus John Foster, who served in Washington, D.C., as the British secretary of legation from 1804 through 1808, visited Princeton in 1805 and left a lengthy report of the restored facility; an extract was published by William H. Gaines, "The Aftermath of Rebellion; or, Princeton in 1807 [actually 1805, as shown by internal evidence]," *PULC* 19 (1957): 47–50.

letters each year on college business. In his report, Smith did not mention that he had also played a major role in overseeing the restoration of Nassau Hall.[28]

Until the addition of a new professor lightened his load, John Maclean's duties were almost as arduous. Maclean taught nine different subjects in science and mathematics to juniors and seniors. During the winter of 1803–1804, he directed up to twenty-one recitations per week, each lasting one to two hours, and offered several public experiments, each requiring one to three hours' preparation, besides taking his regular turn in the refectory.

The professor of languages, William Thompson, came to Princeton from Dickinson College in 1802 as the first additional teacher to handle the rising number of students. With the aid of the tutors, he was to instruct the two lower classes in Latin and Greek and to preserve order in the college. In 1804 Thompson was hearing student recitations for six hours a day and remaining in Nassau Hall for purposes of discipline five nights a week until nine o'clock. Unfortunately for the rest of the faculty, Thompson was elderly and infirm and did not have good rapport with the students. When the trustees in October 1807 sent a committee to talk with Thompson about the necessity of vacating his position, they found that he had been ill and reduced to part-time instruction for some time. According to one source, Thompson had earlier suffered some kind of mental collapse, "his mind giving way under the pressure of his arduous duties."[29] Whatever the exact nature of Thompson's infirmities, they only increased the demands upon the other professors.

The only faculty member not overwhelmed with work in 1804 was the new professor of theology, Henry Kollock, who as yet had only four pupils in his elective Hebrew class and whose only other duties were preaching and catechizing on Sundays and three recitations a week to "the Theological class" of perspective ministers.

Faculty overwork and the overcrowding of facilities—even with two new buildings—kept the level of tension relatively high on the Princeton campus. The fire had made trustees even more concerned about the potential for disorder among the students, and so they nervously issued a series of new guidelines—toughening

[28] TM, Apr. 5, 1804; see Maclean, *CNJ*, 2:57–59, for full quotation of this report.
[29] Smith to Ashbel Green, Mar. 23, 1803, Samuel Stanhope Smith Collection, PUL, on Thompson's weakness as disciplinarian; TM, Oct. 1, 1807; quotation from John Frelinghuysen Hageman, *History of Princeton and Its Institutions*, 2 vols. (Philadelphia, 1879), 2:270.

the oath students were to swear to obey campus regulations, specifying "Dice, Cards and Backgammon" as "unlawful games," requiring students who broke furniture to reimburse double the cost, authorizing faculty to defend college property with force, admonishing faculty to enforce attendance at morning prayers, and more.[30] Students on the whole, however, behaved fairly well, even if the faculty was faced with a regular series of disciplinary problems. In 1804 Smith reported that the tutors were spending as much as one day a week "hearing the excuses of such students as have at any time been absent from church or from prayers" and that "their weightiest and most irksome duty is preserving order and decorum in the College building."[31] Occasionally things boiled over, as when a few students, accustomed to celebrating holidays more exuberantly than was the custom at Princeton, blew up the outhouse at 2:00 A.M. on Christmas morning, 1804—"with a terrible explosion," as a North Carolinian noted with glee. Yet swift action by the professors quieted that situation, and within a week, one of the two students suspended in the affair had been readmitted after apologizing and pledging his good behavior.[32]

The greatest difficulty, however, was not student riotousness—though there was perhaps a growing propensity for such behavior. Nor was it even strain on the faculty. The most serious matter brought on by the unprecedented enrollment and by faculty overwork was rather a problem of perception. College authorities were conditioned to understand public disorder as a simple function of private immorality. To this conditioning, principles of Christianity, republicanism, and the Enlightenment all made a contribution. Public disorder was sinful. It was the outgrowth of vicious or tyrannical lust for power. Its whys and wherefores, its roots and fruits, could be understood by moral philosophers who examined social relationships with the precision of Newton in his mechanics. The shock of the fire led Princeton authorities to see their own campus as an arena in which the great moral conflicts of the day were being fought. Student overenrollment and faculty overwork increased the potential for student disorder. But student obstreperousness, as the Princeton circle regarded it, was a function of the

---

[30] TM, Mar. 19, 1802; Dec. 9, 1803; Sept. 27, 1804; Sept. 24, 1805; Apr. 3 and Sept. 24, 1806.

[31] Ibid., Apr. 5, 1804; also in Maclean, *CNJ*, 2:59.

[32] James Iredell to "My dear Friend," Jan. 7, 1805, James Iredell Papers, PUA; FM, Dec. 25 and 26, 1804; Jan. 3, 1805.

age's great crises and not of less complicated physical or psychological distress.

When the apprehensions of the authorities were joined to the stresses on the campus, the result was to transform physical and social problems into moral and religious crises. Student unrest was no longer a simple issue in itself but a symptom of moral failure. Especially in light of other suspicions concerning Stanhope Smith, student disorder could be viewed as a failure of instruction—both, that is, as a failure to discipline the students properly and as a failure of the curriculum. Since disorder flowed from morally deficient character and since education shaped character, the presence of disorder cast in doubt the moral quality of the education.

The story hidden by successful rebuilding after the fire was this tale of moral expectations. The fire frightened the trustees. When crowded conditions on the renovated campus increased disorder, the worst fears of the board were fulfilled. Even if the college was relatively calm, the press of new students concealed dangers that some trustees began to associate with other troubling developments.

ONE SUCH development was Princeton's declining contribution of ministers to the Presbyterian church, or for that matter to any denomination. This problem was rooted in the Revolutionary period but attracted attention only after the turn of the century. It was important because of Princeton's attachment to both religion and the moral economy of republicanism. A steady supply of well-trained ministers was needed to promote Christianity, but also to ensure the well-being of the new country. As republicans, the Princeton authorities understood that the virtue of a people determined its social health. As Christians, they were placing increased emphasis on the religious foundations of virtue. And as participants in the Enlightenment, they perceived clearly the processes whereby proper education inculcated virtue and a properly virtuous people guaranteed good order in the nation. Concern about the shortage of ministers, in brief, involved the same ideologies by which student behavior was interpreted. Neither could remain an isolated matter.

The force of this problem came from the simple facts of geography and population. Presbyterians had promoted missions in "the West" before the Revolution, and they monitored closely the seismic changes taking place in the new nation. The population was not only expanding with unprecedented speed, but it was flowing away from the constraints of the settled East at an alarming rate. The number of people in the United States was doubling every twenty years (from approximately 3.9 million in 1790 to 7.2 million in 1810). Where the population of settled New Jersey grew from about 180,000 to 250,000 in the twenty years after 1790, Tennessee's leaped from 40,000 to 260,000, Ohio's from scattered settlements to 270,000, and Kentucky's from 70,000 to 410,000.[33] While Presbyterians could rejoice at the triumphs of the gospel in the West following the outbreak of revival in 1801, they were still troubled by the hundreds of thousands of settlers who remained untouched by Christian influence. They were also beginning to be uneasy about the fact that Methodist and Baptist preachers, men overly prone to frontier enthusiasm, were responsible for most of the Christian work that occurred.

Princeton trustees were among the leaders of their denomination in promoting the recruitment of ministers. Members of the Princeton circle preached mission sermons, like Samuel Miller's address to the New York Missionary Society on April 6, 1802, in which he recommended "the signs of the times" as a spur to evangelistic endeavor.[34] They undertook preaching tours like John Woodhull's two-week itineration in 1806 from the Jersey shore to Philadelphia, where he found attentive audiences, but also a strip twenty to twenty-five miles wide and eighty miles long with "no settled presbyterian minister besides myself, and very few of any other denomination."[35] And they took every chance to inform their denomination about the need to increase the ministerial supply.

Ashbel Green made the most impassioned appeal of this sort in a stirring speech before the General Assembly on May 27, 1805. "It is a melancholy fact," he reported, that the denomination's interests as well as "the Redeemer's kingdom" suffered "for the want of a greater number of able and faithful ministers of the gospel. . . . 'Give us ministers' is the cry of the missionary regions;— 'Give us ministers,' is the importunate entreaty of our numerous

[33] *Historical Statistics of the United States, Colonial Times to 1957* (Washington, D.C., 1960), 7, 13.

[34] Miller, *A Sermon, Delivered before the New-York Missionary Society* (New York, 1802), 47, with list of awakened areas, 46n.

[35] "The report of John Woodhull to the Presbytery of New Brunswick, who was appointed last summer by said Presbytery as a Missionary for two weeks among the destitute parts of Monmouth County," Manuscripts, Speer Library, Princeton Theological Seminary.

and increasing vacancies—'Give us ministers,' is the demand of many large and important congregations in our most populous cities and towns." The need, moreover, was not just for bodies to fill the ranks but for men of sound learning, since "the possession of vigorous and improved intellect is, in most cases, indispensable to the acceptance, the influence, and the success of [the church's] public teachers." Green's plan to remedy the situation was still evolving, but he did have a suggestion. Presbyteries should select "youths of capacity as well as of piety . . . to be conducted by the Presbyteries through the whole of their academical course and theological studies; and at such schools, and under such teachers, as each Presbytery may choose to employ or recommend."[36]

Statistics collected by the General Assembly were never entirely reliable, but still they indicated the reason leaders like Green were so exercised. Nine college trustees were commissioners to the 1794 General Assembly, where the statistical report showed 167 Presbyterian ministers with churches and 126 vacant preaching stations. In 1802, seven trustees heard that there were now more vacant Presbyterian pulpits (242) than filled ones (181). Within a few years Samuel Miller could speak of "near four hundred vacant congregations within our bounds."[37] No one doubted that the need for ministers was acute.

Given this situation, Presbyterian leaders naturally looked to the College of New Jersey to meet the need. But in the day of battle Princeton blew a feeble trumpet. The number of ministers produced by the college was in fact falling off steeply. In part the decline represented a national trend: republican ideology had captured some of the minds that before the 1770s devoted themselves to Christian theology; westward expansion may have drained away potential ministers; and the general decline of interest in religion during the 1780s and 1790s certainly had a negative effect on efforts to recruit ministers. At Princeton, moreover, Witherspoon's leadership in public affairs and Stanhope Smith's concentration on science and belles lettres seems to have heightened the general trend. Where nearly half (47 percent) of Princeton's graduates under its presidents before Witherspoon entered the ministry, and where an even slightly higher percentage became clergymen in Witherspoon's early years (48 percent from 1769 to 1775), the

[36] *Minutes of the General Assembly of the Presbyterian Church in the United States of America from . . . 1789 to . . . 1820,* (Philadelphia, 1847), 341.

[37] Ibid., 78, 93 (1794), 181, 242 (1802); Miller's comments in ibid., 457 (1810).

Revolutionary period witnessed a rapid decline of interest in the sacred profession. The porportion fell to 21 percent during the war (1776–1783) and to 13 percent for both Witherspoon's last decade (1784–1794) and Smith's tenure before the fire (1795–1802). In the four classes from 1803 to 1806, even with the presence of a new theology professor most of that time, the number of graduates entering the ministry dropped to 9 percent of the total.[38]

Modern historians can calculate the statistics of this situation more accurately than participants at the time, but it did not require comprehensive records to inform leading Princeton trustees that something was wrong. When in May 1802 Green addressed the students who assembled after the fire, he concluded that the many "corrupted" students who had been coming to Princeton "for some years past" may have "gradually, but yet greatly in the issue, warped it from its orginal design and designation." He also went out of his way to remind the undergraduates that "it would coincide precisely with the original design of the seminary, if many of you had in prospect the sacred office of the gospel ministry."[39] Soon Green would conclude that corruption not just in the ranks but at the head kept Princeton from fulfilling this part of its mandate.

The desire to recruit more ministers led to the ongoing discussion, primarily involving Green, about the possibility of erecting a seminary expressly for theological training. In the first years of the nineteenth century, however, that discussion was still amorphous and did not lead to concrete steps until after 1807. Before that time, however, the college itself put forth an effort to remedy the situation. Part of that effort involved more direct lobbying at the General Assembly to promote Princeton as a place of ministerial preparation. More concretely, it involved the establishment of a separate professorship in theology whose primary responsibility

---

[38] *Princetonians 1748–1768*, xxxi–xxxii, 670–72; *Princetonians 1769–1775*, xxvii–xxix, 546–47; *Princetonians 1776–1783*, xxx–xxxii, 463–64; *Princeton University: Catalogue of All Who Have Held Office in or Have Received Degrees from the College of New Jersey* (Princeton, 1896). In Smith's last decade, years of manifest clerical shortages, Princeton College graduated only thirty-nine students who became ministers, and not all of these were Presbyterians. The proportion of Yale students entering the ministry also declined in this period, but not as rapidly—from about one-third in the years 1745–1778 to about 18 percent from 1805 through 1815 (Kelley, *Yale*, 123).

[39] Green, *Address after the burning of the College*, 5, 11.

was to superintend the postgraduate training of candidates for the ministry.

The appointment of the theology professor seemed at first to be a simple task, but it turned out to be complicated and divisive. In fact, it may have been the event that precipitated a division of the board into "old" and "new" factions. It probably contributed to a polarization of goals and an antagonism between individuals that affected the school for twenty years. The personalities most directly involved were Stanhope Smith, Ashbel Green (the board's most influential clergyman), the very important layman Elias Boudinot, and the board's clerical old guard. The stature of these men, combined with the sensitive nature of the problem (meeting the crying need for ministers) and the timing of the appointment (hard on the heels of the fire and increased board nervousness), made this event more than usually significant.

Circumstances dictated the addition of a theology professor, but the board was divided on the best candidate for the position.[40] Stanhope Smith, Richard Stockton (the squire of Morven, who had assumed his father's role as a leading force in the village and on the college board), and a few others favored the appointment of Henry Kollock, who in 1803 was pastor of the Elizabethtown Presbyterian Church. Kollock, son of Shepherd Kollock of Elizabethtown, who published the *New Jersey Journal*, had graduated from Princeton in 1794 at the tender age of fifteen. In 1797 he returned to serve as tutor and prepare for the ministry. He remained for three years, during which time he won a reputation as an unusually gifted preacher. Kollock seems to have leaned toward the Jeffersonianism of his father, but this was the only blemish on an otherwise sparkling record. It is said that he was Stanhope Smith's favorite pupil.[41] He also enjoyed the respect of other senior ministers, especially in the Presbytery of New York, which included Elizabethtown. While some trustees who were approached about

[40] The following story, which does not appear to have been treated in any history of the college, is stitched together from a relatively full record of correspondence, especially the following sequence: Stanhope Smith to Ashbel Green, Mar. 23, 1803, Samuel Stanhope Smith Collection, PUL; Green to Jacob Janeway, Oct. 11, 1803, in *Life of Green*, 568–71; John Rodgers to Green, Oct. 27, 1803, Gratz Collection, HSP; Smith to Green, Nov. 26, 1803, Samuel Stanhope Smith Collection, PUL; Rodgers to Green, Nov. 28, 1803, Gratz Collection, HSP; Smith to Green, Dec. 5, 1803, Samuel Stanhope Smith Collection, PUL; Elias Boudinot to Elisha Boudinot, Dec. 27, 1803, Thorne Boudinot Collection, PUL; and Rodgers to Green, Feb. 15, 1804, Gratz Collection, HSP.

[41] Varnum Lansing Collins, *Princeton* (New York, 1914), 110n.

supporting Kollock for the position demurred on account of his youth and inexperience, Kollock's reputation was such that Smith, without direct authorization from the board, approached Kollock sometime in 1803 on his availability.[42]

Other trustees, however, favored a more mature and better established candidate. Ashbel Green, who had turned forty in the summer of 1802 and who had managed the college competently during Smith's absence in the winter of 1802–1803, was the obvious choice. Both the conduct of the students and their educational progress during Green's interim had been, as he told the board, "highly satisfactory."[43] Green, moreover, was an experienced pastor who also had made a mark as tutor and professor at the college some twenty years before. His administrative abilities had been proven time and again in service to the Presbyterian General Assembly and many other benevolent causes, including the College of New Jersey. Even at this early date, perhaps a few of the trustees also felt the need for a more active advocacy of Christianity at the college, especially from the chair of theology, as a counterweight to the intellectual program of Stanhope Smith.

In the event, the logic behind Green's appointment prevailed over that for Kollock, even though Green had repulsed the idea when it was suggested to him before the regular board meeting of September 1803. The trustees nevertheless voted unanimously on that occasion to create a professorship of theology, and they asked Green to fill the position. The board also requested a committee of distinguished members to treat with Green about coming to Princeton—Elias Boudinot, Richard Stockton, and John Rodgers of New York (senior minister on the board). Green thought he would reject the offer preemptorily, but when Alexander Mac-Whorter and William Mackay Tennent, two respected ministerial veterans, beseeched him at least to consider the appointment, Green took the matter under advisement.[44]

From this point the story becomes more confusing, but it is obvious that Green's appointment touched several sensitive areas involving factions on the board, relations between Green and Smith, and general attitudes toward the college. During the next few months, letters flew back and forth, but resolution did not come

[42] Reported in Rodgers to Green, Nov. 28, 1803. See also the warm recommendation of Kollock by Rodgers to Jedidiah Morse, June 8, 1801, Moore Collection, PUL.

[43] TM, Apr. 12, 1803.

[44] Ibid., Sept. 30, 1803; Green to Janeway, Oct. 11, 1803.

easily. Henry Kollock was hurt that he had not received the call he had been led to expect, and yet a group on the board—identified by John Rodgers as "Mr. Stockton and his friends"—still kept his name alive as an alternative should Green decline the post, as he seemed inclined to do. Rodgers and others appealed fervently to Green, urging him to accept and also assuring him that it was not necessary to respond quickly, since all agreed, including Stanhope Smith, that no further action would occur until the regular board meeting in the spring of 1804. Rodgers also took pains to reassure Green that Smith really did desire Green's service at the college.[45] For his part, Green remained opposed to the appointment, but not without second thoughts caused by the importunity of his clerical friends.

Several developments in late fall 1803 complicated an already knotty situation. When classes began in November, even more students had arrived; John Maclean was now responsible for most of the instruction for nearly one hundred juniors and seniors. Trustee Andrew Hunter, an experienced minister and educator who was then farming near Trenton, let it be known that he would like to change his present circumstances and be considered for a post at the college.[46] A Dutch Reformed Church in Albany approached Henry Kollock with a solid offer to serve as its minister. And Green continued to intimate that he would probably decline the proffered appointment. This combination of circumstances— especially the need for immediate assistance at the college— prompted Stanhope Smith and five other board members (the statutory minimum) to rethink earlier decisions about not making changes hastily and to call for a special board meeting on December 8. The call was specific—to divide Maclean's responsibilities and to name another professor to share his duties.

On December 5 Smith spelled out the reasons for the meeting in a letter to Green, who had apparently written in some heat to question its necessity. The ones who called the meeting, Smith reported, had been informed that Kollock was lost to the Dutch Reformed and that Green was resolved to decline the professorship. The crush of new students, however, made it necessary "to strengthen the Faculty as soon as possible, & before the bad weather of the Winter would render a meeting of the board too

[45] Rodgers to Green, Oct. 27, 1803.
[46] Reported in Smith to Green, Nov. 26 and Dec. 5, 1803. On Hunter, see *Princetonians 1769–1775*, 225–29.

inconvenient." Smith went on to tell Green that the purpose of the special meeting was to call Andrew Hunter as a professor, so that "by a division of Dr. Maclean's department, & by occasional assistance to me, a considerable portion of time might be redeemed by both for other necessary purposes of the institution."[47]

But then after the call for the meeting had gone out, an unexpected development intervened. The Reverend John Rodgers of New York was distressed upon learning of Kollock's call to the Dutch Reformed Church in Albany. Several times he had experienced what he took to be coldness and exclusivity in the Dutch denomination, and he was loath to see a rising star among the Presbyterians lost to that body. Rodgers, therefore, convinced the Presbytery of New York to delay its meeting that had been called to consider Kollock's request for dismissal to Albany. Since Green had responded lukewarmly at best to Rodgers's plea that he take the post at Princeton, Rodgers assumed that the position was still open. And so he wrote a letter that Smith received on December 3 to urge the board to appoint Kollock as professor of theology in order to keep him from being snatched away by the Dutch Reformed. The next February Rodgers told Green that he very much disliked the idea of special meetings and had nothing to do with calling the one for December 1803, even if "some peculiar circumstances" allowed him to be present. Smith, on the other hand, reported to Green on December 5, 1803, that Rodgers—once convinced that Green would not take the position and now having arranged Kollock's availability—urged the speedy appointment of Kollock "before the Pby of N. York shall meet."[48] To add another dimension to an already complicated picture, Rodgers was quite upset with the way that Hunter was put forward as the solution to Maclean's teaching burden. This whole effort was, in Rodgers's words, "to me *highly disgusting*," both because Rodgers did not know if Hunter was properly qualified in mathematics and because it seemed as if his appointment had been arranged and announced before the board could even meet.[49]

At the board meeting of December 8 and 9, 1803, Rodgers's hastily improvised plan prevailed. On Decmeber 8 a letter was read from Green declining the theological post, a letter that seems to have been written only after learning of Rodgers's plan to bring

[47] Smith to Green, Dec. 5, 1803.
[48] I have not been able to locate Rodgers's letter to Smith of Dec. 3, 1803.
[49] Rodgers to Green, Feb. 15, 1804.

forward Kollock to fill what Rodgers assumed was still a vacancy. The board immediately proceeded to elect Kollock. The next day it asked Rodgers and two other members of the New York Presbytery—the Reverend Alexander MacWhorter of Newark and Elias Boudinot's brother, Elisha, of Elizabethtown—to approach Kollock and the New York Presbytery concerning the position. Rodgers, it appears, had arranged ahead of time to secure Kollock's acceptance. Then with a larger faculty secured, the board postponed until its regular April meeting a decision on the division of John Maclean's duties.

Thirteen trustees, the minimum required for a quorum, attended the December meeting: Stanhope Smith, Andrew Hunter, four laymen from the Princeton area, four members of the New York Presbytery (Rodgers, MacWhorter, Elisha Boudinot, and lawyer Aaron Ogden of Elizabethtown), two ministers from the Princeton area, and the Episcopalian Henry Wharton from Burlington. Conspicuously absent were Ashbel Green, Elias Boudinot, and the board's other members from Philadelphia. Many of the trustees were visibly relieved at the results—Smith because he now had some help with instruction, Rodgers because he had saved Kollock from the clutches of the Dutch, and at least some of the ministers because the college had taken steps to strengthen its training of ministers.

Other board members felt very differently. Ashbel Green was especially aggrieved, although it is hard to tell exactly why.[50] Whether because he was being passed over for a position he had begun to consider, because he felt Kollock was not up to the demands of the position, or because of the manner in which the board acted, Green was clearly offended. So also was Elias Boudinot, at the time still residing in Philadelphia as director of the mint. Boudinot wrote to his brother on December 27 that, although Elisha had actually attended the board meeting, he knew "but little of what has passed with regard to the college affairs," especially the fact that "the trustees this way have not been well treated." Boudinot even held that the action of the board was illegal, since it had acted on matters not specified in the call for a special meeting. In addition, Boudinot was even more irritated that the board acted so precipitously to engage Kollock. "If the College could not

---

[50] It is necessary to infer Green's response from letters written to him: Smith to Green, Dec. 5, 1803; and Rodgers to Green, Feb. 15, 1804. The latter epistle mentions Green's letters of Dec. 1 and 5, 1803, which I have not found.

have been kept together without a young Gentl of 25 or 26 years old, it is time it was dissolved." For the overhasty appointment of Kollock, Boudinot blamed Stanhope Smith, who had earlier informed Green (from whom Boudinot received the news) that Kollock had cast his lot with the Dutch Reformed Church. But Boudinot was even more upset with "Dr. Rodgers and Dr. Macwhorter." In September Boudinot had told these two that he would not be able to attend any special meeting, and MacWhorter had assured him that he would himself guarantee that none was held and that, even if one were called, he would make sure that Kollock was not appointed. Rodgers had told Boudinot much the same thing in October. Now in late December Boudinot marveled to his brother, "How the Interests of Religion & the College have so strongly changed in four Months, I am at a loss to find out." The upshot was that Boudinot felt that Green had been "ungenerously & unjustly" treated. And he feared that the action might be "injurious to the College," since "it discovers that the Trustees think the study of Divinity, a subject of small Importance."[51]

The culminating irony of this episode occurred in September 1806, when Henry Kollock resigned his professorship. Discouragement was the keynote in his report to the board: "I flattered myself when I came to Princeton that I might by instructing students of Divinity be of as much service to the Church of Christ as by officiating in any particular Congregation—the number of my students however has been and probably will continue to be so small as to render my labors of little Consequence." Kollock was pained by receiving a regular salary, "whilst I was prescribed by the want of students from making that compensation to it which it was both my duty and my wish to have done."[52] Not only was the plan that had bruised so many egos a failure, but it left the original need unfilled, with three more barren years having passed. Kollock's resignation was a definite defeat for Stanhope Smith; it seems also to have stimulated Ashbel Green to more direct action in organizing a theological seminary.

It is tempting to regard this affair as a soap opera, an event wholly without significance except to illustrate the foibles of the professedly pious. To do so, however, would obscure both important features of the Princeton board and one of the reasons for later difficulty in the Princeton circle. While the trustees were not

[51] Boudinot to Elisha Boudinot, Dec. 27, 1803. Boudinot wanted to appoint Dr. John Henry Livingstone, a Dutch Reformed minister from New York, in order to unite "the two great interests of the Church together."

[52] TM, Sept. 25, 1806.

factionalized as such in 1803, they clearly harbored distinct interests, as suggested by the maneuvering over the theology professor. The group of Princeton-area trustees that acted with Smith to call the special meeting—including Richard Stockton, John Bayard, and Andrew Hunter—was the object of Boudinot's ire, and Boudinot was also upset with the older, influential ministers of the New York Presbytery who rammed through the appointment of Kollock. These same New York ministers, if John Rodgers's remarks are reliable, were not pleased with Smith and the Princeton-area trustees for the way they brought forward Hunter for a teaching position. And Green was upset not only with the same group of older ministers (for veering so rapidly from their ardent solicitation of his services to those of Kollock's) but also with Smith (for bungling the appointment procedure as a whole). In 1803 the various groupings of interest on the board did not adversely affect the trustees' ability to act in concert for the college. But after a few years' time, when the older cohort of trustees passed from the scene, the board's incipient factionalism began to undermine the college's effectiveness as a cultural and educational force.

Misunderstandings over the appointment of a theology professor did not take place in a vacuum. Rather, they occurred at a time when pressure from the outside world intensifed fears within the Princeton circle. And they occurred at a time when the quality of Smith's leadership was coming under increasing scrutiny. With these circumstances, the confusion over the professor of theology became not just a random happenstance but a sign of Smith's slipping competence.

Ashbel Green, at least, had come to such a conclusion. Although he remained on the college board, Green soon became the center of a younger, more activistic group of ministers whose interests turned away from the college toward the promotion of other means to fulfill the religious, intellectual, and social vision inherited from Witherspoon. The wounds that Green had suffered, or felt that he had suffered, seemed to have precipitated a rift of far-ranging consequences with Stanhope Smith. Their deteriorating relationship, in turn, largely defined the trials of the college for the next two decades.

TENSIONS BETWEEN Green and Smith had far-ranging implications because of who Green was and what he stood for.[53] As the

---

[53] Maclean, *CNJ*, 2:219–20, comments briefly on the unfriendly relationship between Smith and Green.

minister of a historic and influential Philadelphia church, as a nationally recognized leader of the Presbyterians, and as one who cultivated a widely flung correspondence, Green was a crucial mediator of news, opinion, and advice to much of the Presbyterian connection. He was eminently a rallying point for all those concerned with the larger mission of the church, now encouraging societies for missions and social reform, now upbraiding his contemporaries for laxity in promoting the gospel. Green, moreover, was the most active minister on Princeton's board for more than a decade after Smith's inauguration. The board itself acknowledged Green's key position by naming him to address the students after the 1802 fire and to serve as interim president during Smith's fund-raising tour.

Green's importance for Princeton rested not just on his general dedication to the college's interests but also on his self-conscious role as a pupil and successor of John Witherspoon. In later years Green would describe Witherspoon as "his venerated master and friend" and say about himself in the third person that he owed more to Witherspoon "than to all other men, and perhaps to all the books he has ever read, for whatever success has attended him through life."[54] Green worked hard to publish Witherspoon's works after the Old Doctor's death, an effort that occasioned the only known disagreement with Smith before 1803.

In retrospect, that disagreement may have been the start of later problems. Stanhope Smith seemed to feel that, although Witherspoon was indubitably a fount of wisdom, his lectures on moral philosophy, proofs of Christianity, eloquence, and other subjects were too hasty and insubstantial to merit publication.[55] Green, on the other hand, while conceding that the lectures contained blemishes, still worked might and main to have them published and eventually became the editor when a publisher was secured. In

[54] Ashbel Green, *The Life of the Revd John Witherspoon*, ed. Henry Lyttleton Savage (Princeton, 1973), 127, 273.

[55] On Smith's lack of eagerness to publish Witherspoon's works, see Smith to Green, Feb. 13 and Mar. 20, 1796; Nov. 14, 1799; Smith to William Woodward, Aug. 1, 1810 (all in Samuel Stanhope Smith Collection, PUL); and Smith, *A Comprehensive View of the Leading and Most Important Principles of Natural and Revealed Religion* (New Brunswick, 1815), iv–v, which criticizes the "editor" of Witherspoon's works directly. Green described his own efforts to edit and publish Witherspoon's writings in his *Life of Witherspoon*, 19. Perhaps as an answer to Smith, he also placed a "recommendation" from John Blair Smith as the first advertisement in the collected works; *The Works of the Rev. John Witherspoon*, 4 vols. (2d ed., Philadelphia, 1802), 1:[1].

Witherspoon's lectures on moral philosophy Green found a better presentation of "the immutable and universal obligation of truth" than any place but the Bible. Green also thought that these same lectures showed that Witherspoon never forgot "his character as a teacher of religion—one of whose principal inducements, in coming to this country, was to educate men for the gospel ministry." Witherspoon, moreover, was an excellent guide for the students, combining firmness and flexibility to establish a nearly ideal campus environment.[56]

The upshot was that Green's conception of an institution inspired by Witherspoon differed considerably from Smith's. To Green, Witherspoon had shaped a college that was more pious, more zealous in structuring religious life, more committed to producing ministers, and more content to proclaim the harmony of religion and science than to practice it. Green demonstrated the sort of institution he felt Witherspoon had left behind when he was called to supervise the winter semester of 1802–1803. He immediately introduced formal Sunday instruction in the Bible and catechisms, which was, surprisingly, an innovation at evangelical Princeton. Green made Paley's *Evidences* a required text for seniors and attempted a close discipline of the students.[57] By these adjustments Green indicated both where he thought Smith's instruction was weak and where he would take the college if he was ever put in charge.

The crucial matter in 1803 was that the effort to prepare more ministers, as far as Green was concerned, had miscarried. This miscarriage, in turn, contributed to a personal breach with far-reaching consequences. Soon Green was intimating to correspondents that Smith's friendliness toward himself was only a sham.[58] He also indicated his changing attitude toward Smith by not sending his own sons to Princeton. While his eldest child, Robert Stockton, had graduated under Smith in 1805, Green directed his next son, Jacob, to the University of Pennsylvania, and the third, James, to Dickinson College.[59]

The lasting significance of Green's antagonism was not on the personal level. It lay rather in Green's creation of an alternative vision for education generally and Princeton College particularly.

[56] Green, *Life of Witherspoon*, 128, 130.

[57] FM, Nov. 30, 1802, to May 12, 1803; Maclean, *CNJ*, 2:51.

[58] E. D. Griffin to Green, Aug. 7, 1805; and Green to Griffin, Sept. 4, 1805; both Gratz Collection, HSP.

[59] *Princetonians 1776–1783*, 409.

Like Stanhope Smith, Green professed loyalty to Witherspoon's legacy. Yet, unlike Smith, Green thought the heart of Witherspoon's inheritance was its religious orthodoxy and its concern for revival. Green perceived the integration of faith and learning in different terms than did Smith and also the implications for society of that integration. When Smith's way of integrating traditional Christianity and modern science began to raise questions in Green's mind and when disruption on the campus continued (and by continuing, called into question the effectiveness of Smith's intellectual effort), Green became increasingly convinced that the legacy of Witherspoon was being slowly and seriously eroded.

Even during the rebuilding and expansion of the college after the great fire, Green saw reason for grave concern. What before seemed only the inconsequential trivialities of Smith's curious erudition now took on a sinister shape. Precisely at this point, while memories of the fire still unsettled the Princeton circle and in the very aftermath of confusion over the appointment of a theological professor, Green received specific—and deeply troubling—information about the dereliction of the Princeton president.

In January 1804 a Virginian, William Hill, wrote to Green with reports of revivals in his region, but also to pass along distressing information about the College of New Jersey. Hill had been given to understand that Stanhope Smith was teaching the students that "polygamy & concubinage are not moral evils" but only violations of civil law. If this charge was true, Hill concluded that no Princeton graduates could be effective missionaries to the Indians, among whom irregular marriages prevailed, and that, if such teaching continued, only the "most profligate" youth would come to Princeton.[60] Green took immediate steps to check out the rumor by writing "in perfect confidence" to tutor John Bradford for a copy of Smith's lectures. Green told Bradford, "If the Dr. & I were on as good terms as we once were, [I] would write to him at once on the subject. But from what [I] have been informed, he would consider my doing this as an [invidious?] attempt to injure him."[61] Bradford complied and sent Green a copy of Smith's lectures, with Bradford's own opinion "that the gentleman of Virginia has not complained without some sufficient grounds." Bradford quoted Smith as saying:

I believe the wisest institution & the greatest happiness & perfection of society are most commonly connected with the law of one wife—

[60] Hill to Green, Jan. 20, 1804, General Manuscripts, PUL.
[61] Green to Bradford, Feb. 1, 1804, Ashbel Green Collection, PUL.

but I cannot suppose that there is natural immorality attached to the law of Polygamy. This opinion is justified by our religion which teaches us that the greatest & most pious men & those who enjoyed the most familiar intercourse with heaven have submitted to this law. . . . Polygamy therefore in certain cases cannot be a vice.[62]

Green then wrote to Hill confirming his suspicion and apparently requesting Hill to file a complaint against Smith in a Presbyterian judiciary. Hill was filled with indignation—"morality & religion are more endangered by such sentiments so taught & propagated, than by all the writings of Paine & his Deistical fraternity together"—but held back from proceeding against Smith because of an unspecified personal connection with the Princeton president.[63] Through Green or another source, other members of the Princeton circle were also upset. The Reverend Robert Finley of Basking Ridge, New Jersey, a young revivalist and educator soon to join the Princeton board, wrote Green in August 1805 to offer "a long Sermon" for the General Assembly's magazine (which Green edited) that would refute "the sentiments [Smith] adopts on the morality of polygamy."[64] But nothing concrete seems to have come of the agitation.

The question of polygamy was a nice one for a group of intellectuals committed both to the law of nature (which might provide evidence either way) and the Scriptures (where the Old Testament tolerates the practice and the New Testament condemns it). It was, in fact, a topic of discussion among the Scottish moralists; David Hume took a position similar to Smith's, and Lord Kames similar to Green's. In the early years of the century, the student societies at the college were also debating "Whether polygamy is consistent with the laws of nature."[65] On such a question the effort to link moral philosophy and faithfulness to the Bible could be precarious.

The lasting significance of this additional contretemps for the period between Princeton's great fire in 1802 and its great rebellion in 1807, however, was to increase the uneasiness of certain trustees with Stanhope Smith's direction of Princeton. After the

[62] Bradford to Green, Feb. 4, 1804, General Manuscripts, PUL. Most of this letter is quoted also in Wertenbaker, *Princeton*, 122. Smith expanded the same general opinions in *The Lectures . . . on . . . Moral and Political Philosophy*, 2 vols. (Trenton, 1812), 2:120–27.

[63] Hill to Green, May 12, 1804, General Manuscripts, PUL.

[64] Finley to Green, Aug. 12, 1805, Gratz Collection, HSP.

[65] Gladys Bryson, *Man and Society: The Scottish Inquiry of the Eighteenth Century* (Princeton, 1945), 181. Harrison, "Young Kentuckian at Princeton," 297.

dreadful fire Princeton succeeded in rebuilding even more spectacularly than after the devastation of the Revolutionary War.
Twice, now, Smith had led the college back from ruin. But this
second time there was no corresponding intellectual and cultural
regrouping. No one recaptured the confidence John Witherspoon
had once inspired. Trustees remained ill at ease about the behavior of students and worried about holding the forces of dissipation
at bay. They had lost none of Witherspoon's belief in the social and
religious power of a good education. But some, with Ashbel Green
as the focal point, had begun to doubt more seriously whether the
aims and principles of Stanhope Smith qualified as a good education.

The Republican Christian Enlightenment of

Samuel Stanhope Smith

A Just Philosophy Grounded on Fact and Experience

D URING THE first decade of the nineteenth century, Stanhope Smith continued to pursue the course begun under
Witherspoon in the late 1760s. As Witherspoon's successor,
he enjoyed considerable deference and not a little respect. Some
students did chafe under his administration, whether for his "political philosophy" or because they felt they were being "treated as
children," both the complaints of a North Carolina student in
1804.[1] More typical, however, was respect for Smith as a venerable
fount of learning. Even his infirmities could strengthen such an
impression. A student from Georgia informed a correspondent in
October 1805 that Smith was not speaking as well as formerly due
to "a disagreeable cough." Smith's physical weakness gave rise to
"his custom of shaking his head gently, at intervals during his address." But this, "by associating itself to the idea of age always has
a happy effect."[2]

Smith's precarious health did not prevent him from fulfilling the
numerous public duties required as the head of a leading college.
Nor did it keep him from fulfilling his tasks as the intellectual successor of Witherspoon. Amid the press of administrative duties
and despite several time-consuming crises, Smith still managed to

[1] William Garnett to Thomas Ruffin, Sept. 24, 1804; Oct. 22, 1804; in *The Papers
of Thomas Ruffin*, vol. 1, ed. J. G. de Roulhac (Raleigh, N.C., 1918), 56, 57.

[2] John W. Walker to Moses Waddel, Oct. 27, 1805, quoted in M. L. Bradbury,
"British Apologetics in Evangelical Garb: Samuel Stanhope Smith's *Lectures on the
Evidences of the Christian Religion*," *Journal of the Early Republic* 5 (1985): 194 n. 39.

publish several major works during the last phase of his career. These works were the stuff of a full-orbed system of thought.

SMITH HAD begun transcribing his lectures in moral philosophy while at Hampden-Sidney, a practice he resumed when he took over the subject from Witherspoon at Princeton around 1790. By 1800 the senior course in moral philosophy was based on these lectures, and in 1812 they were published in two volumes.[3] A similar process attended the composition of an elementary text on Christian evidences, composed "pretty early in my professorial career in the college," as Smith described it much later, and a more advanced theological system that came from the regular meetings with theological students at Princeton. Both sets of lectures were available in manuscript by about 1800 and were published near the end of his active days as a professor. Smith was pleased to acknowledge, "with pride," that notes from Witherspoon on theology (delivered in 1772 and 1773) aided the construction of his own advanced *Comprehensive View of . . . Natural and Revealed Religion.*[4] In addition to his work on these textbooks, Smith also expended considerable effort enlarging his *Essay on the Causes of Variety of Complexion and Figure in the Human Species.* When the fruits of this further labor were published in 1810, the *Essay* had grown to nearly three times its original size. Smith also regularly wrote out his sermons, some of which were published individually at the time of their composition and others posthumously, and he contributed to other literary projects as well. Whatever the state of his health, Smith's busy pen testified to the ongoing vigor of his mind.

As much as he wrote, Smith never departed from the main lines of his intellectual heritage. He was developing, enriching, and broadening the legacy of Witherspoon, but still that legacy defined the content and the direction of his thought. Smith's works testified to wider reading than Witherspoon's, and they certainly dis-

[3] *The Lectures, Corrected and Improved, which have been delivered for a series of years, in the College of New-Jersey; on the Subjects of Moral and Political Philosophy,* 2 vols. (Trenton, 1812). For the dating of these lectures, see Beasley, "Life," 472. Close to the end of his life, Smith wrote a long letter to Ashbel Green that described the circumstances under which all of his major books were written, dated in Green's hand "about the 18th month before his death" (hence ca. Feb. 1818), Gratz Collection, HSP. (Unless indicated otherwise, works cited in this chapter are Smith's.)

[4] *A Comprehensive View of the Leading and Most Important Principles of Natural and Revealed Religion: digested in such order as to present to the pious and reflecting mind, a basis for the superstructure of the entire system of the doctrines of the gospel* (New Brunswick, 1815), iv.

played a self-conscious attention to style that the Old Doctor's published lectures rarely betrayed. But they still expressed the vision that Witherspoon had communicated with such power to the Revolutionary generation.

That vision had changed hardly at all in the decades since Witherspoon's early days in America. It offered a world of harmonies in which philosophy confirmed the Christian faith. The methods of natural philosophy—close observation, inductive reasoning, and strict adherence to facts—opened up the entire world to systematic understanding. When these methods were employed judiciously, they yielded universally valid conclusions, not only for the realm of physical nature, but for human beings as well. Humankind, a unity as demonstrated by observation and confirmed by Scripture, could be studied scientifically. The results of such scientific study proved the validity and usefulness of traditional morality, personal and social. Moral philosophy, therefore, was able to provide a reliable, independent source for truths about the human condition that harmonized with and expanded upon the truths of religion. Chief among these truths was the reciprocal calculus of republicanism—virtue made possible a free and beneficent social order; tyranny subverted virtue and social well-being alike. Because such truths were clear demonstrations of science, sanctioned also by a proper understanding of the Christian Scriptures, knowledgeable observers could use them to understand the causes of public events. And they could also teach them to the rising generation to mold it for enlightened service to church and society. God was supreme over all, revealing his ways through the privileged vehicles of revelation but also, increasingly in that age of light, through the moral and physical sciences.

Smith's four mature works developed this picture of the world fulsomely. They also amounted to an expansion of Witherspoon's original insights. Smith's *Lectures on Moral and Political Philosophy* defined general principles of human nature, discussed methods of scientific observation by which those principles could be applied to society, and set forth a series of rules for governing civil society, for forming government, and for regulating the activities of states among themselves. His *Lectures on the Evidences of the Christian Religion*, a collection of talks that Smith gave to seniors on Sunday afternoons, was meant as an antidote against "the increasing tendency towards infidelity in the present age" and "the poison continually administered to youth in their intercourse with the world." The lectures developed a "science of divine truth" that proved the veracity of Scripture in two ways: by demonstrating the truthfulness of miracles and prophecy through "evidences which propose themselves directly to the senses," and by showing how "the known and immutable principles of human nature" pointed to Christianity's sublimity, its morality, and its contributions to liberty of conscience.[5] Smith's more extensive *Comprehensive View of the Leading and Most Important Principles of Natural and Revealed Religion* incorporated most of the material in his *Evidences*, while also interpreting the Trinity, God's decrees, and human redemption along lines suggested by both the traditions of colonial Presbyterianism and the refinements of the Scottish Enlightenment. Smith's most creative literary effort was the 1810 revision of his *Essay on the Variety of Complexion and Figure in the Human Species*, a work that supplied more evidence to support his thesis that physical forces determined complexion and the external human form, responded at length to criticism of the first edition and offered a fifty-page appendix on how the natural history of American Indians confirmed Smith's main conclusions. Even more than the first edition, the *Essay* was an advertisement for Smith's broad learning and dialectical skill, as well as a demonstration of the main elements of his intellectual system.

THAT INTELLECTUAL system was a complex, finely honed set of convictions involving principles of the Scottish Enlightenment, doctrines of Protestant Christianity, and beliefs about social order. It was a system that transformed Witherspoon's spontaneous insights into fully formed reflections on human nature, religion, the social functions of education, and the relationship of ideas to society.[6] The ideas that Smith developed systematically were the ideas of the Princeton circle at large. As we have already seen, not all of Smith's colleagues approved all his formulations, but such disagreement probably resulted from Smith's ability to define beliefs that were only latent for his fellows. It may also have had something to do with the nature of the beliefs themselves—whatever internal strains were hidden by amorphous or indiscriminate intel-

---

[5] *Lectures on the Evidences of the Christian Religion, Delivered to the Senior Class, On Sundays, in the Afternoon, in the College of New Jersey* (Philadelphia, 1809), iv, 1, 34. For an informative introduction to this work, see Bradbury, "British Apologetics in Evangelical Garb."

[6] On Smith's sophistication, see Elizabeth Flower and Murray G. Murphey, *A History of Philosophy in America*, 2 vols. (New York, 1977), 1:308–11, 318–29.

lectual commitments might be revealed when a patient thinker carefully developed their implications.

Smith's great achievement was to set forth the character of a republican Christian Enlightenment with learning, style, and finesse. Unlike Witherspoon, who was more a skimmer than a scholar, Smith digested thoroughly the works of Europeans that bore on his intellectual interests. For his work on human complexion and form he read, among others, Johann Friedrich Blumenbach, Leibnitz, the Comte de Buffon, and even, for his comments on race, Immanuel Kant.[7] To prepare his theological lectures he digested a different series of authors, including William Paley, Samuel Shuckford, Humphrey Prideaux, and Johann Lorentz von Mosheim.[8] In addition, he worked carefully through the Scottish and British moralists for his principles of mental science. Smith acknowledged a special debt to Francis Hutcheson and Lord Shaftesbury for developing the conception of "the moral sense," or "faculty," which allowed ethicists to construct a science of morals analogous to Newton's physical science.

Smith also made especially careful use of "the learned and profound Dr. [Thomas] Reid of Glasgow."[9] Witherspoon had looked upon Reid as a rival, since by the 1780s the scholarly world was ascribing to Reid the development of "common sense" philosophical principles that Witherspoon felt he had first enunciated in his critique of Lord Kames in 1753.[10] Smith, on the other hand, more easily saw the difference between Witherspoon's fumbling with the concept of a moral sense and Reid's expert analysis of the same subject. Smith's expositions in both moral philosophy and theology reflect careful study of Reid's two major works, *Essays on the Intellectual Powers of Man* (1785) and *Essays on the Active Powers of Man* (1788) as well as his earlier *Inquiry into the Human Mind on the Prin-*

[7] *An Essay on the Causes of the Variety of Complexion and Figure in the Human Species. To Which are added, Animadversions on certain Remarks made on the first edition of this Essay, by Mr. Charles White, in a series of Discourses delivered before the Literary and Philosophical Society of Manchester in England. Also, Strictures on Lord Kaims' Discourse on the Original Diversity of Mankind. And an Appendix*, 2d ed., enl. (New Brunswick and New York, 1810), ed. Winthrop D. Jordan (Cambridge, Mass., 1965), 147n, 155n. Further references to the expanded work are from Jordan's edition.

[8] Smith to Green, ca. Feb. 1818, Gratz Collection, HSP.

[9] *Moral and Political Philosophy*, 1:300; *Natural and Revealed Religion*, 283. On Smith's use of Reid, see also Douglas Sloan, *The Scottish Enlightenment and the American College Ideal* (New York, 1971), 153–54.

[10] Witherspoon, "Remarks on an Essay on Human Liberty," *The Scots Magazine* 15 (1753): 165–70.

ciples of Common Sense (1764). Specifically, Smith followed Reid in arguing (against Locke, Berkeley, and Hume) that "external things are the direct objects of our perception" and that the process of perception does not require the Lockean hypothesis of ideas as intermediaries between our knowledge and the external world.[11] With Smith, it was no longer rough-and-ready intelligence that promoted common sense at Princeton but a mind sharpened by careful study of the most relevant contemporary scholarship.

Smith's attainments exceeded those of his mentor and most of his peers, not just because of his wide reading. To his tasks Smith brought also a discriminating intelligence. He assembled almost as much data about the world as Samuel Miller had done in preparing his lengthy *Retrospect of the Eighteenth Century*, but he far exceeded Miller in scholarly creativity. He understood theology nearly as well as Ashbel Green, but did not allow his theological convictions to foreclose academic curiosity, as they did for Green. While he lacked the fiery eloquence of an Alexander MacWhorter, he was still an accomplished speaker, and by dint of continuous application developed a prose with as much polish as any of his Presbyterian contemporaries. In addition, as a full-time professor from his early years, he enjoyed the long concentration upon academic subjects—though hardly the leisure—that neither Witherspoon nor most of his clerical peers ever experienced. And though his days at Princeton were never tranquil, they still allowed for more systematic nurture of the mind than Witherspoon had enjoyed in the hurly-burly of the Revolution and its aftermath. Smith, in short, possessed the most luminous mind in a Princeton circle distinguished for the number of its diligent intellects. If Smith does not rank with Jefferson, Adams, Madison, or the other premier thinkers of his day, it is partly a comment on his genius, but also a commentary on the nature of the intellectual efforts to which he bent his energies. Neither in his own day nor since has Smith's vision of a republican Christian Enlightenment received the serious attention that has been given to the more strictly theological ideas of his Presbyterian colleagues or the more thoroughly political ideas of the early republic's great statesmen. Whatever the reason for this lack of interest—whether flaws in the ideas themselves or prejudices of historians—the intellectual edifice that

[11] *Moral and Political Philosophy*, 1:20, 137–39, 232. Smith also followed Reid in arguing that free will was "a most obvious dictate of experience" (*Natural and Revealed Religion*, 219, 266–86, with Reid cited by name, 283).

Smith constructed was still imposing. If nothing else, it showed that Witherspoon's disjointed insights were capable of a mature synthesis.

STANHOPE SMITH erected his intellectual system on four principles: that philosophy in a Newtonian mode yielded rewards as rich for the moral world as for the physical world; that human nature was a source of experience from which moral laws could be formed; that moral principles influenced social life directly; and that the results of moral science could be harmonized with an enlightened interpretation of biblical religion. While Smith's "science" was a refinement of Witherspoon's Scottish philosophy, his confidence in its capacity was broader and deeper than his mentor's. Where Witherspoon made his mark guiding Princeton in support of the Revolution, and so was fixed on a course of visible public service, Smith first broke upon the world with his *Essay on the Causes of Variety*, and so was placed on the path of philosophy at the start of his career. Much more thoroughly than Witherspoon, Smith developed the implications of the Scottish moral philosophy. Much more unambiguously, he employed the science of morals as the integrating point of his intellectual efforts.

Smith's reliance upon science—combined with his general optimism about human nature and the advancing course of civilization—sets him apart as a leading figure of the American Enlightenment.[12] While the enthusiasms of the 1780s and 1790s—that science, civilization, and piety could usher in the millennium—cooled somewhat over the course of his career, near the end of his days he still regarded the world with considerable optimism. Not only could he argue that the quantity of good vastly outweighed the quantity of evil in the world, but he could also look back over the period since the Revolutionary War as a period in which the United States was transformed "from a state of feeble and sickly

[12] See Henry F. May, *The Enlightenment in America* (New York, 1976), xiv: "Let us say that the Enlightenment consists of all those who believe two propositions: first, that the present age is more enlightened than the past; and second, that we understand nature and man best through the use of our natural faculties." Smith also fits very well the definition offered in Donald H. Meyer, *The Democratic Enlightenment* (New York, 1976), xiii–xiv, which identifies the assumptions of the Enlightenment as "a new faith in science . . . , a heightened interest in the natural world, including, significantly, human nature . . . , a growing impatience with mystery and 'metaphysics' . . . , [and] new hope for man."

infancy to one of vigorous manhood."[13] The tumults and alarms that Smith himself had experienced at Princeton did not, at the last, shake his faith. The rising of America seemed but to harbinger a more general advance of civilization.

The shape of Smith's Enlightenment was set much more by his specific beliefs about the potential of science than by his more general optimism. It was clear to Smith what proper science entailed and how such a science would open the door to systematic understanding of the world. Valid science, or philosophy (the terms were interchangeable), was the systematic induction of facts presented by the human senses. "Experience," Smith told his students, "and a diligent and attentive observation of the course of nature, and of the actions of mankind in every variety of situation in which they may be placed, is the only legitimate means of attaining a competent knowledge of the laws of either the material or the moral world."[14] Philosophers carefully collected "particular facts"—"fact and experience," "unquestionable facts," "obvious and undeniable events," and "nature and fact" was the litany in Smith's expanded *Essay*—in order to frame their "general laws."[15] Such attention to fact had practical as well as theoretical significance, something that Smith could testify from his own experience. The reason he had been able to treat himself successfully for hemorrhages was because he had allowed "no theory to bias my mind." Instead he had chosen a course of action after close observation of his own experience and careful reasoning toward an inductive conclusion.[16] Facts, as Smith's experience testified, came to us reliably through the senses—indeed, "all our knowledge is originally introduced into the mind through the avenue of the senses." From the diligent study of the facts presented by the senses, philosophers could construct "laws," which deserve to be "deemed universal, till other facts occur to invalidate, or limit the conclusions which have been drawn from them."[17] God was the ultimate source of these laws,

[13] On the quantity of good, see *Moral and Political Philosophy*, 2:32; the quotation from Smith is in a continuation of David Ramsay's *History of the United States, from their First Settlement as English Colonies, in 1607, to the Year 1808*, 3 vols. (2d ed., Philadelphia, 1818), 3:190.

[14] *Moral and Political Philosophy*, 1:11.

[15] Ibid., 14; *Essay on the Causes of Variety* (1810), 14, 38–39, 39, 78.

[16] "An Account of the good Effects of copious Blood-letting in the Cure of an Hemorrhage from the Lungs," *Medical Museum* 2 (1806): 5.

[17] *Moral and Political Philosophy*, 168, 21, and similar professions, 23.

and since God is perfect, so also do the laws operate perfectly.[18] The lawlike character of the world offered more than enough reason to pursue the path of science.

To Smith it was self-evident that proper science set one upon a privileged road to truth. Facts, experience, the senses, and the inductive process generated the "rules . . . which have been followed in natural philosophy ever since the age of the great Newton, with so much advantage to the science."[19] With many of the great thinkers of his age, Smith was mesmerized by Newton's accomplishments and those of other natural scientists. He felt, as did so many of his contemporaries, that the triumphs of Newton established empirical and inductive methods as the unique means for discovering the truth in any sphere.[20] It was, thus, not to be wondered at that Smith began his lectures on moral philosophy with this definition: "Philosophy is an investigation of the constitution and laws of nature, both in the physical and moral world, as far as the powers of the human mind, unaided by the lights of revelation, are competent to discover them."[21] Smith's equation of method "in the physical and moral world" and his assertion that philosophy proceeds "unaided by the lights of revelation" led directly to his most distinctive contributions as a thinker.

In order to demonstrate the analogy between a philosophy of nature and a philosophy of morals, Smith took two additional steps that, because they fell from favor at the end of the nineteenth century, seem somewhat strange today. The first was to regard human consciousness as a variety of sense experience that provided facts to be arranged inductively for discovering general laws about humanity. This perception provided a key ingredient of what Norman S. Fiering has called "the new moral philosophy" of the eighteenth century, a European enterprise prosecuted especially in the Scotland of Francis Hutcheson, Thomas Reid, and Dugald Stewart, and in the American centers that adopted Scottish moral phi-

[18] See *A Discourse on the Nature and Reasonableness of Fasting, and on the existing causes that call us to that Duty* (Philadelphia, 1795), 15; *Moral and Political Philosophy*, 1:21; and *Natural and Revealed Religion*, 266, 537–38.

[19] *Moral and Political Philosophy*, 1:19.

[20] See Winthrop Jordan, "Introduction" to *Essay on the Causes of Variety* (1810), xxvi. The finest treatment of Newtonianism in the early United States is Theodore Dwight Bozeman, *Protestants in an Age of Science: The Baconian Ideal and Antebellum American Religious Thought* (Chapel Hill, N.C., 1977).

[21] *Moral and Political Philosophy*, 1:9.

losophy for their own purposes.[22] Smith's second step was more original. It was his effort to defend scientifically the common origin of all human beings against attacks on the idea of human unity, and so to preserve the validity of the universal laws of human nature divulged by an empirical study of consciousness.

In the first instance, Smith's entire career as a philosopher depended upon his ability to treat consciousness as a source of empirical data. It was, therefore, not surprising that he asserted in strongest terms the ability of careful observers to derive truths about human nature from the examination of their own minds. The first of his lectures in moral philosophy was the occasion for the fullest statement of this position. Because natural philosophers have shown that the relation of cause and effect is "a law of nature," people are able to "study human nature in our own hearts." The result of such inquiry is a philosophy every bit as rigorous and productive as the philosophy of nature.

> The science of moral philosophy, therefore, begins in the study of the human mind—its sensations, perceptions, and generally, its means of acquiring knowledge—its sentiments, dispositions and affections, and generally, its principles of action or enjoyment. . . . From an attentive examination of its various principles and powers, and from carefully remarking their operations either singly, or in combination with others, we may at length form a rational judgment of what man was intended, by his creator, to be, and thence deduce the law of his duty. . . . [By] an attentive induction of facts . . . observing the operations of the human mind . . . we arrive at length, at a knowledge of the laws of our moral nature.[23]

From Hutcheson and Shaftesbury, Smith took the idea of "the moral faculty" or moral "sense," which to him was "the only *organ* . . . of the ideas of duty, and of right, and their contraries, as the eye is of those of color, as the ear of sound."[24]

The ability to reason from these internal sensations was far from a vacuous theoretical curiosity. Rather, the capacity to sense properly and to describe human nature inductively provided Smith with a wealth of critical insight about the moral character of the universe. Early in his career as he was still composing the moral

[22] Norman Fiering, *Jonathan Edwards's Moral Thought and Its British Context* (Chapel Hill, N.C., 1981), 4–7.

[23] *Moral and Political Philosophy*, 1:13–14, 16–17.

[24] Ibid., 300–301. The entire lecture from which this quotation comes, "Lecture 14: The Moral Faculty," expands upon this idea.

philosophy lectures, for example, he told Benjamin Rush that "the common sentiments of mankind" justify capital punishment.[25] Much more obviously, since "in all nations" people upon the inspection of nature have acknowledged "a Supreme Power," we may "justly infer that the belief of existence of God is to be ascribed to an original law of our rational and moral nature."[26] Smith made the most of evidence from self-consciousness in defending the "entire liberty of moral action," a conviction that did not change from his early correspondence with James Madison. Moral free agency is "among the first dictates of reason" and so possesses "the irresistable evidence of our own consciousness, than which no stronger exists for the first truths of science." In his theological lectures he called this idea of free agency one of "the primary sensations of our nature . . . emphatically and happily called *first truths*, or axioms in science. . . . They are the impressions of the hand of God upon the mind; convictions resulting from the very constitution of our nature."[27]

For Smith the human mind—specifically, the moral sense—provided evidence no less compelling in its sphere than the evidences of the physical senses for the natural philosopher. Nothing, therefore, prevented the careful observer from gaining a more accurate knowledge about the workings of human morality as Newton and his successors had gained about the workings of the physical world. The prospect of such knowledge was enthralling. It lay bare the causes and effects of human actions and established reliable laws connecting moral dispositions with public behavior. It gave the acute philosopher more insight than had ever before been available about the workings of the mind and the springs of human action. To construct a *science* of morals was a Promethean achievement. It was to make the sight of humanity as the sight of God.

But of course if a science of morals was to flourish, the unity of humanity was essential. The deliverances of consciousness could not lead to universal moral laws if humankind were not a unified species. A humanity made up of more than one species was a fragmented field of research that could not yield universal moral prin-

---

[25] Smith to Rush, Apr. 10, 1787, Library Company of Philadelphia, HSP.

[26] *Moral and Political Philosophy*, 1:16.

[27] "The Sinner Blinded to Truth, and Hardened Against Conviction, By His Own Sins, and the Righteous Judgment of God," in *The New-Jersey Preacher; or, Sermons on Plain and Practical Subjects* (Trenton and New Brunswick, 1813), 107; *Natural and Revealed Religion*, 284.

ciples. Smith's *Essay on the Causes of the Variety of Complexion and Figure in the Human Species* was therefore a signal contribution to the exercise of moral science because it demonstrated the unity of humanity. This book amounted to the most significant scientific defense of a science of morals in the early history of the United States. While Smith greatly expanded his evidence in preparing a second edition, he never wavered from the conclusion of his 1787 *Essay*. As the even more explicit statement of the the 1810 edition put it:

> The denial of the unity of the human species tends to impair, if not entirely to destroy, the foundations of duty and morals, and, in a word, of the whole science of human nature. No general principles of conduct, or religion, or even of civil policy, could be derived from natures originally and essentially different from one another, and afterwards, in the perpetual changes of the world, infinitely mixed and compounded. The principles and rules which a philosopher might derive from the study of his own nature, could not be applied with certainty to regulate the conduct of other men, and other nations, who might be of totally different species; or sprung from a very dissimilar composition of species. . . . But when the whole human race is known to compose only one species, this confusion and uncertainty is removed, and the science of human nature, in all its relations, becomes susceptible of system. The principles of morals rest on sure and immutable foundations.[28]

By observing that climate and "the state of society" could account for the manifold variety in the human species, Smith scientifically demonstrated the unity of humanity. Not only did that conclusion confirm the biblical account of a common ancestry. It also saved mental science and so made it possible to employ the methods of Newton for discovering the moral laws of human nature.

The second significant claim in Smith's definition of philosophy asserted that science advanced "unaided by the lights of revelation." Far from an indication of Smith's disdain for Christianity, this disclaimer hinted at Smith's strategy for the defense of the faith. In a day when traditions of all sorts were coming under fire—including traditional religion—and in a day that exalted scientific method as the royal road to truth, Smith hoped to establish the claims of Christianity not on deference or tradition but on its scientifically demonstrable veracity. Theology itself, as Smith told

[28] *Essay on the Causes of Variety* (1810), 149. Cf. the first edition (Philadelphia, 1787), 109–10.

successive generations of undergraduates, was "the science of divine truth." Moreover, it was a dignified science, as the efforts of no less a personage than Isaac Newton proved by his persistent efforts to show scientifically the precise fulfillment of biblical prophecies.[29]

Christian faith could still be recommended in an age of Enlightenment because it fully met the demands of genuine science. Smith, that is, believed in "the coincidence of reason, with religion; and [in] the support which science, justly explained, may often render to revelation."[30] Moral science and physical science both demonstrated the truths of religion in general and the teachings of the Bible more particularly. Smith acknowledged the guidance of Samuel Clarke (1675–1729), along with the Scottish moral philosophers, in his efforts to demonstrate the truthfulness of theism by moral science. Clarke had been selected to give the Boyle Lectures twice early in the eighteenth century. On the first occasion he developed a variation of the cosmological argument (things exist, nothing exists without a cause, therefore the existence of things proves the existence of a necessarily existent first cause). On the second he rebutted Thomas Hobbes and sought to prove the reality of the Christian revelation through an examination of human reason and its operations. Following the general line of Clarke and the Scottish moral philosophers, Smith showed his students how the common moral experience of all humans reveals the existence of God.[31] In another typical use of such argumentation, Smith suggested that "intrinsic rectitude and congruity with the state and moral requirements of a rational being" offered scientific demonstration for the value of "temperance, patience, fortitude, the moderation of our passions, the wise improvement of time."[32]

The line for Smith was never hard and fast between these internal proofs from moral nature and external proofs drawn from the physical world. For the latter Smith acknowledged the lead of William Paley, whose works offered Smith's generation the consum-

[29] *Evidences of the Christian Religion,* 1, 227; for the same view, see *Essay on the Causes of Variety* (1810), 3.

[30] *Natural and Revealed Religion,* 286; forceful restatement of this conviction appears also in *Essay on the Causes of Variety* (1810), 21, 186.

[31] *Moral and Political Philosophy,* 1:16, 308–9; 2:10. Elmer Sprague, "Samuel Clarke," in *The Encyclopedia of Philosophy,* 8 vols. (New York, 1967), 2:118–20.

[32] *Moral and Political Philosophy,* 1:308. For the same point, see "Faith the Principle of a Holy Life," in *The New-Jersey Preacher; or, Sermons on Plain and Practical Subjects* (Trenton, 1813), 11.

mate statement of the argument from design, or the reasoning by which evidence for order in the physical world was taken as proof of a Divine Originator of that physical world.[33]

Smith's most compelling statement of the way science supports religion came not from Clarke, Paley, or any other authority but from his own work on the causes of human variety. Where the 1787 edition of his *Essay* had merely touched upon the value of his research for Christianity, Smith treated the subject at length in 1810. Clearly it had become more important in the interval to show how manifestly his science supported religion and the Christian Scriptures. Smith acknowledged that some might think it frivolous to devote over four hundred pages to a topic as recondite as human variation, or wonder more specifically about the wisdom of a clergyman giving such concentrated attention to this theme. But for Smith the project had "an obvious and intimate relation with religion, by bringing in science to confirm the verity of the Mosaic history." In a day when "certain superficial smatterers in physical science" were suggesting that research into nature led to conflict with piety, when the charge had gone forth that Christians relied blindly on authority instead of "on well ascertained facts," Smith wanted to remind the world of the tradition established by "such men as Newton, or Boyle, Bacon or Mede," who were exemplary for learning and piety alike. Smith was as eager in his day, as they were in theirs, to show that "genuine philosophy has ever been found the friend of true religion." Only "spurious pretences to science" array themselves against the Bible. But it is not necessary to appeal blindly to revelation to rebut such claims. When infidelity attempts to show contradictions between natural science and Christianity, it is necessary to see that the impious have not dealt fairly with the evidence. And so Smith has come forward not first as the champion of religion but as a champion of science. In that garb, under the banner of philosophy, he will defend the faith. "I appeal to the evidence of facts, and to conclusions resulting from these facts which I trust every genuine disciple of nature will acknowledge to be legitimately drawn from her own fountain."[34]

[33] Smith's most obvious employment of Paley is in *Natural and Revealed Religion*, 7; *Moral and Political Philosophy*, 2:16, 18; and *Evidences of the Christian Religion*, 192. On Paley's considerable influence in Smith's lifetime, see Wilson Smith, "William Paley's Theological Utilitarianism in America," *WMQ* 11 (1954): 402–24.

[34] *Essay on Variety* (1810), 3. See also Smith to Rush, Aug. 21, 1811, Library Company of Philadelphia, HSP, where Smith complains about the way modern French thinkers pretend submission to the faith while using science to subvert it.

Religion was secure because science could demonstrate its truthfulness, expressly and fully on the question of human unity and, by implication, for the other Christian doctrines as well. "A just philosophy, therefore, grounded on fact and experience, will lead us to the conclusion which the sacred scriptures propose as an elementary principle of our belief"—that God created one race and imbued that one race with a common set of moral principles.[35]

The way in which Smith's Enlightenment defense of religion influenced the specific character of his theology deserves separate consideration. At this point, however, it is important to note how thoroughly committed Smith was to the scientific defense of Christianity and how much his picture of true religion turned upon its scientific demonstration. Real Christianity for Smith was a religion moderated by the judicious use of reason. When Smith preached the funeral sermon for his friend Gilbert Snowden in 1797, he told how Snowden's early religious life had been marked by an excess of zeal. But Smith was pleased to report that "reflection, judgment and acquaintance with the holy scriptures" soon tamed Snowden's passionate faith to "a system of virtue and practical holiness, highly rational and just."[36] The whole point in laboring so hard to demonstrate the truth of Christianity by scientific means, Smith told the undergraduates, was "that our faith may not be merely an enthusiastic and visionary confidence, but a rational offering to truth and reason."[37] Smith's search for a rational piety coincided very well with the general shape of his thought. It was, however, one of the predispositions that eventually posed difficulties for those members of the Princeton circle who, however committed to the ways of John Witherspoon, still longed for the unmediated religion of revival.

Near the end of *Natural and Revealed Religion* and as part of a more general consideration of the Christian sacraments, Smith paused to criticize the Roman Catholic doctrine of transubstantiation. Most of the main features of his religion came into view as he rejected the Catholic formula. "This doctrine contradicts the evidence of all our senses, by which alone we can form an accurate judgment on the qualities of material subjects. If our senses could be so far violated that the essences of flesh and blood could be covered under the sensible qualities of bread and wine, we could

[35] *Essay on the Causes of Variety* (1810), 19.

[36] *A Discourse Delivered on the 22nd of February, 1797, at the Funeral of the Rev. Gilbert Tennent Snowden* (Philadelphia, 1797), 32.

[37] *Evidences of the Christian Religion*, 3.

have no criterion left by which to judge of any miracle; the whole rational evidence of religion would be annihilated by this single position."[38] Transubstantiation was a great evil, not primarily because it misinterpreted the Bible or for other traditional Protestant reasons. Rather, its central proposition—that the elements of communion could be experienced as one thing while truly being another—devastated Smith's fundamental intellectual principles. Things were as they seemed to be. Sense information undergirded rationality. Rational evidence demonstrated the truth of religion. To believe in the enthusiastic irrationality of transubstantiation destroyed both faith and philosophy.

Smith's two great achievements as a thinker of the Enlightenment were to assert the strictest analogy between natural science and moral philosophy and to show how such an analogy could demonstrate the truth of Christianity. The work in which Smith himself showed the most interest—like the creative portions of his *Essay* or the lectures in moral philosophy—was the scientific demonstration of human unity and the encouraging results of such demonstration for a science of morals. On the other hand, the work that spoke most directly to the concerns of the Princeton circle was the apologetic use of science on behalf of religion. To Smith the two tasks were parts of one whole. While other Princeton leaders never disagreed, they seemed to harbor more suspicion about the internal cohesion of Smith's science and his apologetics. None of the Princeton leaders rejected the harmony of science and faith, but some of them reversed the order of Smith's priorities by pouring creative energies into the inculcation of religion while devoting only pro forma attention to the harmonies of science and faith.

DIFFERENCES OF intellectual priority within the Princeton circle never broke out into open controversy, in large part because the entire body of college officials shared common convictions about the way thought influenced life. For Smith and his colleagues, the principles of Enlightenment science that provided structure for moral philosophy and proof for Christianity also offered compelling explanations for public events. If theory operated more self-consciously for Smith than for others in the Princeton circle, it was still the same set of principles with which, in the end, the others analyzed the workings of the world. As a body they stressed training in morals as the key to social well-being. They believed, more-

---

[38] *Natural and Revealed Religion*, 487–88.

over, that a science of morality undergirded the republican social theory to which they all assented. The same moral science also demonstrated that the best way to preserve a republic was to train the rising generation in virtue (as defined by the principles of religion). In lecturing and writing on these matters, Smith did not merely express his own views but spoke for the Princeton circle as a whole.

"It is education chiefly," Smith told Princeton seniors, "which makes man what he is; whether it be well, or ill considered."[39] The benefits of a systematic education were numerous and important. Study of mathematics strengthens the mind.[40] Even more, training in reasoning subdues those passions that destroy lives and disrupt society.[41] But most important, education aims at "the moral and religious cultivation of the heart and manners." The best way to achieve that cultivation is through the science of morals, for the object of moral philosophy is "to propose such general *principles* as may enable a rational and reflecting mind to deduce the point of duty for itself, on every case as it arrises [*sic*] in practice." Since human nature is very pliable, education skillfully applied, can form "the manners, habits, and sentiments of youth . . . to almost any standard."[42]

Education, therefore, played a critical role in the structuring of society. "We may lay it down as an infallible maxim in morals, that right principles truly understood, and firmly believed, will ever be followed by right conduct; and that false principles, on the other hand, tend to vitiate the fountains of virtue and piety in the heart, and lead to many pernicious errors in the habits of life."[43] So absolute was this principle that it applied even to black slaves, as Smith reminded those who, with Thomas Jefferson, felt that slaves were beyond the reach of education. To the contrary, Smith personally knew of several cases "where a good moral education, united with the virtuous, and amiable example of their masters and mistresses, have concurred to cultivate the heart, and produce a certain reserve and refinement in their manners."[44]

The science of morals not only showed the Princeton circle how

[39] *Moral and Political Philosophy*, 2:145.

[40] *An Oration upon the Death of George Washington* (Trenton, 1800), 7.

[41] This theme appears in ibid., 24; *Moral and Political Philosophy*, 1:175, 255; and *Natural and Revealed Religion*, 521–22.

[42] *Moral and Political Philosophy*, 2:146; 1:24; 2:146.

[43] *Natural and Revealed Religion*, 344. The same notion is found in *Moral and Political Philosophy*, 1:25; 2:225–26.

[44] *Essay on the Causes of Variety* (1810), 168n.

important education was and not only supplied the most important content of that education. It also offered the most convincing explanation for the health or debility of society. On such topics, Smith spoke as a conventional republican of the old school: the health of a society depended upon the virtue of its people. It was part of the "order established in the universal system," Smith told the Presbyterian General Assembly in 1800, that "God has connected the knowledge of truth, with the practice of duty, and the duties with the happiness of human nature."[45] With several of his Princeton associates, Smith stressed the religious factor in this standard republican equation. "The universal science of history" testfies to the "maxim, that the prosperity of nations is intimately linked with their virtue, and their decline as certainly associated with the corruption of morals, and the disorder of public manners." All also knew "how much public, and individual manners are affected by the healthful state of religion."[46] Not just ancient history revealed this maxim. Americans knew how the corruption of England's Parliament had yielded "an uncontrollable power to the crown."[47] And especially the contemporary turmoil in France—where impiety, public madness, inflamed passions, levity, vanity, false science, and dissolute public manners had laid waste much of Europe—offered proof positive of the republican equation.[48]

Smith, as an old Federalist very much out of sympathy with the Jeffersonian "revolution" of 1800, warned his students repeatedly about the moral and political dangers of unbridled democracy.[49] The moral problem with unchecked democracy was the way demagogues, representing faction or personal ambition, inflamed public passion and unhinged well-balanced republics.[50] The specifically political issue had to do with the location of power. Because of the flightiness of the mob in the hands of a demagogue, the

---

[45] *Natural and Revealed Religion*, 519. This assertion is also made in *Essay on the Causes of Variety* (1810), 19; and "Faith the Principle of Holy Life," 21; as well as in Lectures 26–29 of *Moral and Political Philosophy*: "Politics," "Government and Its People," "National Policy—Constitution," and "National Policy."

[46] *Natural and Revealed Religion*, 39, with the same connection drawn on p. 52.

[47] *Moral and Political Philosophy*, 2:324.

[48] Ibid., 302–3; *Evidences of the Christian Religion*, 99n; *Natural and Revealed Religion*, 532–33.

[49] *Moral and Political Philosophy*, 2:288–326.

[50] *The Divine Goodness to the United States of America. A Discourse on the Subjects of National Gratitude . . . a Day of General Thanksgiving and Prayer* (Philadelphia, 1795), 28.

franchise should be restricted to landholders, and a republic should ever be on its guard against "the spirit of equality . . . carried to an extreme."[51] On the other hand, civil liberty protected commerce and ensured prosperity. Custom on a flourishing trade would yield a sufficient income for the purposes of government and remove the threat of taxation arising from personal ambition or public passion manipulated by an unscrupulous broker of factions. Such convictions about politics were the norm for the religious Federalists of Smith's day, but for him they amounted to more than simple political reflexes. Smith and the Princeton circle could be confident about these conclusions because they so clearly grew out of the scientific study of human nature.

Princeton reliance on what might today be called normative social theory and the methods of social science culminated in a supreme self-confidence about what it took for American society to flourish. If philosophy demonstrated the truth of religion, if education inculcated virtue, and if a religiously inspired virtue preserved a republic, then nothing could be more important for America than an education shaped by a philosophical religion. When he announced the restoration of the college in 1804, Smith proudly proclaimed that the trustees encouraged students to believe "the truths of religion, as . . . the surest basis of public morals."[52] Nothing was more important "for promoting the tranquility, order, and happiness of society" than instructing "every class of the people" in their "moral and social duties."[53] Train a population in religion, and one will "lay the foundations of society most securely, and . . . promote its civilization."[54] Train slaves in "religious principle and feeling," and "the greater security will you have for your own safety, and the safety of the republic." Train a nation's leaders in "the principles of true political science," and one will ensure "the stability of her government, and the wisdom of its administration."[55] To the Princeton circle nothing could be clearer than the way that their most cherished principles stabililized both thought and practice.

The note that marked Smith and most of his Princeton colleagues as denizens of the Enlightenment was the absolute confi-

[51] *Moral and Political Philosophy*, 2:296, 309–10.
[52] *College of New Jersey* (n.p., [1804]), 3.
[53] *Moral and Political Philosophy*, 2:225–26; and the same on pp. 305–6.
[54] Ibid., 227. A state church, however, encourages corruption and therefore is best avoided (pp. 227–28).
[55] Ibid., 179, 181.

dence that they could discern the relationship between moral cause and public effect. Smith, whose leadership at Princeton would eventually be destroyed by the practical outworking of this moral calculus, nonetheless gave it the strongest possible expression. His enemies were atheism and chance; his confidence lay in God and predictability. "All events," he wrote in his moral philosophy, "depend upon a certain concatenation of causes." And "moral effects," he told his theological students, "are as certain, in their order, as the results of any physical causes whatever."[56] To Smith, "history may be regarded as a volume of moral experiment" where a perceptive observer can trace the causes and effects of human action.[57]

Smith not only repeated such axioms but put them to use in his own contributions to the science of his day. A greatly expanded section of his *Essay*'s second edition demonstrated painstakingly how the "State of Society, and the Habits of Living" affected the human body and human conduct.[58] The argument was that conditions of civilization directly affected not only skin color and the shape of bodily features but also individual character. Blacks taken from equatorial regions to temperate climates thus acquire fairer skin, straighter hair, and civilized manners—if not immediately, then in the course of only a few generations. An examination of the "state of society"—clothing, government, ideas, habits of thought, forms of agriculture—can explain almost any personal and social event. In England, for instance, the relatively even distribution of wealth and the liberty of the British constitution quite naturally account for the fact that English people look, think, and believe alike.[59]

Smith's explicit environmental determinism set him apart in his day, but neither his view of human nature nor his faith in education were unusual within the Princeton circle. His research had convinced him that "the pliant nature of man is susceptible of many changes from the action of the minutest causes." In addition, they had shown "how much the human race might be improved in personal, as it is acknowledged it may be in mental qualities, by proper cultivation." The philosopher who understood cause and effect, scientific law, and the "reciprocal influence" of body and

[56] Ibid., 22; *Natural and Revealed Religion*, 266.

[57] *Moral and Political Philosophy*, 1:12. Again, "reason, as well as history," supplies "the truth" (*Essay on the Causes of Variety* [1810], 12).

[58] *Essay on the Causes of Variety* (1810), 97.

[59] Ibid., 109, 103.

mind could see these minutest causes at work and mark out a pathway to civilization by putting them to good use.[60]

In short, the world that Smith described to his students was a luminous world. To the carefully scientific observer, it was as it appeared to be. Smith's intellectual universe depended, in Gordon Wood's apt phrase, on "a mode of causal attribution based on particular assumptions about the nature of social reality and the necessity of moral responsibility in human affairs." As a Federalist guided by the light of eighteenth-century intellectual discoveries, Smith assumed, again in Wood's words, "the existence of a rational moral order and a society of deliberately acting individuals who controlled the course and shape of events."[61] Smith was unusual for his age only by the heightened self-consciousness of his scientific vocabulary. With his peers he trusted implicitly his own observations and his own moral reasoning. There could be no question, for the one who saw religion and virtue leading with such philosophical certainty to social health, that disorder and infidelity sprang from observable moral actions or definable states of society. So clearly could the trained observer discern the connections among events that no excuse was left to the philosopher whose educational efforts did not produce the desired effects or the Christian whose religion failed to reinforce the health of the church and the order of society. In such a tightly controlled moral universe, either the philosophy or the Christianity must be at fault. And so in this way did Stanhope Smith painstakingly, thread by scientific thread, fashion an intellectual noose for himself.

IN ORDER to clarify the nature of Smith's difficulties with other members of the Princeton circle, we must also look closely at his theology. From a modern vantage point, we might expect Smith's theological conclusions to have brought him grief from his Presbyterian colleagues, since his commitment to principles of the Enlightenment had a liberalizing effect on his religious thought. Compared with predecessors like Jonathan Edwards or Samuel Davies, for example, Smith gave less scope to the person, revelation, and agency of God and more centrality to the lot, science, and agency of humans. As it happened, however, Smith's colleagues rarely raised specific objections to his theology as such. The reason

[60] Ibid., 125, 116, 118.
[61] Gordon S. Wood, "Conspiracy and the Paranoid Style: Causality and Deceit in the Eighteenth Century," *WMQ* 39 (1982): 409, 434.

seems clear. Although many of Smith's fellow trustees were more orthodox (by the standards of the eighteenth century), they shared with him the general convictions of the Christian Enlightenment as popularized by John Witherspoon. Because Smith spoke for the whole Princeton circle as the acknowledged representative of Witherspoon's harmony of science and religion and because his theology was orthodox in its broadest outlines, the other members of the Princeton circle rarely objected to it as such. Problems came rather when these other disciples of John Witherspoon had occasion to question the *results* of Smith's educational leadership. Since they too were largely content with the Enlightenment as baptized by Witherspoon, they were not eager to question the theology of Witherspoon's acknowledged heir, who was, besides, such a formidable champion of both science and religion. But since they also believed in the scientific predictability of moral relationships, they could not ignore failures in preserving social order or in promoting religion—especially with all that such failures involved for the health of individuals and of the republic. These matters, rather than the specifics of Smith's thought, were their greatest concern.

At the same time, Smith's mature theology reveals how much the effort to present Christianity in the forms of the moderate Enlightenment required him to modify the content of revivalistic colonial Presbyterianism. To be sure, Smith was no radical. The continuity of his theology with his Reformed predecessors is apparent whenever he paused for comprehensive definitions of Christianity. As he put the matter to his theological students, "Evangelical Faith, in its most general import, consists in receiving the holy scriptures, with clear understanding, and with inward and profound conviction of their truth, as containing the infallible word of God; and in embracing Jesus Christ, who is the principal subject of them, as the Son of God, and the Saviour of the world."[62] In addition, Smith defended many of the cardinal beliefs of colonial Calvinists as essential principles of religion. While making much of what humans could discover by reason and the study of nature, Smith still maintained the necessity of special revelation in Scripture,[63] and he de-

---

[62] *Natural and Revealed Religion*, 336. Nearly the same words may be found in "Faith the Principle of Holy Life," 14. The list of "those fundamental doctrines on which the whole fabric of christianity rests" that Smith enumerated for the General Assembly in 1800 also had a traditional ring (*Natural and Revealed Religion*, 530).

[63] *Natural and Revealed Religion*, 21n; *Evidences of the Christian Religion*, 9, 29, 31; *Moral and Political Philosophy*, 2:33, 34n, 40.

fended the reality of miracles and prophecy.[64] While emerging as the Princeton circle's unrivaled champion of education, he still was willing to speak of regeneration by the Holy Spirit.[65] And while he proclaimed the sovereignty of natural law, he nonetheless left no doubt as to his belief that God was the creator of law as well as disposer of events.[66] If his explanation of these doctrines emphasized their compatability with nature interpreted scientifically, he nonetheless accorded these traditional Presbyterian beliefs a prominent place in his own firmament.

On the other hand, Smith also propounded theological novelties, at least by the standards of his Calvinist tradition. On these points he followed the liberalizing disposition of the Enlightenment beyond the pale of the earlier orthodoxy.[67] Smith adjusted his theological heritage most obviously by deemphasizing the supernatural. At various points in the development of his natural philosophy and his theology, he took pains to show that what a previous age regarded as God's direct action could now be better described in terms of natural law.[68] Thus, education was nearly as effective as grace in helping overcome reluctance to identify oneself as a Christian.[69] The doctrine of Christ's physical resurrection "contains nothing which violates reason, and which is not even supported and rendered credible by the course of nature." The Holy Spirit always works "by natural means, and never, in the ordinary exercise of the christian life, by immediate impulse, or direct influence, without them."[70] To repeat a point from his *Essay*, the different human languages arose by a natural process, not from a divine act at Babel. The story of rapid Hebrew births in Exodus 1:19 may be explained by natural means, as Cotton

[64] *Evidences of the Christian Religion*, 34–62, 197–284.

[65] *Natural and Revealed Religion*, 397; "Faith the Principle of Holy Life," 16.

[66] *Natural and Revealed Religion*, 266; *Moral and Political Philosophy*, 2:104, 126.

[67] On that orthodoxy, see Fiering, *Jonathan Edwards's Moral Thought*; Frank Hugh Foster, *A Genetic History of the New England Theology* (1907; reprint, New York, 1963), 3–186; Bruce Kuklick, *Churchmen and Philosophers from Jonathan Edwards to John Dewey* (New Haven, 1985), 5–65; Howard Miller, "Evangelical Religion and Colonial Princeton," in *Schooling and Society*, ed. Lawrence Stone (Baltimore, 1976); and Glenn T. Miller, "God's Light and Man's Enlightenment: Evangelical Theology and Colonial Presbyterianism," *Journal of Presbyterian History* 51 (1973): 97–115.

[68] *Moral and Political Philosophy*, 1:153–54, 157n.

[69] *Natural and Revealed Religion*, 340; *Three Discourses* (Boston, 1791), first sermon, 23.

[70] *The Resurrection of the Body* (Washington, D.C., 1809), 9; *Natural and Revealed Religion*, 383.

Mather did concerning a similar phenomenon among the American Indians.[71] And what the Bible calls demon possession is best accounted for as "diseases, chiefly of the melancholic, phrenetic, and epileptic kind."[72]

Especially striking for this scion of New Light Presbyterianism was the way Smith naturalized conversion. While Smith's colleagues like Alexander MacWhorter might continue to speak of the New Birth as Edwards and Whitefield did—"an holy illumination of the understanding, and a new bias of the will"—Smith dispensed with the latter change in favor of the former.[73] "Regeneration is a term entirely of figurative meaning," Smith wrote in his theology; it stands for the moral understanding that the Holy Spirit communicates to believers. While the work of the Holy Spirit is a requirement for the regeneration that no merely "human cultivation" can achieve, that work is "ever conducted according to the laws of the rational system, the laws of human liberty, and the moral laws of the heart. In accomplishing the regeneration of the believers, the blessed Spirit is able . . . imperceptibly to instruct the intellect in divine things. . . but there is, in no instance, any violation of the laws of the moral world."[74] Even in the domain of faith, natural law was nearly everything for Smith.

Smith moved more obviously away from earlier theological formulas and toward the spirit of Enlightenment by changing several specific parts of the Calvinist deposit. Original sin was not an inbred propensity to glorify the self at God's expense—as Jonathan Edwards described it—but rather an abuse of the divinely created constitution.[75] With other Calvinists of his generation, Smith also regarded the Christian doctrine of the atonement as the process by which God's justice was satisfied rather than a sacrifice that placated the divine anger at sin.[76]

Most strikingly, Smith continued to argue the position on moral free agency that he had outlined to James Madison in the early

[71] *Moral and Political Philosophy* 1:104–5n; *Essay on the Causes of Variety* (1810), 172.

[72] *Evidences of the Christian Religion*, 398, with extended discussion, 398–407.

[73] Alexander MacWhorter, *A Series of Sermons, upon the most important principles of our Holy Religion*, 2 vols. (Newark, N.J., 1803), 2:254.

[74] *Natural and Revealed Religion*, 396, 397, 401–2. The same sentiments appear on p. 340 and in *Moral and Political Philosophy*, 1:294.

[75] *Moral and Political Philosophy*, 1:263, 265, 279–80n.

[76] *Natural and Revealed Religion*, 363. On the development of the governmental view of the atonement in New England, see Foster, *Genetic History of New England Theology*, 210–23; and Robert L. Ferm, *Jonathan Edwards the Younger: 1745–1801* (Grand Rapids, Mich., 1976), 114–19.

days of his intellectual development. Smith labored at length to show that free will was an inescapable conclusion of self-awareness and hence a foundation for mental science. "The primary principle, than which there can be no axiom of science more evident," was "that the mind is perfectly free in her volitions. It stands on the same footing with the clearest testimonies of sense and consciousness."[77] Smith used his theological lectures to attempt a reconciliation between "the perfect liberty of human action" and God's "infallible foreknowledge, and preordination of events." He felt that he could appeal, on the one hand, to "the most obvious dictate of experience" and, on the other, to the fact that God ordains "the universal laws of nature so . . . as to attain by their natural operation, every end for which they were evidently designed by the Creator."[78] For Jonathan Edwards's argument that volition is always a function of the strongest motive arising from an individual's character and experience, Smith had only the sharpest criticism. Drawing on Thomas Reid's account of "sensations" common to all humans, Smith merely repeated that moral free agency is among the "*first truths*, or axioms in science."[79]

On the question of the will Smith once again saved both science and Christianity by affirming that things are what they seem to be. Just as the Roman Catholic doctrine of transubstantiation threatened the whole structure of moral science, so too did Edwards's account of the will. If—as Edwards argued on the basis of revelation and his analysis of the language of moral responsibility—our internal sense of free moral agency is illusory, the whole fabric of mental science dissolves. Smith could not tolerate Edwards's position because it led to doubts about self-perception, doubts that destroyed not only control over one's own choices but also the possibility of moral philosophy. Edwards's doctrine of the will had no place in an age of light where the foundations of science rested upon the verities of self-consciousness.

In addition, the kind of God-centered universe for which Edwards had argued was equally out of place in a world resplendent with the accomplishments of human science and dazzled by the prospect of human progress. Again with most of his contemporaries, Smith held that God had fashioned the universe for the

[77] *Moral and Political Philosophy*, 1:292, as summarizing, 283–92. The sense of our freedom "is peculiarly clear. It is among the primary sensations of our nature" (*Natural and Revealed Religion*, 284).

[78] Natural and Revealed Religion, 219, 266.

[79] Ibid., 284.

happiness of humanity and only incidentally for his own glory. The Christian faith itself was, as he put it in a sermon, "adapted to the best, and most excellent feelings of human nature."[80] But this situation was simply part of a larger intention. "The Creator, who appears to have designed the happiness of the human family, has disposed the order of the world for that purpose in a way most consistent with the nature of man."[81] For Smith, to be a theologian in an age of Enlightenment meant the repositioning of human happiness closer to the center of religion than had been the case with Edwards and the other earlier presidents of Princeton.

As Smith's lectures in moral philosophy amounted to the best textbook published outside of New England in the early republic, so his formal theology was the most systematic treatment of religion among the Presbyterians in the first forty years after independence.[82] While that theology certainly followed lines laid down by Witherspoon and his predecessors, it also reflected the learned spirit of the age. Douglas Sloan was correct to note that Smith advanced some of the same alterations to traditional Calvinism that made N. W. Taylor of Yale a controversial religious figure in the 1820s and 1830s.[83] Taylor, however, adjusted his theology in order to make it an engine for revival and social reform. Smith's adjustments came more from a desire to make use of a modern world of thought. Especially his defense of the self-determining power of the will, his orientation of theology around human happiness, and his desire to play down the supernatural as much as possible marked Smith as an advanced thinker, one not afraid to leaven the old lump with modern ideas. If the older theology had to be modified to keep it attuned with the times—particularly with the conventions of an age of moral science—Smith was willing to make the effort.[84]

[80] *Resurrection of the Body*, 13. On the age's general drift to moralistic conceptions of Christianity, see James Turner, *Without God, without Creed: The Origins of Unbelief in America* (Baltimore, 1985), 64–72, 82–95, 142–43.

[81] *Moral and Political Philosophy*, 1:269. Elsewhere in this work Smith describes God's provision of the moral sense as one of his ways of arranging "the happiness of mankind" (pp. 304–7).

[82] For later, more comprehensive works, see D. H. Meyer, *The Instructed Conscience: The Shaping of the American National Ethic* (Philadelphia, 1972); and George M. Marsden, *The Evangelical Mind and the New School Presbyterian Experience* (New Haven, 1970), 7–58.

[83] Sloan, *Scottish Enlightenment*, 166 n. 58.

[84] Later conservative Presbyterians were quick to attack Nathaniel W. Taylor's principles and New England's general propensity for innovations in theology, but

Besides, even if Smith's theology represented a profound, if subtle, change from colonial Calvinism, almost none of his associates seemed to notice. On rare occasions, to be sure, Smith spoke as if his religious views were not acceptable to some of his Princeton colleagues. In 1812, for example, when he sent a copy of the first volume of his moral philosophy lectures to Benjamin Rush, he intimated that "some of my opinions are too philosophical for several of my brethren who are so deadly orthodox, that they cannot find words in the english language, to express their zeal and jealousy upon the subject, & therefore oblige their candidates to swear *ex animo* to all their doctrines."[85] And an occasional student, with sensitive theological antennae, might sense a change in the air. So William Weeks from New England complained in the spring of 1808 that "the favorite work here is *Reid's Essays*, which is strongly recommended by Dr. Smith, our President." New England's consistent Calvinists—Edwards, Samuel Hopkins, Nathaniel Emmons—had no place in the curriculum. Weeks' judgment was not favorable: "*Reid* is grossly Arminian, & advocates a *Self-determining power*, which, if it means anything, means that the creature is independent of the Creator." As it turned out, however, Weeks accommodated himself well enough to instruction at Princeton to remain there after graduation in order to prepare for the ministry under Smith's direction.[86]

ON THE WHOLE, Smith's theology excited little comment as such in the Princeton circle. The reason for this lack of interest seems to be that the other Princeton trustees, though they may have retained more bits and pieces of the old theology, had also accepted many of the same modern assumptions that Smith was explicating so well. Thus, the deliverances of consciousness also showed Ashbel Green the unquestionable necessity of moral free agency, even if he also clung to older views of divine sovereignty. The principal difference between Smith and Green on this one important matter was that Smith several times attempted to defend his view system-

---

they remained silent about similar elements in their own tradition resembling those of Taylor and other New Englanders. The best treatment of this blind spot remains Sydney E. Ahlstrom, "The Scottish Philosophy and American Theology," *Church History* 24 (1955): 265–66.

[85] Smith to Rush, Sept. 27, 1812, Library Company of Philadelphia, HSP.

[86] William Weeks to Eb. Weeks, Apr. 11, 1808; and on staying to study with Smith, Weeks to unknown correspondent, June 10, 1809; both in William Weeks Letters, Sheldon Art Museum, Middlebury, Vt.

atically, while Green simply accepted human free will and divine sovereignty as an unresolvable paradox.[87] Again, Samuel Miller, who, in his *Brief Retrospect of the Eighteenth Century*, shared much of Smith's fascination with the triumphs of modern science—as exemplified by "the stupendous mind of Newton"—proclaimed just as forthrightly "the perfect harmony between the Religion of Christ and genuine Philosophy" and was almost as enthusiastic about the moral philosophy of Thomas Reid and the Scots.[88] While Miller retreated toward more sectarian and conservative positions after the publication of his *Brief Retrospect* in 1803, he continued to share Smith's commitment to eloquence, elegance, and the necessity of learning for ministers.[89] Elias Boudinot, the board's most important layman, believed more strongly than did Smith in the continuing manifestation of the supernatural, but when he reasoned against infidelity or discoursed on social order, his arguments sounded like Stanhope Smith's.[90] Smith certainly moved further away from revivalistic habits of mind than had the board's older ministers like John Rodgers and Alexander MacWhorter, yet with these veterans he shared so many personal, denominational, and patriotic bonds that differences in theology seemed to have been overlooked completely.

In short, Smith's theology accommodated itself generously to the spirit of the Enlightenment, a fact that (we might reason) should have amounted to a real stone of stumbling for his more orthodox colleagues. Yet, since these colleagues also shared the general convictions of Smith's Christian Enlightenment, they were in no position to gibe at theological positions that Smith extrapolated from those general assumptions. An occasional issue with practical implications—like Smith's teaching on polygamy or his views on baptism and the Episcopal church might cause momen-

[87] Green's position on this matter is described in chapter 13.

[88] Samuel Miller, *A Brief Retrospect of the Eighteenth Century*, 2 vols. (New York, 1803), 1:11, iv; 2:11.

[89] See Belden C. Lane, "Democracy and the Ruling Eldership: Samuel Miller's Response to Tensions between Clerical Power and Lay Authority in Early Nineteenth-Century America" (Ph.D. diss., Princeton Theological Seminary, 1976), a broader study than its title implies.

[90] See Elias Boudinot, *Memoirs of the Life of the Rev. William Tennent . . . In which is contained, among other interesting particulars, an account of his being three days in a trance, and apparently lifeless* (Trenton, 1810); Boudinot, *The Age of Revelation; or, The Age of Reason shewn to be an Age of Infidelity* (Philadelphia, 1801); and Mark A. Noll, ed., "The Response of Elias Boudinot to the Student Rebellion of 1807: Visions of Honor, Order, and Morality," *PULC* 43 (1981): 16–22.

tary fits of uneasiness.[91] The general tenor of his bearing—contemplative instead of activistic, rationalistic instead of pious, elegant instead of earnest—might also distance him from his fellows. But these matters do not adequately explain the currents of uneasiness with Smith's administration that gathered strength throughout the last decade of his tenure.

Rather, it was failure in terms of the Princeton worldview that led to difficulty. Virtue preserved social order. Religion ensured virtue. The careful observer could discern the causes and effects of moral action. These shared principles—articulated explicitly by Smith as the fulfillment of John Witherspoon's intellectual vision and accepted implicitly by the Princeton circle—rather than particular differences over theological or philosophical points set the stage for intellectual controversy and institutional decay.

When disorder broke out with a vengeance in 1807, the Princeton circle looked instinctively to Smith's educational practice and to the formulation of his philosophy as the culprit. When the college throughout the first decade of the century failed to produce the ministers so necessary for public order, the Princeton circle eventually began to seek alternatives to Smith's conception of learning, truth, and social well-being. In both cases, however, Smith's colleagues questioned his leadership, not primarily because they doubted the specifics of Smith's philosophy or the details of his educational vision, but precisely because they shared the larger outlines of the republican Christian Enlightenment that Smith constructed from materials first assembled at Princeton by the venerated John Witherspoon.

[91] The tiffs over baptism and Episcopalianism are treated in chapter 12.

Student Rebellion and New Trustees, 1807

Pillars of the Social Fabric Crumbling into Dust

★

THE TURNING POINT for Samuel Stanhope Smith came in 1807. Events unfolding throughout that year marked the end of the era that had begun when John Witherspoon broke upon the American scene in 1768 with such masterful effects on church and nation and with such a complete triumph of the Scottish philosophy over Calvinistic idealism. The critical events of 1807 were of two kinds. The first, a great student rebellion in early April, discredited Smith's leadership and testified to the inadequacy of his teaching. The rebellion caused additional consternation when students used the authorities' treasured language of republicanism to indict *them* for promoting vice and tyranny. At the same time that this dramatic incident embroiled the college—with lasting consequences far more serious than those following the destruction of the war or the fire of 1802—a second, less obvious change was under way. The year witnessed also a major shift in the makeup of the board—in fact, the most rapid turnover in the entire history of the College of New Jersey. More than a fourth of the trustees, including several influential veterans, died or resigned. Their replacements were men whose view of the world and whose aspirations for the college resembled Ashbel Green's much more closely than Stanhope Smith's.

The combination of events—one spectacularly visible, the other scarcely noticed at the time—brought about a major reorientation at Princeton. No one questioned Witherspoon's main achievements, and all still sought, as he had, to forge principles of Christian faith, the moderate Enlightenment, and republican thought into a cohesive and forceful whole. Yet Smith's version of the Witherspoon synthesis, with its supreme commitments to the moral philosophy of the Enlightenment and to the promotion of science, speedily gave way to a version with a much larger role for evangelistic religion and the promotion of the church.

AFTER THE rebellion of March 31–April 1, 1807, students and authorities explained what had happened in ideological terms. Both groups, however, probably underestimated the influence of more mundane circumstances on the college community during the winter semester of 1806–1807. To understand the environmental factors that exacerbated tension at the time of the rebellion requires, however, a sketch of the circumstances of student life during the presidency of Stanhope Smith.[1]

The most obvious fact about the student body in the spring of 1807 was its size. Nearly two hundred students, more than had ever gathered before in the college's history, confirmed the success of rebuilding after the fire, even as they placed great demands on the institution. The students of 1807 still pursued a traditional curriculum, with studies for freshmen and sophomores concentrated in the classical languages, but with preliminary work also in ancient history, mathematics, English grammar, and religion, as well as regular practice in public speaking. The curriculum for juniors and seniors was as diverse as earlier studies were concentrated. Juniors studied mathematics, astronomy, chemistry, natural history, and geography, read some history, and prepared Sunday lessons on Stanhope Smith's *Evidences* and other theological texts. Much of the senior year was devoted to Smith's omnibus course in moral philosophy, but seniors also studied the criticism and composition of speeches, chemistry, astronomy, geography, history, and more texts in religion. Juniors and seniors alike were called upon for frequent orations.[2]

Organization of the days in which students performed these assignments left freshmen and sophomores with very little leisure time. In July 1804, James Iredell wrote home to his sister in North Carolina about his routine as a sophomore.

At six o'clock in the morning the bell rouses us to morning prayers. From this till breakfast (which is always at half past seven) I study the

---

[1] For a fuller description of these circumstances, see Mark A. Noll, "Before the Storm: Life at Princeton College, 1806–1807," *PULC* 42 (1981): 145–64.

[2] A detailed account of sophomore studies is found in William Weeks to Eb. Weeks, Nov. 29, 1806, Sheldon Art Museum, Middlebury, Vt. For an overview of the curriculum in the period, see Darrell L. Guder, "The History of Belles Lettres at Princeton" (Ph.D. diss., University of Hamburg, 1964), 212–67.

recitation. I have to commit to memory, either geography or English grammar. The time between breakfast & nine I spend either in Conversation or reading. At nine the bell rings for all the students to retire to their rooms except the two lower classes which must attend in the recitation room, where we are confined till twelve. From this till dinner (at one o'clock) I generally read. At two we again go to the recitation room & stay till five, when the bell rings for evening prayers. From this till supper (at six o'clock) I study or read & also from supper till seven. Between seven & eight I usually take a walk, & from eight till ten read. At nine the tutor visits the room to see that the students are all in.[3]

Iredell also reported that Sundays were devoted to church and the preparation of a religious recitation. Time off was strictly limited to Saturday afternoons and the first day of each month.

Students were not wildly enthusiastic about such a regimen. Educational reformers like Benjamin Rush felt that it wasted too much time on the classical languages.[4] Stanhope Smith pushed consistently to increase the time available for natural and moral philosophy. Trustees sometimes wondered if there was enough formal instruction in religion. But on the whole, the Princeton circle accepted the traditional curriculum as a given. Moreover, because of Smith's fame as a moral philosopher and Maclean's as a scientist, Princeton enjoyed a better reputation for its curriculum than almost all other American colleges.

Princeton's reputation also rested on its ability to attract the sons of wealthy and influential families. Even students of middling origins could look forward to lives of distinguished public service, for which the study and friendships at Princeton provided useful preparation. The senior class of 1807, for example, included a future United States representative from Pennsylvania, a chancellor of New York University, and a judge for the District of Columbia. The juniors achieved even more numerous distinctions: a congressman from South Carolina, a justice of the United States Supreme Court, a chief justice of the Delaware Supreme Court, a judge on the New Jersey Supreme Court, a president of the Theological School of the Protestant Episcopal Church of Virginia, a vice president of Princeton who became the first president of Cincinnati College, United States district attorneys in New Jersey and

---

[3] Iredell to Anne Iredell, July 28, 1804, James Iredell Papers, PUA.

[4] Rush to Ashbel Green, May 22, 1807, in L. H. Butterfield, ed., *Letters of Benjamin Rush*, 2 vols. (Princeton, 1951), 2:946.

New York, a member of the North Carolina senate, and a secretary of state for Kentucky.[5]

As this list indicates, a large share of the undergraduates at Princeton in 1806 were from the South. The continuing settlement of Scottish and Ulster Presbyterians in Delaware, Maryland, and the back country of Virginia, North Carolina, and South Carolina explains some of Princeton's appeal in that direction.[6] During Witherspoon's tenure Princeton had educated a stream of influential southerners: one president of the United States (James Madison), four members of the Continental Congress, ten United States senators, seven congressmen, nine state governors, one justice of the Supreme Court, and one attorney general. If anything, the connection between Princeton and the South grew stronger after Witherspoon's death, perhaps because of Smith's well-received labors at Hampden-Sidney. In 1805 nearly half the student body came from states south of Pennsylvania. The American Whig Society had been founded by southern and western students in the early 1770s, and it continued to reflect a strong southern influence through the time of the Civil War.[7]

The presence of such a large southern contingent at Princeton created special problems. On the most elementary level, New Jersey's climate often was a rude shock.[8] More important than the southerners' reaction to northern weather was their importation of a distinct system of personal values, which contemporaries described as "disorganizing and loose principles." More recent students of the South have provided a fuller analytic framework to describe the behavior of young southern aristocrats.[9] They suggest

[5] Maclean, *CNJ*, 2:112–17; *General Catalogue*, 117–20; Richard H. Greene, "Alumni of the College of New Jersey Who Have Held Official Position," *New England Historical and Geneological Record* 43 (1889): 47–52.

[6] William Warren Sweet, *Religion on the American Frontier, 1783–1840*, vol. 2, *The Presbyterians* (Chicago, 1936), 2.

[7] *Princetonians 1769–1775*, 49; Wertenbaker, *Princeton*, 115; Jacob N. Beam, *The American Whig Society of Princeton University* (Princeton, 1933), 162–63.

[8] For complaints from a North Carolinian about the cold, see James Iredell to "My dear Friend," Jan. 7, 1805, James Iredell Papers, PUA; from a Kentucky student, Joseph Cabell Breckinridge to his mother, Feb. 8, 1809, in Lowell H. Harrison, "A Young Kentuckian at Princeton, 1806–1810: Joseph Cabell Breckinridge," *Filson Club History Quarterly* 38 (1964): 310.

[9] The contemporary was President Willard of Harvard; Steven J. Novak, *The Rights of Youth: American Colleges and Student Revolt, 1798–1815* (Cambridge, Mass., 1977), 81. Cf. Rhys Isaac, "Evangelical Revolt: The Nature of the Baptists' Challenge to the Traditional Order in Virginia, 1765–1775," *WMQ* 31 (1974): 345–68; T. H. Breen, "Horses and Gentlemen: The Cultural Significance of Gambling

that wealthy southerners possessed an elaborately developed code of personal honor to govern the presentation of self in society. The code encouraged an emphasis on personal confrontation, a passion for the perquisites of position, and a commitment to social distinctions. While this well-developed sense of honor shared some of the characteristics found among northerners, particularly the Federalist lovers of deference, it also differed substantially—often lacking, for example, the evangelical strain that moderated the admittedly robust notions of honor held by some of the Princeton trustees.

Contemporaries often singled out Virginians as the source of student unrest at Princeton.[10] But southern students came into sharpest conflict with the authorities not so much for misbehaving more than their northern peers as for resisting the means of enforcing order. The presence of a large number of southern students in the winter semester of 1806–1807 did not mean that revolt was inevitable. It did mean, however, that southern standards of personal honor were a tinder that sparks of confrontation could ignite.

Southern students were also more likely to be Jeffersonians and thus to smart under the Federalist pronouncements of Smith and his colleagues. While some Democratic-Republicans discovered no cause for complaint, others were offended. In 1804 William Garnett of North Carolina was so upset with "the conduct of Doctor Smith, with respect to politics" that he wrote to friends urging them to go elsewhere to college. Reversing his instructors' political opinions, Garnett in early 1805 joyfully heralded Jefferson's reelection as the victory of "principle" over "corruption."[11] On the whole, however, even students with Jeffersonian sentiments got along well at Princeton.

One of the reasons for Princeton's relative equanimity in politics was the presence of two vigorous student societies, American Whig and Cliosophic, where students enjoyed ample opportunity to defend their political views in unencumbered debate. For many students the societies provided the primary stimulus for intellectual

among the Gentry of Virginia," ibid. 34 (1977): 239–57; Bertram Wyatt-Brown, *Southern Honor: Ethics and Behavior in the Old South* (New York, 1982).

   [10] Beam, *Whig Society*, 72–73; Edwin Monk Norris, *The Story of Princeton* (Boston, 1917), 117; FM, Dec. 25, 1804; Iredell to "My dear Friend," Jan. 7, 1805; "The Great Rebellion at Princeton," *WMQ*, 1st ser., 16 (1907): 119–21.

   [11] Garnett to Thomas Ruffin, Sept. 24, 1804, and Mar. 25, 1805, in *The Papers of Thomas Ruffin*, vol. 1, ed. J. G. de Roulhac (Raleigh, N.C., 1918), 62, 71.

and political expression in their college years.[12] In the society halls on the top floor of the new Library Building west of Nassau Hall, students ruled their lives like adults. Most of the student body belonged to one society or the other; those who did not were scorned as "neuters"; and those expelled from the societies despaired, left college, or both. Whigs and Clios elected their own officers, admitted their own members, maintained their own extensive and well-used libraries, disciplined their own members, staged a never-ending series of debates, and conducted their business in secret.[13]

An incident in January 1806 dramatized the importance of the societies. One of the Whigs, William Hamilton, after being "very impertinent and disobedient to Professor Thompson," was arraigned before the faculty on a Monday. The professors voted to suspend Hamilton but not to announce the sentence to the other students until Wednesday. In the interim the college informed the "censor" of the Whig society that his organization would fall into "disgrace" if it did not suspend Hamilton immediately. When the Whigs met to discuss this proposition, a debate of three hours ensued. Some argued that suspension "was only inflicted on persons guilty of the grossest faults, and not for such a comparatively trivial offense as mere impertinence to a professor." Finally it was decided that the society would merely "publickly admonish" Hamilton. James Iredell was more concerned with the politics of the case than with its merits. "It seemed to me that an agreement with [the faculty's order] would have appeared too much like a mean compliance or submission to the wishes of the faculty, and I thought it necessary that we should shew them that we had the independence to think and act for ourselves in cases that concerned society

[12] The importance of the societies is reflected in the frequency with which they formed the staple of the correspondence for both students and alumni: for example, letters dated July 28 and Aug. 18, 1804; Dec. 1805; Jan. 7 and 13, 1806; July 10 and Dec. 1, 1807; Jan. 18, 1809; in James Iredell Papers, PUA; James Mercer Garnett to his mother, Jan. 30, 1813, Garnett Papers, PUA; Joseph Bloomfield to Nicholas Biddle, May 13, 1805, General Manuscripts, PUL; *The Correspondence of John Henry Hobart, 1757–1797,* ed. Arthur Lowndes (New York, 1911); J. C. Breckinridge to his father, June 1, 1806, in Harrison, "Young Kentuckian at Princeton," 296; Betty Fladeland, *James Gillespie Birney: Slaveholder to Abolitionist* (Ithaca, N.Y., 1955), 9; William Birney, *James G. Birney and His Times* (1890; reprint, New York, 1965), 27; and Thomas P. Govan, "Nicholas Biddle at Princeton, 1799–1801," *PULC* 9 (1948): 52–54.

[13] See Beam, *Whig Society*; and the excellent essay, James McLachlan, "The *Choice of Hercules*: American Student Societies in the Early Nineteenth Century," in *The University in Society,* ed. Lawrence Stone, 2 vols. (Princeton, 1974), 2:449–94.

alone." The faculty did suspend Hamilton but took no action against the Whig society for failing to follow its mandate.[14]

The societies also featured prominently in the patriotic celebrations that structured the ritual ordering of life at Princeton. The Fourth of July was the main event of the year. Traditions established in the days of the Revolution—feasting, speeches, fireworks, illuminations, balls, gunfire—constituted the elements for remembering independence and other patriotic occasions.

In contrast to the power of republican ritual, Christian observance was relatively pallid. Students encountered Protestant ceremonial at three levels during their college life—daily prayers, Sunday services, and church holidays. The daily worship, at 6:00 A.M. and in the late afternoon, could be grim. Morning devotions in winter offered a particularly severe trial, since the sun was not yet up and the prayer hall was unheated. When Ashbel Green prepared his autobiography as an old man, he still could not hide his delight that the students were unusually orderly at the morning prayers he led as a senior in 1783. But such halcyon respites were rare. In an extreme case from 1805, freshman Archibald Mercer, who had been "repeatedly remonstrated . . . by the officers of the College" for lying down during morning prayers, stuck a penknife into John Glascock when the latter sat on Mercer's recumbent head. More typically, students showed their lack of interest by inattention, dozing, or simply staying away.[15]

The vigorous support provided by Princeton leaders for republican rituals may have had something to do with the language students used to present their grievances in the spring of 1807. Trustees wanted students to see the connections between proper religion and a proper society, but their celebrations of independence were much livelier than their commemorations of religion. The result was a student world in which republican values appeared more vivid than Christian values. Even female members of the student generation received the message. Sixteen-year-old Mary Ann Breckinridge visited Princeton in the summer of 1811,

[14] James Iredell to R. S. Green, Jan. 13, 1806, James Iredell Papers, PUA. See also Wertenbaker, *Princeton*, 204–5.

[15] *Life of Green*, 132; FM, Aug. 15, 1805. For a general account of ceremonial at Princeton, see Wertenbaker, *Princeton*, 189–90. The situation at Princeton, with adjustments for its republicanism, is reminiscent of that described by Marvin O'Connell for Europeans more generally at the start of the modern period: "The splendors of ritual, banished from the churches, were lavished on the sovereign" (*The Catholic Reformation* [New York, 1974], 38).

when for the first time in many years the Fourth of July passed quietly. On the previous Independence Day a cannon had exploded, injuring some students and killing a servant. Recent bad feeling between town and residents also made fervent celebration of the Fourth unwise. So, she reported, "for fear of . . . offending Doctor Smith," Independence Day "passes off like a sabbath."[16]

Along with the societies and campus customs, the physical condition of student life may also have had a bearing on the events of 1807. Overcrowding in Nassau Hall certainly did nothing to dampen unrest. The venerable structure of four floors contained about fifty student rooms, of which up to twelve were in the basement, which was dark and often damp. The rooms as rebuilt after the 1802 fire measured about nineteen by twenty feet and were intended to house two or three students, each with his own window and separate sleeping area. In November 1806, however, as many as five students were living in each room, and trustees, in their effort to preserve order, continued to deny requests to board in the village.[17]

The New Jersey climate could add discomfort to the strain of overcrowding. The winter of 1806–1807 especially had not been an easy one. Although cold weather was late in arriving, temperatures hovered below average levels in January and February. The snow and rain that fell in Philadelphia on March 5, 14, and 29 probably also kept the undergraduates indoors at Nassau Hall. Then on the thirty-first itself a storm, which dropped record amounts of spring snow on New York and New England, passed just to the north of Princeton, bringing damaging winds and some precipitation to central New Jersey.[18] Cold and snowy conditions usually prevailed from mid-November to mid-March.[19] And the

[16] Mary Ann Breckinridge to Mary Breckinridge, July 4, 1811, in Harrison, "Young Kentuckian at Princeton," 315 n. 102.

[17] Paul Norton, "Robert Smith's Nassau Hall and President's House," in *Nassau Hall, 1756–1956*, ed. Henry Lyttleton Savage (Princeton, 1956), 16–19, with diagram, 17; TM, Sept. 25, 1806.

[18] David M. Ludlum, *Early American Winters, 1604–1820* (Boston, 1960), 174–77; Charles Peirce, *A Meteorological Account of the Weather in Philadelphia, from January 1, 1790, to January 1, 1847* (Philadelphia, 1847), 15, 37, 56; letter, David M. Ludlum to Mark Noll, Apr. 1, 1980.

[19] By Christmas 1804, snow had been on the ground for two weeks (James Iredell to J. C. Johnston, Dec. 24, 1804, James Iredell Papers, PUA). A friend wrote to Henry Hobart on Nov. 15, 1794, "My fingers are so cold that I can hardly write any more" (*Correspondence of John Henry Hobart*, 101). In 1786 students could be outside for long walks by March 18 and play "basteball" outdoors by March 22 (Nathaniel

coming of winter also reduced the diversion provided by visitors as the flow of travelers between New York and Philadelphia slowed to a trickle or ceased altogether.[20]

Student activity did not cease with the arrival of winter but took a turn that created conflict with the faculty. Forced indoors by the weather, students resorted to makeshift games like "battledore" or "shuttle," species of field hockey played in the long corridors of Nassau Hall.[21] As might be expected, the faculty regarded these games as impediments to study and attempted to suppress them. The result was to increase the sense of confinement. A southern student, who in January 1813 was complaining about "this western Siberia," had almost despaired by the middle of February. "It has not ceased to snow almost every day for a month, and if it continues any longer I shall be forced to run away; for I cannot live without exercise, and Dr. Green has forbidden any noise or romping in the college."[22] But winter gave, even as it took away. If the season circumscribed some outdoor activities, particularly the long walks that were the major form of exercise for the students, it provided occasions for others, like skating and sleigh riding.[23] Where the first of these sports caused little difficulty, the second created problems. Sleigh rides often led to the accommodating inns of neighboring villages, to excessive drinking, and then to the disruption of the college.[24]

In the early nineteenth century the winter semester was a particularly difficult session at Princeton. Major student disturbances occurred either in the dead of winter (January 1800, January 1802, and "the big cracker" of January 1814) or immediately upon the

Burt, "Student Life in Nassau Hall," in *Nassau Hall 1756–1956*, ed. Henry Lyttleton Savage (Princeton, 1956), 121, 123.

[20] John Frelinghuysen Hageman, *History of Princeton and Its Institutions*, 2 vols. (Philadelphia, 1879), 1:229.

[21] Burt, "Student Life in Nassau Hall," 121.

[22] James Mercer Garnett to his mother, Jan. 30 and Feb. 13, 1813, both James Garnett Papers, PUA.

[23] On North Carolinian James Iredell's fondness for skating, see letters to J. C. Johnston, Dec. 24, 1804, and "My dear Friend," Jan. 7, 1805.

[24] Iredell to "My dear Friend," Jan. 7, 1805. On other students who went sleighing, see Govan, "Nicholas Biddle at Princeton," 54; and Hageman, *Princeton and Its Institutions*, 2:42. The practice was also a favorite with the families of college officers, as testified by the many references to "slaying" scattered throughout the journal of Esther Edwards Burr, which she kept during the administration of her husband, President Aaron Burr, in 1756 and 1757 (Carol F. Karlsen and Laurie Crumpacker, eds., *The Journal of Esther Edwards Burr, 1754–1757* [New Haven, 1984]).

coming of spring (April 1807). In 1816 Ashbel Green attempted to explain the source of difficulties to the trustees. "Our winter sessions are always considered as more exposed to difficulty in maintaining good order in the College than the summer session. The confinement occasioned by the winter, the length of the nights, and other circumstances of the season, seem to generate and favour mischievous designs beyond what takes place in other portions of the year." Green added that the presence of many new students for the winter semester contributed to the prevalence of disorder.[25] All of the difficulties associated with winter sessions do not explain the unfolding of rebellion in the spring of 1807. Similarly, the fact that religious revivals in New Jersey during the early nineteenth century usually occurred in the winter season does not by itself account for their occurrence.[26] Yet in both situations, to neglect the seasons is to miss one of the most obvious elements in the day-to-day life of the students and their teachers.

WHILE COLLEGE authorities never lost sight of the physical circumstances of their students, they were much more concerned about their interpersonal environment. In particular, they wanted the students to enjoy the benefits of a sturdy framework of discipline. Trustees looked to the faculty to maintain order. They spelled out their expectations for student conduct in a book of college laws. And they also institutionalized lofty standards of honor as the principal means of encouraging students in the practice of virtue.

One of the most important duties of the faculty was to uphold the college laws, which first appeared in the board minutes in 1748, eight years before the college settled permanently in Princeton; in the early 1760s they were printed in a substantial booklet.[27] After the fire of 1802, the trustees added a series of new regulations designed to keep the peace: the tutors were expressly required to check each room at least once a day, all the faculty were given "the right to enter the rooms and studies of the students at

[25] *Life of Green*, 387.

[26] Martha Tomhave Blauvelt, "Society, Religion, and Revivalism: The Second Great Awakening in New Jersey, 1780–1830" (revision of Ph.D. diss., Princeton University, 1974), 100.

[27] TM, Nov. 9, 1748. On the faculty's responsibility for upholding the regulations, see Ashbel Green, *An Address to the Students and Faculty of the College of New-Jersey* (Trenton, 1802), 15–16; and *Laws of the College of New Jersey* (Philadelphia, 1802), 17.

their pleasure," and the president was required to stop any student who in a speech departed from his previously approved text to "pronounce any thing in public of a censurable nature." The 1802 revision continued a prohibition against student "clubs or combinations" that had as their intent "resisting the authority of the college, interfering in its government, or for concealing or exciting any evil or disorderly design." And it added a requirement for students to "give information" about their disorderly fellows.[28] In 1807 the last two provisions became rocks of offense.

The college laws also spelled out the means by which the institution hoped to preserve order. In so doing, they formalized the procedures that John Witherspoon had used so effectively to control the students. "The punishments of the institution, being wholly of the moral kind," were addressed to the students' "sense of duty and the principles of honor and shame."[29] At all points in their education, students were instructed to act honorably and to seek an honorable end to their time at the college. Letters from parents called upon sons to court distinction and to flee from dishonorable practices and companions.[30] The student societies reinforced the appeal to honor, and the professors allowed the societies to stand upon their honor in relating to the faculty.[31] Injunctions to honor were also the key to discipline at the college.

The carefully calibrated punishments installed under Witherspoon were designed to bring erring students back to their senses and order back to the college. Punishments progressed in gravity from private counsel with a single faculty member to admonishments before the class and then all the students, suspension with a public statement of the case, probationary dismissal, and finally expulsion (which required the approval of at least six trustees). The admonitions, moreover, were to be accompanied by "acknowledgments of the fault and engagements of amendment" (before the class) or "a public confession and profession of penitence" (before

[28] *Laws* (1802), 20, 17, 18, 29, 33–34.

[29] Ibid., 23.

[30] See, for example, Hannah Iredell to James Iredell, July 21, 1804, James Iredell Papers, PUA: Hannah expected her son to graduate from Princeton "enriched with virtue and knowledge" and "improved in wisdom and uncorrupted in morals." Similar sentiments can be inferred from J. C. Breckinridge's reassurances to his mother about his honorable behavior (Harrison, "Young Kentuckian at Princeton," 292–93, 294, 296, 300–301, 309–10). They were also primary in the concerns expressed by Henry Hobart's mother to her son in the 1790s (*Correspondence of John Henry Hobart*).

[31] McLachlan, "The *Choice of Hercules*."

all the students).[32] Virtually no student offense was beyond the pale of forgiveness, except the unwillingness to ask for forgiveness. While the overt purpose of disciplinary action was to restore order, its higher goal was the restitution of the student to an honorable place in the institution. Only in unusual circumstances, as in the spring of 1807, did the system break down.

College officials made use of analagous practices of honor and shame to encourage students in their studies. Laws warned the negligent that "the faculty may mention, before the class, the names of such persons, and administer a reproof to them, and an exhortation to greater diligence in the future; those, on the contrary, who shall appear to excel, shall be mentioned with approbation." The emphasis on public performance that characterized the whole of Princeton only heightened the concern for honor and the fear of shame. Each night after prayers students in regular rotation gave speeches "on the stage in the publick hall" before the faculty and their fellows. The faculty distributed college honors at commencement through the assignment of speeches. The societies held debates and organized orations continually. College examinations were also oral, as classes were called in a body to recite before the assembled faculty, a delegation from the trustees, and "all gentlemen of liberal education who may choose to be present."[33]

Through their laws, trustees attempted to regulate conduct, but they also made a statement about order and honor. The regulations that prevailed in 1806–1807 had been revised after a devastating fire during the first years following the political "Revolution of 1800." Leaders of the college worried about the disorder overwhelming the country, which they feared might sweep over the college. Within the sphere of their authority they meant to do something about it. When students received the bound college laws in formal ceremony, they were put on their honor to preserve order. The stress on honor at Princeton comported better with the college's Whig republicanism than with its evangelical Presbyterianism, a faith that featured the humiliation of the Savior and the sovereignty of God as the source of all human worth. Yet the largely Federalist authorities at Princeton had grown accustomed to thinking of national preservation in terms of national honor. That honor had been won in fields of bloody battle. It had been

[32] *Laws* (1802), 23.
[33] Ibid., 27–28.

preserved at great cost—against the dishonor of those who wished to repudiate debts, against a dishonorable lust for influence (Democratic clubs) or for anarchy (Whiskey Rebellion), and against the dishonorable grasp of foreign nations for the territory and trade of the United States.

During the rebellion of 1807, students stood upon their honor, basing their "dignity as gentlemen" upon their honor as what it meant to show "a proper spirit of resistance and dignified pride."[34] Trained by their teachers in a host of face-to-face challenges to regard honor as a fundamental value, and also aware that national honor had assumed cosmic significance, they took the short step of investing honor with a power to order all reality.[35]

The trustees, for their part, responded by attaching honor more securely to the received traditions of Protestant order and political deference. Princeton authorities perceived the student effort as a transgression of sacred norms that annihilated honor and prostituted patriotism. To Elias Boudinot, honor had no meaning unless it grew from religion, reason, and familial emotion, as well as patriotism. As he put it in the immediate aftermath of the rebellion, "True honor consists in the performance of duty." To the students he would say that, in their situation, "submission is honor—not submission to despotism, which you need not apprehend, but deference to authority, exercised under the guardianship & controul of those, who in the place of your natural Parents, regard your improvement as essential to their happiness; and as Patriots connect your acquirements with the dearest interest & highest destinies of our Country."[36]

The lived realities of the students' lives affected the larger purposes of trustees and faculty almost randomly. Sometimes these realities—like overcrowding in Nassau Hall or the lack of exercise during winter—worked at direct cross-purposes to the larger goals of the Princeton circle. T. J. Wertenbaker was probably correct when he wrote of this period that the encouragement of "interclass

[34] I. W. Bates and Student Committee, Broadside beginning *Dear Sir* (Princeton, Apr. 15, 1807).

[35] The process of making honor the ultimate value led to "all sorts of confusions and self-doubts," especially when the definition of personal worth included the contradictory dictates of religion and self-assertion. A full consideration of such confusion is found in Wyatt-Brown, *Southern Honor*, especially chap. 4, "Gentility," from which this quotation comes, 88.

[36] In Mark A. Noll, ed., "The Response of Elias Boudinot to the Student Rebellion of 1807: Visions of Honor, Order, and Morality," *PULC* 43 (1981): 19–20.

athletics . . . would have worked wonders in keeping the boys contented and in developing their bodies."[37] Other aspects of the weekly round, like participation in the student societies, more generally supported the general aims of the institution. The loyalty inspired by the societies could override loyalty to faculty, but usually it served to channel student ambition along lines approved by the entire community. In the event, however, as tensions rose in the spring of 1807, the general conditions of student life faded into the background. Not how students lived but what they believed was at center stage when the clash occurred.

THE CRUSH of students in the spring of 1807 no doubt contributed to the seventeen disciplinary cases, an unusually large number, that came before the faculty during the semester. Most of these involved public insolence or disruptive behavior due to inebriation.[38] Also during the semester two or three fires were set in the college. While they were extinguished without harm, an outhouse on the grounds was consumed. In response to rising tensions, the professors let word be passed sometime in March that they would request the trustees to address the question of student discipline at their regularly scheduled meeting in early April.[39]

On Tuesday night, March 24, a senior, Francis D. Cummins, was out of his room "at an unlawful time of the night" and was discovered "cursing and insulting some of the peaceable and orderly inhabitants of the town." When the staff investigated the incident, it was discovered that Cummins had "intoxicated himself." And so, "viewing the disorderly state of the College occasioned by the frequent use of strong liquors and going into taverns without permission," the faculty suspended Cummins. Five days later, on Monday, March 30, the faculty adjudicated two other cases. Junior Henry Hyde had cursed tutor Alexander Monteith for trying to quell a disturbance in Hyde's room. Sophomore Francis Matteaus was arraigned for bringing "strong liquor into the college" and for responding insolently to Professor Maclean, who had been trying

[37] Wertenbaker, *Princeton*, 193–94.

[38] FM, Sept. 29, 1806–Mar. 30, 1807.

[39] A full account of the semester's problems and a brief résumé of the faculty minutes concerning the riot is found in John Maclean to Ashbel Green, Apr. 3, 1807, Miscellaneous Papers, PUL. Additional details are supplied by Elias Boudinot to Ashbel Green, Apr. 3, 1807, Elias Boudinot Collection, PUL, most of which is quoted in George Adams Boyd, *Elias Boudinot: Patriot and Statesman, 1740–1821* (Princeton, 1952), 267–68.

to quiet him down. For both students the sentence was suspension and dismissal.[40]

Spring exams and a regular meeting of the board were both planned for Wednesday, April 1. On Tuesday, a group of eight students, "calling themselves a committee of the college appointed to wait on the Faculty[,] handed in a petition," asking the professors to reconsider their recent disciplinary decisions. The three seniors and five juniors on the committee were talented and respected by their peers. None of them had appeared before the faculty for discipline in the course of the semester. All were from well-connected families. Of their number, James W. Wayne later became a member of the United States Congress from Georgia and a justice of the Supreme Court; William Hayward of Maryland also became a congressman; and Abel Parker Upshur of Virginia served as secretary of state under President Tyler.[41]

The petition, signed by as many as 160 students, contended that the faculty had violated "the principles of justice" and had "proceeded precipitately" in suspending Hyde, Matteaus, and Cummins. It "respectfuly" requested the reinstatement of the students, in view of the fact that the faculty acted under the influence of prejudicial or misinformed testimony. The faculty met immediately but was entirely unmoved. "Without hesitation" it rejected the demands of the students. The professors then called upon lawyer Richard Stockton, Jr., of Princeton, "the only trustee in their reach," for advice, before concluding that the student petition was nothing more than the fruit of an illegal conspiracy.[42]

At 5:00 P.M. President Smith proceeded with the usual service of evening prayer in the main room of Nassau Hall. Trustee Stockton followed with "a speech of considerable length" in which students were told that, if they did not "renounce the *principle* of uniting together to control the government of the College according to their humours," they would be suspended.[43] Stockton's words and his bearing, which his Jeffersonian opponents called "haughty and

---

[40] FM, Mar. 25 and 30, 1807.

[41] Ibid., Mar. 31, 1807. A fellow student, William Meade, who later became an Episcopal bishop in Virginia, spoke of the eight leaders as the school's "finest young men" (Maclean, *CNJ*, 2:76). Cf. Alexander A. Lawrence, *James Moore Wayne: Southern Unionist* (Chapel Hill, N.C., 1943); *Biographical Dictionary of the American Congress, 1774–1971* (1971 ed.), s.v. "William Hayward, Jr."; and Claude H. Hall, *Abel Parker Upshur: Conservative Virginian, 1790–1844* (Madison, Wis., 1964).

[42] FM, Mar. 31, 1807, with full transcript of the student petition.

[43] Ibid., further details in Gov. Joseph Bloomfield in behalf of the Trustees, *To the Public* (n.p., [1807]), col. b.

imperious," did not achieve the desired effect.[44] As he spoke, "the disorderly students," according to the faculty minutes, "at several times . . . scraped with their feet on the floor and gave other signs of their disapprobation of what was said." When he finished, Stockton offered the students time to think over "the part they had to play." One or more replied that "they wished an Answer" immediately. Whereupon President Smith proposed to call the roll, informing the students "that those who adhered to the combination should be suspended from the College." But Smith could get out only a single name before "one of the leaders of the association" arose, cried out, and led most of the students from the room "shouting and yelling"—"like drunken Indians" is how trustee Elias Boudinot received the story. To their backs President Smith announced that they were suspended. About 35 students remained, and those of that number who had earlier signed the petition withdrew their names. The faculty then made a list of 126 students "who adhered to the combination in the Hall and were suspended." It included 41 seniors, 48 juniors, 29 sophomores, and 8 freshmen.[45]

Some of the suspended students meanwhile began "to break doors and windows and to commit various other disorders." The faculty soon surrendered Nassau Hall but then called on the local militia to remove the students. The rebels, in the words of a sympathizer, "with the magnaminity of Spartans got clubs and stones, posted themselves in the entries and dared them to a combat. The faculty perceiving that the students were not to be terrified had their troops discharged."[46] The next day, the trustees failed for the first time since 1798 to muster a quorum for their regular spring meeting. The four who did attend, including Richard Stockton, saw that "the state of disorder and confusion" continued and, fearing "fatal mischief, if they remained longer in a body," officially closed the college. An extraordinary meeting of the board was called for April 8, and it was announced that the college would open for the scheduled beginning of the summer session on May 8.[47]

[44] Alfred Hoyt Bill, *A House Called Morven: Its Role in American History, 1701–1954* (Princeton, 1954), 70.

[45] FM, Mar. 31, 1807; Boudinot to Green, Apr. 3, 1807, in Boyd, *Boudinot*, 208.

[46] FM, Mar. 31, 1807; John Campbell to David Campbell, May 2, 1807, Campbell Family Papers, William R. Perkins Library, Duke University, Durham, N.C.

[47] TM, Apr. 1 and 8, 1807.

THE TRUSTEE action sparked a noteworthy reaction from the protesters who remained in Princeton. Students may have begun their agitation out of genuine concern for their dismissed fellows, to blow off steam after a hard winter, or in the hope of somehow avoiding end-of-term examinations, but their struggle soon became something more. The Faculty Minutes for March 31 record that students were already referring to their original petition as "a remonstrance." Almost as soon, the group presenting the petition was termed "the committee of correspondence." And one of the first students to renounce his part in the affair wrote spontaneously of "the late rebellion" and of "those who have rebelled against your Laws."[48]

Nothing in the whole episode is so striking as the students' attempt to justify their actions with the republican vocabulary of the Revolution. Although the clash of will occurred over a relatively insignificant matter, students did not hesitate to interpret the event in terms of grand social theory. College officials responded in kind, not by agreeing that the incident should be dignified with the language of the Revolution, but by treating student pretentions as an affront to a value system embracing not only Whig but also Christian convictions.

Joseph Cabell Breckinridge, a junior, explained his view of the situation in a letter of April 6 to his mother, widow of John Breckinridge (d. 1806), a Kentucky legislator who had served as Jefferson's attorney general. Earlier in his career at Princeton, young Breckinridge, a serious-minded and hard-working scholar, had complained about the distracting influence of his less dedicated classmates. Now, however, he was indignant at the injustices of the faculty, whose conduct was "unjust, tyrannical, and unaccommodating." To the faculty's assertion that the students had "no right to form ourselves into a combination," Breckinridge replied that if "men" could not associate for such purposes, "they had no rights at all." Breckinridge was astounded "that any set of men should be so weak as to make such an observation in a country the fundamental principle of whose government is, liberty of action." Breckinridge went on to tell his mother that, if the faculty trespassed its legal bounds, "we must indubitably have a right to remonstrate . . . against proceedings contrary to truth, justice, humanity, and diametrically opposite to those very doctrines of moral and political

---

[48] FM, Mar. 31, 1807; Bates and Committee, Broadside of Apr. 15, 1807; Henry Hyde to college trustees, Apr. 10, 1807, PUA.

right which you yourselves have inculcated during many precious hours of private recitation."[49]

When the board convened on April 8, it dismissed a note from six members of the original committee expressing the desire "to do any thing which will tend to reconcile so unfortunate a rupture, still keeping in view the principles we have already publickly avowed."[50] The next day trustees communicated their willingness to meet individually with suspended students and appointed a committee to prepare questions for the ones who chose to appear.[51] Much of the next day's sessions was taken up with sixteen-year-old Abel Parker Upshur, whom the committee of correspondence selected as its representative. Upshur, the fourth son of a wealthy planter on Virginia's Eastern Shore, was a capable spokesman. His father, a responsible Episcopalian, community leader, slaveholder, and Federalist, equated Jeffersonianism and "jacobinism" as easily as the Princeton trustees. Before the trustees, Upshur argued for the right to petition for redress of grievances. He also took particular exception to two of the trustees' stated principles—that students owed unquestioned obedience to the college governors and that the student-faculty relationship was a "domestic" one like that of child to parent. To the contrary, he argued, individuals "have a right to resist or even overthrow" a government that exceeds its bounds. Students, moreover, were not required to submit to college authorities in loco parentis.[52]

Although some of the trustees were impressed with Upshur's performance, they proceeded to expel him along with the other leaders of the rebellion and to suspend several more who had taken part. The board drew up a letter to presidents of other col-

[49] Breckinridge to Mary Breckinridge, Apr. 6, 1807, in Harrison, "Young Kentuckian at Princeton," 303–4.

[50] TM, Apr. 8, 1807; the student note of Apr. 8 is reproduced in Bates and Committee, Broadside of Apr. 15, 1807.

[51] TM, Apr. 9, 1807; a fuller manuscript with the questions is in PUA.

[52] Hall, *Upshur*, 11–12, TM, Apr. 10, 1807; Bloomfield, *To the Public*, col. d; The Committee in behalf of the Combination, *To the Public* (n.p., [sometime after Apr. 15, 1807]), Folder labeled "Rebellion of March 1807—Miscellaneous Documents," PUA. The last quotation is from the trustees' broadside. In a strange irony, A. P. Upshur, while secretary of state, was killed on Feb. 28, 1844, when a cannon exploded during the inspection of a new warship, the *Princeton*, captained by the son of Richard Stockton. The story is told, though without reference to the student rebellion of 1807, in Bill, *House Called Morven*, 108–9; and Oscar Handlin, "Explosion on the *Princeton*," in *Chance or Destiny: Turning Points in American History* (Boston, 1955).

leges, requesting them not to admit the ousted students, and another to the parents of suspended students, spelling out conditions under which their sons could reenter the college. They would be requested to "acknowledge their error and criminality in the late riotous and rebellious proceedings" and "pledge themselves to future obedience to submit to such admonitions as the Board of Trustees shall judge expedient." The board also made arrangements to lay its case before the public.[53]

THE BOARD actions led the committee of correspondence to prepare two documents for the press, a short circular letter to students who had left Princeton and a longer broadside, "To the Public." Both were couched self-consciously in the language of 1776. The circular letter recounted Upshur's futile appearance before the trustees and passed on word of the meeting that the board had scheduled for early May to receive the appeals of suspended students. The committee confessed that its prospects at this forthcoming session were not good, "since the adoption of our principles has been deemed a crime, and resolution in supporting them meritorious of expulsion." The circular closed with an emotional appeal, asking all those, who shared "a spirit of freedom and independence . . . to revolt from tyranny and resist oppression."[54] The students were defending due process, the right of petition, and their fundamental honor. They also thought they had a vocabulary, provided by the republicanism of the Revolution, with which to express their complaint.

The student broadside offered a full recitation of events and expanded upon the cause of student grievance.[55] It placed the blame for "this serious and lamentable revolution" squarely upon "the haughtiness of superiority" exercised by the faculty and trustees. "The principle on which we had combined" was due process. The students suspended in the last week of March "were even denied the privilege of an evidence in their own defence." The authorities

[53] TM, Apr. 11, 1807. The account of Upshur's having impressed the trustees, especially President Smith, is in Henry A. Wise, *Seven Decades of the Union* (Philadelphia, 1881), 197. Almost all the college presidents who responded to the Princeton authorities approved their actions. Several added their own comments concerning, as Timothy Dwight of Yale phrased it, "that impatience of controul which we also lament as a strong characteristic of the rising generation" (Dwight to Governor Bloomfield, May 16, 1807, John Maclean Papers, PUA).

[54] Bates and Committee, Broadside of Apr. 15, 1807.

[55] Quotations in this paragraph are from Committee, *To the Public.*

refused to accept the petition and "determined on punishment before they knew of a crime." Their "violence and oppression" compelled "actions of a bolder turn." And now the trustees were dishonoring themselves by spreading injurious reports before the public. Those who formed the committee were not hell-raisers ("for such we do not contend"), nor did they fear the result of the impending examinations. Impressive principles—for example, "the mind is free in its determination and cannot be influenced by the exercise of power"—supported the student stand. The rebels did not "wish to be liberated from the restraints of Law." They were rather "induced . . . to countenance this rebellion," in which "they had nothing to gain and every thing to lose . . . only by a sense of its propriety, from a conviction that no superiority should sanction oppression—that it is a privilege which nature has given us to petition when we think ourselves aggrieved." Infused with republican principles, filled with rhetorical parallels to the Stamp Act Resolves, the Declaration of Independence, the Bill of Rights, and the Kentucky Resolutions, the students felt they had a persuasive case.[56]

Their reasoning needed no further support in some quarters. A friend of the suspended Joseph Cabell Breckinridge wrote of "the arbitrary despotism at Princeton" and of the students who left the college, deeming it "degrading in the lowest degree to apologize for asserting a right which nature had given them." Breckinridge himself scorned the trustee actions. "Once we were all to be shot for rebels, then we were to be prosecuted as rioters, and last of all . . . liable to an arrest and prosecution for the crime of conspiracy."[57]

---

[56] For sources of the students' phrases, see protests against denial of the right to petition in the Resolutions of the Stamp Act Congress (1765), Declaration and Resolves of the Continental Congress (1774), the Declaration of Independence, and the First Amendment to the Constitution; affirmation of the right to present evidence before one's accusers in the Virginia Bill of Rights (1776) and the Fifth Amendment; the Kentucky Resolution's protest against "unlimited submission" and "undelegated and consequently unlimited powers," and its affirmation in support of due process (1798); and the Virginia Resolution's similar protest against illegitimate power forbidden by the Constitution (1798) (Samuel Eliot Morison, ed., *Sources and Documents Illustrating the American Revolution, 1764–1788, and the Formation of the Federal Constitution*, 2d ed. [1929; reprint, New York, 1965], 34, 120, 160, 363, 150, 363; Henry Steele Commager, *Documents of American History*, 2 vols. [8th ed., New York, 1968], 1:178–81, 182–83).

[57] John Campbell to David Campbell, May 2, 1807; Breckinridge to Mary Breckinridge, May 17, 1807, in Harrison, "Young Kentuckian at Princeton," 306.

Even when members of the student generation had doubts about the affair, they were expressed in terms reflecting the ideological framework that the students had appropriated. Thomas Telfair, a graduate of the class of 1805, grasped both serious and comic dimensions of the situation when he wrote in early May to his brother, Alexander, one of the suspended students. "I suppose the heroes of '76 were but pigmies in comparison with those of College—For the first two or three days after the College was dissolved, no doubt more heroes walked the streets of Princeton than did in Paris after the memorable Revolution of France—But now, without any great effort of fancy, I can see them moping about with broken spirits & relenting hearts."[58]

Predictably, the Princeton authorities and their supporters found the student arguments pretentious and offensive. Commenting on the rebellion in its issue of May 19, 1807, the *Troy Gazette* (N.Y.) editorialized that "society would be overthrown by tenets like those manifested by the revolters," tenets "worthy of a Godwin or a Holcroft. . . . The same mental epidemick which has crazed Europe, and is extending its baleful ravages throughout the civilized world, has contaminated these young rights-of-boy-politicians." Support for the trustees came also from parents of suspended students like Charles Worthington of Georgetown, who wrote on April 25 to apologize for his son's conduct and to rue the "times like the present when principles of immorality, Revolution & disorganization are so prevalent." These convictions echoed the judgment of trustees like Ashbel Green, who, unable to attend the board's special session in early May, wrote President Smith to urge the most unbending response to student demands, or otherwise "the institution is ruined."[59]

The Princeton authorities treated the rebellion as both an exercise in youthful dissipation and an expression of pernicious principles. Their response to dissipation was to control student access to money and drink. Their response to pernicious principles was to invoke a hallowed set of religious convictions. These reactions nicely illustrated the intellectual world of the trustees. On the one hand, they were sustained by an Enlightenment confidence in the ability of nearly mechanical remedies to counteract the fall from

[58] Thomas Telfair to Alexander Telfair, May 2, 1807, Edward Telfair Papers, Perkins Library, Duke University.

[59] "Revolt at Princeton College," *Troy Gazette*, May 19, 1807, copy in PUA; Worthington to Governor Bloomfield, Apr. 25, 1807, John Maclean Papers, PUA; Green to Smith, May 5, 1807, PUA.

private venality to public disorder.[60] On the other hand, however, they were compelled as Christians to seek otherworldly explanations for sin and its effects.

The trustees' published statements described the riot as a disruption in the mechanics of moral order. Students had too much money, they drank too much, they visited taverns too frequently, they were ill-mannered, and they refused to act as witnesses to the disruptive behavior of their fellows.[61] Abel Parker Upshur's argument, which "spoke much of *rights*, comparing the College to a state of civil society," was absurd. The right each student enjoyed was to withdraw from the college, "but while he remains in it, and subject to its laws, his *right* is obedience."[62] Trustees felt they faced a clear choice: "either to govern their own institution by their own officers, or resign it to the government of inconsiderate boys, and passionate young men." They were resolved to "humble that indocile and usurping spirit, which tramples on the wholesome restraints of all legitimate authority, and which has led to the late unhappy disorders." And they set themselves to exert "that paternal discipline . . . to fix [students] in habits of diligence, of virtue and order, the sole aim and tendency of which are, to prepare them for usefulness and distinction in this life, and for a higher state of happiness in a better world."

The board directed positive efforts toward counteracting "the evils" arising "from young men possessing, in too great abundance, the means of dissipation." It specified necessary college expenses ($188.32 per year) and proposed a suitable allowance ($250–$280) for clothes, furniture, and miscellaneous expenses. It explained that a new officer, the bursar, would act "as the legal guardian" for the students' money. And it provided a form for parents to promise not to provide any money to their sons except through the bursar.[63]

---

[60] These reactions fit neatly into the assumptions about causality and Providence described in Gordon S. Wood, "Conspiracy and the Paranoid Style: Causality and Deceit in the Eighteenth Century," *WMQ* 39 (1982): 408–11, 434–35, 439–41, with specific reference to Stanhope Smith, p. 413.

[61] Summaries and quotations in this paragraph are from Bloomfield, *To the Public*.

[62] An illuminating discussion of how students and faculty differed in their conception of college governance in the the period is found in McLachlan, "The *Choice of Hercules*," 2:462–66.

[63] Joseph Bloomfield (for trustees) to parents, Apr. 10, 1807, printed in *Troy Gazette*, June 2, 1807, copy in PUA. Not all parents appreciated this effort to regulate the flow of funds; in a letter of May 5, 1807, Jared Ingersoll and four other fathers

Trustees approached the problem of drink more indirectly. At the close of its special session in early April, they dispatched a committee to the New Jersey legislature with a request that the lawmakers "prohibit . . . tavern keepers, storekeepers and all other persons" from selling liquor to students. Later that year the board appointed a numerous delegation of its own members to present the model act to the legislature. And shortly thereafter such a bill became law.[64]

Elias Boudinot, then in his thirty-fifth year as a board member, offered the college's religious interpretation of the disturbance when he addressed the approximately 110 students who appeared in Princeton on May 8 to begin the summer semester. Boudinot blamed the rebellion on the dishonorable willingness of students to violate their oaths to uphold college regulations. "Where truth & honor remained in the smallest degree," good order could have been expected in the college. But "when the moral principle is wanting," disorder must result. He defended the severe actions of the trustees against the rebels as springing "only from an honorable zeal for Literature & Religion, the two main pillars of the social Fabric, which without sound principles in the rising generation, must crumble into dust."[65]

Boudinot's speech drove home once again the Princeton worldview—sound principles encouraged virtue and order, fallacious beliefs led to vice and disorder. The returning students who sought "the light of Reason, Science & Revelation" would find lives of honor and duty. By contrast, those who led the revolt had set their course by more dangerous guides: "The clumsy sophistry of Godwin; the pernicious subtilties of Hume, and the coarse vulgarities of Paine, have been exposed at once in all their loathsome deformity." According to Boudinot, "these boasted Systems" were responsible for the dissolution manifested in the rebellion—"originating in the wantonness & pride of human intellect, marking their progress by desolation & infamy; sapping all the foundations of Society, & levelling all the props of morality; aiming, in a word, at the perfection of Man by extinguishing every Sentiment which raises him above the Brute." Students should flee such principles in favor of "that blessed *System of Life & Immortality*, which has been brought to light by the divine Messenger from Heaven, and which

from Philadelphia told Bloomfield that the plan presented "insuperable difficulties" (Individual Autograph Manuscripts, PUA).

[64] TM, Apr. 11 and Oct. 1, 1807; Maclean, *CNJ*, 2:80.

[65] In Noll, "Response of Elias Boudinot," 17–19.

it has allways been, and I trust allways will be, the principal Aim of this Institution, to impress upon your minds & establish in your hearts."[66]

To the college authorities, nothing was clearer than that the rebellion, however garnished by the language of the Revolution, was a dangerous expression of anti-Christian dissipation. The rebellion manifested an absurd attempt to use republican slogans for the unsettling of an order established by Christian faith, enlightened reason, and a correct understanding of Revolutionary values. It was self-evident to them that, properly understood, the republican virtues of the Revolution supported good order and were aligned with the dutifulness inspired by Christian faith. They not only could not understand, they were greatly offended by the attitudes and arguments of the rebels.

Their viewpoint was shared by a small number of the students. The pious William Weeks, who had come to Princeton from New England to prepare for the ministry, wrote home in early May about the "pretty serious consequences" from the "rebellion." To Weeks, however, rights were irrelevant to what had gone on. "I was so fortunate as to keep clear, as did about all who make any pretentions to religion: But near 7 eighths of the whole number of students were more or less concerned in it. It owed its origin, probably, to the spirit of dissipation & impatience of restraint which was very prevalent."[67] Like the trustees, whose active concern for religion he shared, William Weeks looked through the Revolutionary rhetoric of the rebellious students to the dissoluteness that he assumed was the source of their error.

STUDENTS AND authorities disagreed sharply about the meaning of the rebellion, but observers then and since have concurred that it was a disaster for the college.[68] The number of students dropped immediately to little more than half of those present before 1807; for thirty-three years Princeton did not graduate as many students

---

[66] Ibid., 20.

[67] Weeks to Sally Weeks, May 10, 1807, Sheldon Art Museum, Middlebury, Vt. Another pious student who regretted the whole affair was William Meade, the future Episcopal bishop (Maclean, *CNJ*, 26–27).

[68] Wertenbaker, *Princeton*, 143 ("the injury done by the riot of 1807 can hardly be overestimated"); Maclean, *CNJ*, 2:82; W. Frank Craven, "Samuel Stanhope Smith," in *Princetonians 1769–1775*, 49–50; Howard Miller, *The Revolutionary College: American Presbyterian Higher Education, 1707–1837* (New York, 1976), 270; Novak, *Rights of Youth*, 33–37; and Varnum Lansing Collins, *Princeton* (New York, 1914), 116–17.

as it did in 1806. Soon the loss of students forced the college to cut back its faculty, so that, by the end of 1807, after two forced resignations and the earlier loss of Henry Kollock, Stanhope Smith and John Maclean once again were the only professors. Even sympathetic friends such as Benjamin Rush had to admit that "Princeton has lately lost its popularity among us."[69]

Although the loss of students, faculty, and public reputation was a severe blow, the rebellion's effect on trustee attitudes toward their own institution was even more serious. Trustee decisions about the course of higher education would become the dominant factor in Smith's last years at the college, but even in the first months after the rebellion it was obvious that board members were shaken by the event. At its April meeting the board appointed a standing committee to oversee college life, and the committee fulfilled its charge compulsively. In September it reported that the president had read the college laws three different times during the semester at evening prayer and that the change in the refectory from cider to "Molasses beer" had proven useful. Yet, serious problems had also surfaced: the pavement around Nassau Hall's lowest story was in a "filthy state," some students had violated the prohibition against frequenting taverns on public occasions, the faculty minutes were occasionally unintelligible (a serious lapse in the event that the minutes were ever required in court), a tutor had once been absent without permission, another had once entertained "a party of Ladies in his chambers," and the cut-up desks of the sophomores revealed "a great want of proper discipline." Never in the history of this active board had surveillance been carried to such lengths.[70]

The meaning of the student rebellion extended beyond a crisis in student discipline and the immediate loss of students. The college trustees of 1807 tolerated no doubts about the essential har-

[69] Rush to John Montgomery, July 5, 1808, in Butterfield, *Letters of Rush*, 2:970. A former trustee, William Shippen, could make only a feeble denial to a Virginia correspondent who wrote late in 1807, "Our University is rising very fast whilst Princeton is in decline" (quoted in Burt, "Student Life in Nassau Hall," 125). On the decline in attendance, see *General Catalogue*, 119–24; Collins, *Princeton*, 109, 115, 121; F. H. Skinner to James Iredell, July 16, 1809, James Iredell Papers, PUA; and McLachlan, "The *Choice of Hercules*," 2:473.

[70] TM, Oct. 1, 1807. At this same gathering the board asked trustees of the Princeton Presbyterian Church, where the commencement was held, to keep "hucksters' booths" away from the church, to exile the customary refreshment wagon to the far reaches of the campus, and to provide local constables for standing guard throughout the day.

mony between republicanism, which nourished social order through political liberty, and Christianity, which promoted the same end through liberation from sin. Student arguments that seemed to disregard this basic harmony confronted a deeply ingrained tradition. The trustees' own promotion of Revolutionary ritual and their constant repetition of its verities no doubt stimulated students to think that they too could work the republican calculus for their own benefit, even at the expense of their teachers and examples. Trustees, of course, saw it differently. The rebellion symbolized much more the failure of their instruction than its success.

Or at least it signaled the failure of Stanhope Smith's instruction. The rebelling students were trifling with a cherished legacy, challenging a carefully wrought synthesis between republican and Christian values, exploiting for disorder a political ideology that the trustees held to be the foundation of order, and trampling upon the educational possibilities opened up by the War for Independence. In short, everything that the trustees held sacred in their own national history and all that was most important in their oversight of Princeton seemed to be at risk. Who should bear the primary responsibility for this disaster but the one charged with communicating these most basic values to the students?

As individuals and as a body the trustees never indicted Stanhope Smith in these terms, but their actions spoke clearly. Smith had failed on two accounts. The lower-order problem was a failure of education. His teaching, perhaps for pardonable reasons of health, had not taken hold. Student disorder indicated that the rising generation was not learning its lessons. The higher-order failure concerned the lessons themselves. Was it possible that Smith's infirmity was intellectual as well as physical, that his ardent advocacy of Enlightment science—or perhaps the way he aligned Christian faith and moral philosophy—had somehow poisoned the good stock handed down from Witherspoon? As they assessed problems at Princeton, the trustees did not abandon the methods of diagnosing public disorder they had learned from Smith's predecessor. Rather, their allegiance to those methods, the very methods to which Smith was so scrupulously loyal, led them to an unpleasant conclusion. The nearly fatal fever of April 1807, as well as the festering problem with the production of ministers, suggested to at least some trustees that disease at the College of New Jersey was widespread and malignant.

THE BOARD in which such suspicions grew after 1807 was a markedly different body from the group that rebuilt the college after the fire of 1802. The large turnover of 1807 marked the passing of a generation whose goals for the school had been shaped by Witherspoon and the exuberant inspiration of the Revolutionary era. It also significantly weakened personal ties joining lay and clerical trustees and paved the way for a sharp increase in the activity and influence of ministers on the board. Almost as decisively as reactions to the student rebellion, the new orientation of the trustees sealed the fate of Stanhope Smith's republican Christian Enlightenment.

When the Princeton board met on April 6, 1808, its ranks included six new men. Three of the old trustees had died during the previous year: John Bayard, the Reverend William Boyd, and the Reverend Alexander MacWhorter. Three others, bowing to the infirmities of old age, had resigned: ministers John Rodgers (age 80) and Azel Roe (69) and layman Jonathan Bayard Smith (65). Far more than a mere shuffling of interchangeable parts occurred when replacements for these men took their seats on the board. The new trustees of 1807, and the four others who joined them in the next three years, rapidly took the lead in directing the school. The turnover of trustees, combined with the great activity of the new board members, meant that substantially new leadership guided Princeton into the second decade of the nineteenth century.

To be sure, the new trustees came from the same networks that had supplied the old.[71] Samuel Bayard of Princeton, an active Federalist, a judge, editor, experienced diplomat, and husband of Elias Boudinot's niece, replaced his father, John Bayard. Andrew Kirkpatrick, chief justice of the New Jersey Supreme Court and Samuel Bayard's brother-in-law, was named to the position relinquished by Jonathan Bayard Smith. The four new clergymen were Samuel Miller of New York City, who took the place of his mentor and senior colleague, John Rodgers; Robert Finley of Basking Ridge, a Princeton graduate (1787) who had studied for the ministry under Ashbel Green and Witherspoon; James Richards, a transplanted New Englander who had pastored the Presbyterian church in Morristown since 1794; and George Spafford Woodhull

[71] Biographical sources are cited for individual trustees in the Bibliography. A fuller account of the new board is found in Mark A. Noll, "The Princeton Trustees of 1807: New Men and New Directions," *PULC* 41 (1980): 208–30.

of Cranberry, who graduated from Princeton in 1790 and then trained for the ministry with his father, John, a trustee since 1780. Although these new men were already members of the broader Princeton circle before they joined the board, their presence still signaled several important changes.

In the first instance, the retiring and deceased members took with them more than just the wisdom of age and a combined total of 168 years on the board. The two Bayard laymen with ministers Rodgers, Roe, and MacWhorter had been living links to a rapidly vanishing world. These five were veterans of the Revolution, contemporaries and friends of George Washington and John Witherspoon. Only a rapidly diminishing corps of similarly aging relics knew firsthand the exalted vision of the nation's founding. Aspirations for a "Christian Sparta" or "a Republic of Christian Virtue" did not entirely pass away with the passing of the Revolutionary generation,[72] but the ways in which educational leaders perceived godliness and freedom, morality and the safety of the republic, were changing as the United States moved into its third decade.

As a group, the new trustees lacked the comprehensive vision that the contemporaries of Witherspoon shared. They were, rather, particularists, expert in forming voluntary societies, eager to press the claims of Presbyterianism, and anxious to professionalize the ministerial calling. In the face of these interests the comprehensive purposes of Witherspoon and Samuel Stanhope Smith became secondary concerns.

The role of the new trustees in founding a Presbyterian theological seminary was the most obvious manifestation of the new attitude. But the new trustees also departed in other ways from the more cosmopolitan disposition of their predecessors. Older trustees were active Presbyterians, but the new men, especially Samuel Miller and Robert Finley, became much more aggressive champions of the denomination's distinctives. In addition, many of the new trustees were promoters of revival. Where earlier ministers had combined a concern for revival with broader interests in the general life of society, revival became a more exclusive preoccupation in the early nineteenth century. Trustee involvement in many new voluntary agencies also led to a situation where the college became just one of the many causes its board members sup-

[72] Gordon S. Wood, *The Creation of the American Republic, 1776–1787* (Chapel Hill, 1969), 114–18; Nathan O. Hatch, *The Sacred Cause of Liberty: Republican Thought and the Millennium in Revolutionary New England* (New Haven, 1977), 97–138.

ported. Under these influences, Princeton's catholicity began to dissipate.

In sum, the trustees who joined the board in 1807 were part of a vanguard searching for new solutions to American problems. While none professed to repudiate the Revolutionary ideals that had held sway at Princeton since the 1770s, all were willing to adapt the mission of the college to the particularistic, denominational, and voluntaristic currents rapidly gaining ascendency among the country's educated and religious elite.[73]

Another reason for the new character of the Princeton board was that ties between its ministers and laymen were weakened by the passing of the old trustees.[74] In addition, ministers came to exert an increasing influence on the board. Under Witherspoon and during Smith's early years, laymen—the Bayards, Boudinots, and Stocktons—were clearly the most active and influential board members. After 1807 clerical involvement increased rapidly until clergymen dominated the board's decisions. Historians of Princeton have treated the student rebellion of 1807 as the occasion for trustees to exercise a stifling oversight of the institution. Board members did indeed tighten their control as a result of the disturbance. At the same time, however, it was a substantially new board that did the tightening. Ironically, it was a board in which clergymen took a larger share of the leadership at the same time that they directed their major interests toward the founding of a theological seminary. After 1807 fewer of the board's ministers had intimate ties of kinship or shared interests with its laymen. The older lay trustees were either reducing their participation in college affairs or turning their attention in other directions. The board's newer laymen had neither the vision for the school nor the single-minded commitment that the preceding generation had displayed. The result was a turn by the college to directions ordained by the board's ministers.

Under the influence of the new trustees, the college began to

[73] See Donald G. Mathews, "The Second Great Awakening as an Organizing Process, 1780–1830," *American Quarterly* 21 (1969): 23–43; and Robert H. Wiebe, *The Opening of American Society: From the Adoption of the Constitution to the Eve of Disunion* (New York, 1984), 229–32.

[74] In particular, ministers John Rodgers and Alexander MacWhorter had served as crucial mediators between lay and clerical interests. The removal of these two stalwarts, in conjunction with the death of Elizabeth Stockton Green, Ashbel's wife, also in 1807, meant that the Stockton-Boudinot-Bayard network of lay trustees had no remaining bonds of blood with the kin network of influential clerical trustees. See genealogies, Appendix B.

move away from the ideals that had dominated Princeton since the Revolution. Ties to the past were strained. While the new members were no less eager to save the nation and strengthen the church, they looked for new means to accomplish those goals. Now it would be through voluntary agencies, revival, and ministerial education, instead of through Revolutionary idealism and an organic union of political and religious aspirations. The trustees were still concerned about the flourishing of the college, but they had other vineyards to till. Moreover, for as long as Stanhope Smith continued to lead Princeton, suspicion would becloud its future.

The Domination of Ministers, 1808–1812

Not the Understanding, but the Heart

★

D URING STANHOPE SMITH'S last years as president, the College of New Jersey continued to reel from the effects of the great rebellion and to suffer from continued lack of confidence in Smith himself. The college limped along with about half the number of students that had been present before 1807 and with enough disorder in Nassau Hall to keep the authorities on edge. Trustees took unprecedented measures to regulate the college, and a few of them continued to skirmish with Smith over his views on incidental theological questions. That skirmishing was inconclusive for the specific questions, but it did testify to a growing divide between Smith's expansive educational vision and the growing sense of Presbyterian sectarianism among his colleagues.

Cause-and-effect relationships are complex, but the loss of political power to the Jeffersonians after 1800 as well as disillusionment with earlier national optimism seem to have nudged the Princeton circle away from its earlier cosmopolitanism toward a greater particularism. Preoccupation with revival, the formation of voluntary societies, and the distinctives of Presbyterianism loomed larger during the first decade of the century at the expense of the nationalistic, political, and enlightened vision of the 1780s and 1790s. As an indication of this trend, the great enterprise for the Princeton circle in Smith's last years as president was the creation of a Presbyterian theological seminary. Not only did this venture manifest a desire for new strategies to meet the needs of the hour, but it also had the broadest possible implications for Stanhope Smith's intellectual vision and the College of New Jersey.

ABOUT 110 students returned to Princeton on May 8, 1807, to resume their studies after the rebellion. That number did not increase under Stanhope Smith and indeed declined to under 100 in both 1810 and 1812.[1] Princeton continued to attract young men from well-connected families who went on to responsible positions in American life. The 171 graduates from 1808 through 1812 included, for example, one future vice president of the United States (George Mifflin Dallas, 1810), one Supreme Court justice, two senators, two governors, ten United States congressmen, one Episcopal bishop, and two moderators of the Presbyterian General Assembly.[2] Yet it was obvious to most observers that the college was laboring. Its faculty was reduced to Smith, Maclean, and one or two tutors. And it was impossible to hide the extent of dissatisfaction with the school among the board members themselves. Public confidence in Princeton was clearly shaken; its former glory had departed.

Recurring episodes of student unrest did nothing to assuage uneasiness. Reports were rosy in the immediate aftermath of the 1807 rebellion, so much so that Smith could tell a former student in December 1808 that "the order & the diligence prevailing in the college this session far exceeds anything of the kind you have ever seen in it. . . . The remains of Jacobinism appear to be totally extirpated."[3] This apparent order was but calm before storm. Less than three months later a combination of winter sleigh rides and excessive drinking brought disorder back to Nassau Hall. A tutor was harassed, "an attempt was made by some person unknown to burn the college in the day time," and when Smith tried to remove a suspended scholar on March 7, 1809, he was menaced by a group of students, one of whom hurled tongs at him from the top of a stairwell.[4] The next winter drinking again led to problems, and Smith was forced to report that an undergraduate had threatened a ministerial student with a pistol. The summer thereafter a student was complaining that "the discipline of college was given up by the tutors appointed to preserve it."[5]

[1] TM, Apr. 5, 1810; Oct. 1, 1812.

[2] *General Catalogue*, 120–24.

[3] TM, Sept. 29, 1808; Smith to William Hamilton, Dec. 10, 1808, copy in Samuel Stanhope Smith Collection, PUL, from William S. Hamilton Papers, Southern Historical Collection, University of North Carolina Library, Chapel Hill.

[4] FM, Feb. 24, 1809; TM, Apr. 5, 1809; Betty Fladeland, *James Gillespie Birney: Slaveholder to Abolitionist* (Ithaca, N.Y., 1955), 10; on the college's "considerable degree of dissipation," see Joshua M. Wallace to John Mayo, Apr. 12, 1809, General Manuscripts, PUL.

[5] TM, Apr. 5, 1810; John K. Rodgers to college trustees, Sept. 25, 1810, John Maclean Papers, PUA. In 1810 Smith had the embarrassment of telling the trustees

Problems with student restlessness were not aided by the condition of Smith's health. A trustee report on the disturbances of February 1809 pointed out that Smith was ill then and thus had been for some time handicapped as a disciplinarian.[6] In January 1812 Smith suffered a slight stroke or attack of palsy that further compromised his ability to maintain discipline.[7] Nor did Smith's demeanor toward the students help him to restrain their excesses. Individuals still occasionally expressed their appreciation for some special attention from the president, like Joseph Cabell Breckinridge, one of the students suspended in 1807 for whom Smith made special intercession, or an unnamed lad in 1809 with suicidal tendencies to whom Smith devoted special attention.[8] But on the whole, Smith behaved "very cooly to the students," as one scholar put it in 1809 who had expected a livelier social scene on the campus.[9] Unlike his predecessor, Witherspoon, or Yale's Timothy Dwight, the two college presidents of the era most respected for rapport with students, Smith lacked the hardy bonhomie, the evangelical solicitude, or whatever it took to overcome the riotous spirit of the age.[10]

Further bickering over Smith's opinions also continued to poison the atmosphere at Princeton. This time it was his comments in a sermon on baptism that irritated members of the constituency and led to further questions about his orthodoxy. The subject and its theological context were sensitive ones for Presbyterians in this age. Aggressive evangelistic efforts by Baptists had put Presbyterians, with their practice of infant baptism, on the defensive. In addition, a fresh outbreak of debate among New England Congregationalists on the old controversy of baptismal qualifications for

that a fight was taking place in the refectory while they were meeting in special session (TM, June 6, 1810).

[6] TM, Apr. 5, 1809.

[7] Beasley, "Life," 472; William White to Alexander Griswold, Jan. 30, 1812, General Manuscripts, PUL.

[8] Lowell H. Harrison, "A Young Kentuckian at Princeton, 1806–1810: Joseph Cabell Breckinridge," *Filson Club History Quarterly* 38 (1964): 308; Smith to Benjamin Rush, May 20, 1809, Library Company of Philadelphia, HSP.

[9] Thomas Shippen to William Shippen, Mar. 4, 1809, quoted in M. L. Bradbury, "British Apologetics in Evangelical Garb: Samuel Stanhope Smith's *Lectures on the Evidences of the Christian Religion*," *Journal of the Early Republic* 5 (1985): 180 n. 6. A similar assessment was reported by James Garnett to his mother, July 11, 1812, James Mercer Garnett Papers, PUA.

[10] On Dwight's effectiveness, see Steven J. Novak, *The Rights of Youth: American Colleges and Student Revolt, 1798–1815* (Cambridge, Mass., 1977), 131–32; and Brooks Mather Kelley, *Yale: A History* (New Haven, Conn., 1974), 120–22.

church membership sparked a corresponding discussion among Presbyterians. That issue was whether the baptism of infants should be restricted only to the children of those who had made profession of faith or be opened more broadly to all parents who desired the rite for their children. Members of the Princeton circle worried about both matters but defended infant baptism and also relatively loose standards for those who wanted their children baptized.[11]

When Smith contributed to the fray in 1808 with his monograph *Discourse on the Nature, the Proper Subjects, and the Benefits of Baptism, with a Brief Appendix, on the Mode of Administering the Ordinance*, he was met with an unanticipated rebuff. A person or persons unknown began circulating the charge that the sermon verged into heterodoxy, not because of its statements on baptism, but because of its offhand comments about faith. Smith took the criticism seriously enough to write a lengthy letter for the denomination's monthly magazine that criticized the way some guardians of orthodoxy damagingly blended "their philosophical systems with the simple rules and prescriptions of the gospel."[12] Smith's critics had suggested that he made human faith into a good work meriting salvation, a change that Smith denied with careful attention to Pauline language in the Book of Romans.[13] They also objected to a weak concept of original sin, especially in Smith's contention that baptized children who died in infancy were necessarily redeemed. Smith turned back this attack by arguing that baptized infants were saved because of Christ's intercession on their behalf, not on the basis of original innocence.[14] Once more the details of the issue are less important than the contemporary perception that Smith was wavering in his Calvinism, weak on the sovereignty of God in salvation, and shaky in defending original sin. Whoever was responsible for criticism of this sermon shared the feeling of Ashbel

[11] For the situation in New England, see Williston Walker, *The Creeds and Platforms of Congregationalism* (1893; reprint, Philadelphia, 1960), 241–44, 287. The flavor of Presbyterian concern is revealed in essays on baptismal standards in *The General Assembly's Missionary Magazine; or, Evangelical Intelligencer* 3 (Jan. 1807): 18–22; (Feb. 1807): 55–61; n.s., 1 (July 1807): 12–17; (Oct. 1807): 156–60.

[12] Smith, letter, *Evangelical Intelligencer*, n.s., 2 (Mar. 1808): 104. See also the expression of Smith's distaste for theological squabbling of this sort in a letter to Ashbel Green, editor of the *Evangelical Intelligencer*, Mar. 20, 1808 (Samuel Stanhope Smith Collection, PUL).

[13] Smith, *Discourse on the Nature, the Proper Subjects, and the Benefits of Baptism* (Philadelphia, 1808), 7, 19; letter, *Evangelical Intelligencer*, 104–5.

[14] Smith, *Discourse on Baptism*, 32–33; letter, *Evangelical Intelligencer*, 105–8.

Green and his friends that collegiate instruction from such a source had dubious implications for the church.

The most obvious sign of distress at the College of New Jersey, however, was the tightened trustee control of its affairs. To a degree unprecedented in the history of the college, the board took on immediate oversight of its life. Special committees were appointed in 1808 to examine the state of the college and to regularize bylaws and rules, a "board of visitors" was named in 1810 to visit Princeton periodically to help preserve order, and several other committees were charged with various tasks usually carried out by the faculty.[15] Where the board had met an average of 1.8 times per year during Witherspoon's last fifteen years as president, it met 3.3 times each year in the period 1807 to 1812. The board gathered for special session only twelve times from 1779 to 1806, but from 1807 to 1812, eight special meetings were called. Along with this increased frequency of meeting came also a more dominant role for the board's clergymen. Where laymen had taken responsibility for most of the board's actions before 1801, clergymen began to perform an increasing share, until from 1807 to 1812 they were discharging more than half of the board's officially designated duties.[16] In June 1810 the board launched a fund-raising effort to solicit an endowment for a new vice president and professor of theology, a scheme that may have had Smith's blessing but that was advanced primarily to remedy his failures.[17]

The pattern of board activity after 1807 suggests that previous harmony between lay and clerical trustees was strained or breaking down. Ministers hatched plans among themselves for concentrated action, and laymen occasionally sniped at what they perceived as clerical impracticality. So Elias Boudinot could tell a minister in 1809, "I have wished, among other improvements in Theological Studies, a Professorship of Common Sense & Prudence was established in our Seminaries. I really have known so many ruinous Errors in practice, among our pious & zealous Ministers, for want of

[15] TM, Apr. 6 and 8, 1808; June 6 and Sept. 27, 1810; Sept. 26, 1811; June 30, 1812. John Maclean, the son of Smith's colleague (who also suffered from this supervision), left no doubt about his opinion on this turn of events: "Under no other administration of the affairs of the College did the Trustees ever interfere so much with the discipline; undertaking to direct in all matters, and leaving but little to the judgment of the Faculty,—an unwise course for any Board of Trustees to pursue, and which in this case did no good" (Maclean, *CNJ*, 2:82).

[16] See Appendix C for a summary of board meetings and lay/clerical activity.

[17] TM, June 6, 1810.

this celestial quality, that I am sure it is of more importance than is generally believed."[18] Boudinot's comment was hardly a sign of absolute rupture between the laymen and the ministers on the Princeton board. Yet its utterance at a time of increasing clerical dominance at Princeton suggests that Boudinot was sensing the altered circumstances that prevailed after the tumultuous events of 1807.

The board's tightened supervision of the college, combined with heightened clerical concern for Smith's leadership, finally led in 1812 to Smith's resignation, the first such event in the history of Princeton. In June 1812, two years after it had appointed a regular committee of visitors, the board met again in special session and asked a new extraordinary committee "to take into consideration the general state of the College and to report to the Board whether any and what measures are necessary to be adopted for the good of the Institution at this meeting of the Board." On July 1, 1812, that committee recommended the appointment of a vice president to be "especially charged with the internal discipline and order of the College," but always "subject to the controul and direction of the Board when it shall be thought proper to interfere."[19] The board then adjourned until August, when it proposed to appoint this officer.

From their lack of subtlety, as well as from private communications, it had become apparent that the trustees wanted a fresh start. Finally the message got through. When it assembled again in August, the board received a letter from John Maclean, resigning his position as professor of chemistry and natural philosophy after seventeen years of service.[20] Then, after Elias Boudinot personally arranged a financial settlement with the president, Smith submitted his resignation on August 14. Impaired health, Smith wrote, necessitated this move "after the fatiguing & I hope, faithful service of thirty three years."[21] The board accepted Smith's resignation and ratified the provisions for retirement that Boudinot had worked out, which included the purchase of Smith's library, his continuation in the president's house, and an annuity of $1,250 per year. It then proceeded immediately to elect Ashbel Green as

[18] Boudinot to E. D. Griffin, Oct. 24, 1809, in George Adams Boyd, *Elias Boudinot: Patriot and Statesman, 1740–1821* (Princeton, 1952), 282.

[19] TM, June 30 and July 1, 1812.

[20] Ibid., Aug. 13, 1812. Maclean moved to William and Mary to continue his teaching but died soon thereafter, in 1814.

[21] Boyd, *Boudinot*, 269–70; TM, Aug. 14, 1812.

the college's new president by a unanimous vote. For some time before the meeting Samuel Miller of New York, with perhaps one or two other young clerical trustees, had been canvassing the board members, both to ease Smith out and to move Green in.[22] And therein lies a tale.

That story involves a larger world in which events at the college were part of the greater drama being played out in the Princeton circle. Even as trustees bore down on Smith and Princeton, they were devoting increasing attention to other remedies for the republic's ills. Clerical trustees especially had been busy, even as they worked to reform the college. The events that led to Smith's resignation, therefore, belong to a more comprehensive narrative that includes an account of Princeton's perceptions of its world and of the remedial labors promoted by members of the Princeton circle. The founding of a theological seminary for Presbyterians was the most important of those efforts. That subject, in turn, eventually leads us back to the dissatisfaction with the state of Princeton College under Stanhope Smith.

DURING THE early nineteenth century Princeton's disillusionment with the course of American politics combined with an apocalyptic understanding of world events to produce a largely pessimistic outlook. At the same time, however, hope was also growing that an invigorated Presbyterian self-consciousness, new voluntary organizations, and the spread of revival might hold back the tide of evil and advance the Kingdom of Christ. In the process, attitudes toward education underwent a subtle shift as perceptions of the world continued to evolve.

For larger geopolitical affairs the Princeton circle held out little hope during the early years of the century. Elias Boudinot, for example, strummed only one note in his dirge for America's political fortunes—Jeffersonians came to power in 1801 because of votes from "the deluded Multitude." Things did not improve with the rise of Napoleon abroad or with the turmoils within Jefferson's administration. In 1807 Boudinot bemoaned "the Political Horrors of Europe and America" and opined that the American gov-

[22] Green professed to have no knowledge of this backstage maneuvering (*Life of Green*, 338–40). For Miller's activity, see Samuel Miller, Jr., *The Life of Samuel Miller*, 2 vols. (Philadelphia, 1869), 1:336–38; and Miller to Green, Oct. 2, 1812, Samuel Miller Papers, PUL. At least one student considered Green's profession of reluctance "nothing more than an electioneering trick" (James Garnett to his mother, Sept. 5, 1812, James Mercer Garnett Papers, PUA).

ernment was too weak to stand up against the plots of Aaron Burr. The next year his fears turned to the Constitution, which he looked upon as the last bulwark against "anarchy and confusion."[23]

Boudinot's political opinions may have reflected a measure of personal pique, for he and his colleagues were almost completely shut off from national political leadership after the turn of the century. In the years of transition between Witherspoon and Smith, 1794–1796, the ten laymen on the Princeton board included, besides the governor of New Jersey, one United States senator, two congressmen, an associate justice of the United States Supreme Court, the director of the United States Mint, the mayors of New Brunswick and Burlington, New Jersey, a New Jersey legislator, the New Jersey secretary of state, a Philadelphia alderman, and the auditor general of Pennsylvania. By contrast, the ten laymen on the board from 1808 to 1810 included only the chief justice of the New Jersey Supreme Court and two judges of local courts of common pleas.[24]

Whatever the exact role played by the frustration of personal ambition, many members of the Princeton circle joined Boudinot in his bleak analysis of the age. Even if the stock phrases of sermonic jeremiads had become conventions, ministers in the Princeton circle still went to great lengths to convince congregations of the decadence of the day. In 1802 Samuel Miller portrayed his age as "a time of great degeneracy and distress."[25] When Federalist Aaron Ogden won the New Jersey governorship in 1812, his fellow trustee the Reverend John Woodhull wrote that, even though "we" had won in New Jersey, "the present awful state of the country" was still a matter of grave concern."[26] Joseph Clark's message was just about the same in a fast-day message to his New Brunswick congregation in that election year. With the Old World immersed in blood and England too now drawn into the conflict, with rumors of war and the blight of party spirit at loose in America, Clark felt that ingratitude and rebellion against God were reaping a bitter harvest. Where once the new American Israel, "a land of Bibles and Sabbaths," had glowed in the purity of its Revolution

[23] Boudinot to Elisha Boudinot, Jan. 7, 1801, and Jan. 9, 1807, both in Thorne Boudinot Collection, PUL; letter of June 3, 1808, quoted in Boyd, *Boudinot*, 277.

[24] Biographical information is from sources cited in the Bibliography.

[25] Samuel Miller, *A Sermon, Delivered before the New-York Missionary Society* (New York, 1802), 7. In 1805 it was *"the pollutions* which surround and assail you" (Miller, *The Guilt, Folly, and Sources of Suicide* [New York, 1805], 6).

[26] Woodhull to Ogden, Nov. 9, 1812, Gratz Collection, HSP.

and the strength of its Constitution, the nation, especially its youth, now reveled in vice and sought "the contagion of . . . infidel philosophy."[27] More than one Princeton trustee was coming to the conclusion that Elias Boudinot's brother, Elisha, expressed in 1810: "The storm of the Almighty's wrath appears to be shaking the old world to its centre—and I am apprehensive that we shall not escape."[28]

The response of the Princeton circle to the perception of a public crisis was not more politics but less. Significant withdrawal from political involvement in favor of more spiritual warfare became the order of the day. Ministers like Alexander MacWhorter and John Rodgers, who had preached with great conviction about political concerns into the 1790s, now directed their attention more specifically to spiritual subjects.[29] Ashbel Green now spoke about politics only in the vaguest of terms. By the end of Jefferson's second term in 1809, Samuel Miller had almost completed his disengagement from political involvement.[30] For his part, Stanhope Smith continued to comment on political matters privately but was silent in public.[31] The board as a whole, after a long tradition of bestowing almost as many honorary doctorates on political leaders as on clerics, from 1807 through 1812 gave out seventeen honorary D.D.'s and no honorary LL.D.'s.[32] Clearly, the Princeton circle no longer expected political exertions to lead into the Promised Land. Instead, the unstable will of the people and the machinations of leaders heralded the final outpouring of divine wrath.[33]

[27] Joseph Clark, *A Sermon, Delivered . . . on Thursday, July 30, 1812. Being the Day set apart . . . for Fasting, Humiliation, and Prayer* (New Brunswick, 1812), 10, 14.

[28] Elisha Boudinot to E. D. Griffin, Dec. 19, 1810, Gratz Collection, HSP. Another close associate of the Boudinot family, C. H. Wharton, wrote much the same to Elias Boudinot, Aug. 1, 1809 (Stimson Boudinot Collection, PUL).

[29] For example, Alexander MacWhorter, *A Series of Sermons, upon the most important principles of our Holy Religion*, 2 vols. (Newark, N.J., 1803); John Rodgers, *The Presence of Christ the Glory of A Church* (New York, 1808). Samuel Miller made it a point to praise Rodgers, after his passing, for the latter's detachment from politics, for not voting, and for keeping his political sentiments to himself (*Memoirs of the Rev. John Rodgers* [New York, 1813], 333–34).

[30] Miller, *Life of Samuel Miller*, 1:129–33.

[31] See, for example, Smith's disquiet about the way Jefferson and the Congress were going about strengthening the army (Smith to William Hamilton, Dec. 10, 1808).

[32] Cf. 1780–1794 (27 D.D.'s, 16 LL.D.'s), 1795–1801 (10 D.D.'s, 7 LL.D.'s or M.D.'s) and 1802–1806 (9 D.D.'s, 7 LL.D.'s), from *General Catalogue*, 399–408.

[33] Fred J. Hood, *Reformed America: The Middle and Southern States, 1783–1837*

Princeton leaders, however, were far from passive as they engineered their retreat from politics. Energies now were redirected to different ends. Earlier trustees had of course been active in the Presbyterian church, but after the turn of the century, and especially after the new cohort of younger ministers joined the board in 1807, members of the Princeton circle sharpened their defense of Presbyterian distinctives. For this effort Samuel Miller led the way. In 1807 and 1809 he published lengthy defenses of Presbyterian ordination against New York Episcopalians, including the rising advocate of American high church principles, John Henry Hobart, himself a Princeton graduate and friend of Stanhope Smith.[34] Robert Finley also published two expositions of Presbyterian baptism in the same period over against these same foes.[35] As later developments demonstrated, Presbyterian particularism did not rule out an ecumenical Christian nationalism.[36] Since the time of Witherspoon, however, strictly Presbyterian concerns had attracted less attention at Princeton than the common American task of protecting the spiritual and political health of the new nation as a whole. Now, however, the earlier expansiveness was giving way to a narrower denominationalism.

Princeton's concern for national well-being did not simply decay in the flight from politics and the cultivation of the denomination. Rather, it came to new expression in the promotion of Christian voluntary agencies, organizations looking not for the mobilization of government but more directly to human needs themselves. Princeton trustees were in fact among the early leaders in the formation of the mission, Bible, tract, and reforming societies of the

---

(University, Ala., 1980), dates the turn from politics a little later than this but still describes it in much the same terms.

[34] Samuel Miller, *Letters Concerning the Constitution and Order of the Christian Ministry* (New York, 1807); *A Continuation of Letters concerning the constitution and order of the Christian ministry* (New York, 1809). On Miller's efforts against the Episcopalians, see also Miller to Ashbel Green, Mar. 12, 1805, Samuel Miller Papers, PUL; Miller to unknown correspondent, Dec. 27, 1808, Gratz Collection, HSP; and Miller, *Life of Samuel Miller,* 1:190–93, 211. On Hobart's efforts to promote a "higher" view of the ministry, see Robert Bruce Mullin, *Episcopal Vision/American Reality: High Church Theology and Social Thought in Evangelical America* (New Haven, Conn., 1986), 36–46, 66–72.

[35] Robert Finley, *A Sermon on the Baptism of John, Shewing it to be a Peculiar Dispensation, and No Example for Christians* (Elizabethtown, N.J., 1807); *A Discourse on the Nature and Design, the Benefits and Proper Subjects of Baptism* (Philadelpia, 1808).

[36] A good survey is found in Louis Weeks, "Faith and Political Action in American Presbyterianism, 1776–1918," in *Reformed Faith and Politics,* ed. Ronald H. Stone (Washington, D.C., 1983).

early nineteenth century that sprang up to civilize and Christianize American society.[37] Some of the older trustees, like Elias Boudinot—a founding member of the New Jersey Bible Society (1809) and first president of the American Bible Society (1816)—took an active part in this business.[38] In general, however, the younger trustees were even more active in the voluntary societies as they led the way in promoting missionary work,[39] relief for the poor,[40] and even manumission for slaves.[41]

A modified view of the relation between nature and grace, human agency and divine activity, fueled the Princeton turn toward voluntarism. While never abandoning trust in reason properly employed, the Princeton circle came gradually to reassert the importance of the spiritual over against the natural. If the harmonies between church and nation seemed to be strained, so also the earlier confidence was shaken that science or philosophy simply by itself would always come out right in the end. In 1795 Elias Boudinot had responded to the skepticism of Tom Paine by appealing to "evidence," "rational inquiry," "sound learning and pure science," and "facts or principles."[42] The buffeting of subsequent years did not decrease Boudinot's confidence in learning, properly

[37] On the general process, see Lois W. Banner, "Presbyterians and Voluntarism in the Early Republic," *Journal of Presbyterian History* 50 (1972): 187–205; and Donald G. Mathews, "The Second Great Awakening as an Organizing Process, 1780–1830," *American Quarterly* 21 (1969): 23–43.

[38] On the involvement of Princeton trustees in the formation of Bible societies, see John Frelinghuysen Hageman, *History of Princeton and Its Institutions*, 2 vols. (Philadelphia, 1879), 1:230; Elias Boudinot, *Address of the New-Jersey Bible Society to the Publick* (New Brunswick, 1810); Charles H. Wharton to Samuel Bayard, Dec. 4, 1809, Gratz Collection, HSP; and Elias Boudinot to Elisha Boudinot, Jan. 10, 1808, Thorne Boudinot Collection, PUL.

[39] Miller, *Sermon before New-York Missionary Society*; Ashbel Green, *Glad Tidings* (Philadelphia, 1804), 4; and James Richards to Ashbel Green, Mar. 13, 1810, Gratz Collection, HSP, on missionary work among the Cherokee.

[40] Samuel Miller, *A Sermon . . . for the Benefit of the Society instituted in the City of New-York, for the relief of Poor Widows, with Small Children* (New York, 1808); John B. Romeyn, *The Good Samaritan: A Sermon . . . for the Benefit of the New-York Dispensary* (New York, 1810).

[41] See especially Robert Finley's role in promoting the American Colonization Society (Isaac V. Brown, *Biography of the Rev. Robert Finley* [1819; reprint, New York, 1969]). Several trustees were also involved in other voluntary societies; see, for instance, the ten board members listed as officers in Joshua M. Wallace, *Constitution of the New-Jersey Society for the Suppression of Vice and Immorality, and for the Encouragement of Virtue and Good Morals* (New Brunswick, 1818).

[42] Elias Boudinot, *The Age of Revelation; or, The Age of Reason shewn to be an Age of Infidelity* (Philadelphia, 1801), vi, xx, 323.

applied, but it did bring about a certain reorientation of his loyalties. In early 1808, for example, a Boudinot more subdued about the utility of reason wrote to his brother: "When I see so many, who have rec[eive]d the best Education, under the most pious Instructors, turn out the greatest opposers of the Kingdom of Christ in the World, I am fully convinced of the truth of the Gospel, that our sufficiency must be in Christ."[43]

The same modification marked the public statements of Samuel Miller. While his *Brief Retrospect of the Eighteenth Century* in 1803 had been more than merely a hymn to science and reason, it nonetheless made much of natural learning, applauded the scientific breakthroughs achieved by "infidels," contended that modern education was constantly improving the quality of life, and praised at length the good results that came from abandoning flighty hypotheses for solid empiricism.[44] Miller never entirely set such views aside, but in the first decade of the century he came more and more to assert the preeminence of faith over reason. As early as 1802 he deprecated any hope for humanity not resting on "the future prevalence and influence of the gospel." In 1805 he considered the outbreak of suicides in New York City (nine in three months) and offered as a remedy not physical, psychological, or social remedies but "the power of godliness" alone.[45] The journey that would take Miller from expansive cosmopolitan to conservative sectarian was well under way by this time.

Ashbel Green had never been quite as sanguine as Boudinot or Miller about the power of natural learning, and so there was less obvious movement in his thought. But Green's key position on the Princeton board made his views on the relationship of religion and reason especially important during Smith's last years. Among the Presbyterians, Green was the leader in promoting religious remedies, specifically missions and revival, for the nation's ills. In 1808 he wrote to Jedidiah Morse, congratulating Morse and his colleagues on the successful establishment of Andover Theological

[43] Boudinot to Elisha Boudinot, Jan. 10, 1808.

[44] Samuel Miller, *A Brief Retrospect of the Eighteenth Century*, 2 vols. (New York, 1803), 1:v, xii; 2:272, 442, with reservations about unrestricted learning, 2:295–96.

[45] Miller, *Sermon before the New-York Missionary Society*, 51; Miller, *The Guilt, Folly, and Sources of Suicide*, 66. On Miller's general drift toward less optimistic views of reason and education, see Belden C. Lane, "Democracy and the Ruling Eldership: Samuel Miller's Response to Tensions between Clerical Power and Lay Authority in Early Nineteenth-Century America" (Ph.D. diss., Princeton Theological Seminary, 1976).

Seminary. Green was confident that Andover would strike a mighty blow against the newfangled Harvard Unitarianism, but he did not rest his confidence in the strength of reason. Rather, "It is not the understanding, but the heart, which needs to be addressed on this subject—It is not argument, but piety which is requisite to exterminate this heresy."[46] Green, along with Boudinot and Miller, never abandoned a firm commitment to science, reason, and philosophy, but in the first years of the new century, the Princeton circle began to look more fervently to piety, faith, and revelation as the foundation of their efforts to sustain the church and revive the republic.

With this turn toward piety Princeton republicanism continued to display the more religious tone it had assumed in the mid-1790s. Religious foundations seemed more than ever necessary, since, as Joseph Clark put it at the funeral of William Paterson, the ranks of the *"real patriots of '76; . . . [the] tried friends* of virtue and your county . . . are fast thinning away."[47] In 1802 Samuel Miller claimed flatly that all social betterment rested on the gospel. "The public institutions of religion," echoed Ashbel Green three years later, "are unspeakably beneficial—perhaps I should rather say they are absolutely essential, to civil society. . . . Abolish the observance of the Sabbath and its public worship, and you shall see men rapidly decline into barbarism, rapine, and every ferocious and abominable vice." In 1812 the same note was sounded from Joseph Clark's New Brunswick pulpit: rebellion against God and its consequent immorality threatened the peace and plenty, the sound Constitution, the political harmony, and the social stability of the United States.[48] If the country could be saved, if the nation's people could be turned from vice to virtue, it would be a religion of the heart that did the job.

The view of the world held by most members of the Princeton circle in the first decade of the nineteenth century was the heir of both colonial evangelical Presbyterianism and the Christian Enlightenment of John Witherspoon. If, in the tumult of the times, evangelicalism was once again coming to the fore at the expense of

[46] Green to Morse, May 27, 1808, Gratz Collection, HSP.

[47] Joseph Clark, *A Sermon on the Death of the Hon. William Paterson* (New Brunswick, 1806), 22.

[48] Miller, *Sermon before New-York Missionary Society*, 51; Green, *A Discourse, Delivered at the Opening for Public Worship, of the Presbyterian Church, in the Northern Liberties of Philadelphia; April 7th, A.D. 1805* (Philadelphia, 1805), 19; Clark, *Sermon for Fasting, Humiliation, and Prayer.*

Enlightenment, and if narrowly focused Christian activity was edging aside broadly conceived public service, the fundamental desire to enlist religion and learning for the cause of the church and the nation had not altered. What did change, however, in these early years of the century was the concord between Samuel Stanhope Smith and other leaders of the Princeton circle. Smith and his colleagues shared the same inheritance, but his application of that legacy was beginning to diverge more obviously from other influential Princetonians. Smith continued to display the same confidence in reason that infused the moral philosophy of Witherspoon, even though his colleagues were beginning to make more of Witherspoon's Presbyterian evangelicalism. Where gloom settled more thickly over other members of the Princeton circle as they surveyed public life, Smith recovered his spirits after the initial distress at the triumph of infidelity abroad and Jefferson at home.[49]

The growing antagonism between Smith and Ashbel Green testified to this disengagement within the Princeton circle, as did the even sharper divide between Smith and Samuel Miller. Smith remained on good terms with his Episcopalian students, especially John Henry Hobart, at the very time when Miller was attacking Hobart and the Episcopalians for errors of church organization and practice.[50] Smith continued, moreover, to practice the harmony of nature and grace, with nature predominating, while Miller reversed the emphasis. Smith bled a student troubled by suicidal intentions, while Miller urged godliness as an antidote to suicide.[51] For Smith, history was "a volume of moral experiment"; for Miller it had become "but a development of prophecy."[52]

Differences between Smith and other members of the Princeton circle were not as obvious as those with Miller or Green, and indeed some Princetonians never expressed dissatisfaction with him or his work. Nor was even the chasm between Smith and Miller unbridgeable. It was, after all, Miller who, on the day of Smith's retirement, October 1, 1812, proposed a resolution that the board

[49] Smith, continuation of David Ramsay's *History of the United States*, 3 vols. (rev. ed., Philadelphia, 1818), 3:118, 190.

[50] *The Correspondence of John Henry Hobart, 1757–1797*, ed. Arthur Lowndes (New York, 1911), cix.

[51] Smith to Benjamin Rush, May 20, 1809; Miller, *Guilt, Folly, and Sources of Suicide*, 66.

[52] Smith, *The Lectures . . . on the Subjects of Moral and Political Philosophy*, 2 vols. (Trenton, 1812), 1:12; Miller, *Sermon before New-York Missionary Society*, 47.

as a body visit Smith "for the purpose of expressing to him in person, their tender sympathy on the infirm state of his health—their highly respectful and grateful sentiments, towards him, for his long and faithful services—and their fervent wishes for his welfare and happiness in retirement."[53] That all was not harmonious within the Princeton circle, however, is obvious by the fact that this same Miller had for years been criticizing Smith's direction of the college and for months had been campaigning to replace him with Ashbel Green. But as Miller's perhaps not entirely insincere gesture at Smith's retirement suggests, there still existed a common framework of means and ends to constitute a Princeton circle.

THE PRACTICAL question that loomed larger than all others within that circle after the turn of the century was the question of educating ministers. How should it be done? Who should control it? How could it produce the leaders so desperately required by the Presbyterian church? The response to these questions led eventually to the founding of a separate Presbyterian theological seminary. But since that seminary was founded in considerable part because of dissatisfaction with results from the College of New Jersey and since its founders were for the most part influential members of the college board, the establishment of Princeton Theological Seminary also marks an important chapter in the story of Princeton College.

Although efforts to train ministers had begun in America almost as soon as the first churches were established, the emergence of the theological seminary as a special institution for that purpose was a development of the early nineteenth century.[54] Ashbel Green, as we have noted, was writing to close friends as early as January 1800 with "a plan to educate men for the ministry in an

53 TM, Oct. 1, 1812.

54 On the training of ministers before 1800, see Mary Latimer Gambrell, *Ministerial Training in Eighteenth-Century New England* (1937; reprint, New York, 1969); and Archibald Alexander, *The Log College* (1851; reprint, London, 1968). The foundation of seminaries in the early nineteenth century is the subject of William Warren Sweet, "The Rise of Theological Schools in America," *Church History* 6 (1937): 260–73; and Natalie A. Naylor, "The Theological Seminary in the Configuration of American Higher Education: The Ante-Bellum Years," *History of Education Quarterly* 17 (1977): 17–30. For an earlier attempt at ministerial education by Ashbel Green's father, see Mark A. Noll, "Jacob Green's Proposal for Seminaries (1775)," *Journal of Presbyterian History* 58 (1980): 273–86. Some of the material that follows is abridged from my essay "The Founding of Princeton Seminary," *Westminster Theological Journal* 42 (1979): 72–110.

institution by themselves."[55] Over the next several years he floated several alternative plans, including "a Divinity School in the College" (i.e., Princeton), and an apprenticeship program involving service by young ministers in rural areas.[56] The shortage of Presbyterian ministers lent urgency to these vague plans, especially for Green, Samuel Miller, and their colleague in Newark, the Reverend E. D. Griffin.

With that need uppermost in his mind, Green felt constrained to submit the overture to the General Assembly of May 1805, which contained his ringing appeal, "Give us ministers!"[57] The assembly responded by putting the question of ministerial training on its agenda for 1806. Green meanwhile drafted an extensive plan for such an institution and circulated it among his closest associates. He did not want simply "to abandon to more worldly men institutions which the friends of religion contributed largely to establish, & which are now rich & well furnished with libraries and apparatus," since that would leave these institutions to become "nurseries of infidelity, heresy & vice." Yet the need for ministers was so great and the absence of a school training young men "in *presbyterian* principles" so manifest that Green could see no other option than proceeding toward a theological seminary.[58]

In the event, the 1806 General Assembly did call on Presbyterians "to use their utmost endeavors to increase . . . the numbers of promising candidates for the holy ministry . . . , choosing for them such schools, seminaries and teachers, as they may judge most proper and advantageous." At the same assembly the delegates also received a message from Stanhope Smith outlining the advantages that Princeton College offered as a place to prepare for the ministry.[59] Neither action in 1806, however, satisfied the needs felt by many for improved ministerial training. The presbyteries lagged in implementing the General Assembly's direction, and Presbyterian confidence in Princeton College was at a low ebb.

The need for better education for more ministerial candidates continued to be a staple in the correspondence of Miller, Green,

[55] Green to E. D. Griffin, Jan. 13, 1800, Gratz Collection, HSP.

[56] John Rodgers to Green, Nov. 28, 1803, responding to Green's letter of Nov. 8; Rodgers to Green, Nov. 30, 1804, both Gratz Collection, HSP.

[57] *Minutes of the General Assembly of the Presbyterian Church in the United States of America from . . . 1789 to . . . 1820* (Philadelphia, 1847), 341.

[58] Green to E. D. Griffin, Nov. 18, 1805, with lukewarm response from the latter in Griffin to Green, Dec. 13, 1805, both Gratz Collection, HSP.

[59] *Minutes of the General Assembly*, 366, 362–63.

and a handful of their associates,[60] but not until 1808 did the drive for a seminary take on new life. In that year two significant events jarred the Presbyterians into action. The retiring moderator, Archibald Alexander, chose to open the 1808 General Assembly with a sermon on 1 Corinthians 14:12 ("seek that ye may excel to the edifying of the church"). Alexander at the time was pastor of the Third Presbyterian Church in Philadelphia, where he had been called the previous year after service as a revivalist and pastor in Virginia, and in succession to Stanhope and John Blair Smith as president of Hampden-Sidney College. Alexander had been educated privately by the Reverend William Graham, Princeton class of 1773 and an ardent disciple of Witherspoon.[61] At one remove, therefore, Alexander received some of the same lessons in piety, science, and political philosophy that inspired both Ashbel Green and Stanhope Smith in their different ways. Alexander was one of the great extempore preachers of his day and yet also a careful thinker. Now in 1808 he was drawing on his experience as pastor and educator to guide the Presbyterians along the path of edification. For our purposes, the important thing about his address was an appeal for greater diligence in training ministers. Alexander criticized the existing colleges for pursuing a course of study "little adapted to introduce a youth to the study of the sacred Scriptures." There would be no change for the better, contended Alexander, "until every Presbytery, or at least every Synod, shall have under its direction a seminary established for the single purpose of educating youth for the ministry."[62]

Arresting as this sermon was, it was not as important as the example provided by the founding of Andover Theological Seminary later that year. Trinitarian Congregationalists, stung by the appointment in 1805 of a Unitarian to the Hollis Professorship of Divinity at Harvard, had responded by coordinating the energy of orthodox ministers and the money of orthodox laymen for the es-

---

[60] See, for example, Miller to Green, Mar. 12 and May 13, 1805, in Miller, *Life of Samuel Miller*, 1:190–97; John Rodgers to Jedidiah Morse, Jan. 31, 1807; Rodgers to Green, Sept. 9, 1807, both Gratz Collection, HSP; and an enthusiastic recommendation from Benjamin Rush in a letter to Green, May 22, 1807, in L. H. Butterfield, ed., *Letters of Benjamin Rush*, 2 vols. (Princeton, 1951), 2:946–47.

[61] See James W. Alexander, *The Life of Archibald Alexander* (New York, 1854); and Lefferts A. Loetscher, *Facing the Enlightenment and Pietism: Archibald Alexander and the Founding of Princeton Theological Seminary* (Westport, Conn., 1983). See also the article on William Graham by W. Frank Craven, *Princetonians 1769–1775*, 289–94.

[62] Quoted in Alexander, *Life of Archibald Alexander*, 314–15.

tablishment of a theological school.[63] By the end of its first year, Andover's endowed faculty of three had admitted thirty-six students and was well on the way to creating a major educational institution. Presbyterians from the middle states contributed encouragement and one of their number, Edward Dorr Griffin of Newark, to the new seminary. For its part, Andover gave the Presbyterians a model for religious higher education.[64]

In 1809 the Presbytery of Philadelphia, under the leadership of Ashbel Green, overtured the General Assembly to establish "a theological school." The proposal was assigned to a committee that asked the presbyteries if they preferred one central school, two schools for the northern and southern parts of the church, or a school in each of the four synods.[65] Over the winter of 1809–1810, Miller and Green corresponded on how to promote the idea of one central seminary, the plan that Miller in particular felt was best suited to promote the learning and unity of the church.[66]

When the presbyteries responded in 1810, the results were not conclusive. Ten favored each of the first and third plans (one central seminary, one seminary in each synod), one favored two schools north and south, six did not feel that it was time to start any seminaries, and the other nine made no response. Samuel Miller, however, was the chairman of the committee to report on the balloting, and by a feat of legerdemain he converted the confused voice of the denomination into a clarion call for one, centrally located seminary.[67] Miller's committee then proposed that this seminary be organized under the control of the General Assembly with three professors. It asked for a committee to "prepare a plan of a Theological Seminary" and suggested the names of Ashbel Green, Samuel Miller, Archibald Alexander, and four other ministers to compose this committee. It then named forty-two agents to solicit funds for the new seminary, again including Green, Miller, and Alexander. And it called on Samuel Miller and

[63] See Joseph W. Phillips, *Jedidiah Morse and New England Congregationalism* (New Brunswick, 1983), 138–40; Naylor, "Theological Seminary," 19–21; and Elwyn A. Smith, *The Presbyterian Ministry in American Culture* (Philadelphia, 1962), 107–11.

[64] For indications of interest in Andover within the Princeton circle, see John Rodgers to Jedidiah Morse, Jan. 31, 1807; Ashbel Green to Jedidiah Morse, May 27, 1808; Green to Griffin, Aug. 3, 1808, all Gratz Collection, HSP; and Elias Boudinot (from Boston with a glowing report of the new school) to Elisha Boudinot, Aug. 9, 1808, Thorne Boudinot Collection, PUL.

[65] *Minutes of the General Assembly*, 417, 430–31.

[66] Miller to Green, Jan. 16, 1810, in Miller, *Life of Samuel Miller*, 1:280–83.

[67] *Minutes of the General Assembly*, 453–54.

one other minister to draft a letter to the Presbyterian churches of the country in order to ask their support for the venture. In response, the assembly named a committee to draw up a plan for the seminary, and the letter went out to the churches.[68]

Before the delegates dispersed from Philadelphia, Ashbel Green was selected by his committee to draft a scheme for the seminary. Four months later, during commencement at Princeton, Green presented the committee with his work. The committee made virtually no changes and forwarded Green's proposal to the 1811 assembly. This plan, most of which was adopted in 1811, left full control of the seminary in the hands of the General Assembly, acting through a board that it elected. This board was to exercise close oversight over the faculty, even to the extent of approving changes in the courses taught by the professors. It called for its professors to "solemnly, and *ex animo* adopt, receive, and subscribe the Confession of Faith, and Catechisms of the Presbyterian Church in the United States." Students were to be trained thoroughly in the Bible, learning "to explain the principal difficulties which arise in the perusal of the Scriptures . . . from apparent inconsistencies . . . or objections arising from history, reason, or argument" and being taught the main arguments of "the deistical controversy" in order to become defenders of the faith. The plan called upon students to cultivate personal piety; it made clear that they were to exercise due respect for the faculty and to live temperate, honorable lives. Students were also to swear an oath that they would obey the laws and the officials of the school. The only two parts of Green's plan for the seminary that were not approved by the 1812 assembly were a section on the library and one calling for the establishment of a "theological academy," a college designed specifically for the special needs of students preparing for seminary and the ministry.[69]

Meanwhile, the trustees of Princeton College, despite the lack of enthusiasm for President Smith's message in 1806, had not abandoned their effort to contribute ministers for the cause. With their overwhelmingly Presbyterian character—twenty-one out of twenty-three members—the board was naturally much interested in schemes for educating Presbyterians. And so they apppointed their own committee at the 1810 commencement to meet with rep-

[68] Ibid., 457–59.

[69] *Life of Green*, 334; Green, *The Plan of a Theological Seminary Adopted by the General Assembly . . . 1811* (Philadelphia, 1811).

resentatives of the General Assembly about how they could coop-
erate in starting a theological seminary. The members of this committee were themselves all sometime delegates to the General
Assembly and could be expected to act as sincerely on behalf of
the denomination as of the college.[70]

Early in 1811 a group of trustees from Princeton College, led by
Governor Bloomfield, put forth a plan that would have joined the
new seminary organically to the college. This proposal foresaw an
institution not unlike the Harvard and Yale divinity schools
(founded in 1815 and 1822, respectively), which were constituent
parts of the larger colleges.[71] In Princeton's case, however, the college trustees proposed "that the principal direction of the college
in its instruction, government, and discipline, be gradually turned
to promote the objects of the theological institution."[72] The college
trustees were offering, in effect, to subordinate the undergraduate
program to the theological one. Attractive as this offer was for
many Presbyterians, it involved two insuperable difficulties: the
proposal could not transfer control of the institution to the General Assembly, but left it by virtue of its articles of incorporation in
the hands of a self-perpetuating board; and it could not altogether
efface the suspicions that several influential leaders, including
some of the college trustees themselves, harbored concerning the
college, its personnel, and its programs.

The General Assembly of 1811 deliberated at length on the subject of a seminary. Finally, it approved the essentials of the plan
that Green had drawn up. It named Alexander chairman of a committee to meet with representatives from Princeton College and
authorized it to seek "a union with the Trustees of that College . . .
which shall never be changed or altered without the mutual consent of both parties [General Assembly, college board], provided
that it should be deemed proper to locate the Assembly's Seminary
at the same place with that of the College."[73] The assembly instructed Alexander's committee, however, that in its negotiations

---

[70] TM, Sept. 27, 1810.

[71] Samuel Miller considered Bloomfield's plan "a prodigious thing" but also felt
it labored under very great difficulties (Miller to Green, Apr. 22, 1811, in Miller,
Life of Samuel Miller, 1:307–8). On the type of seminary that developed in New
England, see Roland H. Bainton, *Yale and the Ministry* (New York, 1957), 80; and
Conrad Wright, "The Early Period (1811–40)," in *The Harvard Divinity School*, ed.
George Huntson Williams (Boston, 1954), 26.

[72] Quoted in Wertenbaker, *Princeton*, 148.

[73] *Minutes of the General Assembly*, 470–71.

with the college, it could not contravene the plan for the seminary approved by the assembly. The assembly also appointed a three-man committee under the leadership of Green and Miller to solicit funds for the project. And, after considerable debate, it mandated that the new seminary be located between the Raritan and Potomac rivers.

Less than a month after the close of this assembly, the committee of the Presbyterians met with a committee from the college board. This latter group was chaired by Ashbel Green, and its five members also included two other Presbyterian ministers who had long been active in General Assembly affairs. Given the nature of the personnel on the two committees, it was not surprising that an accommodation was worked out between the college and the new seminary. Nor was it surprising that, within the guidelines provided by the General Assembly, this accommodation offered great advantages to the new theological institution.

The agreement, approved unanimously on June 26, 1811, by the seventeen college trustees present at a specially called meeting, placed the seminary in Princeton but stipulated that the General Assembly would retain full control over its operation. It gave the assembly the right to erect the buildings of the seminary on college land, and it offered the use of existing college buildings until the seminary could construct its own. The college agreed to handle funds for the seminary and to divert college endowments for ministerial candidates to seminarians. The assembly retained its right to move the seminary from Princeton, and the college agreed not to hire a theology professor as long as the seminary remained there.[74] On the whole, it was an agreement that provided the best of all worlds for the seminary: it gained the use of the college's facilities, while retaining its own autonomy.

From this point events moved rapidly toward the actual beginning of instruction. Ministers corresponded in the fall and winter, 1811–1812, about the choice of the first professor. In April 1812 the college trustees appointed a committee chaired by Green and including Miller to urge the General Assembly to approve the decisions of June 26, 1811. College trustee Richard Stockton offered four acres of his land in Princeton to the seminary if it should settle there.[75]

At the 1812 General Assembly, meeting as usual during May in

---

[74] TM, June 25 and 26, 1811; *Minutes of the General Assembly*, 499–501.
[75] TM, Apr. 12, 1812; *Minutes of the General Assembly*, 501.

Philadelphia, the Presbyterians approved the agreement between the college and the General Assembly's committee reached the previous June, and it agreed to locate their seminary, at least temporarily, in Princeton. It took Richard Stockton's offer of land under advisement. Elections were then held for the first board of directors, as a result of which Green, Miller, Alexander, eighteen other ministers, and nine laymen were elected. The next day the assembly chose Alexander as first professor of didactic and polemic theology.[76]

The seminary directors then held their first meeting at Princeton on June 30. After hearing Ashbel Green's opening sermon, they elected him president of the board, an office he held until 1848. The trustees of Princeton College, meeting in special session at the same time, allowed the seminary board to use the college library for its gathering.[77]

The inauguration of Archibald Alexander and the formal opening of the seminary took place on August 12, at services in Princeton's Presbyterian church. Samuel Miller delivered the principal address, on 2 Timothy 2:2. In it he described "a faithful ministry" as one characterized by "Piety, Talents, Learning, and Diligence," and he expounded at length upon how the church should provide for such a ministry. Alexander took John 5:39 ("search the Scriptures") as the text for his inaugural address and spoke learnedly on what he perceived as the two main tasks in studying the Bible: "to ascertain that the scriptures contain the truths of God: and to ... ascertain what these truths are." The ceremonies came to a conclusion with a charge to professor and students that reiterated the assembly's desire for "a learned, orthodox, pious, and evangelical Ministry."[78]

The seminary's student body was not large at first. Alexander began his labors with just three students, although six more came by the time of the board's first annual report to the General Assembly, and five more arrived before the start of the second full year. The General Assembly of 1813 heard from the board that the program of study had gone as planned, though not without

[76] *Minutes of the General Assembly*, 508–9, 512.

[77] TM, June 30, 1812.

[78] [Archibald Alexander,] *The Sermon, Delivered at the Inauguration of the Rev. Archibald Alexander, D.D., As Professor of Didactic and Polemic Theology, in the Theological Seminary of the Presbyterian Church, in the United States of America. To Which are Added, the Professor's Inaugural Address, and the charge to the Professor and Students* (New York, 1812), 12, 62, 108.

some difficulty in obtaining "suitable compends on the several branches which they attempted to pursue." Relationships with the college had been good. Divinity students roomed in the college ("for the most part they have been room mates") and took their board there at a separate table. The 1813 assembly also voted to establish the seminary permanently in Princeton and to accept the offer of land from Richard Stockton.[79] The assembly, recognizing the need for an additional professor, elected Samuel Miller to the professorship of ecclesiastical history and church government.

The seminary that Green and Miller founded with the aid of Alexander and a number of other dedicated Presbyterians, clerical and lay, has had a distinguished history. The close bond with the College of New Jersey was sustained for most of its first century.[80] Still, the harmony characterizing relations between Princeton College and Princeton Seminary throughout the nineteenth century should not obscure the tensions between the college's defenders and the supporters of the new institution during the period before its founding. That these tensions were found primarily within the college's board of trustees and that they arose as part of the ambiguous inheritance from John Witherspoon only makes it more important to understand why Princeton Seminary was founded as an alternative to the College of New Jersey.

THERE WOULD have been no Princeton Seminary—or at least its establishment would have taken a very different course—had not its founders been dissatisfied with Princeton College. As Green, Miller, and Alexander viewed the situation, the college had ceased to produce a significant number of ministers. It was a hotbed of student disorder. Its curriculum overvalued science and undervalued the Scripture. And its president, respected and learned though he was, encouraged suspect thinking. The weight of this indictment was increased by the fact that Green (since 1790) and Miller (since 1807) were serving as trustees of the college and were engaged in an effort to restore that institution to their vision of its

[79] *The Centennial Celebration of the Theological Seminary of the Presbyterian Church in the United States of America at Princeton, New Jersey* (Princeton, 1912) includes a copy of that first report; *Minutes of the General Assembly,* 533.

[80] In light of the importance of that bond for both institutions, especially in the nineteenth century, it has been the subject of surprisingly little attention; an overview is included in an essay by Thomas J. Wertenbaker, "The College of New Jersey and the Presbyterians," *Journal of the Presbyterian Historical Society* 36 (1958): 209–16.

founding ideal. Ironically, their efforts to bring about reform at Princeton College, which in theory should have lessened the need for a seminary, finally succeeded at the very moment that their plans for a new theological seminary reached fruition.[81]

The letter that Stanhope Smith submitted to the General Assembly of 1806 provides an indirect means for understanding the difficulties with theological education at the college. This appeal, offered one year after Green's cry for more ministers, explained in detail "the most generous provision" that the trustees had made "for the support of theological students." After rebuilding from the fire of 1802, the college went out of its way to show how it could then "offer more ample encouragements than usual" to undergraduates preparing for the ministry. Now in 1806 Smith spelled out to the General Assembly what Princeton could provide to college graduates preparing for ordination. Theological students were given a reduced rate for board, one dollar per week. They enjoyed "the assistance of the President and Professor of Theology" without fee. The theological professor offered a regular course of lectures twice a week on the various parts of divinity. A "Theological Society" convened each week under the direction of the theology professor and President Smith, at which time ministerial candidates were joined by interested undergraduates "for the discussion of important questions, immediately relative to the science of divinity." Finally, Smith recommended the "emulation and encouragement communicated by a variety of fellow students, the opportunity of cultivating any branch of science, and an access at all times to a large and well selected theological library."[82]

As it happened, however, the passing of time turned Smith's recommendations into liabilities. Henry Kollock, professor of theology, resigned in September 1806 for lack of students. The rebellion of 1807 and continuing reports of student unrest called into serious question the "emulation and encouragement" that Princeton undergraduates could offer graduate students in theology.[83] The lack of confidence in the college is suggested by the fact that,

[81] Green's account of his efforts to found the seminary leaves out all hints of dissatisfaction with Smith (*Life of Green*, 332–37).

[82] The announcement after the fire is in Stanhope Smith, *College of New Jersey* (n.p., [1804], Shaw-Shoemaker no. 7162), 5; the 1806 report, *Minutes of the General Assembly*, 362–63.

[83] This fear of corruption from the undergraduates loomed large for Benjamin Rush (Rush to Ashbel Green, May 22, 1807, in Butterfield, *Letters of Benjamin Rush*, 2:946–47).

when the board in 1810 proposed to raise funds for the support of a theology professor, the effort fell flat.[84] Well before 1810, moreover, confidence in Smith was so shaken as to compromise any effort by the college to meet the challenge for more ministers.

In sum, the leading clerical trustees simply did not believe that the college could meet the needs of ministerial training. Well before the 1807 rebellion, Ashbel Green and Samuel Miller expressed to each other their fears about the soundness of the institution. "Many doubts" troubled Miller in 1805 about various proposals "to extend the plan and increase the energy of the Princeton establishment" so as to produce more ministers.[85] A few months later Green was telling E. D. Griffin that it may be necessary to work up an entire plan of higher education "ab initio" in order to avoid the worldliness and heresy, "the contamination . . . from youths of another description," prevailing at the College of New Jersey.[86]

After the rebellion, antagonism toward Smith and the college mounted even higher. The year of Archibald Alexander's public, if nonspecific, attack on Presbyterian higher education also witnessed private, explicit denunciations of Princeton. Miller, for example, wrote to Green in May 1808, pursuing a conversation that had begun at a college board meeting.

> Nothing can be done at Princeton at present, and perhaps not for ten years. I doubt whether a divinity-school there, with ever so able and eminent a professor at its head, could be made, in the present state of the college, to command the confidence and patronage of the Presbyterian Church. . . . Under the most favorable arrangement of the college that can be expected, I fear the theological students would not be the better for habitual intercourse with the students in the arts. . . . In short, if it be desired to have the divinity-school uncontaminated by the college, to have its government unfettered, and its orthodoxy and purity perpetual, it appears to me that a separate establishment will be on many accounts advisable.[87]

In October, Green told E. D. Griffin, who was considering a call to the new Andover Seminary, that, while plans for a Presbyterian theological institution were still indefinite, "I have . . . no expecta-

---

[84] TM, June 6 and Sept. 27, 1810; Sept. 27, 1811; a copy of the circular seeking to raise funds is with the John Maclean Papers, PUA.

[85] Miller to Green, Mar. 5, 1805, in Miller, *Life of Samuel Miller*, 1:192.

[86] Green to Griffin, Nov. 18, 1805, Gratz Collection, HSP.

[87] Miller to Green, May 10, 1808, in Miller, *Life of Samuel Miller*, 1:241.

tion or wish that the School should ever be connected with Princeton College."[88] Both Green and Miller continued to work on schemes for ministerial education that included plans for an undergraduate "theological academy," for an institution, that is, that would have made the College of New Jersey entirely superfluous for the theological training of Presbyterians.[89]

Alexander's speech before the General Assembly in 1808 addressed directly another complaint harbored by several Presbyterian leaders against the college: the way it concentrated on science. The difficulty here was not so much that the Presbyterian leaders disliked the study of science. Ashbel Green was inordinately proud of the scientific accomplishments of his son Jacob. Archibald Alexander argued in his inaugural address that ministers needed to know about science in order to perceive the unity of truth and to be an effective "advocate" for the Bible.[90] The problem, rather, was that the college seemed to advance its concern for science at the expense of theology. Alexander stated the matter bluntly in 1808 in a criticism that all who had ears to hear realized was meant for Princeton College. "It is much to be doubted whether the system of education pursued in our colleges and universities is the best adapted to prepare a young man for the work of the ministry. The great extension of the physical sciences, and the taste and fashion of the age, have given such a shape and direction to the academical course, that I confess, it appears to me to be little adapted to introduce a youth to the study of the sacred Scriptures."[91] Such general misgiving with the thrust of the college curriculum only added to the suspicion that especially Ashbel Green had long harbored about Smith's spiritual soundness.

The problems that Green, Miller, and Alexander saw in Princeton College—reduced production of ministers, corrupting under-

[88] Green to Griffin, Aug. 3, 1808, Gratz Collection, HSP.

[89] Green, *Plan of a Theological Seminary*, 20–22; Miller to Green, May 14 and Sept. 4, 1810, in Miller, *Life of Samuel Miller*, 1:243–44, 287. Miller wrote to Green on Sept. 6, 1809, commending another minister who "coincides with you and me . . . that he estimates the importance of colleges by the degree in which they subsume the interests of the church" (*Life of Samuel Miller*, 1:276). Miller also wrote a memorial for Green's autobiography in which he summarized Green's purposes as president with these words: he hoped to make the college "subservient to its great original purpose, that of promoting learning in union with piety; and thus preparing an enlightened and devoted ministry for the service of the Church of Christ" (*Life of Green*, 529).

[90] [Alexander,] *Sermon at the Inauguration*, 84.

[91] Quoted in Alexander, *Life of Archibald Alexander*, 315.

graduate behavior, an overemphasis on science, and the suspect theology of President Smith—led them to seek a root-and-branch reform of that institution at the same time that they maneuvered to establish a separate school for the study of theology. Jockeying for power among the trustees of Princeton College in the early years of the century was complicated, but one thing is clear. From the time of the student rebellion in 1807, trustees allied with Green and Miller gradually assumed leadership on the board until they were able to bring about the resignation of President Smith and all of the faculty members whom he had recruited. In fact, the death throes of the Smith administration coincided exactly with the birth pangs of the seminary. The first meeting of the seminary board of directors, at which Green was chosen president, took place at Princeton on June 30, 1812. That very day the college trustees also met in special session, with ten directors of the seminary on their board, "to take into consideration the general state of the College."[92] Events set in motion by that meeting led to a further special session on August 13, one day after Alexander's inauguration and the launching of the seminary. On that occasion the college board received the resignation of President Smith and, after effective lobbying by Samuel Miller, elected Ashbel Green to take his place.[93] The establishment of the seminary thus preceded by only hours the final clerical efforts to reform the college. From that point until after the Civil War, the college joined the seminary in promoting the interests of the Presbyterian ministry largely as Green, Miller, and Alexander defined them. Yet because of Presbyterian disillusionment with the college at the start of the century, that promotion now took place in two formally distinct institutions.

STANHOPE SMITH's last years as president of Princeton were not as obviously tumultuous as those earlier in the decade. Yet they must have been painful for him nonetheless. The grand synthesis of Enlightenment, Christianity, and republicanism that he had fashioned with so much toil from the inheritance of Witherspoon—and that he was offering to the world through mature publications in those very years—had lost its audience. The rising generation of students seemed fixated on its rights and privileges to the exclusion of all else. Smith's most influential colleagues on the Princeton board, inspired by a narrower intellectual vision,

[92] TM, June 30, 1812.
[93] Ibid., Aug. 13, 1812; Miller, *Life of Samuel Miller*, 1:276.

turned against him with wounding criticism of his ideas and his leadership alike. These critics took responsibility for the training of ministers from his hands and deposed him as head of the college. Now, after a last gala commencement in September 1812,[94] he could but sit idly by in the president's house, nestled close to Nassau Hall—wasted in body, frustrated in purpose—and observe a new regime righting what it considered to be his wrongs.

[94] Described in *Charleston Times* (S.C.), Oct. 30, 1812; reprinted as "Changing Presidents in 1812," *Princeton Alumni Weekly*, Apr. 6, 1928, 751–52; and quoted liberally in Samuel Holt Monk, "Samuel Stanhope Smith [1751–1819]: Friend of Rational Liberty," in Thorp, *Lives*, 107.

13

Ashbel Green and the New Regime

What Its Pious Founders Intended It to Be

★

THE ESTABLISHMENT of Princeton Theological Seminary and the nearly simultaneous inauguration of Ashbel Green as president of the College of New Jersey opened a new chapter in the history of the Princeton circle. With Green at the college and Samuel Miller soon to join Archibald Alexander at the seminary, a trio of forceful leaders pointed the conservative Presbyterians of the middle and southern states in new directions. They looked to Christian voluntary agencies, instead of to the nation as such, for the renewal of American society. They welcomed the seminary and its professionalization of the ministry as a better way of strengthening the church than earlier, less formal methods of clerical training. With greater enthusiasm than Witherspoon or Smith had ever displayed, they gave themselves to the agency of revival as the primary means for strengthening piety.

At the same time, the changes may not have moved the Princeton circle as far from previous expressions as these leaders thought they did. For all his eagerness to straighten the course of the college, Green was still a devoted pupil of John Witherspoon. For Green, therefore, reform meant going back to a pure fount of wisdom more than it did moving on down the stream. In addition, although Alexander and Miller were not pupils of Witherspoon as such, their activity as scholars and ministers depended upon the worldview that Witherspoon proposed and Stanhope Smith developed. From a historical perspective, in fact, the most enduring achievement of this trio was to solidify a general view of American life and general attitudes toward faith and reason that preserved the intellectual world of Witherspoon for over fifty years at Princeton College and for over a century at the seminary.

In 1812, however, Green was concerned only with the immediate future. Reform was the order of his day. Green may or may not have been reluctant to succeed Smith, but once having accepted the job, he set himself to a task that, as he described it, amounted to Hercules before the Augean stables.

MANY YEARS LATER, Green looked back on his arrival at Princeton as a perilous occasion. "I knew before I left my pastoral charge that the College was in a most deplorable state; and I went with the resolution to reform it, or to fall under the attempt; and truly it seemed for some time to be questionable, which part of the alternative would be realized."[1] Green was an intense, even driven individual—"an erratic mixture of eighteenth-century piety and sentimentalism," a "proto Victorian," in the words of James Mc-Lachlan, the most perceptive historian of Green's period at the college.[2] Part of Green's problem was physical, including bouts of melancholy, attacks of kidney stone, and recurring dizziness that, after a fainting spell in the pulpit in 1796, made preaching traumatic.[3] In addition, Green's domestic life had also experienced severe dislocation. His first wife, Elizabeth Stockton, cousin of Richard Stockton, Sr., died in 1807. Two subsequent marriages also ended in the death of his wives (1814 and 1817). These family tragedies undoubtedly contributed to what McLachlan called Green's "astonishingly volatile inner life."[4] At the same time, Green's diligence, his probity, his piety, and his capacity for detail made him the indispensable man for many of the projects of the Presbyterians in the early republic. While never beloved, he was a respected minister and potent ecclesiastical force in Philadelphia, Princeton, and beyond for over half a century.[5]

Green arrived in Princeton in early November 1812, shortly be-

---

[1] *Life of Green*, 345.

[2] James McLachlan, "The *Choice of Hercules*: American Student Societies in the Early Nineteenth Century," in *The University in Society*, ed. Lawrence Stone, 2 vols. (Princeton, 1974), 2:462.

[3] *Life of Green*, 285, 299; Maclean, *CNJ*, 2;216; and on the "dreadful dizziness in my head," see Green to E. D. Griffin, Sept. 4, 1805, Gratz Collection, HSP.

[4] James McLachlan, "Ashbel Green," in *Princetonians 1776–1783*, 408.

[5] Maclean (*CNJ*, 2:107), felt that Green's "nervous condition had greatly exaggerated to his own mind the difficulties he was to encounter in conducting the government of the College." James McLachlan observes, however, that Maclean was not an unbiased witness, since Green's negative comments on Smith reflected also on Maclean's father, who was Smith's longtime colleague (*Princetonians 1776–1783*, 413).

fore the opening of the fall semester. Conditions, as he described them to his son Robert, a young lawyer in Philadelphia, were deplorable. The house provided by the college was "a perfect wreck," the college itself "was on the point of ruin," and Green "had myself no conception, till I came here, of the prostrate state of *everything.*" Still, he was resolute, and after a day of prayer on November 16, Green set down on paper the ideals that would govern his conduct as president.

> Resolved, 1st . . . to endeavour to be a father to the institution. . . . 2d. To pray for the institution as I do for my family . . . and especially that [God] may pour out his Spirit upon it, and make it what its pious founders intended it to be. 3d. To watch against the declension of religion in my own soul . . . to which the pursuits of science themselves may prove a temptation. . . . 10th. To view every officer of the College as a younger brother, and every pupil as a child.[6]

The experiences of his first semester only confirmed Green's belief that he had arrived just in time. For the trustee meeting of April 1813, Green prepared a ninety-six-page report on the degenerate condition of the college at his arrival.

> The state of the college establishment, in general, . . . was, at least in my apprehension, in a high degree disastrous & discouraging. In whatsoever direction I looked, it seemed as if *ruins,* was the proper inscription for all that I beheld. Not only in one department, but in every department, not merely in one particular, but in every particular—errors were to be corrected, or confusion to be methodized, or obscurities were to be explained, or dilapidations were to be repaired, changes were to be introduced, or reformation was to be attempted. It was, & is, my settled opinion, that the establishment could not have continued another year, without a change; & the wonder is that it continued as long as it did.

Green's bill of particulars was no less daunting: Discipline at the college, as well as "the state of religion & morals . . . were completely prostrate." The state of "classick learning" had fallen so low that graduates could not even translate their diplomas. And "the religious instruction of the college was in a state the most mournful of all."[7]

---

[6] Green to Robert Green, Nov. 6, 1812, Gratz Collection, HSP; *Life of Green,* 343–44.

[7] Green, Report to the Trustees, Apr. 1813, Green Family Papers, PUL, 4–5, 13, 64, 68.

Somehow, despite these opinions, Green managed to maintain a cordial front toward his predecessor, perhaps because Smith enjoyed good relations with the Bayards, the Stocktons, and Princeton's other leading families with whom Green had to get on. Green did express the private wish that Smith would move to in-laws in Kentucky. And Green was probably not disappointed when Smith chose to attend the Presbyterian church in Princeton rather than continue to worship at the chapel connected with the college and the seminary.[8] Beneath the polite surface of Princeton, however, antagonisms ran deep and needed only unusual circumstances to come to the fore.

Green's new-modeling of the college included a tightening of discipline and a renovation of the curriculum. He immediately issued a new edition of the college laws that stiffened the already rigorous provisions of the 1802 version. Now tutors were to enter each student's room three times a day, more limits were placed on Sunday activities, students were expressly forbidden to consort with their suspended peers, and special permission was required to rent horses or sleighs for outings.[9] Green himself set up regular meetings of the faculty to review the state of discipline and also personally kept its minutes and those of the board. In addition, he began the practice of sending written reports of student behavior and academic progress to parents, which was something of an innovation in American higher education.[10]

In most areas of the curriculum, Green continued to use the same materials as his predecessor. He did not stint the sciences, and in fact eventually came to grief with the trustees over his support for their place at the institution. His solicitude for Greek and Latin did no more than refurbish the basic curriculum as it had existed since the time of Witherspoon. Green's principal alteration was to reinstall Witherspoon's lectures in moral philosophy for those of Smith, and to replace Smith's published *Lectures on Christian Evidences* and his as yet unpublished notes, "Natural and Revealed Religion," with Paley's *Evidences* and *Natural Theology* as the basic texts in religion.[11] If this decision was more a change in form

---

[8] *Life of Green*, 408. Green to Robert Green, Nov. 6, 1812; Sprague, *Annals*, 3:340.

[9] *Laws of the College of New Jersey; Revised, Amended, and Adopted by the Board of Trustees, September 30, 1813* (Trenton, 1813), 7, 19, 23, 24.

[10] FM, no date, ca. Nov. 1812; Maclean, *CNJ*, 2:150; *Life of Green*, 346.

[11] Darrel L. Guder, "The History of Belles Lettres at Princeton" (Ph.D. diss., University of Hamburg, 1964), 233–35; Maclean, *CNJ*, 2:412; Green, Report to the Trustees, Sept. 29, 1814, Green Family Papers, PUL.

than in substance, it at least satisfied Green's desire to reduce Stan-hope Smith's presence at the college.

Green expended the greatest energy, however, not in remodel-ing discipline or studies but in promoting piety. Reflecting Green's own language, his student John Maclean wrote of this period: "In every way that he could, officially and unofficially, in public and in private, he labored to promote the spiritual welfare of his pupils; and he never lost sight of the great object for which the college was founded."[12] For the first time in Princeton's history, the Bible be-came a part of formal study, with each student assigned five chap-ters weekly for recitation on Sunday afternoons. This assignment was in addition to recitations from Paley and to the requirement that each student memorize, in Latin, the catechism of the church to which his parents belonged. In cooperation with the seminary faculty, Green also promoted the organization of student volun-tary societies for distributing religious literature, organizing Sun-day schools, and providing scholarships for the indigent.[13] Coop-eration with the seminary loomed large during Green's tenure. He was himself president of its board of directors and spent a great deal of time promoting its interests, managing its funds, oversee-ing its building projects, and providing for its endowment.[14] At various times, Green invited the seminary professors to lead wor-ship or other religious meetings in the college, and most of the tutors who served under him were also students of the seminary or its recent graduates.[15]

Although Green's conviction about the college's need for spirit-ual renewal was firmly fixed when he arrived in Princeton, it was strengthened even further by a tragic event in the fall of 1813.

[12] Maclean, *CNJ*, 2:198.

[13] Green, "Historical Sketch of the College through Witherspoon's Inaugura-tion," in *Discourses, Delivered in the College of New Jersey; addressed chiefly to candidates for the first degree in the arts; with notes and illustrations, including a historical sketch of the college* (Philadelphia, 1822), 290–92 (hereafter cited as *Discourses*); Green, Report to the Trustees, Apr. 9, 1816, Green Family Papers, PUL; Green to William B. Sprague, Apr. 10, 1832, Letter 18 in "Appendix" to Sprague's *Lectures on Revivals of Religion* (1832; reprint, London, 1959), Appendix, p. 133; Guder, "Belles Lettres at Princeton," 240–41; Minutes of the Bible Society, first meeting Feb. 27, 1813, PUA; and Maclean, *CNJ*, 2:197–98.

[14] *Life of Green*, 336, 390, 422. Green also arranged for seminarians to be sup-ported from the part of the college endowment that was designated for the educa-tion of ministers (Maclean, *CNJ*, 2:163).

[15] Green, in Sprague's *Lectures on Revivals*, Appendix, p. 135; nine of his thirteen tutors were concurrently seminary students (*General Catalogue*, 51–52).

Green's oldest son, Robert Stockton, had graduated from Princeton in 1805 after a distinguished undergraduate career. He then studied law and began a practice in Philadelphia that flourished from the start. Robert was clearly the apple of his father's eye, not only because of his winning personality ("frank, candid, facetious, hospitable and kind") and his public presence ("a handsome and eloquent speaker") but also because of his profound learning. Said Green with characteristic mingling of self-assertion and scrupulousness: "He had acquired more knowledge, and of more various kinds, than any other individual of his years, that I have personally known; not so much, however, as several extraordinary youths of whom I have read." As his father had done many years before, Robert Green in 1813 embarked on an educational tour of New England. Unlike his father, he did not return, for he fell ill during the journey and died on September 28, 1813. Green was crushed. He had lost "a beloved first-born," the treasured memorial of the wife of his youth.[16]

Green's greatest distress was that "my son was not what we call a professor of religion." Robert Green did believe in the Bible and "the doctrines of grace" and was a forceful advocate of orthodoxy against Unitarians and deists. But whether this interest in religion "had ripened into vital practical piety," Green could not say.[17] At the end he could only conclude that, if the son had been "unequivocally and eminently pious," it would have afforded much more comfort than could be derived "from all the brilliant talents and attainments by which he was unquestionably distinguished." His son's death led Green to resolve "to think less than I have done of the attainments of science and of intellectual distinction, when not connected with religion." He concluded that he had sinned "in having my heart unduly set on my children being what my eldest was in intellectual wealth, without considering . . . that this also is vanity unless sanctified by divine grace. . . . I have certainly been in a degree, an idolator of science. God has taken my idol."[18] Smitten by the uncertainty of his son's eternal future, Green turned with fresh fervor to his tasks at the college. He did not forget, nor did he want his students to forget, the lessons he had learned so

[16] Green, "Note H [on Robert Green]," in *Discourses*, 416–18.
[17] Green to E. D. Griffin, Oct. 5, 1813, Stauffer Collection, HSP; Green, "Note H," 418.
[18] Green, "Note H," 418; *Life of Green*, 355.

painfully about accumulating intellectual riches on earth and neglecting to lay up treasure in heaven.[19]

As he set about reforming the college, Green felt that he was only bringing the institution back to its condition under Witherspoon, who remained the greatest influence on his public life.[20] Green's veneration for Witherspoon led him eventually to transform the Old Doctor into an image of himself. Thus, although in fact Witherspoon was always cool toward student revival and in fact was (in America) a nonpartisan churchman, Green transformed him into a promoter of revival and, during the divisive Presbyterian debates of the 1830s, described him as a "Calvinistic divine of the Old School."[21] It was to remake the college as Witherspoon had shaped it that Green set his hand to the task.

AT FIRST, however, Green's fervent efforts made little headway. For some months the board was uneasy, with uncertainty attending the appointment of Green's faculty and his more general direction of the college.[22] In November 1812 the trustees failed to make a quorum to hear Green's inaugural, "The Union of Piety and Science," but they did show enough confidence in their new executive not to renew the committee of visitors.[23] Soon matters with the board were running smoothly, at least for the time being.

Discipline of the students was a more intractable problem. Green's first address to his young men reduced some of them to tears, but he soon discovered that most were "bent on mischief."[24] Students chafed under the tighter regulations of the new regime, and the faculty was kept busy meting out punishments to the drunk, the slanderous, the pyromaniacs, and, if the report of a student can be credited, to a Sabbath-breaker whose only crime was to throw a stone at a tree on the Lord's Day.[25] The same stu-

[19] Green drew lessons for the students from his son's life in "The Word of God the Guide to Youth," in *Discourses*, 124.

[20] Maclean, *CNJ*, 2:226; McLachlan, "Ashbel Green," in *Princetonians 1776–1783*, 406; A. L. Drummond, "Witherspoon of Gifford and American Presbyterianism," *Records of the Scottish Historical Society* 12 (1958): 198.

[21] Green, in Sprague's *Lectures on Revivals*, Appendix, pp. 129–30; Green, *The Life of the Revd John Witherspoon*, ed. Henry Lyttleton Savage (Princeton, 1973), 266.

[22] Elias Boudinot to Green, Oct. 10, 1812, Miscellaneous Manuscripts, New York Public Library; Samuel Miller to Green, no date, ca. Oct. 1812, and Oct. 2, 1812, Samuel Miller Papers, PUL; Maclean, *CNJ*, 2:220.

[23] *Life of Green*, 346; Maclean, *CNJ*, 2:148–49.

[24] *Life of Green*, 344–45.

[25] FM, 1813–1815; James Garnett to his mother, June 5, 1813, James Mercer Garnett Papers, PUA.

dent did not take kindly to Green's prohibition against dancing lessons, which amounted, as he saw it, to carrying "Presbeterian Bigotry and Superstition as far as ever the Baptists or Methodists, against whom [Green and the faculty] have always been so violent."[26] Minor disruptions continued through 1813 until things literally exploded on Sunday, January 9, 1814.[27] Sometime during the day students burned the privy. That evening at nine o'clock, in what one Princeton historian has called "probably the outstanding act of undergraduate insubordination in the history of the College of New Jersey," unruly mischiefmakers detonated "the *big cracker*"—two pounds of gunpowder in a log, set against one of the doorways.[28] The door was blown away, many windows were broken, and much incidental damage resulted. Two of the perpetrators were apprehended and handed over to local magistrates for criminal process. One was fined one hundred dollars and costs.[29] But the sentence did not deter. On April 6 a student discharged a pistol at the door of a tutor, and other lesser disturbances continued.[30] In his fall report to the board, Green put on the best face possible by reporting that most of the winter's troublemakers had been removed and that the remaining students were better behaved. Still, he admitted, problems continued, chiefly from "the unlawful visiting of taverns." Green offered what he considered a possible solution. The trustees should fix an upper limit of 120 students for the college, since any more than two scholars in each of the "60 habitable rooms" rendered discipline nearly impossible.[31]

It was not through such prudential means that the college was reduced to good order, however, but through the longed-for revival. In November 1814 a small group of students began more seriously to consider religion, and then during the second week of January "the divine influence," as Green reported to the trustees, "seemed to descend like the silent dew of heaven; and in about four weeks there were very few individuals in the college edifice who were not deeply impressed with a sense of the importance of spiritual and eternal things." The result, Green wrote to Jedidiah

[26] Garnett to his mother, May 1, 1813, James Mercer Garnett Papers, PUA.

[27] *Life of Green*, 358–59; Maclean, *CNJ*, 2:154.

[28] Henry Lyttleton Savage, "Introduction" to Green's *Life of Witherspoon*, 4. See also *Life of Green*, 360; and Maclean, *CNJ*, 2:155.

[29] FM, Jan. 14, 1814; Maclean, *CNJ*, 2:155.

[30] Green, *Life of Witherspoon*, 135n.

[31] Green, Report to Trustees, Sept. 29, 1814.

Morse, was glorious.[32] Order prevailed, students applied themselves to study as never before, and—what was most important to Green—"there are somewhat more than forty students, in regard to whom, so far as the time elapsed will permit us to judge, favourable hopes may be entertained that they have been made the subjects of renewing grace."[33]

The revival not only made the college more peaceful but also solved the other great problem of the school, for the ranks of the hopefully converted yielded many ministers. One of these was Charles Hodge, who later taught at the seminary and became the principal exponent of a "Princeton theology."[34] Archibald Alexander led the Friday prayer meeting that sustained the movement, and some of his seminarians took part as well. For the rest of 1815 and on into 1816, Green was convinced the battle had been won. Princeton had reformed. Piety, having triumphed over dissolution, slackness, and spiritual decay, was reborn.

Unfortunately for Green, the breech did not hold. As an old man, he admitted his "palpable mistake"—"I had thought that if the College was once reduced to a state of entire order, it would be likely to remain in that state."[35] But the converted students graduated, and their ranks were filled with those who knew not Joseph. In the place of spirituality and order came a renewal of disorder and fresh discouragement. In April 1816 a disciplined student went as far as to threaten the faculty publicly with grievous bodily harm.[36] In Janaury of the next year another major riot swept the campus. The antagonism reached the level of the Great Rebellion of 1807, and the damage to the reputation of the college was also comparable. This riot was played out over four days; it involved armed confrontration, the arrest of seven miscreants, and the expulsion or dismissal of 24 of the 130 students in attendance. Immediately after the affair, only 30 students remained; by late February, 97 were present. Green laid the blame on "the fixed, irreconcilable and deadly hostility of such youth as perpetrated

---

[32] Green, *A Report to the Trustees of the College of New Jersey; Relative to a Revival of Religion Among the Students of said College, in the winter and spring of the year 1815* (Philadelphia, 1815), 6; Green to Morse, April 12, 1815, Ashbel Green Collection, PUL.

[33] Green, *Report Relative to a Revival*, 7.

[34] A. A. Hodge, *The Life of Charles Hodge* (1881; reprint, New York, 1969), 30, with list of other ministers converted in this revival, 34–35.

[35] *Life of Green*, 350.

[36] Maclean, *CNJ*, 2:165.

[the disturbances], to the whole system ... of diligent study, of guarded moral conduct, and of reasonable attention to religious duties."[37]

Others were not so sure. In a letter to his son-in-law, Stanhope Smith for once let slip gentility and vented his irritation fulsomely.

It has been agreed, however, by all who are best acquainted with the college that, different from all other commotions, or discontents which I have seen in it, it has been in a great measure provoked by the austerity and illiberality of Dr. Green, and those tutors, whom he makes, by his manners, as subordinate and submissive as dogs. ... A very long statement has been published by Dr. Green, displaying the violence of the students, and covering the real causes of the outrage. He boasts that, before the sudden eruption, the college never was in so quiet, and studious a state. His own pride and self love would not permit him to see, that his manners were revolted against by the most serious students in the house. ... Indeed not a Winter has passed since his presidency that has not been disturbed by such disorders as the institution has never before seen.[38]

Soon some of the trustees came to share Smith's general opinion.

In the wake of this riot and the stern measures Green took to quell it, public confidence and the confidence of the board were shaken. Green justified his harsh stand in 1817 by referring back to the events of the 1807 rebellion. A failure to crack down at that time was, as he saw it, a nearly fatal mistake. "A total relaxation of government" had caused the earlier revolt, whereupon "the institution instantly sank, & never rose again under the administration in which it occurred."[39] Yet no amount of self-justification or comparison with earlier troubles could hide the fact that the sort of disruptive behavior that undercut the credibility of Green's predecessor, and that Green was commissioned to remedy, had returned to compromise his own leadership.

Student complaints about Green's unbending regimen and further commotions contributed to a growing institutional malaise after 1817. Efforts to raise money and to keep parents from sending surplus cash to their sons both failed.[40] In April 1822, ten years

---

[37] Green, *To the Friends of the College of New-Jersey* (n.p., Feb. 20, 1817), 3. For another full account, see *Salem Gazette*, Feb. 7, 1817, transcript in PUA.

[38] Smith to Joseph Cabell Breckinridge, Mar. 13, 1817, Papers of the Breckinridge Family, Manuscript Division, Library of Congress.

[39] Green to James Richards, June 1817, Ashbel Green Collection, PUL.

[40] John Breckinridge to Robert Breckinridge, June 2, 1819, Papers of the Breckinridge Family, Library of Congress; Maclean, *CNJ*, 2:178, 181, 191.

after the erection of a similar body for similar purposes, the board appointed a special committee of inquiry to assess the general discipline and instruction of the college. Once more, the committee reported, Princeton had suffered a "loss of reputation" because of the inability to control its students.[41] Even while the committee was preparing this report, Green was embroiled in conflict with the board on other matters. One trustee was upset because Green had suspended his son during during the summer term in 1822.[42] Green had also reached a standoff with the board on instruction in mathematics and science, which Green was eager to preserve at previous levels. A series of circumstances had led to the resignation of the mathematics professor. The board then proposed to combine professorships in mathematics and chemistry. This idea was unacceptable to Green in principle and also because it would have meant that his own son, Jacob, who had served since 1818 as chemistry professor but who had no competence in mathematics, would be out of a job.[43] Over this specific issue as well as a more general loss of support, Green submitted his resignation at the fall commencment in 1822.

Once again the conscientious inculcation of high ideals in religion, science, and public affairs had not led to the success that Witherspoon enjoyed. To be sure, Green's concentration on the religious side of Witherspoon's legacy had earned a certain reward. Nothing like the revival of 1815 had been seen since Witherspoon's early days at the college. In addition, Green reversed the trend in clerical vocations. A full quarter of his graduates entered the ministry, compared with well under 10 percent throughout most of Smith's tenure.[44] Green's efforts on behalf of Princeton Theological Seminary also contributed to the rise of that institution as a vital center of diligent learning and Presbyterian thought. Having noted such progress, however, we must conclude that the reformer had failed. The institution still labored with the same problems that had beset Stanhope Smith. Green's restoration of

[41] Maclean, *CNJ*, 2:193. Richard Stockton served on both committees.

[42] Green to James Richards, July 26, 1822, Gratz Collection, HSP.

[43] McLachlan, "Ashbel Green," in *Princetonians 1776–1783*, 416–17; Maclean, *CNJ*, 2:192–95. Jacob Green went on to a distinguished teaching career in Philadelphia (Edgar Fahs Smith, "Jacob Green Chemist, 1790–1841," *Journal of Chemical Education* 20 [1943]: 418–27).

[44] Out of 355 graduates, 89 entered the ministry; *Princeton University: Catalogue of All Who Have Held Office in or Have Received Degrees from the College of New Jersey* (Princeton, 1896), 65–72.

discipline and his adjustment of the curriculum had not produced the desired results, or at least they had not come up to his own expectations and the expectations of the board.

ONE OF THE reasons that Green's tenure resembles the tenure of Stanhope Smith is that Green's view of the world and his conception of the educational task resembled those of his predecessor much more closely than he realized. As much as Green looked upon himself as a new broom sweeping the college clean, the tools with which he set to work and the ideal toward which he strove were virtually those of Stanhope Smith. Both presidents were convinced that the worldview constructed by Witherspoon was sound, both considered themselves his legitimate successor, and both felt that a proper extrapolation of Witherspoon's principles would make the college an engine for the harmonious advancement of Christianity, science, and the public good. If they differed, it was because each appropriated different parts of a single inheritance.

The task of describing the intellectual legacy of John Witherspoon during Ashbel Green's tenure is complicated by the fact that the theological seminary had come onto the scene. Green's intimate involvement with its development and the indirect influence of Witherspoon on Archibald Alexander meant that the work of the seminary took its place alongside the work of the college in defining Princeton's intellectual position during the second decade of the nineteenth century. The new leaders of the Princeton circle certainly reversed Smith's priorities. Where Smith gave attention first to science, Green, Alexander, and Miller turned first to piety. Where he cultivated religion as an inconspicuous given, they treated science much the same way. Yet, principles of harmonizing faith and learning and expectations for results were almost exactly the same. In their own pious way they carried on the heritage of John Witherspoon. In so doing they promoted more a variation of, than an alternative to, the intellectual vision of Samuel Stanhope Smith.[45]

The essential continuity from Witherspoon through Smith to Green is suggested most readily by the themes of their inaugural

[45] Especially perceptive on these continuities is Douglas Sloan, *The Scottish Enlightenment and the American College Ideal* (New York, 1971), 181–82. They are also traced with considerable skill in John C. Vander Stelt, *Philosophy and Scripture: A Study in Old Princeton and Westminster Theology* (Marlton, N.J., 1978), 65–83, 88–89; and M. L. Bradbury, "Adventure in Persuasion: John Witherspoon, Samuel Stanhope Smith, and Ashbel Green" (Ph.D. diss., Harvard University, 1967).

addresses—Witherspoon, "The Connection and Mutual Influences of Learning and Piety"; Smith, "Whether it be profitable to connect piety with all the others arts which belong to a liberal education"; Green, "The Promotion of Science in Union with Piety."[46] The similarities ran much deeper than merely the words. Green, like his predecessors, felt that learning and religion could be joined for the promotion of the church and society. Moreover, he felt, as they had, that careful observers could chart accurately the outworking of private principle into public behavior.

On questions of epistemology and religious apologetics, Green and Alexander carried on entirely in Smith's train. Like Smith, Green made much of the empirical value of self-consciousness. He even reiterated Smith's claim that freedom of the human will was the key matter showing the revelatory power of self-consciousness. As Green told his students, the case for free will rests on the fact that one "is conscious of it . . . that the whole organization and arrangements of human society are, and must be, built upon it, as a conceded, or self-evident truth." On the more general use of common-sense intuitions, Alexander at the seminary was saying the same thing, albeit more eloquently and at greater length: "To prove that our faculties are not so constituted as to misguide us, some have had recourse to the *goodness* and *truth of God*, our creator, but this argument is unnecessary. We are as certain of these intuitive truths as we can be."[47]

Alexander and Green, moreover, followed Smith in the ways they put common-sense intuitions to use in arguing for the faith. As Alexander put it, "We must be sure that we exist, and that the world exists, before we can be certain that there is a God, for it is from these *data* that we prove his existence." Green recommended Christianity because of "the reasonableness of the thing itself," where "the proper office of reason . . . is to take facts as she finds them, explain and harmonize them as far as she can."[48] Smith's Baconian-Newtonian model was good enough as well for Green

[46] Collins, *Witherspoon*, 1:113; Smith, *Oratio Inauguralis* (Trenton, 1817), 1; Green, "The Promotion of Science in Union with Piety," Ashbel Green Collection, PUL.

[47] Green, "Word of God Guide to Youth," 98; Archibald Alexander, "Theological Lectures, Nature and Evidence of Truth, October 1812," Speer Library, Princeton Theological Seminary, transcribed in Mark A. Noll, ed., *The Princeton Theology, 1812–1921: Scripture, Science, and Theological Method from Archibald Alexander to Benjamin Warfield* (Grand Rapids, Mich., 1983), 65.

[48] Alexander, "Theological Lectures," 65; Green, "A Plea for Early Piety," in *Discourses*, 166; Green, "Word of God Guide to Youth," 95.

and Alexander. The way to defend Christianity was by the facts, discovered through rigorous scientific procedures and organized by the careful use of reason.

Alexander's inaugural sermon in 1812 suggests how similar the new regime was to the old. He began his exposition of John 5:39 ("search the Scriptures") not by examining the Scriptures themselves but with an attack upon those who detracted from the Bible. That is, before Alexander discussed the interpretation of Scripture and its main themes, he mounted a scientific defense of the Bible's inspired character. In this effort he took particular care, as Witherspoon had also done in similar circumstances, to refute the arguments of David Hume, "the most insidious enemy of Christianity."[49] Hume notwithstanding, it *was* still possibly to demonstrate the truths of Christianity.

Earlier in his career, Alexander had gathered materials to refute Tom Paine's *Age of Reason* (1794), though he did not publish his response. Ever after he maintained an intense interest in countering the arguments of infidelity, whether they came from Hume, Paine, William Godwin, Elihu Palmer, or other infidels.[50] In this concern he was joined by Miller and Green. Miller, while still in the more liberal phase that produced his *Brief Retrospect of the Eighteenth Century*, was much concerned about "those theories, falsely called philosophy, which pervert reason, contradict Revelation, and blaspheme its divine AUTHOR." Green, for his part, took over Alexander's methods and almost his very words in demonstrating the reliability of the Bible to the undergraduates.[51]

The structure of the seminary curriculum, which Green drafted and Alexander and Miller implemented, reflected this approach to the defense of the faith. While second- and third-year students exegeted the New and Old Testaments, prepared sermons, and studied theology, church history, and pastoral theology, first-year students concentrated on the evidences of natural and revealed religion and on mental and moral science. The latter subjects con-

[49] [Archibald Alexander,] *The Sermon, Delivered at the Inauguration of the Rev. Archibald Alexander . . . To Which are Added, the Professor's Inaugural Address* (New York, 1812), 69–70.

[50] John De Witt, "Archibald Alexander's Preparation for His Professorship," *Princeton Theological Review* 3 (1905): 583, 586; Raleigh Don Scovel, "Orthodoxy in Princeton: A Social and Intellectual History of Princeton Theological Seminary, 1812–1860" (Ph.D. diss., University of California, Berkeley, 1970), 49.

[51] Samuel Miller, *A Brief Retrospect of the Eighteenth Century*, 2 vols. (New York, 1803), 1:iv; Green, "Word of God Guide to Youth," 94.

sisted mostly of the epistemology and ethics that Alexander had learned from his Virginia preceptor, William Graham, as Graham in turn had learned them from John Witherspoon at Princeton College.[52] One of the great needs felt by the founders of Princeton Seminary was for a learned defense of the faith against rampant infidelity in America. As they set about this defense, they did so undergirded by the philosophical perspective of Witherspoon and Smith. Green could even sound like Stanhope Smith in his *Essay on Variety in the Human Species* when he told students that "science is *the chief instrument*, by which religion is to be defended against its learned, malignant and Potent adversaries."[53]

When Green and his colleagues applied this thinking to the larger social order, they once again followed Stanhope Smith. Green continued the retreat from practical politics that had begun late in the previous century, but nothing had altered the fervent conjunction of republican patriotism and Christian piety. And the Fourth of July remained the ceremonial highlight of the year.[54] In addition, underlying assumptions about the workings of society were also the same. "Unsanctified science" was "the source and curse" that wrought destruction in France, but sound learning allied with piety established personal and social stability. "Civil society," as Green told the undergraduates, "is held together by religion."[55] Furthermore, sound principles and their opposite were known by their fruit. Green, like his predecessors, insisted on the essential premise of the Enlightenment that the properly disciplined observer could accurately read the springs of actions in their products. Immoral principles produced disorder. Moral exertions produced stability. Even the manifest confusion of moral ends and means could not shake this conviction, as Green testified immediately after the 1817 riot by concluding: "We are comforted by the confidence that the smiles of Heaven, which give true prosperity, will never be withheld from a faithful and steadfast discharge of duty, and from constant endeavours, however humble, to promote these interests which in the eye of God are the most precious and important."[56] Green, no less than Smith, asked for the soundness of his principles to be judged by their results.

---

[52] Scovel, "Orthodoxy in Princeton," 43, 114–15; De Witt, "Alexander's Preparation for His Professorship," 580–81.

[53] Green, "The Union of Piety and Science," in *Discourses*, 15.

[54] Green, "Historical Sketch of the College," 294: Wertenbaker, *Princeton*, 210.

[55] Green, *Discourses*, 16, 295, 10.

[56] Green, *Friends of the College*, 4.

The refomers also had much of Smith's concern for self-control, dignity, and eloquence. Green warned the undergraduates about "the dangers of intemperate indulgence—whether it be of particular appetites, or of a general love of pleasure."[57] His whole approach to the discipline of Princeton represented an external corollary to Smith's steely efforts to master himself. Meanwhile, at the seminary Samuel Miller was saying about the same things publicly concerning the necessity for dignity and stateliness that Smith had passed on in correspondence with the Blairs and Benjamin Rush. A seminary was necessary, Miller wrote to the Presbyterians in 1810, in order to prepare ministers for the advanced state of modern society. "Vital and experimental" religion was of course the most important qualification for a minister, but now piety alone would not make a good minister, "if his knowledge be scanty, and his literature circumscribed." A minister's reputation depends upon "confidence in the minds of others."[58] Stanhope Smith could not have put it better.

A catalogue of instances showing continuity between Smith and his successors is not meant to suggest that there were no serious differences. Smith worked out his thought systematically and published philosophical treatises, while Alexander and Miller published theological works and Green left only addresses to students as the intellectual memorial of his presidency. Smith found it difficult to admit an intellectual conundrum, while Green more than once confessed that he was unable to see the whole picture.[59] To nurture the rising generation, Green trusted piety attended by faithful learning, Smith the reverse. And Providence still had some of the mystery for Green it had largely lost for Smith.[60]

At the end of the day, however, Smith and Green were intellectual siblings, or at least half-brothers. In Smith, the republican Christian Enlightenment of Witherspoon appeared as a systematic devotion to science. In Green, it came to expression in a more obviously Christian shape. The difference was important, as was also

[57] Green, "The Man of False Honour," in *Discourses*, 214.

[58] *Minutes of the General Assembly of the Presbyterian Church in the United States of America from . . . 1789 to . . . 1820* (Philadelphia, 1847), 457–58. Miller's sermon at Alexander's installation noted that clergymen increased the "polish" of "civil society" as well as its "regularity, peace, . . . and strength" ([Alexander,] *Sermon at the Inauguration*, 9).

[59] See *Life of Green*, 194; and Green, "Word of God Guide to Youth," 98–99.

[60] Green, Sermon on James 5:16, Ashbel Green Collection, PUL; Green, "Word of God Guide to Youth," 99.

the difference in their personalities. But neither was as significant as the legacy they shared from John Witherspoon.

THE TWILIGHT of Green's career as president of the college corresponded with the twilight of Smith's life. Archibald Alexander remembered Smith's declining years as "a beautiful old age surpassing any that we have known. He was tall, slender and feeble, but erect." Smith faded slowly. A student reported on June 2, 1819, that Smith looked unusually well, but the end was near and arrived on August 21 of that same year.[61] Alexander and Miller, but not Green, joined four other clerical members of the college board as Smith's pallbearers. Miller also wrote the inscription for Smith's tombstone and paid for the stone ($187.64) on behalf of the college trustees.[62]

Green's departure from Princeton was less peaceful, in part because he remembered so clearly the circumstances of Smith's retirement. Green resented, among other things, the board's providing generously for his predecessor's old age—more than twenty thousand dollars in various compensations during Green period as president—while, as the situation worsened in 1822, no one said a word to him about financial provisions for his departure. More generally, Green complained of being "treated in an unjust, unfair & unreasonable manner by the trustees."[63] After his resignation the board offered Green its first clerical vacancy, but he declined to serve.[64] Instead, he turned his energy to the denomination, where he continued as a considerable influence from Philadelphia until his death in 1848.

Green eventually joined Smith in doubting whether he had left a lasting impact on the college. Green's later reflections on his time as president were defensive, stressing his faithful discharge of duty, his efforts to promote religion, and his resolution in the face of student dissipation. He protested much more than someone who was satisifed with the work he had done. For his part, Smith was characteristically philosophical. In probably his last communi-

---

[61] James W. Alexander, *The Life of Archibald Alexander* (New York, 1854), 322; John Breckinridge to Robert Breckinridge, June 2, 1819, with a report of Smith's death and funeral in J. Breckinridge to R. Breckinridge, Aug. 26, 1819, both Papers of the Breckinridge Family, Library of Congress.

[62] Samuel Miller, Jr., *The Life of Samuel Miller*, 2 vols. (Philadelphia, 1869), 2:40; bill for Smith's tombstone, Oct. 11, 1820, Samuel Stanhope Smith Collection, PUL.

[63] Green to James Richards, July 26, 1822.

[64] Maclean, *CNJ*, 2:197.

cation to Green, he closed by noting how, at the very institution to which he had given his life, his own books "became unnecessary, by the will of providence, and the change of system in the college."[65]

Green and Smith both erred, however, if they thought their work had been in vain. Life at the College of New Jersey—intellectual as well as moral, religious, and social—continued for nearly half a century within the framework they established. While neither as intellectually adventuresome as Smith nor as unreservedly devout as Green, leaders of the college bore their general stamp for several decades. Under the long tenure of Smith's pupil James Carnahan (1823–1854), and during the presidency of John Maclean (1854–1868), Green's pupil and the son and namesake of Smith's longtime colleague, the college did languish.[66] But it still exerted a by no means inconsiderable national influence through professors like Joseph Henry, later to found the Smithsonian, and the geologist Arnold Guyot, as well as through a continuing stream of elite students. The general outline of that influence was along the lines that Smith and Green had set down.

In addition, Princeton Seminary continued to reflect the work of Smith and Green for an even longer time. In fact, the presence at Princeton after 1812 of two tightly knit, yet still institutionally distinct, agencies fulfilled more exactly the vision of John Witherspoon than either a college or a seminary by itself could have done. Witherspoon had joined in his person a deep commitment to religion and the liberal arts, but he never succeeded in spelling out exactly how the two should relate to each other, without one being reduced to the other. In Scotland, he opposed evangelical Christianity to a moderate form of the Enlightenment. In America, he came close to reinterpreting religion as a product of common sense. Now, years after his demise, the coupled but separate institutions in Princeton carried on his tradition by linking in one place two institutions that were never fully integrated.

Ashbel Green bears much of the credit for the creation of Princeton Theological Seminary and its early rise to prominence. Throughout the first two-thirds of the nineteenth century, the seminary was a religious and intellectual influence in America rivaled only by comparable institutions at Andover and New Ha-

---

[65] Smith to Green, ca. Feb. 1818, Gratz Collection, HSP.

[66] Wertenbaker, *Princeton*, 153–83, held that the college reached its nadir under Green. I am following McLachlan, "Ashbel Green," in *Princetonians 1776–1783*, 418, in dating that trough after Green's tenure.

ven.[67] During its golden age in the nineteenth century, the seminary lived off capital invested by John Witherspoon and his students. Its dominant voice, Charles Hodge, was trained by Green and Alexander and thus was Witherspoon's intellectual grandchild twice over. Ashbel Green wrote the seminary's charter and strongly influenced the character of its religious experience. Not as obviously, the seminary wrestled with its intellectual pursuits as much in the style of Smith as of Green.

A summary glance at the career of Charles Hodge shows these connections. He reunited, in effect, the parts of Witherspoon's legacy that had gone separate directions with Smith and Green. Hodge's mien, his spiritual instincts, and his religious aspirations were of Ashbel Green, but his mental abilities, his approach to the world of thought, and his intellectual ambition were of Stanhope Smith. And so it came to pass that, at the end of his life and at the height of his influence, Hodge was still defending a picture of the world that the Princetonians of his youth had painted. During the Civil War, Hodge's influential analyses of Southern disloyalty and Northern probity reembodied the confidence of Witherspoon, Smith, and Green in the ability to track public conditions to private convictions.[68] In the last decade of his life, Hodge published the two books for which he is best known. He introduced his *Systematic Theology* (1872–1873) with a panegyric to Baconian method that breathed the spirit of Smith's lectures on moral philosophy. His exercise in physico-theology, *What Is Darwinism?* (1874), attempted to defend traditional religion against the depredations of unbelieving scientists as forcefully as anything that had appeared in Princeton since Smith's *Essay on Variety in the Human Species*. It did so, moreover, with the same distinctions between fact and hypothesis, reason and speculation, that Smith had expounded in his earlier work. Whatever the exact genealogy, the Princeton theology carried on where both Green and Smith had left off.[69]

The age of Witherspoon and his students faded away toward the end of the nineteenth century. The arrival of another president from Scotland in 1868, exactly one hundred years after Wither-

[67] For a general picture, see Bruce Kuklick, *Churchmen and Philosophers from Jonathan Edwards to John Dewey* (New Haven, 1985).

[68] William S. Barker, "The Social Views of Charles Hodge (1797–1878): A Study in Nineteenth-Century Calvinism and Conservatism," *Presbyterion: Covenant Seminary Review* 1 (1975): 1–22; and David Neil Murchie, "Morality and Social Ethics in the Thought of Charles Hodge" (Ph.D. diss., Drew University, 1980).

[69] Especially helpful at this point is Vander Stelt, *Philosophy and Scripture*, 120–47.

spoon, marked a singificant change. James McCosh introduced a note of philosophical idealism into the college's long entrenched commitment to common sense and a greater sensitivity to changing academic discussions from Europe.[70] At about the same time, the growing impact of modernity on American religion altered the framework within which the theologians of Princeton Seminary did their work. These changes diffused the influence of the earlier generations, but still they lived on, at least in mutated form. Echoes remained in the actions of the college's supporters who in 1866 created a professorship for the harmony of science and revealed religion and who supported the work of Charles Woodruff Shields in that chair for nearly forty years.[71] At the seminary they could be discerned in the work of Benjamin Breckinridge Warfield, the nation's most capable theological conservative at the end of the nineteenth century, who contended that "faith, in all its forms, is a conviction of truth, founded as such, of course, on evidence. . . . Christianity has been placed in the world to *reason* its way to the dominion of the world."[72] They were still present in the lectures of the college's first new president in the twentieth century, Woodrow Wilson, who reembodied John Witherspoon's vision of putting liberal and Christian learning to use for the advancement of civilization and the renovation of society.[73]

Well before the end of the century, however, the Princeton circle was moving in new directions. America was changing. Hints of Witherspoon's pursuit of the unified virtues of Christianity, republicanism, and a moderate Enlightenment could still be seen. But it was now a different story when once his students and the students of his students had passed from the scene.

[70] J. David Hoeveler, Jr., *James McCosh and the Scottish Intellectual Tradition: From Glasgow to Princeton* (Princeton, 1981).

[71] Wertenbaker, *Princeton*, 284–85.

[72] Warfield, review of Herman Bavinck's *De Zekerheid des Geloofs* (The certainty of faith), *Princeton Theological Review* 1 (1903): 146–47. On these continuities and their importance more generally in American religious history, see especially George M. Marsden, *Fundamentalism and American Culture: The Shaping of Twentieth Century Evangelicalism, 1870–1925* (New York, 1980), 109–18.

[73] Arthur S. Link, "Woodrow Wilson: Presbyterian in Government," in *Calvinism and the Political Order*, ed. George L. Hunt (Philadelphia, 1965); and Wilson's own "Address on the Bible" (May 1911), in *The Papers of Woodrow Wilson*, vol. 23, *1911–1912*, ed. Arthur S. Link (Princeton, 1977), 12–20.

14

Conclusion

Retrogression, the New Nation, and a Republican Christian Enlightenment

★

THE HISTORY of Stanhope Smith and the Princeton circle from 1768 to 1822, or at least the history as I have told it, confirms the theses sketched in the introduction. John Witherspoon's achievement was personal and temporary rather than intellectual and lasting. Samuel Stanhope Smith's very success in fulfilling the ideological vision of Witherspoon largely accounted for his failure. The Revolution promised more to the Princeton circle than it could deliver. And Enlightenment confidence in a science of human nature obscured the world as much as it illuminated the world.

To the extent that such conclusions are justified, there is little in the history of Stanhope Smith's Princeton to support the once-popular opinion that American higher education entered a period of retrogression after about 1800. The retrogression argument arose early in the twentieth century when progressive historians, enthralled by the luminous prospects of scientific democracy and appalled by the crabbed character of nineteenth-century American religion, set about tracing the rise of modern education.[1] This view received its most forceful statement in 1955 from Richard Hofstadter in *The Development of Academic Freedom in the United States*. Hofstadter's rendition in turn struck the interpretive key for later studies, including substantial books in which Princeton figures prominently.[2]

---

[1] Difficulties in the progressive interpretation are spelled out with admirable clarity in Bernard Bailyn, *Education in the Forming of American Society: Needs and Opportunities for Study* (Chapel Hill, N.C., 1960).

[2] Richard Hofstadter, with Walter P. Metzger, *The Development of Academic Freedom*

It is now apparent that Hofstadter's interpretation in this instance, as with several other provocative sallies, revealed as much about the fate of American liberalism after World War II as about the early history of the United States.[3] Problems with the notion of retrogression are numerous. American colleges in fact did much better during the antebellum period at educating "scholars who were not gentlemen" than they had done during the eighteenth century.[4] College graduates did contribute fruitfully to American society and were not hamstrung by ties to the denominations.[5] Moreover, the rise of the theological seminary gave America its first graduate professional schools and became "a functional equivalent of the university in ante-bellum America."[6] Colleges contributed to what Lawrence Cremin called "the signal achievement of popular education during the first century of the Republic," which was "to help define an American *paideia* and teach it to a polyglot population spread across a continent."[7] In short, ideological precommitments made it difficult for Hofstadter and like-minded historians to recognize the considerable strengths of antebellum higher education.

Recent criticism of the retrogression thesis has concentrated more on the state of higher education in the early nineteenth cen-

in the United States (New York, 1955). Wertenbaker, *Princeton*, anticipates Hofstadter's general position in his chapters on developments after about 1800. A too-ready acceptance of Hofstadter's argument mars the otherwise outstanding work of Howard Miller, *The Revolutionary College: American Presbyterian Higher Eduction, 1707–1837*, especially part 3, "Retrogression (1795–1820)."

3 See the strictures concerning Hofstadter's account of the "paranoid style" in Leo P. Ribuffo, *The Old Christian Right: The Protestant Far Right from the Great Depression to the Cold War* (Philadelphia, 1983), 240–47; and concerning Social Darwinism in Jim Moore, "Socializing Darwinism: Historiography and the Fortunes of a Phrase," in *Science as Politics*, ed. Les Levidow (London, 1986), 54–57.

4 David F. Allmendinger, Jr., *Paupers and Scholars: The Transformation of Student Life in Nineteenth-Century New England* (New York, 1975), 7.

5 James McLachlan, "The American College in the Nineteenth Century: Toward a Reappraisal," *Teachers' College Record* 80 (1978): 287–306, with a solid assessment of the aims of Hofstadter and his colleagues. Painstaking study of the colleges throughout the country in the early national period led Colin B. Burke to this conclusion: "The critics' focus upon what they did not want higher education to be in their own time also led them away from recognizing the social and economic contributions of the alumni of the colleges" (*American Collegiate Populations: A Test of the Traditional View* [New York, 1982], 5).

6 Natalie A. Naylor, "The Theological Seminary in the Configuration of American Higher Education: The Ante-Bellum Years," *History of Education Quarterly* 17 (1977): 27.

7 Lawrence A. Cremin, *American Education: The National Experience, 1783–1876* (New York, 1980), 507.

tury than on its development in the period of the Revolution. Yet the history of Princeton under Witherspoon and Smith provides a different reason for questioning the concept of retrogression. The "heights" that Witherspoon and his generation are supposed to have scaled are curious heights. To be sure, no one can question Witherspoon's effectiveness as a public figure or as an agent of institutional renewal. The problem, rather, is intellectual. On that level, the "achievement" of Witherspoon turns out to be, both formally and materially, an illusion.

On a formal level, Witherspoon was not a distinguished thinker. He made his reputation by linking up republicanism, Enlightenment science, and Calvinistic Christianity. Yet in his lectures and public pronouncements, rhetoric often took the place of reason, intuition became a god-of-the-gaps filling in critical missing pieces, and the enterprise as a whole merely confirmed a predetermined vision of social order. Stanhope Smith did better than Witherspoon at knitting together the disparate elements of his mentor's worldview, but Smith's successes at unifying the science of the Enlightenment and the traditions of Christianity for the good of the republic were repeatedly compromised by intellectual weaknesses inherited from his predecessor. Without the enthusiasm of the Revolution and its perception of a tyrannical external threat, the worldview of Witherspoon floundered. In point of fact, proponents of the new moral philosophy failed to identify clearly the springs of public disorder; a science of human nature did not lead to the control of social processes; and religion was undermined as much as it was bolstered by the confidence in nature. The history of Princeton under Stanhope Smith is a record of how far the views of Witherspoon could be carried but also of their serious limitations. Where Hofstadter suggested that "perhaps the root cause of the retrogression was the persuasive national reaction from the Enlightenment,"[8] it fits the historical circumstances just as well to say that the root cause of intellectual retrogression in early America was the pervasive national embrace of the Enlightenment.

A historical account is not the place to address the material question: Was it, in fact, possible to blend the Enlightenment, Calvinism, and classic republicanism in such a way as to strengthen the nation, extend the church, and advance civilization? Many have tried throughout America's history to fashion such a synthesis.[9]

[8] Hofstadter, *Development of Academic Freedom*, 209.
[9] They include, besides Witherspoon and Smith, Lyman and Henry Ward Beecher, Woodrow Wilson, Reinhold Niebuhr, and Robert Bellah.

Yet it still may be asked if the science of the Enlightenment, with its large claims for the human autonomy of perception and action, could ever rest comfortably with traditional Reformed Protestantism, given the Calvinistic vision of both divine mystery and intractable human sinfulness. Nor is it self-evident that, even if a suspension could be compounded of moderate Calvinism and the Didactic Enlightenment, it would ensure the health of the body politic.[10] The material question is important, but it is not one that yields easily to historical study. Nor is Princeton necessarily the best place to address the issue as an intellectual and religious question. In Scotland, for example, intellectual leaders during the early nineteenth century may actually have been more successful at bringing together the convictions of republicanism, Calvinism, and the Enlightenment than were the leaders of Princeton.[11]

THE STORY of the Princeton circle in the age of Witherspoon, Smith, and Green is illuminating quite apart from its place in the debate over retrogression, an issue with Whiggish overtones, no matter how it is worried. In the first instance, that story illustrates the great importance of the American Revolution in the national period, as both an occasion for institutional revitalization and a source for ideological creativity. At Princeton the Spirit of 1776 was ever present. It created a ritual order for the calendar. It offered a rich fund of rhetoric for ceremonial occasions. It opened careers of responsibility and honor to graduates. It sustained a perpetual preoccupation with politics. It quickened memories nearly to the time of the Civil War. Its utopian vision established a long-lasting norm for social harmony. And it provided the stuff for a renewed providential understanding of history. To study the College of New Jersey in these decades is to study the impact of the American Revolution.

At the same time, this history also opens up the national debate that occurred in the early republic over what the Spirit of 1776 actually meant. Princetonians joined other Americans in promot-

[10] Doubts about the coalescence of the Enlightenment and Christianity have been raised by, among others, Samuel Hopkins, Nathaniel Hawthorne, Herman Melville, William Lloyd Garrison, Abraham Lincoln (in the Second Inaugural Address), H. Richard Niebuhr, and perhaps most sharply by two twentieth-century authors in books of unusual force, Joseph Haroutunian, *Piety versus Moralism: The Passing of the New England Theology* (New York, 1932); and Douglas W. Frank, *Less than Conquerors: How Evangelicals Entered the Twentieth Century* (Grand Rapids, Mich., 1986).

[11] See Stewart J. Brown, *Thomas Chalmers and the Godly Commonwealth in Scotland* (New York, 1982).

ing their own interpretations of independence and the new nation's destiny. Reactions of the Princeton circle to events beyond the campus testify to the strength of alternative visions. If Princeton, in the phrase of Stanhope Smith, stood for the "patrician" interpretation, others advocated a "plebian" reading.[12] Since neither is understandable without the other, those today who would better grasp plebian, Jeffersonian democracy (which eventually triumphed) will benefit from a surer understanding of patrician, Federalist centers like Princeton. In addition, just as recent studies have begun to show how thoroughly a commitment to Jeffersonian democracy affected religious life in America,[13] so the story of Princeton reveals further dimensions of the tie between religion and public life for republican Federalists. Witherspoon and his students joined their Harvard contemporaries in opposing mobocracy, but they emphasized more strongly the role of religion in nourishing republican virtue than did their Massachusetts contemporaries.[14] By comparison with the Connecticut Congregationalists, Princeton Presbyterians were less troubled by the separation of church and state and more restrained in pursuit of revival.[15] Over against opponents and as a variation on themes shared by allies, Princeton leaders fashioned a republican Christian Enlightenment that was a consequential force in the ongoing struggle to define the blessings of liberty.

Princeton's history also suggests how important general intellectual considerations were for the working politics of the new nation. Witherspoon and Smith were pioneers who exerted great energy in formulating ideals for the republic. Smith especially has been a neglected figure for such concerns. The students he taught provided respected leadership in church and society for southern and mid-Atlantic states during the first half-century of the nation's ex-

---

[12] Smith to Jonathan Dayton, Dec. 22, 1801, Samuel Stanhope Smith Collection, PUL.

[13] See especially Nathan O. Hatch, "The Christian Movement and the Demand for a Theology of the People," *Journal of American History* 67 (1980): 545–67; and Gordon S. Wood, "Evangelical America and Early Mormonism," *New York History* 61 (1980): 359–86.

[14] Cf. Daniel Walker Howe, *The Unitarian Conscience: Harvard Moral Philosophy, 1805–1861* (Cambridge, Mass., 1970), chap. 5, "Moral Man and Moral Society."

[15] Cf. John R. Fitzmier, "The Godly Federalism of Timothy Dwight, 1752–1817: Society, Doctrine, and Religion in the Life of New England's 'Moral Legislator' " (Ph.D. diss., Princeton University, 1987), 159–211; and Stephen E. Berk, *Calvinism versus Democracy: Timothy Dwight and the Origins of American Evangelical Orthodoxy* (Hamden, Conn., 1974).

istence. His own writing and teaching, though now largely overlooked, also made a telling contribution. No other thinker of his
generation, for example, wrote as learnedly about the unity of humanity, a far from esoteric concern in the eighteenth century. To
glimpse the importance of that contribution it is enough to note
that Smith presented his defense of human unity before Philadelphia's American Philosophical Society less than four months before the Constitutional Convention convened in that city. As he
did so, his friend James Madison was preparing for that convention by studying the history of ancient republics in order to define
universal principles of political behavior.[16] Smith's moral philosophy, in other words, offered a theoretical foundation for the
Founders' practical appeal to "a science of politics."[17] Historians
rightly study Madison and the framers of the Constitution as central actors of their age. Even with a concern simply for such matters, they could benefit from closer observation of the Princeton
circle. Not only did many of the Constitution writers come from
the College of New Jersey, their teachers also gave intellectual
shape to the age.

In the end, the story of Princeton under Witherspoon, Smith,
and Green is most important for historians as a chapter in American thought.[18] The ideology they fashioned was a compound of
four basic convictions: that the old religion and the new science
could be harmonized, that such a harmony could be taught in educational institutions, that it could ground personal virtue and social order, and that careful observers, through scientific procedures, could accurately diagnose the state of society. During the
era of Stanhope Smith the Princetonians both constructed this picture of the world and acted upon it. It set the terms for their en-
gagement with the wider society, and it provided standards for
judging events at Princeton itself. In the eyes of those who accepted this ideology, Witherspoon was a success. Stanhope Smith,
after a promising start, eventually failed because he gave the new

[16] Madison, "Lessons of History: Of Ancient and Modern Confederacies," in
Marvin Meyers, ed., *The Mind of the Founder: Sources of the Political Thought of James
Madison* (rev. ed., Hanover, N.H., 1981), 47–56.

[17] For "the science of politics," see Madison's *Federalist* No. 47, reprinted in ibid.,
127.

[18] For a solid argument concerning the influence exerted by the principles of
Witherspoon and Smith in the middle and southern states between the Revolution
and the Civil War, see Fred J. Hood, *Reformed America: The Middle and Southern
States, 1783–1837* (University, Ala., 1980), with concentrated attention to Witherspoon and Smith, pp. 7–47.

science too much scope. Ashbel Green, who was sound enough in his opinions, lacked the necessary skill as an educator to fulfill the ideal. Whatever later historians may conclude about these judgments, they still should recognize the inner logic by which they were made.

IN CONCLUSION, it is possible to highlight the ironies of the Princeton search for a republican Christian Enlightenment.[19] Princetonians looked to the merger of colonial Calvinism and the republicanism of the Revolution as the hope for a new nation, only to turn toward voluntaristic revivalism when the nation was lost to more democratic interpreters of the Revolution. They enlisted the procedures of the Enlightenment as apologetic means to sustain the Christian faith and thereby opened the door to the spread of naturalistic thought in America.[20] With great optimism they affirmed their ability to discern the ends and means of social well-being and to engineer events for the perpetuation of public virtue. Yet principles accepted eagerly as if to herald the millennium soon showed them the decay of their own institutions and the prospect of apocalypse. Merely to chronicle these ironies, however, is demeaning to a circle of such great industry and accomplishment.

Far better to explore their history for understanding than for irony. Such exploration does reveal that we now see some aspects of the Princetonians' lives more clearly than they themselves did— for example, the way in which passage through the stages of life affects the perception of history,[21] or the way economic potential shapes political discourse,[22] or the way social disruption arises from material as well as ideological causes.[23] Yet the same exploration also shows how difficult it is to grasp more than a shadow of the reality that the Princeton circle experienced. Even in outline

[19] I have explored this possibility in "The Irony of the Enlightenment for Presbyterians in the Early Republic," *Journal of the Early Republic* 5 (1985): 149–78.

[20] For a fine study of this general development, see James Turner, *Without God, without Creed: The Origins of Unbelief in America* (Baltimore, 1985), 35–167.

[21] For possible connections, see Peter Charles Hoffer, *Revolution and Regeneration: Life Cycle and the Historical Vision of the Generation of 1776* (Athens, Ga., 1983); and Steven J. Novak, *The Rights of Youth: American Colleges and Student Revolt, 1798–1815* (Cambridge, Mass., 1977), 167–69.

[22] See Joyce Appleby, *Capitalism and a New Social Order: The Republican Vision of the 1790s* (New York, 1984).

[23] The ability to see more, and at the same time less, of past realities than the historical participants themselves is the theme of Bernard Bailyn, "The Challenge of Modern Historiography," *American Historical Review* 87 (1982): especially 9–11.

that reality is sobering. For nearly fifty years at the College of New Jersey, a dedicated band searched diligently for a republican Christian Enlightenment, a construct rich in intellectual possibility and potent in practical outworking. It was a heroic quest. If it failed—and failed most obviously under Samuel Stanhope Smith, who pursued it most successfully—we are left with a chilling word for those today who pursue, with ignorance about the springs of action hardly less profound, visions of reality manifestly more self-serving and sectarian.

Appendix A
Number of Graduates, 1748–1830

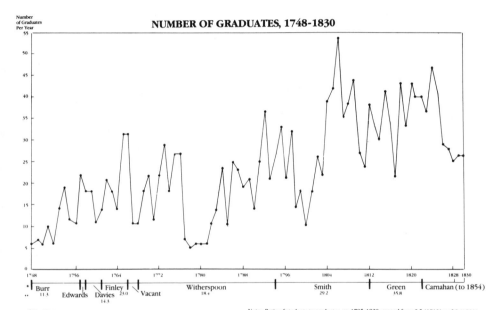

NUMBER OF GRADUATES, 1748-1830

Number of Graduates Per Year

* Presidents
** Average number of graduates per year during president's term

Note: Ratio of students to graduates, ca. 1795-1820, ranged from 2.5 (1813) to 6.8 (1803). Attendance after 1807 into the 1830s ranged from ca. 80 to ca. 165.

Source: **General Catalogue of Princeton University, 1746-1906** (Princeton, 1908).

Appendix B
Trustee Genealogies

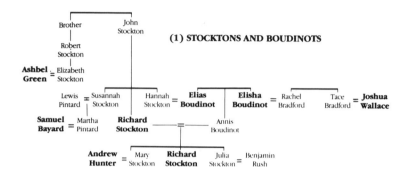

(1) STOCKTONS AND BOUDINOTS

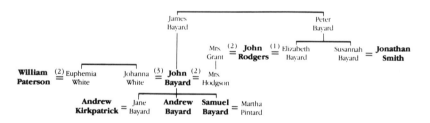

(2) BAYARDS

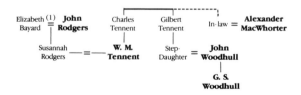

(3) MINISTERS

Note: Trustees of the College of New Jersey appear in boldface type.

Appendix C

Number, Attendance, Participation: Board Meetings, 1779–1812

The figures in this table support the conclusion that the board of trustees exercised increasingly tight control over the College of New Jersey during the first years of the nineteenth century (rows 3 and 6). They also show that ministers became more active on the board over the same years (rows 10 and 12). The periods represent Samuel Stanhope Smith's years at Princeton while Witherspoon was still president (1779–1794), the years between Smith's inauguration and the fire of 1802 (1795–1801), the years between the fire and the Great Rebellion (1802–1806), and the years from the riot to the resignation of President Smith (1807–1812). "Active" trustees are those who were given more than one assignment, who performed more than one task at any one meeting, or who performed a single act of obviously great significance on behalf of the board. Source: Trustee Minutes.

	1779-1794	1795-1801	1802-1806	1807-1812
(1) Years	16	7	5	6
(2) Number of meetings	28	15	12	19
(3) Meetings/year	1.8	2.1	2.4	3.2
(4) Total attendance	368	186	170	267
(5) Attendance/meeting	13.1	12.4	14.2	14.1
(6) Number of special meetings	6	3	3	8
(7) Special meetings/year	0.4	0.4	0.6	1.3
(8) Total active trustees	59	53	68	134
(9) Active trustees/meeting	2.1	3.5	5.7	7.1
(10) Total active ministers	15	11	30	68
(11) Total active laymen	44	42	38	66
(12) Percent ministers of active trustees	25%	21%	44%	51%

Bibliography, with a Prosopography of the
Princeton Circle

MANUSCRIPTS

The fullest nonpublished sources for the Princeton circle in the years of Witherspoon, Smith, and Green are found in the Manuscript Divison of the Firestone Library at Princeton University, the University Archives in Princeton's Seeley G. Mudd Manuscript Library, and the Pennsylvania Historical Society in Philadelphia. The Manuscript Division of Firestone contains extensive holdings in the papers of Stanhope Smith, Elias Boudinot, Ashbel Green, Samuel Miller, and other individuals who figure large in the accounts of this book. The Princeton University Archives houses the Trustee and Faculty Minutes and also contains extensive holdings of student correspondence (especially the James Iredell File and the James Mercer Garnett Letters). In addition, the archives has a rich collection of miscellaneous records on the history of college events. At the Pennsylvania Historical Society the superb collection of letters by ministers, first gathered by Simon Gratz, has been nicely augmented by several other collections with letters from many members of the Princeton circle.

Other depositories with useful records include the Manuscript Room of the Library of Congress (with materials for Elias Boudinot, William Paterson, the Breckinridge family, and student life in the 1780s), the New York Public Library (Elias Boudinot), the Presbyterian Historical Society in Philadelphia (Stanhope Smith), and Princeton Theological Seminary (Samuel Miller, Archibald Alexander). Archivists at the William R. Perkins Library of Duke University, the Southern Historical Collection at the University of North Carolina in Chapel Hill, and the Sheldon Art Museum in Middlebury, Vermont, kindly sent me photocopies of letters by Princeton students of the period.

THE PRINCETON CIRCLE

This section lists relevant published works by and about the trustees and professors of the College of New Jersey for the years 1779 through 1812, printed sources on students of the period, and more general works on Princeton (the college, the seminary, and the community). Ministers are

Presbyterians, and all locations are in New Jersey unless otherwise indicated.

Besides relying on the shortened forms listed above in Abbreviations and Short Titles, I abbreviate as follows the sources of biographical information for the members of the Princeton Circle:

Fischer = David Hackett Fischer, "Appendix II: Federalist Leaders," in *The Revolution of American Conservatism* (New York, 1965)

Princeton (with year of graduation) = entry in *Princetonians 1748–1768*, *Princetonians 1769–1775*, or *Princetonians 1776–1783*

Sprague = Sprague, *Annals*

Yale (with year of graduation) = entry in Franklin Bowditch Dexter, *Biographical Sketches of the Graduates of Yale College*, 6 vols. (New York, 1885–1912)

Faculty and Trustees

ALEXANDER, ARCHIBALD (1772–1851; minister, Virginia, and teacher, Princeton; professor at seminary 1812–1851; *DAB* 1:162; Sprague 3:612)

————. *A Sermon Delivered at the Opening of the General Assembly of the Presbyterian Church in the United States, May 1808*. Philadelphia, 1808.

————. *The Sermon, Delivered at the Inauguration of the Rev. Archibald Alexander . . . in the Theological Seminary of the Presbyterian Church . . . To Which are Added, the Professor's Inaugural Address, and the charge to the Professor and Students*. New York, 1812.

Alexander, James W. *The Life of Archibald Alexander*. New York, 1854.

De Witt, John. "Archibald Alexander's Preparation for His Professorship." *Princeton Theological Review* 3 (1905): 573–94.

Loetscher, Lefferts A. *Facing the Enlightenment and Pietism: Archibald Alexander and the Founding of Princeton Theological Seminary*. Westport, Conn., 1983.

Mackay, John A. "Archibald Alexander (1772–1851): Founding Father." In *Sons of the Prophets: Leaders in Protestantism from Princeton Seminary*, ed. Hugh T. Kerr. Princeton, 1963.

ARMSTRONG, JAMES FRANCIS (1750–1816; minister, Trenton; trustee 1790–1816; Princeton 1773; Sprague 3:389)

ARTSDALEN, JACOB VAN (1745–1803; minister, Kingston and Springfield; trustee 1793–1802; Princeton 1765)

BAYARD, ANDREW (1762–1832; banker, Philadelphia; trustee 1708–1832; Fischer 345; Princeton 1779)

BAYARD, JOHN (1738–1807; merchant and legislator, Philadelphia and New Brunswick; trustee 1778–1807; *DAB* 2:67)

"John Bayard." *The General Assembly's Missionary Magazine*, n.s., 1 (July 1807): 1–7.
Wilson, James Grant. "Colonel John Bayard (1738–1807) and the Bayard Family of America." *New York Genealogical and Biographical Record* 16 (1885): 49–72.

BAYARD, SAMUEL (1767–1840; lawyer, Princeton; trustee 1807–1810; *DAB* 2:69; Fischer 328; Princeton 1784)
———. *Funeral Oration, Occasioned by the death of Gen. George Washington.* New Brunswick, 1800.
———. *An Abstract of those Laws of the United States which relate chiefly to the Duties and Authority of the Judges of the inferior state courts.* New York, 1804.
———. *A Digest of American Cases on the Law of Evidence.* Philadelphia, 1810.
Sterbrig, David L. "A Federalist Opposes the Jay Treaty: The Letters of Samuel Bayard." *WMQ* 18 (1961): 408–24.

BEATTY, JOHN (1749–1826; physician and legislator, Princeton; trustee 1785–1802; *DAB* 2:100; Fischer 321; Princeton 1769)

BLOOMFIELD, JOSEPH (1753–1823; lawyer, soldier, legislator, and governor, Burlington; trustee 1793–1812, 1819–1823; *DAB* 2:385)

BOUDINOT, ELIAS (1740–1821; lawyer and legislator, Elizabethtown, Philadelphia, and Burlington; trustee 1772–1821; *DAB* 2:479; Fischer 321)

———. *The Age of Revelation; or, The Age of Reason shewn to be an Age of Infidelity.* Philadelphia, 1801.
———. *Address of the New Jersey Bible Society to the Publick.* New Brunswick, 1810.
———. *Memoirs of the Life of the Rev. William Tennent.* Trenton, 1810.
Boudinot, J. J., ed. *The Life, Public Services, Addresses, and Letters of Elias Boudinot.* 2 vols. 1896. Reprint, New York, 1971.
Boyd, George Adams. *Elias Boudinot: Patriot and Stateman, 1740–1821.* Princeton, 1952.

BOUDINOT, ELISHA (1749–1819; lawyer, Newark; trustee 1802–1819; Fischer 322)

BOYD, JAMES (1743–1814; minister, Bucks County, Pa.; trustee 1781–1800; Princeton 1763)

BOYD, WILLIAM (1758–1807; minister, Lamington; trustee 1800–1807; Princeton 1778; Sprague 3:444)

BRAINERD, JOHN (1720–1781; minister and missionary, N.J.; trustee 1754–1781; *DAB* 2:593; Sprague 3:149; Yale 1746)

CALDWELL, JAMES (1734–1781; minister, Elizabethtown; trustee 1769–1782; *DAB* 3:408; Princeton 1759; Sprague 3:222)

CHAPMAN, JEDIDIAH (1741–1813; minister, Orange; trustee 1795–1800; Yale 1762)

CLARK, JOSEPH (1751–1813; minister, New Brunswick; trustee 1802–1813; Princeton 1781; Sprague 3:446)

———. *A Sermon on the Death of the Hon. William Paterson.* New Brunswick, 1806.
———. *A Sermon, Delivered in the City of New-Brunswick, on . . . the Day set apart by the General Assembly . . . for Fasting, Humiliation, and Prayer.* New Brunswick, 1812.
Craven, W. Frank. "Joseph Clark and the Rebuilding of Nassau Hall." *PULC* 41 (1979): 54–68.

CONDICT, IRA (1764–1811; Reformed and Presbyterian minister, New Brunswick; trustee 1804–1809; Princeton 1784; Sprague 9:79)

———. *A Funeral Discourse . . . for paying solemn honor to the memory of Gen. George Washington.* New Brunswick, 1800.

DUFFIELD, GEORGE (1732–1790; minister, Philadelphia; trustee 1777–1790; *DAB* 5:489; Princeton 1752; Sprague 3:186)

ELMER, JONATHAN (1727–1807; minister, New Providence; trustee 1782–1795; Yale 1747)

FINLEY, ROBERT (1772–1817; minister, Basking Ridge; trustee 1807–1817; *DAB* 6:391; Princeton 1787; Sprague 4:126)

———. *A Sermon on the Baptism of John.* Elizabethtown, 1807.
———. *A Discourse on the Nature and Design, the Benefits and Proper Subjects of Baptism.* Philadelphia, 1808.
Brown, Isaac V. *Biography of the Rev. Robert Finley.* 1819. Reprint, New York, 1969.

FRELINGHUYSEN, FREDERICK (1753–1804; lawyer and legislator, Somerset County; trustee 1802–1804; *DAB* 7:15; Princeton 1770)

GREEN, ASHBEL (1762–1848; minister and educator, Philadelphia and Princeton; professor of mathematics and science 1785–1787, trustee 1790–1812, president 1812–1822; *DAB* 7:536; Princeton 1783; Sprague 3:479)

———. *An Oration, Delivered July 4, 1789 . . . To which is added, A Prayer . . . by the Rev. Ashbel Green.* Philadelphia, 1789.
———. *A Sermon Delivered . . . the 19th of February, 1795, Being the Day of General Thanksgiving Throughout the United States.* Philadelphia, 1795.
———. *Obedience to the Laws of God, the sure and indispensable Defence of Nations.* Philadelphia, 1798.
———. *A Pastoral Letter from a Minister in the Country, to Those of His Flock who remained in the City of Philadelphia during the Pestilence of 1798.* Philadelphia, 1799

————. *An Address to the Students and Faculty of the College of New-Jersey, Delivered May 6th 1802—the day on which the students commenced their Studies, after the burning of the College Edifice.* Trenton, 1802.

————. *Glad Tidings; or, An Account of the State of Religion, within the bounds of the General Assembly of the Presbyterian Church . . . and in other parts of the world.* Philadelphia, 1804.

————. *The Life and Death of the Righteous . . . the Funeral of the Rev. Dr. William M. Tennent.* Philadelphia, 1811.

————. *A Report to the Trustees of the College of New Jersey; Relative to a Revival of Religion Among the Students of said College, in the winter and spring of the year 1815.* Philadelphia, 1815.

————. *Discourses, Delivered in the College of New Jersey.* Philadelphia, 1822.

————. "Letter 18." In *Lectures on Revivals of Religion,* ed. William Sprague. 1832. Reprint, London, 1959.

————. *The Life of Ashbel Green, V.D.M., Begun to be written by himself in his eighty-second year and continued to his eighty-fourth. Prepared for the press at the author's request by Joseph H. Jones.* New York, 1849.

Lewis, Robert E. "Ashbel Green, a Venerable Presbyterian (1762–1848)." Typescript prepared for Ph.D. diss., University of Pittsburgh, ca. 1949 (copy at Presbyterian Historical Society, Philadelphia).

————. "Ashbel Green, 1762–1848: Preacher, Educator, Editor." *Journal of the Presbyterian Historical Society* 35 (1957): 141–56.

McLachlan, James. "Ashbel Green." *Princetonians 1776–1783,* 404–20.

Wilgers, Larry Martin. "Ashbel Green: Advocate of Practical Christianity." Ph.D. diss., Vanderbilt University, 1973.

HALSEY, JEREMIAH (1733–1780; minister, Lamington; trustee 1770–1780; Princeton 1752)

HARRIS, ROBERT (1735/8–1815; physician and merchant, Philadelphia and Cape May; trustee 1761–1815; Princeton 1753)

HILLYER, ASA (1763–1840; minister, Orange; trustee 1811–1840; Sprague 3:533; Yale 1786)

HOUSTON, WILLIAM CHURCHILL (1746–1788; lawyer, teacher, and legislator, Princeton and Trenton; professor of mathematics and science 1771–1783; *DAB* 9:267; Princeton 1768)

HOWELL, RICHARD (1754–1802; lawyer and governor, Trenton; trustee 1792–1801; *DAB* 9:304)

HUNTER, ANDREW (1751/2–1823; minister and teacher, N.J. and Washington, D.C.; trustee 1788–1804, 1808–1811, professor 1804–1808; Princeton 1772)

JOHNS, TIMOTHY (1717–1794; minister, Morristown; trustee 1748–1788; Yale 1737)

KIRKPATRICK, ANDREW (1756–1831; lawyer and judge, New Brunswick; trustee 1807–1831; *DAB* 10:435; Fischer 324; Princeton 1775)

KOLLOCK, HENRY (1778–1819; minister, N.J. and Savannah, Ga.; professor of theology 1803–1806; Sprague 4:263)

LIVINGSTON, WILLIAM (1723–1790; legislator and governor, Elizabethtown; trustee 1768–1790; *DAB* 11:325; Yale 1741)

MACLEAN, JOHN (1771–1814; teacher, Princeton; professor of chemistry, mathematics, and science 1795–1812; *DAB* 12:126)

———. *Two Lectures on Combustion . . . Containing an Examination of Dr. Priestley's Considerations on the Doctrine of Phlogiston, and the Decomposition of Water.* Philadelphia, 1797.
Bullough, Vern L. "John Maclean." In *Dictionary of Scientific Biography*, 8:612–13. New York, 1973.

MACWHORTER, ALEXANDER (1734–1807; minister, Newark; trustee 1772–1780, 1781–1807; *DAB* 12:175; Princeton 1757; Sprague 3:208)

———. *A Festival Discourse, Occasioned by the Celebration of the Seventeenth Anniversary of American Independence.* Newark, 1793.
———. *The Blessedness of the Liberal: A Sermon Preached . . . before the New York Missionary Society.* New York, 1796.
———. *A Funeral Sermon . . . for the universally lamented, General Washington.* Newark, 1800.
———. *A Series of Sermons, upon the most important principles of our Holy Religion.* 2 vols. Newark, 1803.
———. *A Century Sermon, Preached in Newark, New Jersey, January 1, 1801; containing a Brief History of the Presbyterian Church in that Town.* Newark, 1807.
"Alexander MacWhorter." *The General Assembly's Missionary Magazine*, n.s., 1 (Oct. 1807): 145–56.

MASON, JOHN (1734–1792; Associate Reformed minister, New York City; trustee 1779–1785; Sprague 9:4)

MILLER, ALEXANDER (1739–1820; minister, N.J. and N.Y.; trustee 1785–1790; Princeton 1764)

MILLER, SAMUEL (1769–1850; minister and teacher, New York City and Princeton; trustee 1807–1850, professor at seminary 1813–1850; *DAB* 12:636; Sprague 3:600)

———. *A Sermon Preached in New York, July 4th, 1793, Being the Anniversary of the Independence of America.* New York, 1793.
———. *A Discourse Delivered . . . Before the Grand Lodge of the State of New York.* New York, 1795.
———. *A Sermon Delivered . . . Before, the Mechanic, Tammany, and Democratic Societies, and the Military Officers.* New York, 1795.

———. *A Discourse, Delivered . . . before the New-York Society for Promoting the Manumission of Slaves.* New York, 1797.

———. *A Sermon, Delivered May 9, 1798 . . . a day of general Humiliation, Fasting, and Prayer.* New York, 1798.

———. *A Sermon . . . a Day of Thanksgiving, Humiliation, and Prayer on account of the removal of a Malignant and Mortal Disease.* New York, 1799.

———. *A Sermon . . . Occasioned by the death of General George Washington.* New York, 1800.

———. *A Sermon, Delivered before the New-York Missionary Society.* New York, 1802.

———. *A Brief Retrospect of the Eighteenth Century, Part First.* 2 vols. New York, 1803.

———. *The Guilt, Folly, and Sources of Suicide.* New York, 1805.

———. *Letters Concerning the Constitution and Order of the Christian Ministry.* New York, 1807.

———. *A Sermon . . . for the Benefit of the Society . . . for the Relief of Poor Widows with Small Children.* New York, 1808.

———. *A Continuation of Letters concerning the constitution and order of the Christian ministry.* New York, 1809.

———. *The Divine Appointment, the Duties, and the Qualifications of Ruling Elders.* New York, 1811.

Chinard, Gilbert. "A Landmark in American Intellectual History: Samuel Miller's *Brief Retrospect of the Eighteenth Century.*" *PULC* 14 (1953): 55–71.

Lane, Belden C. "Democracy and the Ruling Eldership: Samuel Miller's Response to Tensions between Clerical Power and Lay Activity in Early Nineteenth Century America." Ph.D. diss., Princeton Theological Seminary, 1976.

Miller, Samuel [Jr.]. *The Life of Samuel Miller.* 2 vols. Philadelphia, 1869.

Stephens, Bruce M. "Samuel Miller (1769–1850): Apologist for Orthodoxy." *Princeton Seminary Bulletin* 67 (1975): 33–47.

MINTO, WALTER (1753–1796; teacher, Princeton; professor of mathematics and science 1787–1796; *DAB* 13:32)

———. *An Inaugural Oration; or, The Progress and Importance of the Mathematical Sciences.* Trenton, 1788.

Eisenhart, Luther P. "Walter Minto and the Earl of Buchan." *Proceedings of the American Philosophical Society* 94 (1950): 282–94.

OGDEN, AARON (1756–1839; lawyer, legislator, and governor, Elizabethtown; trustee 1803–1813, 1817–1839; *DAB* 13:636; Fischer 327; Princeton 1773)

OGDEN, ROBERT (d. 1786; politician, Elizabethtown; trustee 1764–1786)

PATERSON, WILLIAM (1745–1806; lawyer, legislator, and governor, Raritan; trustee 1787–1803; *DAB* 14:293; Fischer 325; Princeton 1763)

———. *The Charge of Judge Paterson to the Jury, in the Case of Vanhorne's Lessee against Dorrance*. Philadelphia, 1796.

Boyd, Julian P. "William Paterson (1745–1806): Forerunner of John Marshall." In Thorp, *Lives*.

Kraus, Michael. "William Paterson." In *The Justices of the United States Supreme Court, 1789–1969: Their Lives and Major Opinions*, vol. 1, ed. Leon Friedman and Fred L. Israel. New York, 1969.

O'Connor, John E. *William Paterson: Lawyer and Statesman, 1745–1806*. New Brunswick, 1979.

READ, ISRAEL (1718–1793; minister, Boundbrook; trustee 1761–1793; Princeton 1748)

REED, JOSEPH (1741–1785; lawyer and legislator, Philadelphia; trustee 1781–1785; *DAB* 15:451; Princeton 1757)

RICHARDS, JAMES (1767–1843; minister, Morristown and Newark; trustee 1807–1824; Sprague 4:99)

RODGERS, JOHN (1727–1811; minister, New York City; trustee 1765–1807; *DAB* 16:74; Sprague 3:154)

———. *Holiness the Nature and Design of the Gospel of Christ. A Sermon*. Hartford, 1780.

———. *The Divine Goodness displayed, in the American Revolution*. New York, 1784.

Anderson, Charles A. "Letters of John Rodgers, Preacher and Patriot." *Journal of the Presbyterian Historical Society* 27 (1949): 195–205.

Handy, Robert T. "John Rodgers, 1727–1811: 'A Life of Usefulness on Earth.'" *Journal of the Presbyterian Historical Society* 34 (1956): 69–82.

Miller, Samuel. *Memoirs of the Rev. John Rodgers*. New York, 1813.

ROE, AZEL (1738–1815; minister, Woodbridge; trustee 1778–1807; Princeton 1756; Sprague 3:232)

ROMEYN, JOHN BROADHEAD (1777–1825; Reformed and Presbyterian minister, New York City; trustee 1809–1825; Sprague 4:216)

———. *A Funeral Oration, in Remembrance of George Washington*. Poughkeepsie, N.Y., 1800.

———. *A Sermon Delivered by Appointment of the Committee of Missions of the General Assembly*. Philadelphia, 1808.

———. *Two Sermons . . . being the day recommended by the General Assembly . . . for Fasting, Humiliation, and Prayer*. Albany, 1808.

———. *The Danger and Duty of Young People*. New York, 1810.

Bibliography

————. *The Good Samaritan . . . A Sermon . . . for the Benefit of the New York Dispensary.* New York, 1810.

RUTGERS, HENRY (1745–1830; squire, New York City; trustee 1804–1817; *DAB* 16:255)

SCUDDER, NATHANIEL (1733–1781; physician, soldier, and legislator, Freehold; trustee 1778–1781; *DAB* 16:524; Princeton 1751)

SHIPPEN, WILLIAM (1736–1808; physician, Philadelphia; trustee 1765–1797; *DAB* 17:117; Princeton 1754)

SMITH, JONATHAN BAYARD (1742–1812; merchant and legislator, Philadelphia; trustee 1779–1807; *DAB* 17:308; Princeton 1760)

SMITH, ROBERT (1723–1793; minister, Pequea, Pa.; trustee 1772–1793; Sprague 3:172)

————. *The Detection Detected; or, A Vindiction of the Revd. Mr. Delap, and New Castle Presbytery.* Lancaster, Pa., 1757.

————. *A Wheel in the Middle of a Wheel; or, Harmony and Connexion of Various Acts of Divine Providence.* Philadelphia, 1759.

————. *The Obligation of the Confederate States of North America to Praise God.* Philadelphia, 1782.

————. *Three Sermons, on the Nature and Excellency of Saving Faith.* Lancaster, Pa., 1791.

————. "The Principle of Sin and Holiness." In *Sermons and Essays by the Tennents and Their Contemporaries,* ed. Samuel D. Alexander. Philadelphia, 1855.

Beam, Jacob Newton. "Dr. Robert Smith's Academy at Pequea, Pennsylvania." *Journal of the Presbyterian Historical Society* 8 (1915): 145–61.

"Robert Smith." *The General Assembly's Missionary Magazine,* n.s., 2 (Jan. 1806): 1–6.

SMITH, SAMUEL STANHOPE (1751–1819; teacher, Virginia and Princeton; professor of moral philosophy and theology 1779–1812, president 1795–1812; *DAB* 17:344; Princeton 1769; Sprague 3:335)

————. *A Funeral Sermon, on the Death of the Hon. Richard Stockton.* Princeton, 1781.

————. *An Essay on the Causes of the Variety of Complexion and Figure in the Human Species. To which are added Strictures on Lord Kaim's Discourse, on the Original Diversity of Mankind.* Philadelphia, 1787.

————. *Three Discourses.* Boston, 1791.

————. *A Discourse on the Nature and Reasonableness of Fasting, and on the existing causes that call us to that Duty.* Philadelphia, 1795.

————. *The Divine Goodness to the United States of America. A Discourse on the Subject of National Gratitude.* Philadelphia, 1795.

————. *A Discourse Delivered . . . at the Funeral of the Rev. Gilbert Tennent Snowden.* Philadelphia, 1797.

————. *Sermons*. Newark, 1799.

————. *An Oration upon the Death of George Washington, Delivered in the State-House at Trenton*. Trenton, 1800.

————. "An Account of the good Effects of copious Blood-letting in the Cure of an Hemorrhage from the Lungs." *Medical Museum* 2 (1806): 1–6.

————. *A Discourse on the Nature, the Proper Subjects, and the Benefits of Baptism*. Philadelphia, 1808.

————. "Letter on Baptism." *Evangelical Intelligencer* 2 (Mar. 1808): 103–8.

————. *Lectures on the Evidences of the Christian Religion, Delivered to the Senior Class, On Sundays, in the Afternoon, in the College of New Jersey*. Philadelphia, 1809.

————. *The Resurrection of the Body; A Discourse*. Washington, 1809.

————. *An Essay on the Causes of the Variety of Complexion and Figure in the Human Species. To Which are added, Animadversions on certain Remarks made on the first edition of this Essay, by Mr. Charles White, in a series of Discourses delivered before the Literary and Philosophical Society of Manchester in England. Also, Strictures on Lord Kaims' Discourse on the Original Diversity of Mankind. And an Appendix*. 2d ed., enl. New Brunswick and New York, 1810.

————. *The Lectures, Corrected and Improved, which have been delivered for a series of years, in the College of New-Jersey; on the Subjects of Moral and Political Philosophy*. 2 vols. Trenton, 1812.

————. *The New-Jersey Preacher; or, Sermons on Plain and Practical Subjects*, ed. George S. Woodhull and Isaac V. Brown. Trenton and New Brunswick, 1813.

————. *A Comprehensive View of the Leading and Most Important Principles of Natural and Revealed Religion: digested in such order as to present to the pious and reflecting mind, a basis for the superstructure of the entire system of the doctrines of the gospel*. New Brunswick, 1815.

————. *Oratio Inauguralis, a Samuele Stanhope Smith*. Trenton, 1817.

————. *History of the United States . . . By David Ramsay, M.D., Continued to the Treaty of Ghent, By S. S. Smith, D.D. and LL.D., and Other Literary Gentlemen*. 3 vols. 2d ed. Philadelphia, 1818.

————. *Sermons of Samuel Stanhope Smith, D.D., Late President of Princeton College, New Jersey. To which is prefixed, A Brief Memoir of his Life and Writings*. 2 vols. Philadelphia, 1821.

Aldridge, A. Owen. "Massillon and S. S. Smith: French-Inspired Sermons in Early American Literature." *French-American Review* 6 (1982): 147–59.

————. "An Early American Adaptation of French Pulpit Oratory." *The Eighteenth Century: Theory and Interpretation* 28 (1987): 235–47.

[Beasley, Frederick.] "An Account of the Life and Writings of the Rev. Samuel Stanhope Smith, D.D., LL.D., Late President of

Princeton College." *Analectic Magazine*, n.s., 1 (June 1820): 443–74; 2 (July 1820): 3–18. (This "Life" is also prefaced to Smith's *Sermons* of 1821.)

Bowers, David F. "The Smith-Blair Correspondence, 1786–1791." *PULC* 4 (1943): 123–34.

Bradbury, Miles LeRoy. "Adventure in Persuasion: John Witherspoon, Samuel Stanhope Smith, and Ashbel Green." Ph.D. diss., Harvard University, 1967.

———. "Samuel Stanhope Smith: Princeton's Accommodation to Reason." *Journal of Presbyterian History* 48 (1970): 189–202.

———. "British Apologetics in Evangelical Garb: Samuel Stanhope Smith's *Lectures on the Evidences of the Christian Religion*." *Journal of the Early Republic* 5 (1985): 177–95.

"Changing Presidents in 1812." *Princeton Alumni Weekly*, April 6, 1928, pp. 751–52.

Craven, Wesley Frank. "Samuel Stanhope Smith." In *Princetonians 1769–1775*, 42–51.

Crowson, E. T. "Samuel Stanhope Smith: A Founder of Hampden-Sydney College." *Virginia Cavalcade* 24 (Autumn 1974): 53–60.

Hudnut, William H., III. "Samuel Stanhope Smith: Enlightened Conservative." *Journal of the History of Ideas* 17 (1956): 540–52.

Jordan, Winthrop D. "Introduction" to Smith's *Essay on the Causes of the Variety of Complexion and Figure in the Human Species* (1787). Cambridge, Mass., 1965.

Kraus, Michael. "Charles Nisbet and Samuel Stanhope Smith—Two Eighteenth Century Educators." *PULC* 6 (1944): 17–36.

Monk, Samuel Holt. "Samuel Stanhope Smith (1751–1819): Friend of Rational Liberty." In Thorp, *Lives*.

Shipton, Clifford K. "Samuel Stanhope Smith." In *Biographical Sketches of Those Who Attended Harvard College in the Classes 1768–1771*. Boston, 1975.

Sloan, Douglas. "Education, Progress, and Polygamy: Samuel Stanhope Smith." In *The Scottish Enlightenment and the American College Ideal*. New York, 1971.

SMITH, WILLIAM PEARTREE (1723–1801; lawyer and legislator, Elizabethtown and Newark; trustee 1748–1793; Yale 1742)

SNOWDEN, ISAAC (?–?; Phildelphia and Princeton; trustee 1782–1808)

SPENCER, ELIHU (1721–1784; minister, Trenton; trustee 1752–1785; *DAB* 17:447; Sprague 3:165; Yale 1746)

STOCKTON, RICHARD [SR.] (1730–1781; lawyer and legislator, Princeton; trustee 1757–1781; *DAB* 18:45; Princeton 1748)

STOCKTON, RICHARD [JR.] (1764–1828; lawyer and legislator, Princeton; trustee 1791–1828; *DAB* 18:47; Fischer 328; Princeton 1779)

TENNENT, WILLIAM MACKAY (1744–1810; minister, Abington, Pa.; trustee 1785–1808; Princeton 1763)

VANCLEVE, JOHN (1776–1826; physician, Hunterdon County; trustee 1810–1826; Fischer 331; Princeton 1797)

WALLACE, JOSHUA MADDOX (1752–1819; lawyer, Burlington; trustee 1798–1819; Fischer 327)

———. *Constitution of the New Jersey Society for the Suppression of Vice and Immorality, and for the Encouragement of Virtue and Good Morals.* New Brunswick, 1818.

WHARTON, CHARLES HENRY (1748–1823; Episcopal minister, Burlington; trustee 1800–1816; *DAB* 20:26; Sprague 5:335)

WITHERSPOON, JOHN (1723–1794; minister and teacher, Scotland and Princeton; president and professor of theology 1769–1794; *DAB* 20:345; Sprague 3:288)

———. "Remarks on an essay on human liberty." *The Scots Magazine* 15 (Apr. 1753): 165–70.
———. *An Annotated Edition of Lectures on Moral Philosophy by John Witherspoon*, ed. Jack Scott. 1802. Reprint, Newark, Del., 1982.
———. *Lectures on Moral Philosophy*, ed. Varnum Lansing Collins. 1802. Reprint, Princeton, 1912.
———. *The Works of the Rev. John Witherspoon, D.D., LL.D., Late President of the College at Princeton, New Jersey.* 4 vols. Edited by Ashbel Green. 2d ed. Philadelphia, 1802.
Atwater, Lyman. "Witherspoon's Theology." *Biblical Repertory and Princeton Review* 35 (1863): 596–610.
Barnes, Timothy M., and Robert M. Calhoon. "Moral Allegiance: John Witherspoon and Loyalist Recantation." *American Presbyterians* 63 (1985): 273–83.
Butterfield, L. H. *John Witherspoon Comes to America: A Documentary Account Based Largely on New Materials.* Princeton, 1953.
Collins, Varnum Lansing. *President Witherspoon: A Biography.* 2 vols. Princeton, 1925.
Drummond, A. L. "Witherspoon of Gifford and American Presbyterianism." *Records of the Scottish Historical Society* 12 (1958): 185–201.
Fechner, Roger J. "The Godly and Virtuous Republic of John Witherspoon: Thought and Action in the American Revolution." In *Ideas in America's Cultures: From Republic to Mass Society*, ed. Hamilton Cravens. Ames, Iowa, 1982.
Green, Ashbel. "Dr. Witherspoon's Administration at Princeton College." *Presbyterian Magazine* 4 (1854): 466–72.
———. *The Life of the Revd. John Witherspoon, D.D., LL.D., with a brief review of his writings: and a summary estimate of his character and talents*, ed. Henry Lyttleton Savage. Princeton, 1973.

Gummere, Richard M. "A Scottish Classicist in Colonial America." *Publications of the Colonial Society of Massachusetts* 35 (1944): 146–61.

Landsman, Ned. "John Witherspoon and the Problem of Provincial Identity in Eighteenth-Century America." In *Scotland and America in the Age of Enlightenment,* ed. Richard B. Sher and Jeffrey Smitten. Edinburgh, forthcoming.

McAllister, James A. "John Witherspoon: Academic Advocate for American Freedom." In *A Miscellany of American Christianity: Essays in Honor of H. Shelton Smith,* ed. Stuart C. Henry. Durham, N.C., 1963.

Nichols, James Hastings. "John Witherspoon on Church and State." *Journal of Presbyterian History* 42 (1964): 66–74.

Rich, George Eugene. "John Witherspoon: His Scottish Intellectual Background." Ph.D. diss., Syracuse University, 1964.

Smylie, James H. "Madison and Witherspoon: Theological Roots of American Political Thought." *PULC* 22 (1961): 118–32.

———. "Presbyterian Clergy and Problems of 'Dominion' in the Revolutionary Generation. *Journal of Presbyterian History* 48 (1970): 161–75.

Tait, L. Gordon. "John Witherspoon as Sage: 'The Druid' Essays of 1776." *New Jersey History* 100 (1982): 30–46.

———. "John Witherspoon, American Intellectual Leader." *Journal of Religious Studies* (Ohio) 12 (1986): 1–13.

Wertenbaker, Thomas Jefferson. "John Witherspoon (1723–1794): Father of American Presbyterianism, Maker of Statesmen." In Thorps *Lives.*

WOODHULL, GEORGE SPAFFORD (1773–1834; minister, Cranberry; trustee, 1807–1834; Princeton 1790)

———. and Isaac V. Brown, eds. *The New Jersey Preacher; or, Sermons on Plain and Practical Subjects.* Trenton and New Brunswick, 1813.

WOODHULL, JOHN (1744–1824; minister, Freehold; trustee 1780–1824; Princeton 1766; Sprague 3:304)

———. *A Sermon, for the Day of Publick Thanksgiving.* Trenton, 1790.

Students

BIDDLE, NICHOLAS (graduated 1801)

Govan, Thomas P. "Nicholas Biddle at Princeton, 1799–1801." *PULC* 9 (1948): 49–63.

BIRNEY, JAMES GILLESPIE (1810)

Birney, William. *James G. Birney and His Times.* 1890. Reprint, New York, 1969.

Fladeland, Betty. *James Gillespie Birney: Slaveholder to Abolitionist.* Ithaca, N.Y., 1955.

BRECKINRIDGE, JOSEPH CABELL (1810)

Harrison, Lowell H. "A Young Kentuckian at Princeton, 1806–1810: Joseph Cabell Breckinridge." *Filson Club History Quarterly* 38 (1964): 285–315.

CALDWELL, JOSEPH (1791)

Wagstaff, Henry M., ed. *The Harris Letters.* The James Sprunt Historical Publications, vol. 14, no. 1. Durham, N.C., 1916.

HOBART, JOHN HENRY (1793)

Lowndes, Arthur, ed. *The Correspondence of John Henry Hobart, 1757–1797.* New York, 1911.

LINDSLEY, PHILIP (1804)

Pomfret, John Edwin. "Philip Lindsley (1786–1855): Pioneer Educator in the Old Southwest." In Thorp, *Lives.*

MADISON, JAMES (1771)

Brant, Irving. *James Madison.* Vol. 1, *The Virginia Revolutionist.* Indianapolis, 1941.
Ketcham, Ralph. "James Madison at Princeton." *PULC* 28 (1966): 24–54.

RUFFIN, THOMAS (1805)

Roulhac, J. G. de, ed. *The Papers of Thomas Ruffin,* vol. 1. Raleigh, N.C., 1918.

SMITH, JOHN RHEA (1787)

Woodward, Ruth L. "Journal at Nassau Hall: The Diary of John Rhea Smith, 1786." *PULC* 46 (1985): 269–91; 47 (1985): 48–70.

UPSHUR, ABEL PARKER (1807)

Hall, Claude H. *Abel Parker Upshur: Conservative Virginian, 1790–1844.* Madison, Wis., 1964.

WAYNE, JAMES M. (1808)

Lawrence, Alexander A. *James Moore Wayne: Southern Unionist.* Chapel Hill, N.C., 1943.

The College of New Jersey, Princeton Seminary, the Village of Princeton

Alexander, Samuel Davies. *Princeton College during the Eighteenth Century.* New York, 1872.
Beam, Jacob N. *The American Whig Society of Princeton University.* Princeton, 1933.

Bill, Alfred Hoyt. *The Campaign of Princeton, 1776–1777.* Princeton, 1948.

———. *A House Called Morven: Its Role in American History, 1701–1954.* Princeton, 1954.

[Blair, Samuel]. *An Account of the College of New-Jersey. In which are described the methods of government, modes of instruction, manner and expences of living in the same, etc.* Woodbridge, 1764.

Bost, George H. "Samuel Davies as President of Princeton." *Journal of Presbyterian History* 26 (1948): 165–81.

Broderick, Francis I. "Pulpit, Physics, and Politics: The Curriculum of the College of New Jersey, 1746–1794." *WMQ* 6 (1949): 42–68.

Burr, Nelson R. "Connecticut Yankees on the Princeton Campus, 1748–1905." *PULC* 45 (1984): 122–49.

Butterfield, L. H. "Morven: A Colonial Outpost of Sensibility, with Some Hitherto Unpublished Poems by Annis Boudinot Stockton." *PULC* 6 (1944): 1–15.

———. "Annis and the General: Mrs. Stockton's Poetic Eulogies of George Washington." *PULC* 7 (1945): 19–39.

Cohen, Sheldon S. and Larry R. Gerlach. "Princeton in the Coming of the American Revolution." *New Jersey History* 92 (1974): 69–92.

Coleman, Earle E. "*A Dialogue on Peace* (1763) and Princeton Commencements." *PULC* 46 (1984): 231–36.

College of New Jersey at Princeton. *A General Account of the Rise and State of the College, Lately Established In the Province of New-Jersey, In America: And of the End and Design of its Institution.* New York, 1752.

———. *Laws of the College of New Jersey.* Revised. Trenton, 1794.

———. [Broadside Circular]. N.p., 1796.

———. *The Memorial and Petition of the Trustees of the College of New Jersey.* N.p., 1796.

———. *Laws of the College of New Jersey.* Revised. Philadelphia, 1802.

———. *Catalogue Collegii Neo-Caesariensis.* Trenton, 1804.

———. *College of New Jersey.* N.p., 1804.

———. *The Students to the Public.* N.p., 1807.

———. *Trustees to the Public.* N.p., 1807.

———. *Laws of the College of New Jersey.* Revised. Trenton, 1813.

———. *Charter of the College of New Jersey, with Amendments, and the Laws of New Jersey Relative to the College.* Newark, 1868.

———. *Catalogue of All Who Have Held Office in or Have Received Degrees from the College of New Jersey at Princeton in the State of New Jersey.* Princeton, 1896.

———. *General Catalogue of Princeton University, 1746–1906.* Princeton, 1908.

Collins, Varnum Lansing. *The Continental Congress at Princeton.* Princeton, 1908.

———. *Princeton.* New York, 1914.

———. *Princeton Past and Present.* Revised. Princeton, 1945.

Come, Donald R. "The Influence of Princeton on Higher Education in the South before 1825." *WMQ* 2 (1945): 359–96.

Craven, Wesley Frank. "On the Writing of a Biographical Dictionary." *Proceedings of the American Philosophical Society* 12 (1978): 69–74.

Davies, Samuel. *Little Children Invited to Jesus Christ: A Sermon . . . With an Account of the late, remarkable Religious Impressions among the Students in the College of New-Jersey.* Boston, 1765.

Gaines, William H. "The Aftermath of Rebellion; or, Princeton in 1807." *PULC* 19 (1957): 41–51.

"Glimpses of Old College Life." *WMQ*, 1st ser., 8 (1900): 213–27.

" 'The Great Rebellion' at Princeton." *WMQ*, 1st ser., 16 (1907): 119–21.

Greene, Richard H. "Alumni of the College of New Jersey Who Have Held Official Position." *New England Historical and Genealogical Record* 43 (1889): 47–52.

Guder, Darrell Liskens. "The History of Belles Lettres at Princeton: An Investigation of the Expansion and Secularization of the Curriculum at the College of New Jersey, with Special Reference to the Curriculum of English Language and Letters." Ph.D. diss., University of Hamburg, 1964.

Hageman, John Frelinghuysen. *History of Princeton and Its Institutions.* 2 vols. Philadelphia, 1879.

Harrison, Richard A., ed. *Princetonians 1769–1775: A Biographical Dictionary.* Princeton, 1980.

———, ed. *Princetonians 1776–1783: A Biographical Dictionary.* Princeton, 1981.

Hoeveler, J. David, Jr. *James McCosh and the Scottish Intellectual Tradition: From Glasgow to Princeton.* Princeton, 1981.

Hogendorp, Gijsbert Karel van. *The College at Princeton, May 1784.* Edited by Howard C. Rice. Princeton, 1949.

Humphrey, David C. "The Struggle for Sectarian Control of Princeton, 1745–1760." *New Jersey History* 91 (1973): 77–90.

Kerr, Hugh T. "The Seminary and the College: The First Twenty-Five Years." *Princeton Seminary Bulletin* 6 (1985): 116–22.

Link, Arthur S., ed. *The First Presbyterian Church at Princeton: Two Centuries of History.* Princeton, 1967.

McLachlan, James. "The *Choice of Hercules*: American Student Societies in the Early Nineteenth Century." In *The University in Society*, vol. 2, ed. Lawrence Stone. Princeton, 1974.

———, ed. *Princetonians 1748–1768: A Biographical Dictionary.* Princeton, 1976.

Maclean, John. *History of the College of New Jersey, from Its Origins in 1746 to the Commencement of 1854.* 2 vols. Philadelphia, 1877.

Miller, Howard. "Evangelical Religion and Colonial Princeton." In *Schooling and Society*, ed. Lawrence Stone. Baltimore, 1976.

————. *The Revolutionary College: American Presbyterian Higher Education, 1707–1837.* New York, 1976.

Murrin, John M. "Princeton and the American Revolution." *PULC* 38 (1976): 1–10.

Noll, Mark A. "The Founding of Princeton Seminary." *Westminster Theological Journal* 42 (1979): 72–110.

————. "The Princeton Trustees of 1807: New Men and New Directions." *PULC* 41 (1980): 208–30.

————. "Before the Storm: Life at Princeton College, 1806–1807." *PULC* 42 (1981): 145–64.

————. "The Response of Elias Boudinot to the Student Rebellion of 1807: Visions of Honor, Order, and Morality." *PULC* 43 (1981): 1–22.

————. "The Irony of the Enlightenment for Presbyterians in the Early Republic." *Journal of the Early Republic* 5 (1985): 149–76.

Norris, Edwin Monk. *The Story of Princeton.* Boston, 1917.

Novak, Steven J. *The Rights of Youth: American Colleges and Student Revolt, 1798–1815.* Cambridge, Mass., 1977.

Olson, Alison B. "The Founding of Princeton University: Religion and Politics in Eighteenth-Century New Jersey." *New Jersey History* 87 (1969): 133–50.

Paden, Elaine Page. "The Theory and Practice of Disputation at Princeton, Columbia, and the University of Pennsylvania from 1750 to 1800." Ph.D. diss., University of Iowa, 1943.

Princeton College. *See* College of New Jersey at Princeton.

Princeton Theological Seminary. *Report of a Committee of the General Assembly of the Presbyterian Church, Exhibiting the Plan of a Theological Seminary. To be Submitted to the Next Assembly.* New York, 1810.

————. *The Plan of a Theological Seminary Adopted by the General Assembly of the Presbyterian Church . . . Together with the Measures Taken to Carry the Plan into Effect.* Philadelphia, 1811.

————. *Fourth Report of the Board of Directors of the Theological Seminary; to the General Assembly of the Presbyterian Church.* Philadelphia, 1816.

————. *The Centennial Celebration of the Theological Seminary of the Presbyterian Church in the United States of America at Princeton, New Jersey.* Princeton, 1912.

————. *Biographical Catalogue of Princeton Theological Seminary, 1815–1954.* Princeton, 1955.

Rice, Howard C., Jr. "Jonathan Edwards at Princeton: With a Survey of Edwards Materials in the Princeton University Library." *PULC* 15 (1953–1954): 67–89.

Savage, Henry Lyttleton, ed. *Nassau Hall, 1756–1956.* Princeton, 1956.

Schmidt, George P. *Princeton and Rutgers: The Two Colonial Colleges of New Jersey.* New York, 1964.

Scovel, Raleigh Don. "Orthodoxy in Princeton: A Social and Intellectual

History of Princeton Theological Seminary, 1812–1860." Ph.D. diss., University of California, Berkeley, 1970.

Sheridan, Eugene R., and John M. Murrin, eds. *Congress at Princeton: Being the Letters of Charles Thomson to Hannah Thomson, June–October 1783.* Princeton, 1985.

Simpson, Lowell. "The Little Republics: Undergraduate Literary Societies at Columbia, Dartmouth, Princeton, and Yale, 1753–1865." Ed.D. diss., Teachers College, Columbia University, 1976.

Wertenbaker, Thomas Jefferson. *Princeton, 1746–1896.* Princeton, 1946.

———. "The College of New Jersey and the Presbyterians." *Journal of the Presbyterian Historical Society* 36 (1958): 209–16.

ESSAY ON SECONDARY AUTHORITIES

The most immediately useful materials for the purposes of this study were the wealth of manuscripts and publications from members of the Princeton circle as well as the quantity of sturdy modern scholarship on Princeton itself. Hardly less important, however, were a number of twentieth-century works—on political history and ideology; on American religion generally and the Presbyterians specifically; on science, philosophy, and education—that provided a broader context for my interpretation of the republican Christian Enlightenment at Princeton. From a vast quantity of available material on this period and this theme, the works mentioned below were especially helpful; some also provide authoritative interpretations of relevant themes, persons, and problems of the period.

Key Books and General Works

Four books more than any others shaped my approach to the subject. D. H. Meyer, *The Instructed Conscience: The Shaping of the American National Ethic* (Philadelphia, 1972), awoke me from dogmatic slumbers on the subject of antebellum Protestant thought. George M. Marsden, *The Evangelical Mind and the New School Presbyterian Experience: A Case Study of Thought and Theology in Nineteenth-Century America* (New Haven, 1970), showed what could be done by treating the discourse of Presbyterian ministers as a serious object of study in the unfolding of American culture. Henry F. May, *The Enlightenment in America* (New York, 1976), provided a much-appreciated mapping of religion, science, and political thought for the second half of the eighteenth century. Norman Fiering, *Jonathan Edwards's Moral Thought and Its British Context* (Chapel Hill, N.C., 1981), offered a most instructive example of how to interpret the relationship between older and newer forms of ethical thought in the American context.

Other more general works that proved immensely useful were Elizabeth Flower and Murray G. Murphey, *A History of Philosophy in America*, vol. 1 (New York, 1977), which includes a fine section on philosophy at Princeton under John Witherspoon and Stanhope Smith; and John C. Greene, *American Science in the Age of Jefferson* (Ames, Iowa, 1984), a book that supplements the historical coverage of Brooke Hindle, *The Pursuit of Science in Revolutionary America* (Chapel Hill, N.C., 1956), and George H. Daniels, *American Science in the Age of Jackson* (New York, 1968), while going well beyond these still helpful volumes in describing connections among science, religion, social expectations, and political experience in the early republic. Perry Miller, *The Life of the Mind in America from the Revolution to the Civil War* (New York, 1965), and "From the Covenant to the Revival," in *Nature's Nation* (Cambridge, Mass., 1967), resonate with Miller's characteristic creativity on the intellectual reordering in the shift from colonial to national life.

The Early National Period, the Revolution, Republicanism

On the early national period itself, two older texts in The New American Nation Series still render good service, John C. Miller, *The Federalist Era, 1789–1801* (New York, 1960), and Marshall Smelser, *The Democratic Republic, 1801–1815* (New York, 1968). Much the same good purposes are served by the splendid "life and times" of *Thomas Jefferson* (6 vols., Boston, 1948–1981), by Dumas Malone. I was oriented to controversies of the 1790s that were much on the minds of Princetonians through older articles by Marshall Smelser, "The Jacobin Phrenzy: Federalism and the Menace of Liberty, Equality, and Fraternity," *Review of Politics* 13 (1951): 457–82, and "The Jacobin Phrenzy: The Menace of Monarchy, Plutocracy, and Anglophilia, 1789–1798," *Review of Politics* 21 (1959): 239–58; and by John R. Howe, Jr., "Republican Thought and the Political Violence of the 1790s," *American Quarterly* 19 (1967): 147–65. Carl E. Prince, *New Jersey's Jeffersonian Republicans: The Genesis of an Early Party Machine, 1789–1817* (Chapel Hill, N.C., 1964), and J. R. Pole, "Jeffersonian Democracy and the Federalist Dilemma in New Jersey, 1798–1812," *Proceedings of the New Jersey Historical Society* 74 (1956): 260–92, show more directly how local situations reflected national circumstances. Although the more general study by David Hackett Fischer, *The Revolution of American Conservatism: The Federalist Party in the Era of Jeffersonian Democracy* (New York, 1965), does not dwell extensively on New Jersey politics, its asides and biographical sketches nonetheless provide a primer on the political experience of the Princeton trustees.

Many biographical studies are now available for contemporaries of Stanhope Smith. Of these, I found most instructive for purposes of comparison Richard M. Rollins, *The Long Journey of Noah Webster* (Philadelphia, 1980), Joseph W. Phillips, *Jedidiah Morse and New England Congregationalism* (New Brunswick, 1983), and Joseph J. Ellis, *After the Revolution: Profiles of Early American Culture* (New York, 1979). L. H. Butterfield, ed., *Letters of Benjamin Rush* (2 vols., Princeton, 1951), remains essential for exploring the mind of the period's leading pantheorist and for showing why Stanhope Smith's inquiring spirit would feel so much at home in Rush's intellectual world.

Study of the early national period draws one back inevitably to the ideas and experiences of the Revolution. At Princeton, as throughout the United States, the story of the post-Revolutionary generation is the story of coming to terms with the ideology of the Revolution, especially with its republicanism, a theme whose ambiguities and even contradictory impulses has been the focus of an increasingly sophisticated literature over the last two decades. Bernard Bailyn, *The Ideological Origins of the American Revolution* (Cambridge, Mass., 1967), and Gordon S. Wood, *The Creation of the American Republic, 1776–1787* (Chapel Hill, N.C., 1969), remain the places to take one's bearings on the subject. But the demurrals of others, who see a "liberal" republicanism looming larger than the "classical" or "Whig" variety, are important for suggesting the complexity and diversity of ideology in the early United States. Joyce Appleby, in several essays and in the seminal book *Capitalism and a New Social Order: The Republican Vision of the 1790s* (New York, 1984), and Isaac Kramnic, "Republican Revisionism Revisited," *American Historical Review* 87 (1982): 629–64, have made the most carefully nuanced criticisms of the thesis that a republicanism of classical virtue meant more than Lockean commercial individualism in the Revolutionary and post-Revolutionary periods. At Princeton, "classical" forms of republicanism generally prevailed over "liberal" forms, but as I tried to show in the body of the book, tension between the two was a dynamic part of the Stanhope Smith years.

Other particularly insightful writings on the the nature, workings, and implications of the republicanism(s) of the Revolutionary and post-Revolutionary periods are found in John M. Murrin, "The Great Inversion; or, Court versus Country: A Comparison of the Revolution Settlements in England (1688–1721) and America (1776–1816)," in *Three British Revolutions: 1641, 1688, 1776*, ed. J.G.A. Pocock (Princeton, 1980); Douglass Adair, *Fame and the Founding Fathers*, ed. Trevor Colbourn (New York, 1974); and Robert E. Shalhope, "Republicanism and Early American Historiography," *WMQ* 39 (1982): 334–56. Moses Coit Tyler could not benefit from modern discussions of Revolutionary republicanism, yet his *Literary History of the American Revolution, 1763–1783* (2 vols., New York, 1897), is still a bracing study of the subject. Larry R. Gerlach, *Prologue to Independence: New Jersey in the Coming of the American Revolution* (New Brunswick, 1976), offers a reliable guide to the part that such thinking played in the unfolding of the Revolution in and around Princeton. The importance of republicanism for the men who wrote the Constitution, many of whom were graduates of the College of New Jersey, is one of the major subjects in several of the excellent recent books on that venerable document, including Forrest McDonald, *Novus Ordo Seclorum: The Intellectual Origins of the Constitution* (Lawrence, Kans., 1985), and Richard Beeman et al., *Be-*

yond Confederation: Origins of the Constitution and American National Identity (Chapel Hill, N.C., 1987). On what it meant for many Americans to live through the War for Independence and its aftermath, Robert Middle-kauf, *The Glorious Cause: The American Revolution, 1763–1789* (New York, 1982), is very useful. That book goes far by itself to explain why the impact of the Revolutionary period could be so great, a subject considered in the terms of *religionsgeschichte* by Catherine L. Albanese, *Sons of the Fathers: The Civil Religion of the American Revolution* (Philadelphia, 1976), and in more conventional political and social terms by Michael Kammen, *A Season of Youth: The American Revolution and the Historical Imagination* (New York, 1978). Two essays by Gordon Wood, "The Democratization of Mind in the American Revolution," in *The Moral Foundations of the American Republic*, ed. Robert H. Horwitz (2d ed., Charlottesville, Va., 1979), and "Conspiracy and the Paranoid Style: Causality and Deceit in the Eighteenth Century," *WMQ* 39 (1982): 401–41, are the finest analyses I have read of how the resistance theory of the Revolution shaped the intellectual assumptions of the early national period.

The Enlightenment—America and Scotland

During the half century after the Revolution, America's intellectual history was fully political, both in the sense that experiences of war and social ordering provided the stuff for mental activity and in the sense that reflection on first-order questions was inspired by the needs of nation building. The books by May, Fiering, Flower and Murphey, and Meyer, mentioned above, along with Meyer's *The Democratic Enlightenment* (New York, 1976), are outstanding guides to many of the period's pressing intellectual issues. One of the strengths of these studies is their awareness that, for most American intellectuals of the period, it was important to incorporate both the old religion of Reformation Protestantism and the new sciences of Newton and Locke in their cautious embrace of the Enlightenment. That subject is the direct consideration of three books that treat the effort to construct a rational, scientific, and socially useful religion in the early decades of the nation's history: Theodore Dwight Bozeman, *Protestants in an Age of Science: The Baconian Ideal and Antebellum American Religious Thought* (Chapel Hill, N.C., 1977), E. Brooks Holifield, *The Gentlemen Theologians: American Theology in Southern Culture, 1795–1860* (Durham, N.C., 1978), and Herbert Hovenkamp, *Science and Religion in America, 1800–1860* (Philadelphia, 1978). These books tell interrelated stories, for which Witherspoon's intellectual accomplishment at Princeton is the prologue. Bruce Kuklick, *Churchmen and Philosphers from Jonathan Edwards to John Dewey* (New Haven, 1985), is a broadly cast history of philosophy that, while focusing more on New England than the middle states, still is very helpful for describing the most important formal intellectual issues faced by the members of the Princeton circle. Also useful on one of the important tributaries to the stream of American intellectual life is Wilson Smith, "William Paley's Theological Utilitarianism in America," *WMQ* 11 (1954): 402–24.

At Princeton and most other intellectual centers in the early United States, the thought of Francis Hutcheson, Thomas Reid, and other Scottish exponents of a common-sense realism was much more important than Paley's. That philosophical orientation is described for modern philosophers by S. A. Grave, *The Scottish Philosophy of Common Sense* (Oxford, 1960). Sydney Ahlstrom, "The Scottish Philosophy and American Theology," *Church History* 24 (1955): 257–72, remains a solid introduction to the Scottish influence on American religious thought. Douglas Sloan performs the same service in splendid fashion for American educational theory in *The Scottish Enlightenment and the American College Ideal* (New York, 1971). The place of the Scottish philosophy among conservative Presbyterianism is the subject of John C. Vander Stelt, *Philosophy and Scripture: A Study in Old Princeton and Westminster Theology* (Marlton, N.J., 1978), and more generally among American evangelicals of my "Common Sense Traditions and American Evangelical Thought," *American Quarterly* 37 (1985): 216–38. Very useful for comparative purposes is Daniel Walker Howe's account of the deep influence that the Scottish philosophy exerted in a different environment, *The Unitarian Conscience: Harvard Moral Philosophy, 1805–1861* (Cambridge, Mass., 1970). An older essay that has born the test of time well, John Clive and Bernard Bailyn, "England's Cultural Provinces: Scotland and America," *WMQ* 11 (1954): 200–13, provides suggestive comparisons for those who would trace an intellectual trajectory from Scotland to the New World in the age of Enlightenment.

A wealth of recent works on the Scottish Enlightenment has made it possible to see more clearly the environment in which John Witherspoon came of age and to note similarities and differences with America. One older work that made an excellent start on that effort was Gladys Bryson, *Man and Society: The Scottish Inquiry of the Eighteenth Century* (Princeton, 1945). More recently, our understanding of how social, religious, political, and scientific concerns related to each other in eighteenth-century Scotland has been measurably increased by the essayists in N. T. Phillipson and Rosalind Mitchison, eds., *Scotland in the Age of Improvement* (Edinburgh, 1970); and Istvan Hont and Michael Ignatieff, eds., *Wealth and Virtue: The Shaping of Political Economy in the Scottish Enlightenment* (Cambridge, 1983); by Nicholas Phillipson, "The Scottish Enlightenment," in *The Enlightenment in National Context*, ed. R. Porter and M. Teich (Cambridge, 1981); and especially by Richard B. Sher, *Church and University in the Scottish Enlightenment: The Moderate Literati of Edinburgh* (Princeton, 1985). The way the purposes of the "Moderates" and the protests of the "Evangelicals" affected Scotland's institutional religion is the subject of Andrew L. Drummond and James Bulloch, *The Scottish Church, 1688–1843: The Age of the Moderates* (Edinburgh, 1973). J. David Hoeveler, Jr.,

James McCosh and the Scottish Intellectual Tradition: From Glasgow to Princeton (Princeton, 1981), is a fine intellectual biography of another Scottish immigrant and proponent of the Scottish philosophy, who began his influential presidency at Princeton exactly one hundred years after Witherspoon arrived. For connections between Scotland and America before Witherspoon's migration, a most helpful study is Ned C. Landsman, *Scotland and Its First American Colony, 1683–1765* (Princeton, 1985).

Religious Culture

The Enlightenment in America took a different course than it did in Scotland in large part because religious culture in America—institutions, forms of organization, habits of thought, and relations with other cultural entities—was different from its counterpart in Scotland. The study of religious culture in post-Revolutionary America is in many ways only just beginning. Nonetheless, it is already clear that the subject is as complex as it is central to antebellum life in general. Religious culture in the middle states—with no heritage of establishment; with simultaneous exposure to New England, the South, and the frontier West; and with a manifest pluralism of nations, tongues, and forms of Christianity—was significantly different from religious culture in New England. The story of Princeton also reflects the significant fact that the New Jersey Calvinists were descended from Scottish Presbyterians rather than from the English Puritans who populated New England. For purposes of comparison, however, it is still useful to observe how many of the fears and aspirations were shared by the intellectual elites of New England and the middle states. Works like Howe's study of the Harvard Unitarians, Phillips's biography of Jedidiah Morse (both mentioned previously), the older work by Vernon Stauffer, *New England the Bavarian Illuminati* (New York, 1918), or more recent efforts such as K. Alan Snyder, "Foundations of Liberty: The Christian Republicanism of Timothy Dwight and Jedidiah Morse," *New England Quarterly* 56 (1983): 382–97, offer instructive points of comparison with the Princeton intellectuals.

For religious as well as for political culture, the way in which republican themes shaped discourse during and after the Revolution has been a major concern of recent scholarship. Nathan O. Hatch, *The Sacred Cause of Liberty: Republican Thought and the Millennium in Revolutionary New England* (New Haven, 1977), was a pioneering work whose conclusions fit just about as well for the Presbyterian Federalists of New Jersey as for the Congregational Federalists of Massachusetts. More recently, in a book with a broader import than its title suggests, Ruth Bloch, *Visionary Republic: Millennial Themes in American Thought, 1756–1800* (New York, 1985), provides a careful periodization of the interaction between republicanism and religious thought at the end of the eighteenth century. Melvin B. Endy, Jr., "Just War, Holy War, and Millennialism in Revolutionary America," *WMQ* 42 (1985): 3–25, argues that it is possible to overstress the influence of republican themes in American religion at the time of the Revolution, an argument suggesting that some of the same complexity may be present in the religious thought of the period that the political historians are discovering in their work. Useful guides for considerations of religion and the public sphere for the entire period are provided in a book and review article by John F. Berens, *Providence and Patriotism in Early America, 1640–1815* (Charlottesville, Va., 1978), and "Religion and Revolution Reconsidered: Recent Literature on Religion and Nationalism in Eighteenth-Century America," *Canadian Review of Studies in Nationalism* 6 (1979): 233–45.

Religious developments in the early national period still need both more factual study and more creative interpretation. At least two major developments seemed to have occurred in this era. The first was a massive turn toward broadly republican language as the means to express doctrine and piety. The turn tended to be more "classical" for elites, more "liberal" for popular movements, but in both cases a secularization of mind was at work as resources from the realm of politics replaced indigenous religious sources. These recondite intellectual developments accompanied, second, a massive Christianization of the populace. The analysis in de Tocqueville's *Democracy in America*—that religion in the United States turned in a leftward, democratic direction and so avoided Europe's alienation between a rightward-looking religious establishment and the revolutionary aspirations of intellectuals and "the people"—still seems sound, but it is a theory that needs to be checked by thorough study of the periods, regions, and themes of the early republic. Many of the biographical and intellectual studies mentioned above are helpful in advancing a clearer picture of the period. A number of articles are also at hand to flesh out the story, like Gary B. Nash, "The American Clergy and the French Revolution," *WMQ* 22 (1965): 392–412; Charles F. O'Brien, "The Religious Issue in the Presidential Campaign of 1800," *Essex Institute Historical Collection* 107 (1971): 82–93; and James H. Smylie, "Charles Nisbet: Second Thoughts on a Revolutionary Generation," *Pennsylvania Magazine of History and Biography* 98 (1974): 189–205, to mention just three that are relevant to events at Princeton. In addition, a growing sophistication characterizes the literature on the "Second Great Awakening," after the turn of the century. Both comprehensive essays, like Donald G. Mathews, "The Second Great Awakening as an Organizing Process, 1780–1830," *American Quarterly* 21 (1969): 23–43, and Lois W. Banner, "Religious Benevolence as Social Control: A Critique of an Interpretation," *Journal of American History* 60 (1973): 23–41, and more specific studies, like Thomas Templeton Taylor, "Samuel E. McCorkle and a Christian Republic," *American Presbyterians* 63 (1985): 375–85, build upon an earlier generation of books that had tended to isolate considerations of social control as the major issue in the revivals. Social control, as illustrated by this study of the Princeton circle, was by no means an insignificant concern for the new nation's religious leaders, but it touched so many other matters—philosophical and spiritual, scientific and political—that a disservice is done when social control is asked to bear the whole freight of meaning for the period.

Helpful as work on the Second Great Awakening has been, we still have only fragmentary hints as to what a more fully comprehensive religious history of the early national period might look like. It may be difficult ever to reveal the full complexity of lived experience, yet the historians of political culture have shown the pervasive importance of ideological and social concerns in the period, and hence how necessary it is to integrate them into the religious story. The two best examples of what such an integration might entail are provided by Gordon S. Wood, "Evangelical America and Early Mormonism," *New York History* 61 (1980): 359–86, and Nathan O. Hatch, "The Christian Movement and the Demand for a Theology of the People," *Journal of American History* 67 (1980): 545–67. These studies indicate how fruitful it is to regard religious life both as a subject with intrinsic integrity and as a cultural expression deeply embedded in the experiences, conceptions, and structures of the wider society.

Studies of the Presbyterians between the Revolution and the Civil War already show some of the richness possible for religious history conceived on a broader compass. For the purposes of this book, I was especially aided by the effort of George Marsden, cited above, who treats intra-Presbyterian debates as intellectually significant. Also helpful on the Presbyterians are Leonard J. Trinterud, *The Forming of an American Tradition: A Re-examination of Colonial Presbyterianism* (Philadelphia, 1949), an older study that takes seriously the need to understand intellectual and social elements of the Presbyterian tradition; and Fred J. Hood, *Reformed America: The Middle and Southern States, 1783–1837* (University, Ala., 1980), a book that, if it overemphasizes the theme of social control, still succeeds in showing how republican and Calvinist elements intermingled in the intellectual culture for which Princeton was so important. Since Presbyterians are careful folk who specialize in taking minutes, historians have access to a panoply of their records. It is, therefore, not surprising to find useful works of synthesis for the denomination. Of modern studies relevant to my research, I have benefited especially from Elwyn A. Smith, *The Presbyterian Minister in American Culture: A Study in Changing Concepts, 1700–1900* (Philadelphia, 1962); Smith, "The Forming of a Modern American Denomination," *Church History* 31 (1962): 74–94; Lois W. Banner, "Presbyterians and Voluntarism in the Early Republic," *Journal of Presbyterian History* 50 (1972): 187–205; and Glenn T. Miller, "God's Light and Man's Enlightenment: Evangelical Theology of Colonial Presbyterianism," *Journal of Presbyterian History* 51 (1973): 97–115. A dissertation by Martha Tomhave Blauvelt, "Society, Religion, and Revivalism: The Second Great Awakening in New Jersey, 1780–1830" (Princeton University, 1974), is the best work on the Presbyterians of New Jersey during the period of my interest.

Educational History

Like religious historians, historians of education in the last quarter century have made much more serious efforts at treating their subject as part of a more general history of culture. In the conclusion to this book, I comment briefly on several opinions concerning higher education in the early republic. This bibliography is the place to acknowledge my debt to the newer educational history for works that, while often oriented to different questions than mine, still enabled me to have a fuller sense of how to study an institution of higher learning in broader compass. James Axtell, *The School upon a Hill: Education and Society in Colonial New England* (New Haven, 1974), provides a good example for an earlier time and different place of how to study education as the transmission of culture. Closer to the concerns of this book is the educational history of the early national period, a subject enjoying a virtual renaissance of serious scholarship. The best of these works include the volumes by Howard Miller and Steven Novak, cited in the list of Princeton sources, and the following works: Wilson Smith, ed., *Theories of Education in Early America, 1655–1819* (Indianapolis, 1973); David F. Allmendinger, Jr., *Paupers and Scholars: The Transformation of Student Life in Nineteenth-Century New England* (New York, 1975); James McLachlan, "The American College in the Nineteenth Century: Toward a Reappraisal," *Teacher's College Record* 80 (1978): 287–306; Lawrence A. Cremin, *American Education: The National Experience, 1783–1876* (New York, 1980); Colin B. Burke, *American Collegiate Populations: A Test of the Traditional View* (New York, 1982); and David W. Robson, *Educating Republicans: The College in the Era of the American Revolution, 1750–1800* (Westport, Conn., 1985). I have also benefited from books on individual colleges. Brooks Mather Kelley, *Yale: A History* (New Haven, 1974), and David C. Humphrey, *From King's College to Columbia, 1746–1800* (New York, 1976), are instructive recent examples of college histories executed with faithfulness to both an institutional record and more comprehensive interactions with American life. Helen Lefkowitz Horowitz, *Campus Life* (New York, 1987), provides a wide-ranging and perceptive effort to trace the shifts in student culture from about the period of my study to the present.

Solid as these recent histories are, older, more narrowly conceived works also remain useful, like Franklin Bowditch Dexter, "Student Life at Yale in the Early Days of Connecticut Hall" and "Student Life at Yale College under the First President Dwight (1795–1817)," in *A Selection from the Miscellaneous Historical Papers of Fifty Years* (New Haven, 1918). Dexter showed that, compared to Witherspoon, Stanhope Smith, and Ashbel Green, Yale's Dwight was less adventuresome intellectually but more successful at pointing students to evangelical vocations. Questions of "older" or "recent" become irrelevant in the face of some works that, for grasp of material and winsomeness of prose, seem impervious to aging. Such a book is Samuel Eliot Morison, *Three Centuries of Harvard, 1636–1936* (Cambridge, Mass., 1936), which early in my study of Princeton offered a great deal of enjoyment and not a little inspiration.

The grail of fully satisfying cultural history entices historians of the early republic, even as it does historians of other times and places. The recent flourishing of political, intellectual, religious, and educational studies for the period of Stanhope Smith's Princeton does not necessarily bring the grail within reach. Such works, however, do provide splendid assistance for the effort to narrate the story of a specific locale like Princeton and to interpret the thought of a specific group like the Princeton circle. In the end, these works, with insights and limitations alike, are their own best testimony to the significance of the quest.

Index

The following abbreviations are used in the Index; CNJ = College of New Jersey, AG = Ashbel Green, SSS = Samuel Stanhope Smith, JW = John Witherspoon.

Adams, John, 28, 34, 137, 138, 149, 150
Adams, John Quincy, 165
Alexander, Archibald, 62n.10, 108, 269, 272, 280, 306; and founding of Princeton Theological Seminary, 260–66; and intellectual legacy of JW, 283–88
Alison, Francis, 30, 31, 40–41, 43, 48, 49
Allmendinger, David, Jr., 293
American Revolution, 4–5, 292, 295–96; battle of Princeton during, 10, 12, 73–74; bibliography for, 324; celebration of, in Princeton, 82–83, 106–7, 220–21; impact on trustees of, 14, 79–80, 225–26, 241
Andover Theological Seminary, 255–56, 260–61, 289
Appleby, Joyce, 8
Armstrong, James Francis, 79, 306
Artsdalen, Jacob van, 306

Bailyn, Bernard, 8, 57, 142
Banning, Lance, 8
Bavarian Illuminati, 148
Bayard, Andrew, 306
Bayard, John, 14, 90, 113, 179, 240–41, 307
Bayard, Samuel, 240, 307
Beasley, Frederick, 63–64, 65, 73, 108, 135n.27
Beattie, James, 64
Beatty, John, 307
Belcher, Jonathan, 35
Bellamy, Joseph, 19, 25, 44, 58
Berkeley, Bp. George, 25, 31, 36–39, 45, 63–64

Biddle, Nicholas, 152, 317
Birney, James Gillespie, 317
Blair, John, 37, 63
Blair, Samuel, Sr., 59–60
Blair, Samuel, Jr., 26, 111–13
Blair, Susan Shippen, 111–13
Bloomfield, Joseph, 147, 263, 307
Blumenbach, Johann Friedrich, 189
Boudinot, Elias, 80, 91, 93–97, 127, 129n.8, 139–40, 150, 151, 161, 164, 212, 226, 236–37, 248–49, 250–51, 307; and appointment of theology professor, 173–79; in opposition to Tom Paine, 145, 254–55; as president of Continental Congress in Princeton, 82–85; and the Revolution, 14, 33–34, 79
Boudinot, Elisha, 177–78, 252, 307
Boyd, James, 307
Boyd, William, 240, 307
Brackenridge, Hugh Henry, 32
Bradford, Ebenezer, 43–44
Bradford, John, 182–83
Brainerd, John, 307
Breckinridge, Joseph Cabell, 165, 230–31, 233, 246, 315
Breckinridge, Mary Ann, 220–21
Bryan, John, 161
Buffon, Comte de, 189
Burke, Colin B., 293n.5
Burr, Aaron, Sr. (president of CNJ), 17, 21, 44, 48, 50, 57
Burr, Aaron, Jr. (vice president of the U.S.), 139, 157, 160, 165, 251
Burr, Esther Edwards, 222n.24

Caldwell, James, 14, 307
Caldwell, Joseph, 318

Calvinism, 9, 42–43, 206–11, 294–95. *See also* Christianity

Carnahan, James, 289

Chapman, Jedidiah, 43, 308

Chauncy, Charles, 29, 43

Christianity, 10, 20, 143–44, 199, 220–21, 236–37; in early republic, 327–30; and learning, 145–46; and republicanism, 5, 8–9, 79–80, 144. *See also* republicanism: and religion

Church of Scotland, 23–25

Cincinnati, Society of, 79

Clark, Joseph, 80, 141, 160–62, 251–52, 256, 308

Clarke, Samuel, 197

College of New Jersey: call of JW as president of, 25–27; and commencement of 1779, 12–15; Continental Congress at, 81–86; continued tensions at, after 1807, 244–49; devastated by American Revolution, 73–75; discipline of students at, in early nineteenth century, 223–27; early purposes of, 20–21; and education of Presbyterian ministers in early nineteenth century, 258–66; and efforts to rebuild, 159–62; faculty of, overworked after 1802, 166–68; and fire of 1802, 158–59; and founding of Princeton Theological Seminary, 266–70; AG replaces SSS as president of (1812), 249–50; AG's early presidency of, 273–78; AG's successes and failures at, 278–83; growth of, after 1802, 162–66; harmful effects of rebellion on, 237–40; historians of, 4, 7, 318–22; history of, before JW, 16–22; and importance of college's history, 295–99; instruction at, under JW, 34–58; and long-term legacy of JW, SSS, and AG, 288–91; and new professorship of theology, 172–79; and optimism during 1780s, 91–93; and politics of American Revolution, 32–34, 47–54; and the Presbyterians, 18–19, 30–31, 87–90, 169–79, 258–70; and the Princeton circle, 3, 305–18; and promotion of religion and patriotism in 1780s, 104–8; and the question of retrogression, 292–95; rebuilding of,

after Revolution, 86–87, 99–103; and a republican Christian Enlightenment, 6–8; responses of, to student rebellion, 230–37; SSS succeeds JW as president of (1795), 125–29; SSS's early success as president of, 129–31, 133–35; and during SSS's time as student and tutor, 62–66; student life at, in early nineteenth century, 215–23; and student rebellion of 1807, 227–29; and student unrest of late 1790s, 150–52; and tension between SSS and AG (1802–6), 179–84; trustees of, 77–81; and turnover of trustees in 1807, 240–43; JW's early activity in, 29–30; and JW's influence on SSS and AG, 283–88. *See also* curriculum; students; trustees

common-sense philosophy, 6, 11, 142–43; and AG, 211–12, 284–86; and Charles Hodge, 290; and SSS, 102, 117–23, 188–91, 193–94, 209, 211–12; and JW, 25, 36–43

Condict, Ira, 153, 308

Congregationalists, 18, 19, 148, 260–61, 296

Constitution of the United States, 90–91, 297

Craven, Wesley Frank, 9n.11, 59n.1

Cremin, Lawrence A., 293

Cummins, Francis D., 227–28

curriculum, 20–21; under AG, 275–76; under SSS, 100–102, 215–16; under JW, 35–36, 75

Cuvier, Georges, 122

Dallas, George Mifflin, 245

Davies, Samuel, 17, 21, 25, 35, 48, 66, 114, 133, 205

Democratic-Republicans, 139–41, 147, 148, 162, 165, 218, 250

Democratic Societies, 126, 136, 226

Dickinson, John, 32, 84

Dickinson, Jonathan, 17, 18

Duffield, George, 80, 308

Dwight, Timothy, 232n.53, 246

Eby, John, 138

Edwards, Jonathan, 17, 19, 50, 51, 63; theology of, in relation to SSS's the-

ology, 71, 133, 205, 208, 209; theology of, in relation to JW's theology, 36, 37, 38, 43–47
Edwards, Jonathan, Jr., 21, 37
Ellsworth, Oliver, 21
Elmer, Jonathan, 308
Enlightenment: bibliography, 325–27; at Princeton, 10–11, 142–43, 168–69, 200–206, 234–36, 256–57, 286, 294–95, 298; in Scotland, 23. *See also* science at CNJ; Smith, Samuel Stanhope—intellectual life: advocate of science; Witherspoon, John—themes: promoter of science
Erskine, John, 25

Fiering, Norman, 43, 193, 322
Finley, Robert, 183, 240–41, 253, 308
Finley, Samuel, 17, 21, 25, 35, 48, 62, 113
Fischer, David Hackett, 4
Floding, Matthew, 17n.3
Fourth of July: celebrations of, at CNJ, 82–83, 106–7, 220, 286
Fredrickson, George M., 142n.45
Frelinghuysen, Frederick, 308
French Revolution, 94–95, 136, 140–41, 202
Freneau, Philip, 32

Galloway, Joseph, 32
Garnett, James Mercer, 222, 305
Garnett, William, 218
Geertz, Clifford, 141–42n.44
Genet, Citizen, 136, 148
George II (king of England), 84
Glascock, John, 220
Godwin, William, 236, 285
Graham, William, 66, 260, 286
Green, Ashbel
—career: as student, tutor, and professor at CNJ, 83–84, 102, 220; as trustee under SSS, 90, 126, 159–60, 172, 174–79, 234, 242n.74; as interim president (1802–3), 161; declines chair of theology in 1802, 174–79; helps found Princeton Theological Seminary, 258–70; as president of CNJ (1812–22), 222, 249–50, 269, 273–83, 288–89; bibliography, 308–9
—themes, activities, relationships: as

biographer and historian, 28–29, 37, 53, 54n.59, 74, 104–5, 223, 278; his concern for educating ministers, 155–56, 170–72, 258–66; convictions of, 94, 137–38, 164–65, 180, 211–12, 252, 255–56, 269, 282; as intellectual heir of JW, 10, 56, 115, 180–82, 272, 278, 283–88; legacy of, 289–91; promoter of revival, 164–65, 276–78, 279–80; relationship with SSS, 108–9, 179–83, 247–48, 257–58, 266–70, 275, 283–88; and science, 269, 282; and Scottish common-sense philosophy, 211–12
Green, Elizabeth Stockton (wife of AG), 273
Green, Jacob (father of AG), 50, 258n.54
Green, Jacob (son of AG), 269, 282
Green, Robert Stockton (son of AG), 277–78
Greene, John C., 116n.40
Griffin, Edward Door, 259, 261
Grove, Henry, 44
Guyot, Arnold, 289

Halsey, Jeremiah, 309
Hamilton, Alexander, 93, 122n.60
Hamilton, William, 219
Hampden, John, 67
Hampden-Sidney Academy, 66–68, 217
Hancock, John, 32
Harris, Robert, 309
Harvard College, 7–8n.9, 16, 17n.2, 21, 256, 260, 263, 296
Hatch, Nathan O., 4, 241
Hayward, William, 228
Henry, Joseph, 289
Henry, Patrick, 68
higher education, history of in early United States: bibliography, 330–31; and notion of retrogression, 292–95
Hill, William, 182–83
Hillyer, Asa, 309
Hobart, John Henry, 91, 253, 257, 318
Hodge, Charles, 280, 290
Hofstadter, Richard, 292–94
Hoge, Moses, 73
Hogendorp, G. K., 86, 100–101
Home, Henry. *See* Kames, Lord

honorary degrees, 32, 84, 87, 92–93, 149, 165, 252

Hood, Fred J., 55n.60, 252–53n.33

Hopkins, Samuel, 19

Houston, William Churchill, 13, 35, 40n.27, 75, 102, 309

Howell, Richard, 309

Hume, David, 25, 31, 39, 42, 45, 133, 183, 236, 285

Hunter, Andrew, 163, 175–79, 309

Hutcheson, Francis, 23, 193; and SSS, 189, 194; JW's shifting attitude toward, 24, 40–43, 45, 48, 52n.53, 58

Hyde, Henry, 227–28, 230

Iredell, James, 107, 168, 215–16, 219–20, 305

Jay, John, 136

Jay Treaty, 136, 139

Jefferson, Thomas, 5, 92, 93, 139, 143, 160, 165, 250; correspondence with SSS, 68–69; SSS's later opinions of, 126, 150

Johns, Timothy, 309

Jordan, Winthrop, 116

Kames, Lord, 25, 119–22, 131, 133, 183, 189

Kant, Immanuel, 189

Kent, James, 5

Kirkland, Samuel, 21

Kirkpatrick, Andrew, 240, 309

Kollock, Henry, 167, 173–78, 238, 267, 309

Lafayette, Marquis de, 92

Landsman, Ned, 58n.66

Lavoisier, Antoine, 131

Leibnitz, Gottfried Wilhelm, 189

liberalism, political, 143

Lindsley, Philip, 134–35, 318

Livingstone, John Henry, 178n.51

Livingstone, William, 90, 309

Locke, John, 38–39, 45, 190

Log College: of William Tennent, 18

Lyon, Matthew, 140

McCosh, James, 56, 291

McLachlan, James, 255n.62, 273, 289n.66

Maclean, John, Sr. (colleague of SSS), 131, 164, 167, 175–77, 238, 249, 310

Maclean, John, Jr. (historian and president of CNJ), 134n.25, 248n.15, 273n.5, 276, 289

MacWhorter, Alexander, 79–80, 93–95, 97, 136, 153, 160–62, 190, 212, 240–42, 252, 310; and appointment of theology professor, 174–79

Madison, James, Sr., 32

Madison, James, Jr. (president of the United States), 32, 62, 91, 92, 123n.60, 217, 297, 318; correspondence with SSS, 69–72

Marsden, George M., 322

Marshall, John, 165

Martin, Luther, 21

Mason, John, 310

Mather, Cotton, 46

Matteaus, Francis, 227–28

May, Henry F., 6n.7, 142, 191n.12, 322

Meade, Bp. William, 228n.41, 237n.67

Mercer, Archibald, 220

Meyer, Donald H., 191n.12, 322

Miller, Alexander, 310

Miller, Samuel, 92, 115, 137, 138n.35, 170, 171, 240–41, 272, 310–11; author of *Brief Retrospect of the Eighteenth Century*, 120n.51, 190, 212; on the bond among religion education, and health of society, 93–96, 97, 145–46, 250–58; continues legacy of JW, 283–88; criticism of SSS, 266–70; and founding of Princeton Theological Seminary, 258–66

ministerial training, 31, 163; faulted under SSS, 266–70; overshadowed by interest in politics, 36, 52–54; rejuvenated by AG, 180–82; and shortage of pastors among Presbyterians, 169–73, 181, 258–66. *See also* Princeton Theological Seminary

Minto, Walter, 40n.27, 102–4, 130, 311

Mondboddo, Lord, 133

Morse, Jedidiah, 5, 148, 158

Mosheim, Johann, 189

Murrin, John, 4

Napoleon, 139, 164, 250

Nassau Hall, 15, 73–75, 100, 158, 167, 221

natural philosophy. *See* science
Naylor, Natalie A., 293
Newton, Isaac, 41, 103, 128, 193, 197, 212
Newton, John, 93

O'Connell, Marvin, 220n.15
Ogden, Aaron, 177, 251, 311
Ogden, Robert, 311
Oswald, James, 37, 64

Paine, Tom, 133, 137, 138, 139, 150, 236, 285
Paley, William, 181, 189, 197–98, 275
Palmer, Elihu, 285
Paterson, William, 65, 79, 90–91, 140–41, 145, 157, 311
Patton, F. Landey, 56
Peale, Charles Willson, 28, 84, 164
Pemberton, Ebenezer, 37
Periam, Joseph, 37, 63, 64
Pickering, Timothy, 149
Pinckney, Charles, 92
Pocock, J.G.A., 8
polygamy, 182–83
Presbyterians, 5, 87–88, 129, 132, 138, 159, 253; formation of General Assembly, 89–90; ministers from CNJ, 18, 169–73; and tension between New Sides and Old Sides, 17–19, 30–31, 40
Prideaux, Humphrey, 189
Priestley, Joseph, 131, 149–50
Princeton College. *See* College of New Jersey
Princeton Theological Seminary, 7, 276, 280, 289–90; founding of, 258–70

Ramsey, David, 21, 116
Reed, Joseph, 87, 312
Reid, Thomas, 36–37, 42, 131n.17, 193, 211, 212; and SSS, 102n.6, 189–90, 209; and JW, 25, 45, 64
republicanism, 8–9, 142, 225; and assumed link between private virtue and public order, 51–52, 81, 95–96, 144–45, 154, 168, 187, 201, 213, 237, 239, 289; bibliography, 324–25; and learning, 97–98, 128–29, 145–47, 200–205; and religion, 5, 8–9,

79–80, 127, 144, 168–69, 202, 220–21, 256, 286; and SSS, 200–205; and students, 10, 230–34; and JW, 57–58
Revolution. *See* American Revolution
Richards, James, 240, 312
Rittenhouse, David, 35, 74, 92, 126, 134
Robbins, Caroline, 8
Rodgers, John, 32, 79, 85, 90, 126, 137, 212, 240–42, 252, 312; and apppointment of theology professor, 174–79
Roe, Azel, 240–41, 312
Romeyn, John B., 312–13
Rousseau, Jean-Jacques, 133
Ruffin, Thomas, 318
Rush, Benjamin, 26, 73, 101, 111, 113–15, 130, 152n.66, 216, 238
Rutgers, Henry, 313

Saint Mery, Moreau de, 108
science at CNJ, 10–11, 21, 269; and religion, 46–47, 103, 145–46; under JW and SSS, 35–36, 40, 101–4. *See also* Green, Ashbel—themes: and science; Smith, Samuel Stanhope—intellectual life: advocate of science; Witherspoon, John—themes: promoter of science
Scott, Jack, 41
Scottish philosophy of common sense. *See* common-sense philosophy
Scudder, Nathaniel, 14, 313
Shaftesbury, Lord, 189, 194
Shields, Charles Woodruff, 291
Shippen, William, 238n.69, 313
Shuckford, Samuel, 189
Sidney, Algernon, 67
Silliman, Benjamin, 131
Sloan, Douglas, 9n.11, 58n.67, 72, 111, 121n.54, 210
Smith, Ann Witherspoon (wife of SSS, daughter of JW), 13, 67, 111, 112n.31
Smith, Elizabeth Blair (mother of SSS), 60
Smith, John Blair (brother of SSS), 62, 67, 68, 134, 180n.55, 260
Smith, John Rhea, 318
Smith, Jonathan Bayard, 14, 113, 240–41, 313

Smith, Robert (father of SSS), 13, 62, 63, 74, 90, 133, 313; biographical sketch, 59–61

Smith, Samuel Stanhope
—career: family and early years, 59–62; as student and tutor at CNJ, 62–66; in Virginia (1773–79), 66–67; his correspondence with Jefferson on education, 68–69; his correspondence with Madison on free will, 69–72; appointed professor at CNJ, 13, 73; early years as professor, 14–15, 73–76, 108–10; elected president of CNJ, 126; reaction to fire of 1802, 158–59; as fundraiser after fire, 160–61; duties in 1804, 166–67; and controversial selection of theology professor, 173–79; during rebellion of 1807, 228; and problems after rebellion, 239, 243–44; resignation in 1812, 244–50; withdrawal from politics, 252; and founding of Princeton Theological Seminary, 258–66; in retirement, 270–71, 275; death of, 288; legacy of, 289–91; bibliography, 313–15
—intellectual life: advocate of science, 101–2, 104, 117–18, 128–30, 146, 154, 166, 187, 191–93; alarmed at election of 1800, 148–49, 158–59; confident of education, 68–69, 98, 149–50, 201–3; defends harmony of religion and science, 196–200; defends unity of humanity, 117–22, 195–96; describes climate as source of change in complexion, 115–24, 198; devoted to Enlightenment, 111–15, 200–205, 212; fears extreme democracy, 88, 126, 202–3; liberalizes Calvinist theology, 110–11, 112, 120, 205–12; links morality and social order, 200–205; manifests general optimism about humanity, 97, 191–92; neglected importance, 9, 296–97; opposes Jonathan Edwards and James Madison on free will, 69–72, 195, 208–9; promotes Scottish common-sense philosophy, 63–64, 70–72, 189–91; promotes toleration, 91, 113; refines intellectual program of

JW, 10, 15, 56, 76, 115, 180, 185–213, 270, 283–88, 294; regards consciousness as source of moral law, 193–95; seeks a republican Christian Enlightenment, 10, 76, 185–213, 270; supports the Constitution, 88; supports modernization of curriculum, 101; teaches about polygamy, 182–83; values dignified style in speech and writing, 150, 190
—themes, activities, relationships: Archibald Alexander's opinion of, 108; his cordial relations with Episcopalians, 66–67, 91, 253, 257; his dignity of person, 64–65, 72, 108, 134, 246, 287; his friendship with Benjamin Rush, 113–15; William Paterson's opinion of, 65; his persistent ill health, 72–73, 109, 185, 246; Moreau de Saint Mery's opinion of, 108; as scholar, 189–91; service to Presbyterians, 88, 132; student opinions of, 134–35, 154–55, 165, 185, 211; tension with AG, 179–83, 247–48, 257–58, 266–70, 275, 281; George Washington's opinion of, 3, 135n.27
—works: Comprehensive View of Religion, 186, 188; "Connexion of Principle with Practice," 153–54; Discourse on Baptism, 247–48; Discourse on Fasting, 126–27; Divine Goodness of the United States, 127; Essay on Complexion (1787 ed.), 115–24, 198; Essay on Complexion (1810 ed.), 117, 186, 188, 196, 198; Funeral Sermon for Richard Stockton, 76; Lectures on Evidences, 186, 187–88; Lectures on Moral Philosophy, 186, 187; Oratio Inauguralis, 127–29; Oration on Death of Washington, 152–53, 155; Sermons (1799), 132–33

Smith, William Peartree, 315
Smylie, James M., 33n.13
Snowden, Gilbert, 199
Snowden, Isaac, 90, 315
Spencer, Elihu, 44, 74, 315
Stewart, Dugald, 122, 193
Stockton, Annis Boudinot, 75, 83
Stockton, Richard, Sr., 12, 26, 74, 75–76, 273, 315
Stockton, Richard, Jr., 12, 113, 140,

173–79, 228–29, 264–66, 315
students, at CNJ: daily life of, ca. 1805, 215–17; numbers, 12–13, 15, 100, 125, 161, 162–63, 215, 237–38, 244–45, 280–81, 301; their opinions of SSS, 134–35, 154–55, 185, 211; public service as graduates, 135, 216–17; rebelliousness of, 6, 67–68, 99, 151–52, 168–69, 227–31, 245, 279, 280–81; regulations for, 100, 223–27, 275, 278–79; religious life of, 105–6, 220–21; republicanism of, 106–8, 220–21, 230–34; societies of, 183, 218–19; southerners among, 217–18, 222

Taylor, N. W., 210
Telfair, Thomas, 234
Tennent, Gilbert, 17n.3, 21, 25, 114
Tennent, William, Sr., 18, 37
Tennent, William Mackay, 162, 174, 316
Thompson, William, 167, 219
Thomson, James, 37
trustees, at CNJ, 1, 15, 25, 40, 77–81, 129, 151–52, 179, 240–43, 252, 302, 303–17; convictions of, 79–80, 97–98, 136–40, 152–54, 164, 250–58; and creation of Presbyterian General Assembly (1789), 88–90; as Federalists, 140–41, 147, 162, 251; and founding of Princeton Theological Seminary, 262–66; governmental positions of, 78–79, 140–41, 251; as Presbyterians, 19, 78; their response to rebellion of 1807, 234–39, 248–50; their service during Revolution, 14, 79–80, 241; their support of CNJ after fire of 1802, 158–62, 168; and writing of the Constitution, 90–91
Tyler, Moses Coit, 29

Upshur, Abel Parker, 228, 231–32, 235, 318

Vancleve, John, 316
Voltaire, 115–16

Wallace, Joshua Maddox, 129n.8, 316

Warfield, Benjamin Breckinridge, 291
War for Independence. *See* American Revolution
Washington, George, 3, 12, 29, 79–80, 89, 126–27, 135n.27, 136, 150; funeral orations for, 152–53; at Princeton with Continental Congress, 82–85
Washington Benevolent Societies, 79
Wayne, James W., 228, 318
Webster, Noah, 5
Weeks, William, 211, 237
Weld, Isaac, Jr., 134
Wertenbaker, Thomas Jefferson, 52, 226–27
Wharton, Charles Henry, 129n.8, 177, 316
Whig thought. *See* republicanism
Whitefield, George, 21, 37, 59
Whiskey Rebellion, 126, 226
William and Mary, College of, 17n.2, 68–69
Wilson, Woodrow, 56, 291
Witherspoon, David (son of JW), 67
Witherspoon, Elizabeth (wife of JW), 26
Witherspoon, John
—career: in Scotland, 22–26; as president of CNJ, 15, 27–29, 34–36, 43–44, 48–56, 81, 217, 224, 246; as American political leader, 13, 32–34, 48–54, 81; as leader of American Presbyterians, 30–31, 90; his ill-fated trip to Britain (1783–84), 87, 109; death of, 124, 125; bibliography, 316–17
—themes: advocate of Scottish common-sense philosophy, 25, 36–43, 47, 189, 289; his legacy for SSS and AG, 10, 154, 156, 160, 180–82, 185–87, 191, 206, 213–15, 239, 256, 266, 272, 278, 283–88, 289–91; promoter of science, 35, 49, 54, 57, 102, 122, 146; synthesis of a republican Christian Enlightenment, 10, 34–43, 206, 289; use of Francis Hutcheson's ideas, 40–41, 45, 48–49, 58; weaknesses of thought, 56–58, 294–95
—works: "An Address to the natives of Scotland residing in America," 49;

Witherspoon, John (*con't.*)
 "The Dominion of Providence over the Passions of Men," 33, 49; *Ecclesiastical Characteristics*, 23–24, 27; *Lectures on Divinity*, 40, 52–53; *Lectures on Moral Philosophy*, 38–40, 46–47, 48–49, 51–52, 180–81, 275; "Remarks on an essay on human liberty," 25, 189; sermons in Scotland, 24–25; "Thoughts on American Liberty," 33
Wolcott, Oliver, 149

Wood, Gordon S., 4, 8, 142, 205, 235n.60, 241
Woodhull, George Spafford, 240–41, 317
Woodhull, John, 90, 93–96, 170, 241, 251, 317
Worthington, Charles, 234
Wyatt-Brown, Bertram, 226n.35

Yale College, 7n.9, 16, 17n.2, 22, 30, 53n.58, 162n.13, 163n.17, 172n.38, 263